CHECK LIST FOR REVISION

IN GENERAL, CHECK YOUR PAPER AGAINST THESE QUESTIONS:

MS
Is your handwriting legible?
Have you observed proper margins?

PLAN
Does the title fit the discussion?
Is the beginning direct, pertinent?
Does the ending give the impression of completeness?

¶S
Is the topic sentence clear in each paragraph?
Does each sentence in each paragraph relate to the topic sentence?

SS
Are there any clumsy, incomplete sentences?
Are there too many short, simple sentences?
Are there too many "and" sentences?

IN PARTICULAR, CHECK YOUR PAPER FOR THESE ERRORS:

GR
(plural subject) is, was, has,
everyone . . . their
these kind for this kind or these kinds

¶S
one-, two-, or three-sentence paragraphs
no paragraphs at all

LOG
"is when," "is where," "is because"
never, always, when you mean seldom, usually

DICTION
deadwood, such as aspects, type, kind of, in case of

SP
seperate for separate
recieve for receive
it's for its; loose for lose; to for too

P
failure to underscore (italicize) titles
, when you need a . or a ; (comma splice or comma fault)
. when you need a , (period fault)

PRENTICE-HALL

Handbook for Writers

GLENN LEGGETT

University of Washington

C. DAVID MEAD

Michigan State University

WILLIAM CHARVAT

Ohio State University

THIRD

PRENTICE-HALL

Handbook

for

Writers

EDITION

PRENTICE-HALL, INC.
Englewood Cliffs, New Jersey

Leggett, Mead, and Charvat

PRENTICE-HALL HANDBOOK FOR WRITERS

Third Edition

Designed by Walter Behnke

Sixth printing......May, 1962

69564–C

Preface

Y ou will find this handbook useful both as a guide and a reference work. As a summary of grammatical usage and elementary rhetoric, it provides the essentials of clear writing. The *Introduction* sketches the growth of English to its present character and discusses the standards of good English. *Manuscript Mechanics* (sections 1-4) describes the conventions of manuscript form, the writing of numbers, abbreviations, and word division (syllabication). *Grammar* (sections 5-9) outlines basic material—parts of speech, case, principal parts, and so forth. *Basic Sentence Faults* (sections 10-18) discusses sentence fragments, misplaced and dangling constructions, shifts, faulty agreement, and faulty reference. *Punctuation* (sections 19-30) offers solutions to the persistent problems of punctuation.

Larger Elements (sections 31-32) discusses the planning and organization of the complete paper and the structure of paragraphs. *Effective Sentences* (sections 33-36) describes the principles of rhetorically sound sentences, from the elementary one of "subordination" to the more subtle one of "emphasis." *Logic* (section 37) discusses briefly how illogical thinking interferes with clear and honest communication. Information on dictionaries and ways of improving vocabulary appears in the first two sections (38-39) under *Words;* a special test to measure vocabulary is provided also. The last sections under *Words* (40-44) discuss the three principles of word choice (exactness, directness, appropriateness), include a glossary of troublesome words, and provide both exhortation and practical help for poor spellers.

The Library (section 45) describes the organization of a library and its facilities for research. *The Research Paper* (section 46) gives instruction on research technique and provides two facsimile papers, each with a comment and analysis. Section 47 discusses the principles of summarizing, or *précis*-writing. Section 48 describes the requirements of conventional business and social letters. Section 49 provides as supplementary exercises a number of specimen papers for analysis. Section 50, the last, is an *Index to Grammatical Terms*.

Throughout the book the emphasis is on the practical problems of what you need to know and consider when you are writing. The introductions to the main divisions are designed to explain many of the basic assumptions underlying the standards of writing—to show you why most of the "rules" of writing are necessary.

It is as a reference work, however, that this book will be most useful to you, for it was designed primarily to help you correct and revise your own writing more quickly and accurately. It classifies the standards and conventions of writing and provides reference to them in four ways: (1) through the index; (2) through the table of contents; (3) through the charts on the endpapers of the book; and, most quickly of all, (4) through the tab index. (In this last system a colored tab appears on the edge of the first right-hand page of each numbered section; the tabs in the text align with those on the two key pages—one for sections 1-30, the other for sections 31-50—thus providing a visual device for ready reference.) Each major rule is given a number, and each subrule is designated by the number of the major rule and an alphabetical letter (5a, 16b, 22c, etc.) Your instructor may wish to use these numbers to mark errors on your papers, so that you can refer to the proper section of the handbook and revise your paper accordingly.

For an illustration of this procedure, consider the two copies of the specimen paper on the next pages. Specimen A shows the paper after it had been marked with handbook numbers by an instructor. Specimen B shows the paper after it had been revised by the writer.

Specimen Paper A

THE IDEAL EDUCATION   (31b)

More than ever before, a good education is required if one is
going to seek the fortunes of opportunity. The past few years college   (17a)
enrollments have been increasing steadily because people are realizing
the importance of higher education. The best jobs are held by people
who have an advanced education, therefore the value of education can-   (11a)
not be stressed too much.

(16b)   In choosing a college to enter, the differences of colleges must
be considered. For instance, a student considering Normal State must
(44a)   realise that this university has many thousands of students. When a
student comes to State, he feels as though he is coming to live in a
(26c)   new town. Right away he finds that he is on his "own." He feels that
high school was more like kindergarten. The college with a small enrollment is more compact, which helps the new student considerably at   (13c)
(37b)   first. He always receives more personnel attention from the faculty   (44d)
than he would at a college as large as Normal St.   (3b)

(14b)   Now that we have seen the big differences between large and small
universities, you probably see that there are advantageous aspects to   (41a)
both or they would not be in existence. At Normal State the student
(44d)   sacrifices personnel attention for the better equipment he has to work
with. At a small college the situation is reversed. Irregardless, the   (41c)
fact remains that the student coming from high school is facing a new   (41a)
situation and needs guidance in many cases.

Specimen Paper B

A Small College or a Large University?

~~THE IDEAL EDUCATION~~ (31b)

More than ever before, a good education is required if one is going to seek the fortunes of opportunity. *In* ~~T~~he past few years college (17a) enrollments have been increasing steadily because people are realizing the importance of higher education. *Because* ~~T~~he best jobs are held by people who have an advanced education, ~~therefore~~ the value of education cannot be stressed too much. (11a)

In choosing a college to enter, *one must consider* ~~the differences of colleges must be considered~~. For instance, a student considering Normal State must *realize* ~~realize~~ that this university has many thousands of students. When a student comes to State, he feels as though he is coming to live in a new town. Right away he finds that he is on his "own." He feels that high school was more like kindergarten. The college with a small enrollment is more compact, *a circumstance* which helps the new student considerably at first. He *usually* always receives more *personal* personnel attention from the faculty than he would at a college as large as Normal *State* St. (16b) (44a) (26e) (13c) (37b) (44d) (3b)

Now that we have seen the big differences between large and small universities, *we* you probably see that there are ~~advantageous aspects~~ *advantages* to both or they would not be in existence. At Normal State the student sacrifices ~~personnel~~ *personal* attention for the better equipment he has to work with. At a small college the situation is reversed. ~~Irregardless~~, *Regardless* the fact remains that the student coming from high school is facing a new situation and needs *may* guidance ~~in many cases~~. (14b) (4/a) (44d) (4/c) (4/a)

Acknowledgments

For suggesting ways to improve the second edition of the HAND-BOOK FOR WRITERS, we are grateful to many persons, but especially to Paul R. Sullivan, Georgetown University; C. A. Bender, City College of New York; Garry N. Murphy, University of Cincinnati; Richard E. Madtes, State University College of Education, New Paltz, New York; Dale S. Bailey, Brigham Young University; Elinor Yaggy, University of Washington; Robert Kirk, El Camino College; Ben Gray Lumpkin, University of Colorado; Lucile Clifton, Ball State Teachers College; Alex Fischler, Whitman College; and John Heide, Wisconsin State Teachers College.

Special thanks are due to Mrs. David Bothun for help in editing the manuscript and to Mrs. Thomas Churchill and Mrs. Roy F. Hollingsworth for typing it.

In addition, we are grateful to Miss Jean Buck (now Mrs. Ralph Brooks) for giving us permission to reprint her library paper.

We wish also to thank the following for their permission to reproduce copyrighted material in the revised *Handbook:*

George Allen and Unwin, Ltd.: the selection from "The ABC of Relativity," in *Selected Papers,* by Bertrand Russell, used by special permission of George Allen and Unwin, Ltd.

The American Historical Association: the selection from "History," by Carl Becker, reprinted from *The American Historical Review* of January, 1932, and used by special permission of the American Historical Association.

Appleton-Century-Crofts, Inc.: the selection from *English Words and Their Background,* by G. H. McKnight, copyright 1923 by Appleton-Century, Inc., and used by special permission of Appleton-Century-Crofts, Inc.

The Bobbs-Merrill Company, Inc.: the selections from *Lake Erie,* by Harlan Hatcher, copyright 1945, and used by special permission of The Bobbs-Merrill Company, Inc.; the selection from *The Life of Andrew Jackson,* by Marquis James, copyright 1938, and used by special permission of The Bobbs-Merrill Company, Inc.

Brandt and Brandt: the selection from "a man who had fallen among thieves," by e e cummings, copyright 1926 by Horace Liveright, published by Harcourt, Brace and Company, Inc., and used by special permission of Brandt and Brandt.

Columbia University Press: the selections from *Five Travel Scripts*, edited by H. W. Troyer, copyright 1933 (Facsimile Text Society), and used by special permission of the Columbia University Press.

Dodd, Mead and Company: the selection from *A Miscellany of Men*, by Gilbert Chesterton, copyright 1912, and used by special permission of Dodd, Mead and Company; and the selection from "Good and Bad Language" in *Essays on Language and Usage*, by Stephen Leacock, used by special permission of Dodd, Mead and Company.

Doubleday and Company, Inc.: the selection from *Winston Churchill: An Informal Study of Greatness*, by Robert Lewis Taylor, copyright 1952, and used by special permission of Doubleday and Company, Inc.; the facsimile entry from the Thorndike-Barnhart *Comprehensive Desk Dictionary*, used by special permission of Doubleday and Company, Inc.

E. P. Dutton and Company, Inc.: the selection from *Science Is a Sacred Cow*, by Anthony Standen, copyright 1952, and used by special permission of E. P. Dutton and Company, Inc.

Mrs. Charles M. Flandrau: the selection from *Viva Mexico!*, by Charles M. Flandrau, copyright 1937, published by D. Appleton-Century Co., Inc., and used with Mrs. Flandrau's special permission.

Grove Press, Inc.: the selection from *Japanese Literature*, by Donald Keene, copyright 1955, and used by special permission of Grove Press, Inc.

Harcourt, Brace and Company, Inc.: the selection from *Seventeenth Century Prose*, edited by R. P. T. Coffin and Alexander Witherspoon, copyright 1929, and used by special permission of Harcourt, Brace and Company, Inc.; the selection from *Collected Poems*, by T. S. Eliot, copyright 1930, 1934, 1936, and used by special permission of Harcourt, Brace and Company, Inc.; the selection from *Main Street*, by Sinclair Lewis, copyright 1920, and used by special permission of Harcourt, Brace and Company, Inc.; the selection from *The Conduct of Life*, by Lewis Mumford, copyright 1951, and used by special permission of Harcourt, Brace and Company, Inc.; the selection from "The Old Order," in *The Leaning Tower and Other Stories*, by Katherine Ann Porter, copyright 1944, and used by special permission of Harcourt, Brace and Company, Inc.

Harper & Brothers: the selections from the *American College Dictionary*, copyright 1947, 1948, 1949, 1950, by Random House, Inc., text edition copyright 1948 by Harper & Brothers and used by special permission of Harper & Brothers; the selection from *The Mind in the Making*, by James Harvey Robinson, copyright 1921, and used by special permission of Harper & Brothers; the selection from Mark Twain's *Europe and Elsewhere*, used by special permission of Harper & Brothers; the selection from Mark Twain's *Life on the Mississippi*, used by special permission of Harper & Brothers; the selections from *One Man's Meat*, by E. B. White, copyright 1950, and used by special permission of Harper & Brothers.

Henry Holt and Company, Inc.: the selections from *Anglo-Saxon Reader*, Fourth Edition, edited by James G. Bright, and used by special permission of Henry Holt and Company, Inc.

Houghton-Mifflin Company: the selection from "The Big Money," in *U.S.A.*, by John Dos Passos, copyright 1930, 1932, 1933, 1934, 1935, 1936, 1937, and used by permission of Houghton-Mifflin Company; the selection from *The Making of the Modern Mind*, Revised Edition, by J. H. Randall, copyright 1940, and used by special permission of Houghton-Mifflin Company.

Alfred A. Knopf, Inc.: the selection from *God, Graves, and Scholars*, by C. W. Ceram, copyright 1952, and used by special permission of Alfred A. Knopf, Inc.; the selection from *In Defense of Women*, by H. L. Mencken, copyright 1918, revised 1922, and used by special permission of Alfred A. Knopf, Inc.; the selection from "The Human Mind," in *Prejudices 6th Series*, by H. L. Mencken, copyright 1929, and used by special permission of Alfred A. Knopf, Inc.; the selection from "Bryan," in *Selected Prejudices*, by H. L. Mencken, copyright 1927, and used by special permission of Alfred A. Knopf, Inc.

J. B. Lippincott Company: the selection from *Sheridan of Drury Lane*, by Alice Glasgow, copyright 1940 by Frederick A. Stokes Company, and used by permission of the present holders of the copyright, J. B. Lippincott Company.

Little, Brown and Company: the selection from *Man Against Myth*, by Barrows Dunham, copyright 1947, and used by special permission of Little, Brown and Company.

Arthur D. Little, Inc.: the selection from *The Turbo-Encabulator*, by J. H. Quick, first published in the *Students' Quarterly Journal*, the Institution of Electrical Engineers, London, England, 1944, and used by special permission of Arthur D. Little, Inc.

The Macmillan Company: the selection from *Life on Other Worlds*, by H. Spencer Jones, copyright 1940, and used by special permission of The Macmillan Company; the selection from *The Aims of Education*, by A. N. Whitehead, copyright 1929, and used by special permission of The Macmillan Company; the selection from *Science and the Modern World*, by A. N. Whitehead, copyright 1925, and used by special permission of The Macmillan Company.

G. and C. Merriam Company: the selection from *Webster's New International Dictionary*, Second Edition, copyright 1934, 1939, and used by special arrangement with G. and C. Merriam Company; the selections from *Webster's New Collegiate Dictionary*, copyright 1949, and used by special arrangement with G. and C. Merriam Company.

The New American Library of World Literature, Inc.: the selection from *Russia: Its Past and Present*, by Bernard Pares, copyright 1943, 1949, by The New American Library of World Literature, Inc., and used by special permission.

Oxford University Press, Inc.: the selection from *The Sea Around Us*, by Rachel Carson, copyright 1951, and used by special permission of the Oxford University Press, Inc.; the selections from *Growth of the American Republic*, by S. E. Morison and H. S. Commager, copyright 1930, 1937, 1942, and used by special permission of the Oxford University Press, Inc.

Prentice-Hall, Inc.: the selection from *Ideas and Men*, by Crane Brinton, copyright 1950, and used by special permission of Prentice-Hall, Inc.; the selection from *The Development of Modern English*, Second Edition, by Stuart Robertson and Frederic G. Cassidy, copyright 1953, and used by special permission of Prentice-Hall, Inc.; the selection from *Foundations of Speech*, by C. M.

Wise *et al.*, copyright 1941, and used by special permission of Prentice-Hall.

Random House, Inc.: the selection from *Track of the Cat*, by Walter Van Til-burg Clark, and used by special permission of Random House, Inc.; the selection from "Delta Autumn," reprinted from *Go Down Moses*, by William Faulkner, copyright 1942, and used by special permission of Random House, Inc.; the selection from *Sanctuary*, by William Faulkner, copyright 1931, and used by special permission of Random House, Inc.; the selections from *Keep It Crisp*, copyright 1943, 1944, 1945, 1946, and used by special permission of Random House, Inc.; the selection from *The Harder They Fall*, by Budd Schulberg, copyright 1947, and used by special permission of Random House.

Rinehart and Company: the selection from *Three Keys to Language*, by Robert M. Estrich and Hans Sperber, copyright 1952, and used by special permission of Rinehart and Company; the selection from *Colonial American Writing*, by Roy H. Pearce, copyright 1950, and used by special permission of Rine-hart and Company.

Charles Scribner's Sons: the selection from *Farewell to Arms*, by Ernest Hem-ingway, copyright 1929, and used by special permission of Charles Scribner's Sons; the selection from "Big Two-Hearted River: II," reprinted from *In Our Time*, by Ernest Hemingway, and used by special permission of Charles Scribner's Sons; the selection from *Look Homeward, Angel*, by Thomas Wolfe, and used by special permission of Charles Scribner's Sons.

William Sloane Associates, Inc.: the selection from *The Desert Year*, by Joseph Wood Krutch, copyright 1952, and used by special permission of William Sloane Associates, Inc.; the selections from *All the Ship's at Sea*, by W. J. Lederer, copyright 1950, and used by special permission of William Sloane Associates, Inc.; the selection from *Back Home*, by Bill Mauldin, copyright 1947, and used by special permission of William Sloane Associates, Inc.; the selection from *Road to Survival*, by William Vogt, copyright 1949, and used by special permission of William Sloane Associates, Inc.

Simon and Schuster, Inc.: the selection from *Van Loon's Geography*, by Hendrik Willem Van Loon, copyright 1932, and used by special permission of Simon and Schuster, Inc.,

Mr. James Thurber: the selections from "There's an Owl in My Room" and "Something to Say," from *The Middle-Aged Man on the Flying Trapeze*, published by Harper & Brothers, and used by special permission of Mr. Thurber.

Charles E. Tuttle Company: the selection from *The Book of Tea*, by Okakura Kakuzo, and used by special permission of Charles E. Tuttle Company.

The Viking Press, Inc.: the selection from *Biography of the Earth*, by George Gamow, copyright 1941, and used by special permission of The Viking Press, Inc.; the selection from *Sons and Lovers*, by D. H. Lawrence, used by special permission of Mrs. Frieda Lawrence, William Heinemann, Ltd., and The Viking Press, Inc.

The World Publishing Company: the selection from Webster's *New World Dic-tionary*, and used by special permission of The World Publishing Company.

The University of Michigan Press: the selection (with revisions) "Radio: Best Source of News," from *Preparation for College English*, edited by Clar-ence D. Thorpe, copyright 1945, and used by special permission of the Uni-versity of Michigan Press.

Contents

xix

PRENTICE-HALL

Handbook for Writers

Blot out, correct, insert, refine,
Enlarge, diminish, interline;
Be mindful, when invention fails,
To scratch your head, and bite your nails.

—JONATHAN SWIFT

All life therefore comes back to the question of our speech, the medium through which we communicate with each other; for all life comes back to the question of our relations with one another.

—HENRY JAMES, *The Question of Our Speech*

Introduction

The origin and growth of English

English is basically a Teutonic language, for it is founded on the speech of the Germanic tribes (Angles, Saxons, and Jutes) who invaded the British Isles in the fifth century A.D. The surviving specimens of this language—now called "Old English" or Anglo-Saxon—hardly seem like English at all.

> Hēr Æðelstān cyning, eorla drihten,
> *Here Athelstan the king, the earls' leader,*
>
> beorna beāhgifa, and his brōðor ēac,
> *the heroes' ring-giver, and his brother also,*
>
> Eadmund aeðeling, ealdor langne tīr
> *Edmund the prince, life-long glory*
>
> geslōgan aet saecce, sweorda ecgum,
> *won at war, by the edges of swords,*
>
> ymbe Brunanburh.
> *at Brunanburh.*
>
> —*Battle of Brunanburh* (A.D. 937)

In the following centuries, this language was greatly altered by the effects of a Danish, and then a Norman French, invasion of the British Isles. Thousands of Latin, Scandinavian, and French words became part of its vocabulary. Spelling and pronunciation changed; the original meanings of words shifted, expanded, and were modified. Syntax—what we now call "sentence structure"—gradually changed. Like Latin, Old English was a highly inflected language, with an involved system of declensions and conjugations. In the course of history, this system was simplified, so much so that, by and large, the order of words in a sentence, rather than the endings of words, came to determine grammatical function, and therefore meaning. The following selections, listed chronologically, illustrate the gradual but steady change:

Ðis gēar cōm Henrī Kīng tō þis lānd. Þā cōm Henrī abbot and
In this year came Henry the king to this land. Then came Henry
wreide þē muneces of Burch tō þē kīng forþī ðat hē wolde under-
the abbot and denounced the monks of Burch to the king for
þēden ðat mynstre tō Clunīe, swā ðat tē kīng was wēl nēh bepaht
that he would subjugate the monastery to Cluny, so that the
and sende efter þē muneces.
king was well nigh deceived and sent after the monks.

—*Peterborough Chronicle* (1132)

A knyght there was, and that a worthy man,
That from the tyme that he first bigan
To ryden out, he loved chivalrye,
Trouthe and honour, fredom and courteisye.

—CHAUCER, *Canterbury Tales, Prologue* (*ca.* 1385)

Hit befel in the dayes of Uther Pendragon, when he was kynge of all Englond, and so regned, that there was a myghty duke in Cornewaill that helde warre ageynst hym long tyme, and the duke was called the duke of Tyntagil.

—SIR THOMAS MALORY, *Morte d'Arthur* (*ca.* 1470)

A Proude Man contemneth the companye of hys olde friendes, and disdayneth the sight of hys former famyliars, and turneth hys face from his wonted acquayntaunce.

—HENRY KERTON, *The Mirror of Man's Lyfe* (1576)

To us these specimens reflect a steady, inevitable progress toward modern English. But to Englishmen living through these centuries it seemed that English would not hold still long enough to have any value as an instrument of communication. Some of them, like Sir Thomas More and Sir Francis Bacon, wrote their most ambitious works in Latin, a safe and stable language. Fortunately other Englishmen, like Geoffrey Chaucer and Sir Thomas Malory, wrote in their native language, staking their future reputations on the chance that it would survive. The development of printing in England toward the end of the fifteenth century, and the growth of a national spirit during the sixteenth, helped to dignify and standardize the language. By the end of the sixteenth century, English was a truly national language, as the English translation of the Bible in 1611 very well indicates.

Since that time English has never ceased to grow and change, but far less radically than before. The widespread use of printing has tended to stabilize the language. The first specimen below, written some 250 years ago, has its oddities of spelling and capitalization, but it is almost "modern" English. And the second selection, written by Oliver Goldsmith almost two centuries ago, is different from modern prose only in its old-fashioned tone and its overuse of the comma.

> The Country, by its Climate, is always troubled with an *Ague* and *Fever;* As soon as ever the Cold fit's over, tis attended with a Hot: and the *Natives* themselves, whose Bodies are Habituated to the suddain changes, from one Extream to another, cannot but confess, They *Freez* in Winter and Fry in Summer.
>
> —[NED WARD], *A Trip to New England* (1699)

> I was ever of the opinion, that the honest man who married and brought up a large family, did more service than he who continued single and only talked of population. From this motive, I had scarce taken orders a year, before I began to think seriously of matrimony, and chose my wife, as she did her wedding gown, not for a fine glossy surface, but such qualities as would wear well. To do her justice, she was a good-natured, notable woman; and as for breeding, there were few country ladies who could show more. She could read any English book without much spelling; but for pickling, preserving, and cookery, none could excel her. She prided herself

5

also upon being an excellent contriver in housekeeping; though I could never find that we grew richer with all her contrivances.

—OLIVER GOLDSMITH, *The Vicar of Wakefield* (1766)

During the eighteenth century, English grammarians set about trying to standardize and refine the language. They prepared dictionaries that fixed the spellings and meanings of words, and some of them tried to force English, still a young and vigorous language, into the rigid mold of Latin. They devised a host of elaborate and artificial rules to govern the use of English in speaking and writing. Some of these rules died of neglect. But others won acceptance and were scrupulously observed by educated Englishmen. Even today a great many users of English feel that the language obeys (or at least ought to obey) a kind of abstract logic instead of doing what it obviously does and must do: follow the actual usage of people who write and speak it. The distaste that purists still feel for split infinitives, for prepositions at the end of sentences, for "It's me," and so on, all grow out of the "eighteenth-century" attitude toward English, an attitude that has passed into the subconsciousness of the English and American people and makes it difficult to discuss the "standards" of modern English realistically.

The standards of modern English

What do we mean by the "standards" of modern English? Remove from your typewriter the letter you have just written to your best friend. Now write another letter to a man you have never seen who can give you a job you are anxious to get. Compare the two letters. In the first, you spoke of the "swell job" you are "after." In the second, the job becomes a "position." In the first, you were sure you "had the stuff to make a go of it." In the second, you "assure" the man that you have had "excellent training" which will "enable you to succeed." In the first you hoped "to get together" with your friend over "Xmas for a blast or two." In the second, you "suggest" that the "Christmas holidays might provide an opportunity for an interview."

You might assume that in the second letter you were writing "good" English, and that in the first you were writing "poor" English. But not everyone would agree. In fact, many of our most distinguished writers and linguists would say that the English in your

6

first letter was better because it was more "natural." But "natural" is a relative term, and really descriptive of the kind of English you were using in both letters. In one letter you were communicating "naturally" with a friend; in the other letter you were unconsciously adjusting your English to a different audience and situation, and being just as "natural."

This adjustment of usage to different audiences and situations is called by John S. Kenyon, a famous editor of dictionaries, "cultural levels and functional varieties of English." By "cultural levels" he means *standard* and *substandard English,* the first describing the writing and speaking habits of cultivated people, the second describing the writing and speaking habits of the uncultivated. In other words, the distinction between the two terms rests on the cultural status (or ambitions) of the people using the language.[*] Here are some illustrations:

STANDARD

Society never advances. It recedes as fast on one side as it gains on the other. It undergoes continual changes; it is barbarous, it is civilized, it is christianized, it is rich, it is scientific; but this change is not amelioration. For everything that is given something is taken. Society acquires new arts and loses old instincts. What a contrast between the well-clad, reading, writing, thinking American, with a watch, a pencil and a bill of exchange in his pocket, and the naked New Zealander, whose property is a club, a spear, a mat, and an undivided twentieth of a shed to sleep under! But compare the health of the two men and you shall see that the white man has lost his aboriginal strength. If the traveller tell us truly, strike the savage with a broad-axe and in a day or two the flesh shall unite and heal as if you struck the blow into soft pitch, and the same blow shall send the white to his grave.

—R. W. EMERSON, "Self-Reliance" (1841)

SUBSTANDARD

So I said to him, I said, you was dead wrong thinking you'd get away with that dough. We had you spotted from the beginning, smart boy. And we was sure when we seen you put that roll in

[*] The words "acceptable" and "unacceptable" are often equated with *standard* and *substandard,* respectively. The equation is frequently accurate, but before assuming that *substandard* English is always unacceptable, we ought to ask "unacceptable to whom?"

your pocket. So I starts to move in on him, easy-like, and all at oncet, he grabs in his pocket and comes out with a gun. Don't nobody move, he yells, and starts for the door. But he trips over his own big feet and goes down, hard. Right then I lets him have it with five quick shots. He was the deadest double-crosser you ever seen.

By "functional varieties of English," on the other hand, Kenyon refers to the different uses or functions of language to which most people instinctively adapt themselves. The chief functional varieties are *informal* and *formal*. In the broadest terms informal describes the English of conversation, of private correspondence, and of ordinary, everyday writing and speaking. Formal describes the English of platform or "pulpit" speech, most legal and scientific writing, and academic and literary prose. Until a generation or two ago most school teachers and textbooks in English recommended formal usage. Formal English was equated with standard English. Informal English, though obviously then as now the real workaday language, was suspected of being not quite proper. This state of affairs was unrealistic, and it led some people to assume that only pretentious-sounding English was "good English." Nowadays we recognize that both informal and formal usage are standard English and that neither is necessarily "more correct" than the other. Everything depends on its suitability to audience and situation; appropriateness is now the real measure of "good" English.

In the examples below, note the oratorical structure of the formal selection, its Latinized vocabulary (exposition, application, mortification), its obviously serious purpose. Then note the relaxed structure, the everyday vocabulary, the modest tone of the informal selection. But if you catch yourself thinking that one is better than the other, remember that the purpose, subject matter, and audience (as well as the temperament) of each author are quite different, and that these differences account for the differences in style.

FORMAL

Dean Donne in the pulpit of old Paul's, holding his audience spellbound still as he reversed his glass of sands after an hour of exposition and application of texts by the light of the church fathers, of mortification for edification, of exhortation that brought tears to the eyes of himself and his hearers, and of analogies born of the study, but sounding of wings,—there was a man who should have had wisdom, surely. For if experience can bring it, this was the man.

—R. P. T. COFFIN *and* A. M. WITHERSPOON,
"John Donne," in *Seventeenth Century Prose*

INFORMAL

Of all the common farm operations none is more ticklish than tending a brooder stove. All brooder stoves are whimsical, and some of them are holy terrors. Mine burns coal, and has only a fair record. With its check draft that opens and closes, this stove occupies my dreams from midnight, when I go to bed, until five o'clock, when I get up, pull a shirt and a pair of pants on over my pajamas, and stagger out into the dawn to read the thermometer under the hover and see that my 254 little innocents are properly disposed in a neat circle round their big iron mama.

—E. B. WHITE, *One Man's Meat*

What about the label *colloquial?* How does it fit in with what we have been saying? This term is sometimes used to refer to *substandard* usage, with a suggestion of disreputability. Technically, however, *colloquial* simply means "spoken." It may refer to any spoken English, whether "culturally" standard or substandard, whether "functionally" formal or informal. Many students of language, however, use the word to refer to a kind of writing that has the easy and unpretentious vocabulary, the loose constructions and contractions, of every-day spoken English. Charles Fries, one of the editors of the *American College Dictionary*, defines *colloquial* as those words and constructions

> . . . whose range of use is primarily that of the polite conversation of cultivated people, of their familiar letters and informal speeches, as distinct from those words and constructions which are common also in formal writing. The usage of our better magazines and of public addresses generally has, during the past generation, moved away from the formal and literary toward the colloquial.

In this sense *colloquial* is really informal.

The existence of "levels" and "varieties" of English means, then, that there is no absolute standard of correctness. But it does not mean that we can do without standards at all, or that what is good enough for familiar conversation is appropriate for all kinds of communication. It is true that if people were to write as naturally as they talk, they would rid their writing of a great deal of affectation. But it is also true that conversational English depends for much of its force upon the physical presence of the speaker. Personality, gesture, and intonation all contribute to the success of spoken communication.* Written English, on the other hand, whether formal or informal, requires a structure that makes for clarity without the physical presence of the writer. It must communicate through the clarity of its diction and the orderliness of its sentence structure. In short, the writer must meet certain standards if he is to get his meaning across.

A handbook somewhat arbitrarily classifies standards of "Good English" into rules or conventions that cannot always be defended on logical grounds. Rather, they reflect the practices—some old, some new—of English and American writers. Most of these conventions are quite flexible. The rules for punctuation, for instance, permit many variations, and so do the standards for diction and sentence structure and paragraphing. The truth is that the rules of writing represent "typical" or "normal" practices. Skillful writers interpret them very loosely and sometimes ignore those that seem too restrictive. For most writers, however, the rules are a discipline and a security. Observing them will not make a writer great, but it will make his writing clear and orderly. And clarity and order are the marks of all good writing.

Books for reference and further study

Aiken, Janet R., *Commonsense Grammar*. New York: Thomas Y. Crowell Co., 1936.

Berry, Lester V., and Melvin Van den Bark, *The American Thesaurus of Slang*. New York: Thomas Y. Crowell Co., 1952.

Bryant, Margaret M., *A Functional English Grammar*. New York: D. C. Heath and Co., 1935.

Curme, George O., *Parts of Speech and Accidence*. Boston: D. C. Heath and Co., 1935.

* Let anyone who disagrees test this assertion by arranging for a tape recording of an ordinary argument or discussion—without informing the speakers. The transcript will probably seem absurd and only partly intelligible.

Curme, George O., *Syntax*. Boston: D. C. Heath and Co., 1931.

Estrich, Robert M., and Hans Sperber, *Three Keys to Language*. New York: Rinehart and Co., 1952.

Evans, Bergen and Cornelia, *A Dictionary of Contemporary American Usage*. New York: Random House, 1957.

Fowler, Henry W., *A Dictionary of Modern English Usage*. New York: Oxford University Press, 1926.

Fowler, Henry W., and F. G., *The King's English*. London: Oxford University Press, 1931.

Fries, Charles C., *American English Grammar*. New York: Appleton-Century-Crofts, 1940.

———, *The Structure of the English Sentence*. New York: Harcourt-Brace and Co., 1952.

Goldberg, Isaac, *The Wonder of Words*. New York: Appleton-Century-Crofts, 1938.

Gray, Louis H., *Foundations of Language*. New York: Macmillan Company, 1939.

Greenough, J. B., and George L. Kittredge, *Words and Their Ways in English Speech*. New York: Macmillan Company, 1923.

Hook, J. N., and E. G. Mathews, *Modern American Grammar and Usage*. New York: Ronald Press Company, 1956.

Jespersen, Otto, *Essentials of English Grammar*. New York: D. C. Heath and Co., 1933.

Kennedy, Arthur G., *Current English*. Boston: Ginn and Co., 1935.

Laird, Charlton, *The Miracle of Language*. New York: World Publishing Co., 1953.

Lloyd, Donald J., and Harry R. Warfel, *American English in Its Cultural Setting*. New York: Alfred A. Knopf, Inc., 1956.

Marckwardt, Albert H., *American English*. New York: Oxford University Press, Inc., 1958.

———, and Fred G. Walcott, *Facts about Current English Usage*. New York: Appleton-Century-Crofts, 1938.

Mathews, Mitford M., *Words: How to Know Them*. New York: Henry Holt & Co., Inc., 1956.

McKnight, George H., *English Words and Their Backgrounds*. New York: Appleton-Century-Crofts, 1923.

Mencken, H. L., *The American Language*. New York: Alfred Knopf, Inc., 1936. Supplement One, 1945. Supplement Two, 1948.

MLA Style Sheet. New York: Modern Language Association.

Myers, L. M., *American English, A Twentieth-Century Grammar.* Englewood Cliffs, New Jersey: Prentice-Hall, Inc., 1952.

Partridge, Eric, *A Dictionary of Slang and Unconventional English,* 3rd edition. New York: Macmillan Company, 1950.

———, and John W. Clark, *British and American English Since 1900.* London: Andrew Dakers Limited, 1951.

Pence, R. W., *A Grammar of Present Day English.* New York: Macmillan Company, 1947.

Perrin, Porter G., *Writer's Guide and Index to English,* 3rd edition. Chicago: Scott-Foresman and Co., 1959.

Pooley, Robert C., *Teaching English Grammar.* New York: Appleton-Century-Crofts, 1957.

———, *Teaching English Usage.* New York: Appleton-Century-Crofts, 1946.

Potter, Simeon, *Our Language.* Baltimore: Penguin Books, Inc., 1950.

Pyles, Thomas, *Words and Ways of American English.* New York: Random House, 1952.

Roberts, Paul, *Patterns of English.* New York: Harcourt, Brace and Co., 1956.

———, *Understanding Grammar.* New York: Henry Holt & Co., 1954.

Schlauch, Margaret, *The Gift of Tongues.* New York: Modern Age Books, Inc., 1942.

Shipley, Joseph, *A Dictionary of Word Origins.* New York: Philosophical Library, Inc., 1945.

Strunk, William, Jr., and E. B. White, *The Elements of Style.* New York: Macmillan Company, 1959.

Summey, George, *American Punctuation.* New York: Ronald Press, 1949.

University of Chicago, *A Manual of Style,* 11th edition. Chicago: University of Chicago Press, 1949.

Whitehall, Harold, *Structural Essentials of English.* New York: Harcourt, Brace and Co., 1956.

It was very pleasant to me to get a letter from you the other day. Perhaps I should have found it pleasanter if I had been able to decipher it.

—THOMAS BAILEY ALDRICH

SECTIONS **1-4**

Manuscript Mechanics = MS

A good many of the rules of written English are merely conventions. Logic alone does not justify them; they represent instead traditional practices and ways of doing things. The "mechanics" of manuscript form, of writing numbers and abbreviations, of word division (syllabication) are such conventions. We observe them chiefly because generations of readers have come to expect writers to observe them. To be ignorant of these conventions, or to violate them, is by no means to commit a cardinal sin—only to make nuisances of ourselves to our readers, who expect that anyone seeking their attention with a piece of writing will have the graciousness at least to do the little things properly.

13

1 MANUSCRIPT FORM = MS

Prepare your manuscripts carefully, write or typewrite them legibly, and arrange them neatly. Proofread them thoroughly before submitting them. After they have been returned, correct them according to your instructor's suggestions.

1a Use suitable materials for your manuscripts.

(1) *Paper.* Your instructor will probably require you to use standard theme paper (8½ by 11 inches). If you write your manuscript in longhand, keep your lines far enough apart to allow space for corrections. Your instructor may ask you to write only on every other line. If you typewrite your manuscript, use either regular unlined typewriter paper or the unruled side of theme paper.

(2) *Pen and ink.* Write only on the ruled side of the paper. Use a good pen and black or blue-black ink.

(3) *Typewriter.* Use a fresh, black ribbon and keep the keys clean.

1b Make sure your manuscripts are legible.

(1) *Handwritten manuscripts.* Provide adequate spacing between words and between lines. Avoid unnecessary breaks between letters and syllables at the ends of lines. Form all letters distinctly, with clear and conspicuous capitals. Cross all *t*'s. Dot all *i*'s with real dots, not with decorative circles. Avoid artistic flourishes. If your handwriting tends to be excessively large and sprawling, or small and cramped, or precariously tipped to right or left, make a conscious effort to improve it.

14

(2) *Typewritten manuscripts.* Use double-spacing to provide room for corrections. Leave one space between words and two spaces between sentences.

1c   Keep your manuscripts physically uniform and orderly.

(1) *Margins.* Leave a uniform one-and-a-half-inch margin on both the right and left side of each page. Resist the temptation to crowd words in at the right or bottom of the page.

(2) *Title.* Center the title about two inches from the top of the page, or on the first line. Leave a blank line between the title and the first paragraph. Capitalize the first word and all other words in the title except the articles *a, an, the,* and short prepositions or conjunctions. Do not underline the title or put it in quotation marks unless it is an actual quotation. Use no punctuation after titles except when a question mark or exclamation point is required. Do not repeat the title after the first page.

(3) *Indenting.* Indent the first line of each paragraph about an inch, or five spaces on the typewriter. Indent lines of poetry one inch from the regular margin, or center them on the page. If you are typewriting, use single-spacing for poetry.

(4) *Paging.* Number all pages, after the first, in the upper right-hand corner. Use Arabic numerals (2, 3, 4, etc.).

(5) *Endorsement.* The endorsement, which usually appears on the outside sheet of the folded (lengthwise) composition, includes your name, the course, the date, plus any information required by your instructor. Below is a specimen:

Fold here → Doe, John
English 101, Section A
October 18, 1960
Instructor: Mr. Brown
Class Paper 2

1d   Carefully proofread your manuscripts before submitting them.

Give every manuscript a close, almost finicky reading before turning it in. Allow a cooling-off period between composition and proofreading. If you know you are poor in spelling, punctuation, or some other area, give your paper a separate reading for each kind of error. If your proofreading reveals a great many errors, rewrite your composition. When rewriting is not necessary, make specific changes as follows:

(1) If you want to delete words, draw a horizontal line through them. Do not use a series of parentheses to cancel words.

(2) If you want to begin a new paragraph within an existing paragraph, put the sign ¶ or *Par.* before the sentence that is to begin the new paragraph. When you want to remove a paragraph division, write *No* ¶ or *No Par.* in the margin.

(3) If you want to make a brief insertion, write the new material above the line and indicate the point of insertion by placing a caret (∧) below the line.

1e   **After your instructor has returned a manuscript, make the necessary corrections and submit it again.**

Correcting your own errors is invaluable practice. Your instructor designates errors by means of numbers or symbols that refer to specific parts of this handbook. Study these parts carefully before making revisions.

For an example of a composition with an instructor's markings, before and after correction, see Specimen Papers A and B, which appear in the Preface.

2   NUMBERS = NOS

In general, use numerals for specific numbers and amounts; write out round or approximate numbers.

2a **Spell out numbers or amounts that can be expressed in one or two words; use numerals for other numbers or amounts.**

He spent two hundred dollars for a camera.
Miriam is twenty-two years old.
The boy saved $4.53.
On their vacation they drove 2,468 miles.

2b **Ordinarily, use numerals for dates.**

The letters *st, nd, rd, th* are not necessary after days of the month.

May 4, 1913; July 2 (or *second,* if the year is not given)

Write out the year only in formal social correspondence.

2c **Use numerals for street numbers, decimals and percentages, chapter and page numbers, and hours followed by** A.M. **or** P.M.

13 Milford Avenue; 57 121st Street.
The bolt is .46 inches in diameter.
The price was reduced 15 per cent.
The quotation was in Chapter 4, page 119.
A train arrived from Chicago at 11:20 A.M.

2d **Except in legal or commercial writing, or when extreme accuracy is required, do not repeat in parentheses a number that has been spelled out.**

COMMERCIAL   The interest on the note was fifty (50) dollars.
UNNECESSARY   The boys caught three (3) fish.
REVISED   The boys caught three fish.

17

2e Spell out numbers that occur at the beginning of a sentence.

AWKWARD   217 bales of hay were lost in the fire.

REVISED   Two hundred and seventeen bales of hay were lost in the fire.

If necessary, recast a sentence to eliminate numerals at the beginning.

AWKWARD   2,655 entries were received in the puzzle contest.

REVISED   In the puzzle contest 2,655 entries were received.

EXERCISE 1. In the following sentences make any necessary corrections in the use of numbers.

1. Franklin died at the age of 84.
2. She retired on January 1st, 1958.
3. 130 families were made homeless by the flood.
4. My profit on the investment was ten per cent.
5. The economics class met at one P.M.
6. My vacation lasted fourteen (14) days.
7. The lump of gold was three and thirteen hundredths inches in circumference.
8. He employed 300 men in his factory.
9. The child spent $.05 for candy.
10. Helen attended college for 2 years.
11. Samuel Johnson was born in the year seventeen nine.
12. 25,000 people listened to the general's address.
13. The jangle of a telephone roused me at three A.M.
14. Our community is sponsoring a celebration on July 4th.
15. Big Harry was sentenced to 25 years in the penitentiary.

3

3 ABBREVIATIONS = **AB**

Use only established and conventional abbreviations.

3a **The following abbreviations are appropriate in both formal and informal writing.**

(1) *Titles before proper names.* Use such abbreviations as *Mr., Mrs., Dr.,* when the surname is given: *Dr. Hart* or *Dr. J. D. Hart.* Use *St.* (Saint) with a Christian name, as in *St. James, St. John.* In informal writing, abbreviations such as *Hon., Rev., Prof., Sen.* may be used before names, but only when both the surname and given name or initials are given: *The Hon. O. P. Jones;* but not *Hon. Jones.* In formal usage spell out these titles and use *The* before *Honorable.*

INAPPROPRIATE	He has gone to consult the Dr.
REVISED	He has gone to consult Dr. Hart (*or* the doctor).
FORMAL	The Reverend W. C. Case delivered the sermon.
INFORMAL	Rev. W. C. Case delivered the sermon.

(2) *Titles after proper names.* Use the following abbreviations only when a name is given: Jr., Sr., Esq., M.D., D.D., LL.D., Ph.D. You may, however, use academic titles by themselves.

He has an M.A. in English and is now studying for his Ph.D.

(3) *Abbreviations used with dates or numerals.* Use the following abbreviations only when specific dates and numerals are given: 42 B.C., 818 A.D., 8:30 A.M., 11:15 P.M., No. 47, $5.79.

INAPPROPRIATE	What was the No. of the play the coach discussed yesterday P.M.?
REVISED	What was the number of the play the coach discussed yesterday afternoon?
APPROPRIATE	He was No. 2 on the list posted at 6:30 P.M.

19

(4) *Latin abbreviations.* In formal writing there is an increasing tendency to use the English equivalents of Latin abbreviations such as *i.e.* (that is), *e.g.* (for example), *etc.* (and so forth). Do not fall into the habit of using *etc.* as a catch-all term or to save yourself the time and trouble of completing your sentences. *Etc.* is meaningless unless the extension of ideas it implies is immediately and unmistakably clear to the reader.

> CLEAR   The citrus fruits—oranges, lemons, etc.—are rich in Vitamin C. (The reader has no difficulty in mentally listing the other citrus fruits.)
>
> INEFFECTIVE   We swam, fished, etc. (The reader has no clues to the implied ideas.)
>
> REVISED   We swam, fished, rode horses, and danced.

Use the ampersand (&) for *and* only in names of firms (Barnes & Noble, Inc., for example).

3b   **In formal writing spell out personal names and the names of countries, states, months, and days of the week.**

> INAPPROPRIATE   Geo., a student from Eng., joined the class last Wed.
>
> REVISED   George, a student from England, joined the class last Wednesday.

3c   **In formal writing spell out the words** STREET, AVENUE, COMPANY, **and references to a** SUBJECT, VOLUME, CHAPTER, **or** PAGE.

> INAPPROPRIATE   The Perry Coal Co. has an office at Third Ave. and Mott St.
>
> REVISED   The Perry Coal Company has an office at Third Avenue and Mott Street.
>
> INAPPROPRIATE   The p.e. class is reading ch. 3 of the textbook.
>
> REVISED   The physical education class is reading the third chapter (*or* Chapter Three) of the textbook.

EXERCISE 2. In the following sentences correct all faulty abbreviations.

1. At six o'clock post meridian the explorers reached the top of the mt.
2. The prof. instructed the class to read ch. 2, p. 43.

3. Thom. Kell began working for the Ace Camera Co. in Oct.

4. After graduating from the U. of Minn. Mister Harper moved to New Eng.

5. The Pres. & Gen. Gale discussed U.S. trade with Gr. Brit.

6. Wm. Greer has opened a garage on Main St.

7. The car's license No. was concealed by rust and mud.

8. During his furlough the capt. visited relatives in Mass.

9. Rev. John Howe's sermons reveal his wide reading in lit.

10. The sts. are slippery because of the big snow this A.M.

11. This book of yrs. on chem. is useless.

12. In the part of the mts. where Roberto went to blow the bridge, Span. was the only language spoken.

13. Geo. had several $$ left from his Feb. paycheck.

14. The sgt. said we would have to march by Tues.

15. At three-thirty P.M. we boarded the plane for Tex.

16. Without a col. educ. you'll never be an elec. eng.

17. You bring the girl; I'll bring the Rev.

18. Prof. Wilson spent most of his time in the Brit. Museum drinking tea with the guards.

19. Rbt. Sellars was sleeping in a hammock when he should have been studying for his exam.

20. Judson Wm.son, however, spent at least eight hrs. a wk. studying hist. and Eng. lit.

4 SYLLABICATION = SYL

Do not divide words awkwardly or unconventionally at the end of a line.

When you find that you can write only part of a word at the end of a line and must complete the word on the next line, divide the word between syllables. Use a hyphen to indicate the break. When you are in doubt about the syllabication of a word, consult a good dictionary.

The following list shows the proper syllabication of a few two- and three-syllable words.

bankrupt	bank-rupt	*grammar*	gram-mar
barren	bar-ren	*hindrance*	hin-drance
collar	col-lar	*pageant*	pag-eant
defraud	de-fraud	*puncture*	punc-ture
either	ei-ther	*theism*	the-ism

antonym	anto-nym	OR	an-tonym
caliber	cal-iber	OR	cali-ber
collective	collec-tive	OR	col-lective
definite	defi-nite	OR	def-inite
malignant	ma-lignant	OR	malig-nant

4a Never divide words of one syllable.

WRONG   thr-ee, cl-own, yearn-ed, plough-ed
REVISED   three, clown, yearned, ploughed

4b Never divide a word so that a single letter is left hanging.

WRONG   wear-y, e-rupt, a-way, o-val
REVISED   weary, erupt, away, oval

22

4c **When dividing a compound word that already contains a hyphen, make the break where the hyphen occurs.**

AWKWARD	pre-Shake-spearean, well-in-formed, Pan-Amer-ican
REVISED	pre-Shakespearean, well-informed, Pan-American

4

EXERCISE 3. Which of the following words may be divided at the end of a line? Indicate permissible breaks with a hyphen.

drowned	enough	walked
swimmer	twelve	automobile
learned	through	exercise
abrupt	acute	open
envelope	ex-President	pre-eminent

MANUSCRIPT REVIEW EXERCISE (Sections 1 through 4). Correct the errors in the following sentences.

1. A discount is offered to consumers who pay their utilities bills within ten (10) days.
2. Mr. Peebles misses the bus every day at exactly seven forty nine A.M.
3. In the absence of the pres., the secy. acted as chmn. of the meeting.
4. A new church is being erected at the corner of Elm and Pine Sts.
5. At the picnic we played ball, pitched horseshoes, etc.
6. 2 soap coupons or facsimiles thereof must accompany each application for a monogrammed pencil.
7. When Bill has no chem. class, he usually sleeps late in the A.M.
8. Mr. & Mrs. Karns are spending the winter in Fla.
9. We visited the shops on Fifth Ave.
10. The town hall was built more than 60 yrs. ago.
11. The bd. of education will meet on the 1st Wed. in Nov.
12. The salesman grudgingly granted a 5 per cent reduction in the price of the property.
13. Semester examinations begin on Mon., June 3rd.
14. This trailer was made by the Wells Mfg. Co. of Detroit, Mich.
15. Princess Pearl set a track record in the race for 3 yr. old fillies.

16. Tad caught a 30 lb. catfish in the Miss. R.
17. Rev. Barnes agreed to deliver a lecture at the Methodist Ch.
18. Columbus Day is celebrated on October 12th.
19. While in Washington we visited the Lib. of Cong.
20. At great personal sacrifice I saved six dollars and seventy five cents for Hilda's birthday present.

Good grammar is not merely grammar which is free from unconventionalities, or even from the immoralities. It is the triumph of the communication process, the use of words which create in the reader's mind the thing as the writer conceived it; it is a creative act. . . .

—JANET AIKEN, *Commonsense Grammar*

SECTIONS **5-9**

Basic Grammar = GR

What is grammar? What does it do? Perhaps the most appropriate question of all is this one: Of what *use* is a knowledge of English grammar? Just this: It tells us how the classes of words (nouns, pronouns, prepositions, etc.) are related to one another (subject-predicate, pronoun-antecedent, etc.), and how they all go together to make up a sentence. In short, grammar shows us how to build meaningful communications out of isolated words and phrases.

English has been subjected to more influences, more haphazardly, than any other major language. Supported on the Anglo-Saxon base of modern English is a superstructure of Latin, Danish, French, and other languages. In linguistic terms, English is chiefly "analytical" and yet partly "inflected." It is chiefly analytical in the sense that the position of words in a sentence, not their endings or changes in form, almost always determines their relationship to one another and hence the meaning of the sentence. It is inflected in that it has declensions (nominative, possessive, and objective forms for pronouns, for example) and conjugations (present, past, and perfect forms for most verbs).

This complication seems all very natural when we look at the history of English and the forces that have influenced it, but it is frankly a nuisance when we are looking for comforting grammatical rules to guide us. Theory dictates that the personal pronoun which follows forms of *to be* must always be in the nominative case (*It is I, It is they,* etc.). But in actual practice the position of the pronoun in the sentence has become more important in deciding its form. *It is me, It is them,* and so on, are now acceptable English. The attraction of the normal English sentence pattern—subject-verb-object—is too compelling; putting the nominative after the verb does not seem quite natural to most people. At the same time, most people feel awkward in starting a sentence with an objective form (*Whom* do you wish to see?); the nominative *who* seems more natural, and so the sentence is often spoken or written "*Who* do you wish to see?" To say that this sentence is "incorrect" would be somewhat unrealistic.

Clearly a tug-of-war is going on between traditional rules of grammar and actual usage. Though actual usage is winning out, the victory is by no means complete, and traditionalists still cling to old rules. No matter which viewpoint prevails, however, the college student needs a working knowledge of correct and acceptable grammar if he is to meet the standards of formal English required in college writing. Though we are aware of choices between older forms and newer usage, we still want to express ourselves correctly, to follow generally accepted practices, and to avoid glaring or embarrassing errors.

Grammar gives us a vocabulary for talking about and criticizing the language we speak and write. It gives us a "trouble-shooting" technique with which we can repair our use of English. Take this

26

sentence: "While enjoying our hamburgers and coffee, the halfback broke away for his third touchdown." Obviously the words "While enjoying our hamburgers and coffee" can modify nothing but the subject of the sentence, "the halfback." But is the sentence really meant to produce a ludicrous picture of a halfback racing for the goal line while munching sandwiches and juggling cups of coffee? Probably not. Grammar requires that the sentence have a subject to which the introductory words can logically apply. Such a subject might be "we": "While enjoying our hamburgers and coffee, we saw the halfback break away for his third touchdown." In other words, *a knowledge of grammar helps us turn nonsense into sense.*

Grammatical analysis of this kind is not an end in itself but a way of identifying and correcting errors. It is a useful servant, not a disagreeable taskmaster.

5 SENTENCE SENSE* = SS

*A sentence is a grammatically independent group of
words that serves as a unit of expression. It normally
contains a subject and a predicate.*

5a Recognizing sentences.

A sentence is grammatically independent and complete. It may
contain words that we cannot fully understand unless we check the
preceding or succeeding sentence, but it is grammatically self-
sufficient even when lifted out of context and made to stand alone.

1. Old Dinger's ghost was said to live in the surrounding hills.
2. It had been seen several times from the tavern window.

Both sentences are grammatically complete. True, the full meaning
of sentence 2 depends on our identifying the subject "it" with its
antecedent "Old Dinger's ghost" in sentence 1. But sentence 2
is structurally independent because the pronoun "it" is an acceptable
substitute for "Dinger's ghost." †

The main ingredients of a typical English sentence are the subject
and the predicate. The *subject* is a noun, a pronoun, or a word or
group of words functioning as a noun. The *predicate* consists of a
verb and its complements and modifiers. The predicate says something about the subject. In the following sentences the subjects are
in italic type, the predicates in small capitals.

---

* The grammatical terms used in these sections are defined in the Index to
Grammatical Terms, Section 50.

† The independence of a grammatically complete sentence is signalized by
means of "end punctuation." See Section 19.

NOUN AS SUBJECT	*Sheep* GRAZE. *Telephones* RING.
PRONOUN AS SUBJECT	*She* IS DANCING. *They* DISAPPEARED.
WORD GROUP (PHRASE) AS SUBJECT	*Over the fence* IS OUT.
WORD GROUP (CLAUSE) AS SUBJECT	*That he failed* IS CERTAIN.

Learning to recognize subject and verb is the first step in analyzing sentences. Normally the subject comes before the verb. But in the inverted sentence they are switched around, with the verb coming first. (Happy AM *I*). In some commands (GO home. SHUT the door.) the subject *You* is not expressed at all but is understood. In questions, the subject may separate the parts of the verb (HAS *he* GONE?); here we can identify the subject by recasting the sentence as a declarative statement (*He* HAS GONE).

EXERCISE 1. Indicate the subjects and verbs in the following sentences by underlining the subjects once and the verbs twice.

1. The wind blows violently.
2. His problems are nearly solved.
3. Are you feeling good today?
4. Tomorrow will be Thursday.
5. Father has been washing his car.
6. Many are the problems of a husband.
7. Where will I find the dishpan?
8. Leave your pistols at the door.
9. He shouldered his pack and trudged into the forest.
10. I think he arrived this morning.
11. Reflected in the mirror was a lovely woman's face.
12. Of all the errors a beginning golfer makes, swinging without watching the ball is probably the most common.
13. Whatever hit me on the head bounced into the lake.
14. To write an epic poem was Dryden's lifelong ambition.
15. That I was driving at a reasonable speed is my only defense.
16. Throwing my shoe at the window, I finally attracted her attention.
17. However, throwing my shoe at the window put my arm out of shape for the next day's game.
18. Grasping at trees and bushes, clawing the earth, pulling great

boulders loose with bleeding hands, the wounded man slid
down the hill and out of sight, his screams echoing distantly
off the canyon walls.

19. Because Milton considered a man who did not act according
to "right reason" a slave to his passions, he felt that such a
man had no right to participate in government.

20. One gadget that will certainly make life easier for the common
man, that will assure the leadership of this country in world
affairs and will secure the lasting respect of all posterity, is
the newly patented electric toothpaste squeezer.

5b   Recognizing parts of speech.

In modern English we recognize eight parts of speech: noun, pronoun, adjective, verb, adverb, preposition, conjunction, and interjection. There are three bases for classifying a word as a particular
part of speech: (1) its grammatical function, such as subject or
modifier; (2) its grammatical form, such as the 's of a possessive
noun; (3) its type of meaning, such as the name of a person or the
statement of an action.

Take the sentence "Lee's army marched." *Lee's* is classified as an
adjective because of its function (modifier of the noun *army*), its
form (noun made into an adjective by addition of the possessive
ending *'s*), and its type of meaning (a descriptive or limiting word).
Army is a noun because of its function (subject of the sentence) and
its type of meaning (name of a thing). *Marched* is recognizable as
a verb because of its function (asserting something about the subject *army*), its form (past tense made with the common ending *ed*),
and its type of meaning (statement of an action).

Many words function in more than one way. For example, the
word *place* may be used as noun, adjective, or verb:

NOUN	The seashore is a restful *place*.
ADJECTIVE	She bought *place* mats for the table.
VERB	*Place* the book on the desk.

The most logical way, then, of identifying a part of speech
correctly is to identify the function of the word in its particular
context.

30

(1) *Nouns*

A noun is the name of a person, place, or thing (*Carl, Detroit, studio, committee, fountain pen, truth*). Nouns normally change their form to make the plural (*boy, boys; man, men;* but *sheep, sheep; deer, deer*). To show the possessive we add an apostrophe (') or *'s* (*Bess' purse, cow's horns*).

(2) *Pronouns*

A pronoun is a substitute for a noun. We can usually discover the full meaning of a pronoun only by referring to the noun that serves as its antecedent. In the sentence "Clara Barton is the woman who founded the American Red Cross," the pronoun *who* refers to its antecedent, *woman*. Occasionally the antecedent is not expressed at all but is implied by the context. In the proverb "He who hesitates is lost," the pronoun *He* refers to any person who hesitates to take action. Indefinite pronouns such as *anybody* or *somebody* are self-sufficient and have no antecedents.

The personal pronouns *I, we, he, she, they,* and the relative or interrogative pronoun *who,* have distinctive forms for the nominative, possessive, and objective cases; *you* and *it* are the same in the nominative and objective cases but have a distinctive form for the possessive. The grammatical problems that arise from the use of these various forms are discussed in "Case," Section 6.

(3) *Adjectives*

An adjective modifies a noun or pronoun. For example: *brown* dog, *Victorian* dignity, *your* coat, *paper* hat, *this* house, *one* football, *the* mountain, *damaging* fire. Predicate adjectives are used to complete the meaning of a verb and to modify the subject. Usually predicate adjectives follow the verbs *be, seem, become, appear,* and the verbs pertaining to the five senses, *look, smell, taste, sound, feel.* (She is *sad*. He looks *happy*.)

Adjectives have no definite forms to show number or case (except pronoun adjectives such as *my, ours*). The special forms by which adjectives show comparison are discussed in "Adjectives and Adverbs," Section 8.

31

(4) Verbs and Verbals

A verb expresses action or state of being. The main function of a verb is to assert something about its subject. Linking verbs (*be, seem, become*, etc.) and verbs pertaining to the senses (*see, smell, taste*, etc.) often serve as connectives between the subject and a predicate noun or a predicate adjective. (He *became* an athlete. The cake *tastes* good.)

A verb may consist of from one to four words, depending on its inflectional form. (The pet duck *eats* too much. It *should have been eaten* long ago.) When a verb is combined with *not* (*cannot*) or with a contraction of *not* (*mustn't*), the *not* or its contraction is regarded as an adverb rather than as part of the verb.

Infinitives, participles, and gerunds, which are derived from verbs, are called *verbals*. Verbs make an assertion. Verbals do not. Though they are actual verb forms, they are used as other parts of speech.

INFINITIVE ("to" form of a verb, used as noun, adjective, or adverb)
To see is *to believe*. (Both infinitives are used as nouns.)
It was time *to leave*. (Infinitive is used as an adjective.)
I was ready *to go*. (Infinitive is used as an adverb.)

PARTICIPLE (verb form used as an adjective)
Screaming, I jumped out of bed. (Present participle)
Delighted, we accepted his invitation. (Past participle)

GERUND ("ing" form of a verb, used as noun)
Swimming is healthful exercise.
His wife enjoyed *nagging* him.

(5) Adverbs

An adverb modifies a verb, an adjective, another adverb, or an entire clause or sentence.

MODIFIER OF A VERB	He stayed *outside*.
MODIFIER OF AN ADJECTIVE	She was *very* sad.
MODIFIER OF AN ADVERB	I walked *quite* slowly.
MODIFIER OF AN ENTIRE SENTENCE	*Fortunately* the accident was not fatal.

Adverbs, like adjectives, have special forms to show comparison; these are discussed in "Adjectives and Adverbs," Section 8.

(6) Prepositions

A preposition relates a noun, pronoun, or phrase to some other part of the sentence.

> He was young *in* spirit. (*Spirit* is related to the adjective *young*.)
> See the shower *of* sparks. (*Sparks* is related to the noun *shower*.)
> I apologized *to* her. (*Her* is related to the verb *apologized*.)
> We ate sukiyaki *with* our wooden chopsticks. (*Our wooden chopsticks* is related to the verb *ate*.)

Over the centuries, English nouns have gradually lost their case endings; noun functions are now shown by the use of prepositions and objects. The object of the preposition is in the objective case (*between you and him; to John and me*). Even the last-remaining use of the inflected noun, the possessive, is often replaced by a preposition and its object (*day's end, end of the day*). Some of the more common English prepositions are *at, between, by, for, from, in, of, on, through, to, with.*

(7) Conjunctions

A conjunction is a word used to join words, phrases, or clauses. Conjunctions show the relation between the sentence elements that they connect.

Co-ordinating conjunctions (*and, but, or, nor, for*) join words, phrases, or clauses of equal grammatical rank. (See 5d, "Recognizing Clauses.") *

WORDS JOINED	We ate ham *and* eggs.
PHRASES JOINED	Look in the closet *or* under the bed.
CLAUSES JOINED	We wanted to go, *but* we were too busy.

Subordinating conjunctions (*because, if, since, when, where, etc.*) join subordinate clauses with main clauses. (See 5d, "Recognizing Clauses.")

> We left the party early *because* we were tired.
> *If* the roads are icy, we shall have to drive carefully.

---

* For a discussion of the punctuation of clauses separated by a co-ordinating conjunction, see Section 20.

33

(8) *Interjections*

An interjection is an exclamatory word that expresses emotion. It has no grammatical relation to other words in the sentence. Mild interjections are usually followed by a comma. *Oh, is that you? Well, well, how are you?* Stronger interjections are usually followed by an exclamation point. *Ouch! You are hurting me. Oh! I hate you!*

EXERCISE 2. Indicate the part of speech of each word in as many of the following sentences as your instructor assigns.

1. We entered the diner, and Higgins served us coffee and rolls.
2. After the others left we had a private talk.
3. From the distance came the wail of a steamboat.
4. Stop! You have trespassed on my property.
5. Washing dishes is a waste of time.
6. He soon recovered from his very severe injuries.
7. The snow-covered Michigan forests are very impressive in winter.
8. The boys clambered up the hill to the lighthouse.
9. The woodsman was angry because somebody had stolen his traps.
10. Galileo disclaimed his support of the theories of Copernicus under the torture of the Inquisitors.
11. Descartes said that there was only one vacuum in the universe, the one in Pascal's head.
12. In reading tales of knights of old you should keep in mind that the medieval doctrine of courtly love is silly and immoral by most modern standards.
13. Some people still believe that men and women have an unequal number of ribs.
14. Having slept through the lecture, he felt himself well qualified to criticize it in detail.
15. "Pshaw!" said old Granny Hoskins, "you don't have to help me get off the horse."
16. Spot the frogs with your flashlight; then shoot before they jump.
17. We watched the phosphorescent water boiling under the stern.
18. Whenever a pocket of air shook the bomber the tailgunner

shouted over the intercom, threatening the pilot with court martial and announcing repeatedly that he was going home.
19. That cave is unsafe; even the bats have left it.
20. Saw off the fence post even with the top of the gate.

5c Recognizing phrases.

A phrase is a group of related words without a subject or predicate and used as a single part of speech. Typical phrases are a preposition and its object (I fell *on the sidewalk*), or a verbal and its object (I wanted *to see the parade*).

Prepositional phrases are classified, according to function, as adjective, adverb, and noun phrases. An adjective phrase modifies a noun or pronoun. (He is a man *of action.*) An adverb phrase modifies a verb, adjective, or adverb. (The train arrived *on time.* We were ready *at the station.*) A noun phrase is used as a noun. (*Before breakfast* is the best time for calisthenics.)

Verbal phrases are classified as participial, gerund, or infinitive phrases. A participial phrase functions as an adjective, modifying a noun or pronoun. (The man *sitting on the porch* is my father. The dog *found in the street* was homeless.) Such phrases are formed with the present participle of a verb (*seeing, calling*) or the past participle (*seen, called*). A gerund phrase is used as a noun. (*Collecting stamps* is my hobby.) Since both gerunds and present participles end in -*ing*, they can be distinguished only by their separate functions as nouns or adjectives. An infinitive phrase is used as an adjective, adverb, or noun. (It is time *to go to bed.* We were impatient *to start the game.* I wanted *to buy a house.*)

> **EXERCISE 3.** In the following sentences identify the prepositional phrases by underlining them once and the verbal phrases by underlining them twice.
>
> 1. The girl with brown eyes is my sister.
> 2. For two years I worked in Chicago.
> 3. The library located on the campus needs repair.
> 4. Keeping a budget requires great patience.
> 5. I am glad to see you.
> 6. He entered the room through the door on the right.
> 7. Paying one's bills is sometimes difficult.

8. John wanted to become an engineer.
9. Playing handball is pleasant exercise.
10. The boy flying the kite was envied by the other children.
11. Twisting to face me, she chewed her already swollen lower lip.
12. Suddenly morning burst, spilling onto the lake, trickling like glowing lava through the forest.
13. Crumpled on the davenport were his tuxedo and his aging topcoat.
14. Having managed to work loose from the wreck, he vaulted the fence and ducked behind a tree, stopping only then to find out who was shooting.
15. To insure quiet in his room while he was studying for the final examinations Roger dropped the radio down the laundry chute.
16. To prevent such drastic action in the future was the purpose of the housemother's rule forbidding use of the laundry chute by anyone but the maid.
17. Passing the examination was more important to Roger than using the laundry chute.
18. Smith wanted to hold the foreman to his promise.
19. He was unable, however, to force him to put vinegar in the plant superintendent's thermos bottle.
20. Reports of flying saucers grew more frequent in the summer.

5d Recognizing clauses.

A clause is a group of words containing a subject and a predicate. The relation of a clause to the rest of the sentence is shown by the position of the clause or by a conjunction. There are two kinds of clause: (1) subordinate or dependent clauses, and (2) main or independent clauses.

(1) Subordinate clauses are frequently introduced by a subordinating conjunction (*as, since, because,* etc.) or by a relative pronoun (*who, which, that*). A subordinate clause functions as an adjective, adverb, or noun, and expresses an idea that is less important than the idea expressed in the main clause. The exact relationship between the two ideas is indicated by the subordinating conjunction or relative pronoun that joins the subordinate and the main clause.

(a) An adjective clause modifies a noun or pronoun.

> This is the jet *that broke the speed record.* (The subordinate clause modifies the noun *jet.*)
>
> Anybody *who is tired* may leave. (The subordinate clause modifies the pronoun *anybody.*)
>
> Canada is the nation *we made the treaty with.* (The subordinate clause modifies the noun *nation* with the relative pronoun "that" understood.)

(b) An adverb clause modifies a verb, adjective, or adverb.

> The child cried *when the dentist appeared.* (The subordinate clause modifies the verb *cried.*)
>
> I am sorry *he is sick.* (The subordinate clause modifies the adjective *sorry* with the subordinating conjunction "that" understood.)
>
> He thinks more quickly *than you do.* (The subordinate clause modifies the adverb *quickly.*)

(c) A noun clause has the function of a noun. It may serve as subject, predicate nominative, object of a verb, or object of a preposition.

> *What John wants* is a better job. (The subordinate clause is the subject of the verb *is.*)
>
> This is *where we came in.* (The subordinate clause is a predicate nominative.)
>
> Please tell them *I will be late.* (The subordinate clause is the object of the verb *tell.*)
>
> He has no interest in *what he is reading.* (The subordinate clause is the object of the preposition *in.*)

EXERCISE 4. Underline the subordinate clauses in the following sentences and identify each as an adjective, adverb, or noun clause.

1. He was a man who never found happiness.
2. When the fire started, I grabbed a bucket.
3. The apples that make the best pies are the sour ones.
4. What you want is hard to obtain.
5. If wishes were horses, beggars would ride.
6. I read the books which he recommended.
7. Hawkeye knew that he was being watched.

8. I was alarmed by what she said.
9. He enrolled in college because he wanted to be a lawyer.
10. What annoyed me was the clerk's indifference.
11. You are the man I am looking for.
12. We went swimming on a day when the sun was bright.
13. While she was gossiping, the supper burned on the stove.
14. His suggestion was that we pool our cash.
15. We left before the concert was finished.

(2) A main clause also has both subject and verb but is not introduced by a subordinating word. A main clause makes an independent statement. Clearly, then, it may never be used as a noun or as a modifier.

The number of main or subordinate clauses in a sentence determines its classification: *simple, compound, complex,* or *compound-complex.*

A *simple sentence* has a single main clause.

The wind blew.

A *compound sentence* has two or more main clauses.

The wind blew and the leaves fell.

A *complex sentence* has one main clause and one or more subordinate clauses.

When the wind blew, the leaves fell.

A *compound-complex sentence* contains two or more main clauses and one or more subordinate clauses.

When the sky darkened, the wind blew and the leaves fell.

EXERCISE 5. Indicate whether each of the following sentences is simple, compound, complex, or compound-complex.

1. Although I am a heavy sleeper, I awoke with a start when the lightning flashed.
2. Taxes are too high.
3. It is his opinion that taxes are too high.
4. A sentence that has a main clause and one or more subordinate clauses is called a complex sentence.

38

5. Although I am a heavy sleeper, I awoke with a start when the lightning flashed, and I rushed to the window to see what had happened.

6. He goes golfing three or four times a week, but his game never seems to improve.

7. Even though he goes golfing three or four times a week, his game never seems to improve.

8. Golf is a sport that requires coordination.

9. Sentence 8 certainly makes a silly statement; is there any sport that doesn't require coordination?

10. The tramp told us that he was homeless.

EXERCISE 6. In the following sentences point out the main and subordinate clauses. Indicate the function of each subordinate clause as an adjective, an adverb, or a noun.

1. After the meeting ended I hurried back to my attic apartment.

2. He has two sons who are excellent horsemen.

3. You may go whenever you wish.

4. Do you remember the night when we first met?

5. The judge wondered why the jury had deliberated so long.

6. A clause is subordinate if it functions as a single part of speech.

7. When I marry I want a wife who can cook.

8. If you will give me your telephone number, I will call you tomorrow.

9. The price that he wanted for the house was too high.

10. A man of action forced into a state of thought is unhappy until he can get out of it.

11. The day I leave this place will be the happiest of my life.

12. It is said that Dryden arrived in London dressed in simple drugget.

13. She cried because I left and she pouted when I came home.

14. Some mothers let their children do whatever they please.

15. As he came in the door he said he could whip any man in the room.

6 CASE = CA

Case is a grammatical property showing the function of nouns and pronouns within a sentence.

In the sentence "He gave me a week's vacation," the nominative case form *He* indicates that the pronoun is being used as subject; the objective case form *me* shows that the pronoun is an object; the possessive case form *week's* indicates that the noun is a possessive.

In some languages, such as German, both adjectives and nouns have special endings to indicate the nominative, possessive, dative, and objective cases. In Anglo-Saxon times the English language too was highly inflected. Case endings were extremely important in showing the function of the word and its meaning in the sentence.

Modern English, however, retains only a few remnants of this complicated system of inflection. Adjectives, once declined in five cases, now have no case endings at all. Consequently, English has had to rely increasingly on word order to show the relation of a particular word to other parts of the sentence. For example, the object of a verb or preposition normally follows the verb or preposition and thus is easily identified. In the following sentences the position of each noun determines its function.

> Jack threw Bill the ball.
> Bill threw Jack the ball.

Modern English nouns have only two case forms, the possessive (*student's*), and a common form (*student*) that serves all other functions. The personal pronouns (*I, you, he, she, it*) and the relative or interrogative pronoun (*who*) are inflected in three cases—nominative, possessive, and objective.

PERSONAL PRONOUNS

SINGULAR

	Nominative	*Possessive*	*Objective*
FIRST PERSON	I	my, mine	me
SECOND PERSON	you	your, yours	you
THIRD PERSON	he, she, it	his, her, hers, its	him, her, it

PLURAL

FIRST PERSON	we	our, ours	us
SECOND PERSON	you	your, yours	you
THIRD PERSON	they	their, theirs	them

RELATIVE OR INTERROGATIVE PRONOUNS

SINGULAR	who	whose	whom
PLURAL	who	whose	whom

NOMINATIVE CASE

6a **Use the nominative case for the subject of a verb.**

We are happy.
He is tired.

There are several types of sentence in which the subject is not easily recognized and is sometimes confused with the object.

(1) *In formal English use the nominative case of the pronoun after the conjunctions* AS *and* THAN *if the pronoun is the subject of an understood verb.*

In informal English there is a growing tendency to use *as* and *than* as prepositions.*

FORMAL   He is taller than *I* (am). (*I* is the subject of the verb *am*, which must be supplied by the reader.)
INFORMAL   He is taller than *me*.

FORMAL   She is as rich as *they* (are).
INFORMAL   She is as rich as *them*.

* When the comparison is negative, *so* replaces *as:*
  She is *as* rich as they.
  She is not *so* rich as they.
See Glossary under *as.*

41

(2) *Remember that the pronoun* WHO *used as subject of a verb will not be changed by parenthetical elements intervening between it and its verb.*

> He is a man *who* I think deserves praise. (*Who* is the subject of *deserves.*)
>
> We invited only the people *who* he said were his friends. (*Who* is the subject of *were.*)

(3) *Use the nominative case for any pronoun that is the subject of a clause, even though the* whole *clause may function as an object of a verb or preposition.*

> I shall welcome *whoever* wants to attend. (*Whoever* is the subject of *wants.* The object of *welcome* is the entire clause *whoever wants to attend.*)
>
> A reward is offered to *whoever* catches the escaped lion. (The entire clause is the object of the preposition *to.*)

6b **In formal English use the nominative case of the personal pronoun after forms of the verb BE, such as IS, ARE, WERE, HAVE BEEN.**

The use of the objective case of the personal pronoun after forms of *be,* however, has gained widespread acceptance in informal usage. "It's me" is freely used by good speakers. The prejudice against *us, him,* and *them* after *be* seems to be yielding to a strong tendency to use the objective form of the pronoun after a verb, regardless of what the verb may be.

> FORMAL   It was *I.* I thought it was *he.* It was not *we.*
>
> INFORMAL   It is *me.* I thought it was *him.* It was not *us.*

6c **In formal English use the nominative case for a pronoun following the infinitive TO BE when the infinitive has no expressed subject.**

Informal English commonly uses the objective case of the pronoun in this construction.

> FORMAL   I would not want to be *he.* (The infinitive *to be* has no expressed subject.)
>
> INFORMAL   I would not want to be *him.*

POSSESSIVE CASE

Generally, use the s-possessive (boy's, Paul's) with nouns denoting animate objects, but use an OF-phrase for the possessive of nouns denoting inanimate objects.

6d

> ANIMATE a man's hat; the ladies' coats; Jack's wife.
> INANIMATE the floor of the house; the power of the machine; the point of the joke.

The *s*-possessive is commonly used in expressions that indicate time (*moment's notice, year's labor*) and in many familiar phrases (*heaven's sake, heart's content*). Which possessive form to use may also depend on sound or rhythm: The *s*-possessive is more terse than the longer, more sonorous *of*-phrase (*morning's beauty, beauty of the morning*).

6e

In formal English use the possessive case for a noun or pronoun preceding a gerund.

In informal English, however, the objective case rather than the possessive case is often found before a gerund.

> FORMAL What was the excuse for *his* being late?
> INFORMAL What was the excuse for *him* being late?
>
> FORMAL He complained of *Roy's* keeping the money.
> INFORMAL He complained of *Roy* keeping the money.

Even in formal English the objective case is frequently used with plural nouns.

> The police prohibited *children* playing in the street.

The choice of case sometimes depends on the meaning the writer intends to convey.

> Fancy *his* playing the violin. (The act of playing the violin is emphasized.)
> Fancy *him* playing the violin. (The emphasis is on *him*. *Playing* is here used as a participle modifying *him*.)

And note the difference in the meaning of the following sentences:

> I hate that *woman* riding a bicycle.
> I hate that *woman's* riding a bicycle.

43

We must confess, however, that the illustrations above are a little abstract. A person wishing to state his dislike for a *woman's riding a bicycle* would say *I hate the way that woman rides a bicycle.*

6f **Use WHICH to refer to impersonal antecedents. However, you may substitute WHOSE in cases where the phrase OF WHICH would be awkward.**

> We saw a house *whose* roof was falling in. (*Compare:* We saw a house the roof of which was falling in.)
>
> This is the car *whose* steering wheel broke off when the driver was going seventy miles an hour. (*Compare:* This is the car the steering wheel of which broke off when the driver was going seventy miles an hour.)

OBJECTIVE CASE

6g **Use the objective case for the object of a verb, verbal, or preposition.**

> OBJECT OF A VERB
>
> I saw *him*. *Whom* did you see?
>
> OBJECT OF A VERBAL
>
> Visiting *them* was enjoyable. (*Them* is the object of the gerund *visiting*.) *Whom* does he want to marry? (*Whom* is the object of the infinitive *to marry*.)
>
> OBJECT OF A PREPOSITION
>
> Two of *us* policemen were wounded. With *whom* were you dancing?

Formal English usage requires "whom" in the objective case. Informal usage permits "who" in similar situations.

> FORMAL   *Whom* are you discussing? (*Whom* is the object of *are discussing*.)
>
> INFORMAL   *Who* are you discussing?
>
> FORMAL   *Whom* are you looking for? (*Whom* is the object of the preposition *for*.)
>
> INFORMAL   *Who* are you looking for?

The following sentences illustrate the use of the pronoun after the conjunction *and*.

44

He found Tom and *me* at home. (Not "Tom and *I*." *Me* is an object of the verb *found*.)

He must choose between you and *me*. (Not "between you and *I*." *Me* is an object of the preposition *between*.)

She had dinner with *him* and *me*. (*Him* and *me* are objects of the preposition *with*.)

(1) *After the conjunctions* THAN *and* AS, *use a pronoun in the objective case if it is the object of an understood verb.*

She needs him more than [she needs] *me*.
I called him as well as [I called] *her*.

(2) *When the infinitive* TO BE *has an expressed subject, use a pronoun in the objective case following the infinitive.*

He took him to be *me*.

EXERCISE 7. In the following sentences correct the errors in case in accordance with formal usage. Be prepared to give the reasons for your corrections.

1. The newspaper told about him finding the treasure.
2. Jane was the kind of secretary who we wanted in the office.
3. I knew it was her.
4. Who do you think you are fooling?
5. He has lived in Cleveland longer than me.
6. I found Harry and she in the park.
7. The barn's roof needs repairing.
8. There was no reason for me staying any longer.
9. He divided the money between Dick and I.
10. I am the one who the committee selected.
11. It was him who we wanted for questioning.
12. We will consider whomever applies for the position.
13. Let's you and I get married, Mabel.
14. Whom do you think is the best candidate?
15. Is it me you are looking for?
16. The truant officer found Don as well as I.
17. Whom shall I say called?
18. I will box with whoever they choose as my opponent.
19. She left without him saying goodbye to her.
20. It wasn't them I was looking for.

7 TENSE AND MOOD = T

Tense is a grammatical property indicating the time of the action expressed by a verb; mood is the manner in which the action of the verb is conceived.

TENSE

PRESENT TENSE (*expressing a present or habitual action*)
He *is talking* to the gun club now. He *talks* to the gun club at least once every year.

PAST TENSE (*expressing an action that was completed in the past*)
He *talked* to the gun club yesterday.

FUTURE TENSE (*expressing an action yet to come*)
He *will talk* to the gun club tomorrow.

PRESENT PERFECT TENSE (*expressing a past action extending to the present and not necessarily completed*)
He *has talked* to the gun club every day.

PAST PERFECT TENSE (*expressing a past action completed before some other past action*)
This morning I saw the speaker who *had talked* to the gun club last month.

FUTURE PERFECT TENSE (*expressing an action that will be completed before some future time*)
He *will have talked* to the gun club before next Thursday.

Except for the present tense (he *talks*) and the past tense (he *talked*), most English verbs show time by means of verb phrases formed with auxiliary or helping verbs (he *is talking*. he *has been talking*, he *has talked*, etc.). All six tenses are formed from the three principal parts of the verbs: the present infinitive (*to talk*), the past

46

(*talked*), and the past participle (*talked*). In most English verbs the past-tense and past-participial forms are indicated by the addition of -*ed: smoked, hammered, played, worked.* Such "regular" verbs are sometimes called "weak" verbs. Other English verbs indicate their past-tense and past-participial forms by more individualistic changes, frequently a vowel change within the word: *grow, grew, grown; swim, swam, swum.* Such irregularly formed verbs are sometimes called "strong" verbs.

A few verbs have only one form for all three principal parts (*burst, cost, split*). These verbs frequently indicate time by an auxiliary verb (I *did split* the wood) or by a modifying word or phrase (I *split* the wood *yesterday*).

In the following conjugation of the verb *to choose,* notice that in the active voice the present and future tenses are based on the present infinitive (*to choose*), and the perfect tenses on the past participle (*chosen*).

INDICATIVE MOOD, ACTIVE VOICE

Present Tense

I choose	we choose
you choose	you choose
he, she, it chooses	they choose

Past Tense

I chose	we chose
you chose	you chose
he, she, it chose	they chose

Future Tense

I shall * choose	we shall choose
you will choose	you will choose
he, she, it will choose	they will choose

Present Perfect Tense

I have chosen	we have chosen
you have chosen	you have chosen
he, she, it has chosen	they have chosen

* In spite of the efforts of teachers to perpetuate the distinction between *shall* and *will,* it is largely ignored by Americans. In all *future* tenses *will* may be substituted for *shall* in the first person singular and plural.

Past Perfect Tense

I had chosen	we had chosen
you had chosen	you had chosen
he, she, it had chosen	they had chosen

Future Perfect Tense

I shall have chosen	we shall have chosen
you will have chosen	you will have chosen
he, she, it will have chosen	they will have chosen

INDICATIVE MOOD, PASSIVE VOICE

Present Tense

I am chosen	we are chosen
you are chosen	you are chosen
he, she, it is chosen	they are chosen

Past Tense

I was chosen	we were chosen
you were chosen	you were chosen
he, she, it was chosen	they were chosen

Future Tense

I shall be chosen	we shall be chosen
you will be chosen	you will be chosen
he, she, it will be chosen	they will be chosen

Present Perfect Tense

I have been chosen	we have been chosen
you have been chosen	you have been chosen
he, she, it has been chosen	they have been chosen

Past Perfect Tense

I had been chosen	we had been chosen
you had been chosen	you had been chosen
he, she, it had been chosen	they had been chosen

Future Perfect Tense

I shall have been chosen	we shall have been chosen
you will have been chosen	you will have been chosen
he, she, it will have been chosen	they will have been chosen

SUBJUNCTIVE MOOD, ACTIVE VOICE

Present Tense

if I choose	if we choose
if you choose	if you choose
if he, she, it choose	if they choose

Past Tense

if I chose, etc.   if we chose, etc.

Present Perfect Tense

if I have chosen, etc.   if we have chosen, etc.

Past Perfect Tense

if I had chosen, etc.   if we had chosen, etc.

SUBJUNCTIVE MOOD, PASSIVE VOICE

Present Tense

if I be chosen	if we be chosen
if you be chosen	if you be chosen
if he, she, it be chosen	if they be chosen

Past Tense

if I were chosen, etc.   if we were chosen, etc.

Present Perfect Tense

if I have been chosen, etc.   if we have been chosen, etc.

Past Perfect Tense

if I had been chosen, etc.   if we had been chosen, etc.

IMPERATIVE MOOD

Present Tense

ACTIVE VOICE	PASSIVE VOICE
choose	be chosen

INFINITIVES

Present Tense

to choose	to be chosen

Present Perfect Tense

to have chosen	to have been chosen

PARTICIPLES

Present Tense

choosing	being chosen

Past Tense

chosen	been chosen

49

Present Perfect Tense

having chosen   having been chosen *

GERUNDS

Present Tense

choosing   being chosen

Present Perfect Tense

having chosen   having been chosen

PROGRESSIVE FORMS, INDICATIVE MOOD

Present Tense

I am choosing, etc.   I am being chosen, etc.

Past Tense

I was choosing, etc.   I was being chosen, etc.

PROGRESSIVE FORMS, SUBJUNCTIVE MOOD

Present Tense

if I be choosing, etc.

Past Tense

if I were choosing, etc.

EMPHATIC FORMS

Present Tense

I do choose, etc.

Past Tense

I did choose, etc.

7a **Make sure that the tense of the verb in a subordinate clause is logically related to the tense of the verb in the main clause.**

ILLOGICAL   As the day *ends*, a few stars *appeared* in the sky.
LOGICAL   As the day *ends*, a few stars *appear* in the sky.
LOGICAL   As the day *ended*, a few stars *appeared* in the sky.

ILLOGICAL   If he *tried*, he could *have avoided* the accident.
LOGICAL   If he *had tried*, he *could have avoided* the accident.

* The active form of the past tense is frequently substituted in journalistic writing for the longer passive. *Chosen as prom queen, Margaret was very proud* means *Having been chosen as prom queen, Margaret was very proud.*

ILLOGICAL	If he *had eaten*, he *had felt* better.
LOGICAL	If he *had eaten*, he *would have felt* better.
LOGICAL	If he *had eaten*, he *would feel* better.

7b **Use a present infinitive after a verb in a perfect tense. A perfect infinitive may sometimes be used after a verb not in a perfect tense.**

ILLOGICAL	I would have liked *to have gone*.
LOGICAL	I would have liked *to go*. (At the time indicated by the verb, I desired *to go*, not *to have gone*.)
LOGICAL	I would like *to have gone*.
ILLOGICAL	I hoped *to have visited you*.
LOGICAL	I had hoped *to visit* you.

7c **Use the present tense in statements that are generally true or that have no reference to time.**

Brevity *is* the soul of wit.

Corn *grows* rapidly in warm, humid weather.

7d **Distinguish carefully between the principal parts of verbs that are similar in meaning or spelling.**

If you are in doubt about the principal parts of a particular verb, go to your dictionary. There you will find the present infinitive (*begin*), the past tense (*began*), and the past participle (*begun*) of irregular verbs. For regular verbs, which form the past tense and past participle simply by adding -*d* or -*ed* (*live, lived, lived*), you will find only the present infinitive.

Be particularly careful with the verbs *lie, lay* and *sit, set*. The correct use of these verbs has become a mark of an educated person. The principal parts of *lie* (meaning *to recline*) are *lie, lay, lain;* the principal parts of *lay* (meaning *to place*) are *lay, laid, laid*. Do not confuse the past tense of *lie* (*i.e., lay*) with the present tense of *lay*. And quite frequently, the nonexistent form *layed* is made up to serve as the past tense of *lay*.

LIE

Correct (present)	*Lie* down for a while and you will feel better.
Correct (past)	The cat *lay* in the shade and watched the dog carefully.

51

Correct (present participle)	His keys were *lying* on the table where he dropped them.
Correct (past participle)	After he *had lain* down for a while, he felt better.

LAY

Correct (present)	*Lay* the book on the table and come here.
Correct (past)	He *laid* the book on the table and walked out the door.
Correct (present participle)	*Laying* the book on the table, he walked out the door.
Correct (past participle)	*Having laid* the book on the table, he walked out the door.

The principal parts of *sit* (meaning *to occupy a seat*) are *sit, sat, sat;* the principal parts of *set* (meaning *to put in place*) are *set, set, set.*

SIT

Correct (present)	*Sit* down and keep quiet.
Correct (past)	The little girl *sat* in the corner for half an hour.
Correct (present participle)	*Sitting* down quickly, he failed to see the tack in the chair.
Correct (past participle)	*Having sat* in the corner for an hour, the child was subdued and reasonable.

SET

Correct (present)	*Set* the basket on the table and get out.
Correct (past)	Yesterday he *set* the grocery cartons on the kitchen table; today he left them on the porch.
Correct (present participle)	*Setting* his spectacles on the table, he challenged John to wrestle.
Correct (past participle)	*Having set* the basket of turnips on the porch, Terry went to play the piano.

The principal parts of some irregular verbs are listed below. Add to the list any other verbs that you may have used incorrectly.

PRESENT INFINITIVE	PAST TENSE	PAST PARTICIPLE
begin	began	begun
bid (*offer*)	bid	bid
bid (*command*)	bade	bidden
bite	bit	bit, bitten
blow	blew	blown
break	broke	broken
bring	brought	brought
burst	burst	burst
catch	caught	caught
choose	chose	chosen
come	came	come
dive	dived, dove	dived
do	did	done
drag	dragged	dragged
draw	drew	drawn
drink	drank	drunk
drive	drove	driven
eat	ate	eaten
fall	fell	fallen
fly	flew	flown
forget	forgot	forgot, forgotten
freeze	froze	frozen
get	got	got, gotten
give	gave	given
go	went	gone
grow	grew	grown
hang (*suspend*)	hung	hung
hang (*execute*)	hanged	hanged
know	knew	known
lead	led	led
lend	lent	lent
lie (*speak falsely*)	lied	lied
lose	lost	lost
pay	paid	paid
prove	proved	proved, proven
raise	raised	raised
ride	rode	ridden
ring	rang, rung	rung
rise	rose	risen
run	ran	run
see	saw	seen
shake	shook	shaken
shrink	shrank	shrunk

PRESENT INFINITIVE	PAST TENSE	PAST PARTICIPLE
sing	sang, sung	sung
sink	sank, sunk	sunk
speak	spoke	spoken
spring	sprang	sprung
steal	stole	stolen
swim	swam	swum
swing	swung	swung
take	took	taken
tear	tore	torn
throw	threw	thrown
wear	wore	worn
weave	wove	woven
wring	wrung	wrung
write	wrote	written

Be especially careful not to substitute substandard verb parts for standard, as *he seen* for the correct *he saw,* or he *had eat* for the correct he *had eaten.* Such substitution is looked upon as an illiteracy.

EXERCISE 8. Correct the verb forms in the following.

1. The housing project was began in the early spring.
2. Before the sun had rose over the hills, Cactus Pete had rode all the way to Cactus Gap.
3. The new dress shrunk when it was washed.
4. He sprung from his seat; a spider had bit him.
5. The defendant denied that he had stole the horse.
6. Mabel run to the gate and welcomed her sister.
7. Snow laid on the barn roof all winter.
8. On her first trip across the lake, the *Morning Mist* has broke the speed record.
9. The Harrisons use to live in Vermont.
10. I remember the day she bid me farewell.
11. I should have liked to have seen the flying saucer.
12. Soon after the fire started, dozens of rats come rushing out of the barn.
13. I hoped to have bought a new car in Detroit.
14. Gertrude Ederle, who swum the English Channel, become one of the great female athletes of her time.
15. She has wore that same old hat for three years.

MOOD

The term *mood* is used to describe three forms of the verb and their distinctive changes in meaning and manner of action. The three moods are the *indicative,* expressing a statement of fact; the *imperative,* expressing a command or entreaty; and the *subjunctive,* expressing doubt, condition, wish, or probability. The distinctions in meaning between the indicative and subjunctive moods are often slight, and the choice of mood depends on the speaker's feelings toward the statement he is making. The subjunctive expresses shades of feeling and meaning that are not expressed by the more direct indicative.

The subjunctive mood is used only occasionally in formal English, and rather rarely in informal English. It occurs in the present tense, first and third person singular and plural, of the verb *to be* (If I be, If he be); in the past tense, first and third person singular, of *to be* (If I were, If he were); and in the third person singular of all verbs (I desire that he *give* a report).

7e   **Use the subjunctive mood in formal idioms.**

> *Suffice it to say* that I am disappointed. (*Suffices* would be the indicative verb form.)
>
> I shall help him *if need be.* (*Is* would be the indicative verb form.)

Such idioms have survived from earlier times, when the subjunctive was more common in English.

7f   **In formal English use the subjunctive in stating conditions contrary to fact, and in expressing doubt, regrets, or wishes.**

> FORMAL   If I *were* tired, I would go home.
> INFORMAL   If I *was* tired, I would go home.
>
> FORMAL   The elm tree looks as if it *were* dying.
> INFORMAL   The elm tree looks as if it *was* dying.
>
> FORMAL   If this man *be* guilty, society will condemn him.
> INFORMAL   If this man *is* guilty, society will condemn him.
>
> FORMAL   I wish that I *were* taller.
> INFORMAL   I wish that I *was* taller.

7g   **Use the subjunctive in** THAT **clauses which express formal demands, resolutions, or motions.**

I demand that he *resign* his position.
Resolved, that Mr. Smith *investigate* our financial condition.
I move that the meeting *be* adjourned.

EXERCISE 9. In the following sentences make whatever changes are demanded by formal usage. Indicate those sentences that would be acceptable in informal English.

1. The track was carefully drug in preparation for the horse races.
2. Bill's books were laying on the table.
3. Our guide lead us into a dense forest.
4. He could have made the team if he would have practiced regularly.
5. If I was a farmer I would raise dairy cattle.
6. I would have liked to have gone to the movies.
7. The swimmer dove into the pool.
8. When the play ended, the audience applaud enthusiastically.
9. He wishes that she was a rich widow.
10. They haven't spoke to each other for years.
11. If you are tired, come in and set a while.
12. The boys seen a flying squirrel.
13. He looks as if he was unhappy.
14. The thirsty children drunk a whole gallon of water.
15. The clown was so funny that we nearly bursted with laughter.
16. After striking the rocks the freighter sunk almost immediately.
17. At the first sound I raised from my pillow.
18. The birds sung all day in the apple tree.
19. Early in life he seen the folly of his ways.
20. Never before had the bishop spoke to such a multitude.

8   ADJECTIVES AND ADVERBS = **AD**

Do not confuse adjectives and adverbs.

Adjectives and adverbs are two different parts of speech with separate and distinct functions. Therefore, the only sound way to distinguish between adjectives and adverbs is to distinguish between their functions. Does the word modify a noun or pronoun? If so, it is an adjective. Does it modify an adjective, adverb, verb, or an entire clause or sentence? If so, it is an adverb.

Although most adverbs end in -ly (*slowly, quickly*), this ending is not a dependable means of identifying an adverb. Some adjectives also end in -ly (*manly, holy*),* while other adjectives have the same form as adverbs (*late, well*). Certain adverbs have two forms (*quick, quickly; slow, slowly*), though in general the form ending in -ly is preferable in formal usage. In informal English the shorter forms are widely used, particularly in commands such as "Drive slow" or "Go fast."

8a   **Do not use an adjective to modify a verb.**

> INCORRECT   He writes *careless.*
> CORRECT   He writes *carelessly.* (The adverb *carelessly* is needed to modify the verb *writes.*)
>
> INCORRECT   She talks *modest.*
> CORRECT   She talks *modestly.* (The adverb *modestly* is needed to modify the verb *talks.*)

---

* The ways in which adjectives are formed from nouns are discussed in Section 39, "Vocabulary."

8b **Do not use an adjective to modify another adjective or an adverb.**

INCORRECT He was *terrible* wounded.
CORRECT He was *terribly* wounded. (The adverb *terribly* is needed to modify the adjective *wounded*.)

INCORRECT She works *considerable* harder than he does.
CORRECT She works *considerably* harder than he does. (The adverb *considerably* is needed to modify the other adverb *harder*.)

The misuse of adjectives is more common in conversation than in formal or informal writing. Indeed, the careless use of the adjective *real* as an emphatic *very* to modify adjectives and adverbs is often heard in the familiar speech of educated people.

FORMAL You will hear from me *very* soon.
COLLOQUIAL * You will hear from me *real* soon.

8c **Use an adjective to modify the subject after a linking verb.**

The linking verbs are: BE, BECOME, APPEAR, SEEM, and the verbs pertaining to the senses: LOOK, SMELL, TASTE, SOUND, FEEL. Modifiers after such verbs often refer back to the subject and should be in the adjectival form. In each of the following sentences, for example, the predicate adjective modifies the subject. The verb simply links the two.

Jane looks *pretty* tonight. (*Pretty* modifies *Jane*.)
The butter smells *sour*. (*Sour* modifies *butter*.)
He appears *jubilant*. (*Jubilant* modifies *He*.)

One of the most frequent errors in this usage is the construction "I feel badly" rather than the correct subject–linking verb–predicate adjective form "I feel bad." This tendency reflects, not the speaker's carelessness, but his zeal to be correct. He feels a "grammatical necessity" to use an adverb after a verb, whatever the verb might be.

FORMAL He feels bad (*ill*).
COLLOQUIAL He feels *badly*.

FORMAL He felt *bad* about it.
COLLOQUIAL He felt *badly* about it.

* We use the term *colloquial* to signify the qualities of familiar spoken English.

8d **Use an adverb after the verb if the modifier describes the manner of the action of the verb.**

> He looked *suspiciously* at me. (The adverb *suspiciously* modifies the verb *looked*. Contrast *He looked suspicious to me.*)
>
> The thief felt *carefully* under the pillow. (The adverb *carefully* modifies the verb *felt*.)

In these examples the verbs *look* and *feel* express action, and must be modified by adverbs. But in constructions like "He *looks* tired" or "He *feels* well," the verbs serve not as words of action but as links between the subject and the predicate adjective. The choice of adjective *or* adverb thus depends on the function and meaning of the verb—in other words, on whether or not the verb is being *used as a linking verb*. Ask yourself whether you want a modifier for the *subject* or for the *verb*.

In some sentences you may use either an adjective or an adverb, with little difference in meaning.

> ADJECTIVE   The sun shines *bright*. I bolted the gate *tight*.
>
> ADVERB   The sun shines *brightly*. I bolted the gate *tightly*.

8e **Distinguish between the comparative and superlative forms of adjectives and adverbs.**

Adjectives and adverbs show degrees of quality or quantity by means of their positive, comparative, and superlative forms. The positive form (*slow, quickly*) expresses no comparison at all. The comparative, formed by adding *-er* or by prefixing *more* to the positive form (*slower, more quickly*), expresses a greater degree or makes a comparison. The superlative, formed by adding *-est* or by putting *most* before the positive form (*slowest, most quickly*), indicates the greatest degree of a quality or quantity among three or more persons or things. Some common adjectives and adverbs retain old irregular forms (*good, better, best; badly, worse, worst*).

Whether to use *more* or *most* before the adjective or adverb, or whether to add the *-er, -est* endings, depends mostly on the number of syllables in the word. Most adjectives and a few adverbs of one syllable form the comparative and superlative with *-er* and *-est*. Adjectives of two syllables often have variant forms (*fancier, more* *fancy; laziest, most lazy*). Adjectives and adverbs of three or more syllables always take *more* and *most* (*more beautiful, most regretfully*). Where there is a choice, select the form that sounds better or that is better suited to the rhythm of your sentence.

Some adjectives and adverbs, such as *unique, empty, dead, perfect, entirely,* are absolute in their meaning and thus cannot logically be compared. There are no degrees of *uniqueness, deadness,* or *perfection.* In the ambiguous area between substandard and informal usage, however, such words are often compared.*

FORMAL	His diving form is *more nearly perfect* than mine.
COLLOQUIAL	His diving form is *more perfect* than mine.
FORMAL	The new stadium is *more nearly circular* than the old one.
COLLOQUIAL	The new stadium is *more circular* than the old one.

8f   **In formal usage, use the comparative to refer only to one of two objects; use the superlative to refer only to one of three or more objects.**

COMPARATIVE	His horse is the *faster* of the two.
SUPERLATIVE	His horse is the *fastest* in the county.
COMPARATIVE	Ruth is the *more* attractive but the *less* good-natured of the twins.
SUPERLATIVE	Ruth is the *most* attractive but the *least* good-natured of his three daughters.

EXERCISE 10. In the following sentences correct any errors in the use of adjectives and adverbs in accordance with formal usage.

1. He should take his profession more serious.
2. The poor fellow sure did feel bad.
3. Owls can see good at night.
4. Little Joe is the biggest of the two dogs.
5. I have been real lucky.
6. Since Sarah's illness, she looks considerable older.
7. This is the emptiest reservoir I have ever seen.
8. We drove slow through the heavy traffic.
9. The music had a most unique melody.

* See the specimen under "Substandard," Section 43b.

10. I get along perfect with my wife.
11. Don't feel badly; occasionally we all make mistakes.
12. A good pitcher throws the ball fast and hard over the plate.
13. They told us that to do good on our jobs we had to do good throughout the community.
14. The book, one of the most unique I every read, probed relentlessly for the motives of the characters and described them candidly.
15. Curtseying, Martha looked prettily at the crowd, seeming more and more confidently as the cheers and applause increased.
16. The clipper ships sailed majestic over the seven seas.
17. She remained constantly to her husband while he was overseas.
18. The more perfect the negative, the better the print will be.
19. Herbert was a sickly child, and therefore seldom played outside except when the weather was real perfect.
20. Our car jerked as the tire blew out and then swerved down the highway, wobbling and dangerously.
21. The hunter aimed careful at the flying ducks.
22. Scarface divided the loot more equal than the boys expected.
23. We are going camping most any day now.
24. Junior's head is rounder than Sister's.
25. I was never more fully insulted in my life.

9 DIAGRAMING

A diagram presents a visual analysis of a sentence that enables you to see clearly how its parts go together. When you are puzzled about a sentence, the moment or two spent in diagraming it may help you determine if it is constructed logically.

A conventional method of diagraming is illustrated below.

9a **Subject and verb.**

Put the *subject and verb* on a horizontal line and separate them with a vertical line.

Flowers bloom.

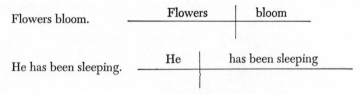

He has been sleeping.

Diagram *questions* in the same manner as declarative sentences.

Are you listening?

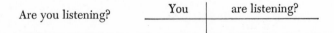

Put *compound subjects or predicates* on parallel horizontal lines.

Susan and Nancy ran.

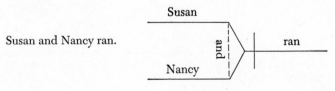

62

Fish swim and splash.

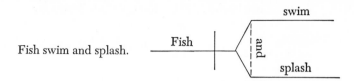

EXERCISE 11. Diagram the following sentences.

1. Dogs bark.
2. John has been swimming.
3. Is she singing?
4. Dogs and cats fight.
5. Girls chatter and giggle.
6. Are you going?
7. Owls hoot.
8. Has she been shopping?
9. Airplanes climb and dive.
10. Revenues and taxes rise.

9b Complements.

To separate the *direct object* from the verb, put a vertical line above the horizontal line.

Ellen loves children. | Ellen | loves | children

Put the *indirect object*, which is usually the implied object of the preposition *to*, on a horizontal line under the verb.

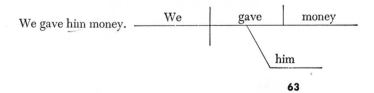

We gave him money.

Give men liberty. (The subject *you* is understood.)

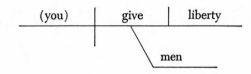

Use a diagonal line sloping toward the subject to show a *predicate noun* or *predicate adjective*.

Henry is treasurer.

| Henry | is \ treasurer |

Mice are rodents.

| Mice | are \ rodents |

March is windy.

| March | is \ windy |

EXERCISE 12. Diagram the following sentences.

1. Goats eat cans.
2. We gave them food.
3. Bring me water.
4. George is shy.
5. Mike is captain.
6. Business is good.
7. Religion offered them peace.
8. Whales are mammals.
9. China attacked Korea.
10. Autumn is invigorating.

9c Modifiers.

Use a diagonal line to join an *adjective* (except a predicate adjective) or an *adverb* to the word it modifies.

The white rooster crowed proudly.

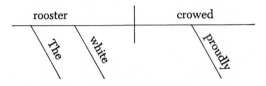

The light blue airplane disappeared very quickly.

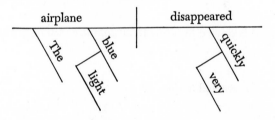

EXERCISE 13. Diagram the following sentences.

1. The farmer bought a fine Jersey cow.
2. The dignified professor reprimanded the student severely.
3. The little girl closed the gate tightly.
4. Our new automobile arrived yesterday.
5. The old mare and her colt suddenly jumped the pasture fence.
6. Many students attended the rally.
7. A rolling stone gathers no moss.
8. The falling leaves gradually covered the grass.
9. The painter carefully sketched the landscape.
10. The tenants and their guests luckily escaped the fire.

9d Verbals.

Place a *participle* under the word it modifies.

Laughing children are playing tag.

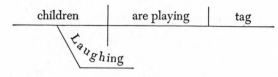

Use this device to indicate a *gerund:*

Walking is fun.

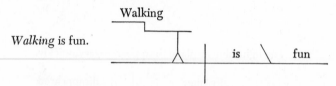

Use this device to indicate an *infinitive used as a noun:*

She wanted *to sing.*

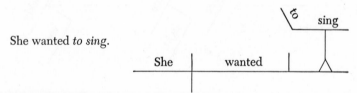

(In this sentence, *to sing* is the direct object.)

In diagraming an *infinitive used as a modifier,* join it to the word it modifies.

We are ready *to go.*

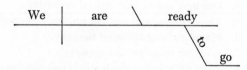

EXERCISE 14. Diagram the following sentences.

1. Falling leaves covered the ground.
2. Swimming is good exercise.
3. The little child wanted to run and play.

4. He is willing to help.
5. Knitting requires patience.
6. Wandering minstrels entertained the court.
7. The witness refused to talk.
8. Our visitors were content to stay.
9. Harvesting is hard work.
10. To work and succeed were his ambitions.

9e Phrases.

Diagram *phrases* as follows:

PREPOSITIONAL PHRASE USED AS AN ADJECTIVE

He is the owner *of the store.*

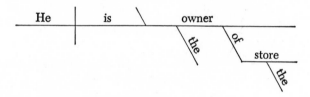

PREPOSITIONAL PHRASE USED AS AN ADVERB

The cow jumped *over the moon.*

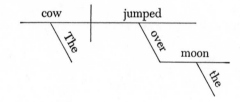

PARTICIPIAL PHRASE

Having made his fortune, he retired.

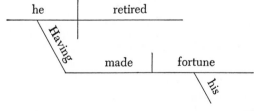

67

GERUND PHRASE

Breaking a forest trail is strenuous work.

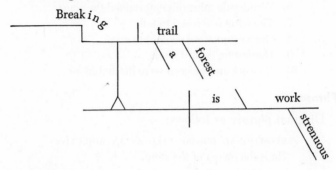

INFINITIVE PHRASE

Kate is learning *to drive an automobile*.

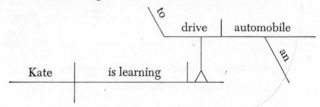

To walk under a ladder requires courage.

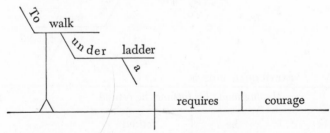

EXERCISE 15. Diagram the following sentences.

1. Swimming the English Channel is a difficult feat.
2. Lillian wanted to catch a large bass.
3. He is the leader of the rebel army.

68

4. Dave led Marguerite out of the woods.
5. Having eaten a large dinner, Jim retired to the veranda.
6. Observing traffic rules is every motorist's responsibility.
7. The angry hornets stung him on the face.
8. Having discovered a clue, Holmes easily solved the crime.
9. Manasseh Cutler was the founder of the Ohio settlement.
10. To refinish old furniture demands much painstaking labor.

9f   Clauses.

To diagram a compound sentence with two or more *main clauses,* diagram each clause separately and then join the diagrams.

The speaker finished his address; the crowd cheered wildly.

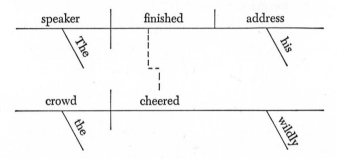

Hawkeye was pursued by Indians, but they did not catch him.

Diagram *subordinate clauses* as follows:

NOUN CLAUSE

His weakness was *that he had no ambition.*

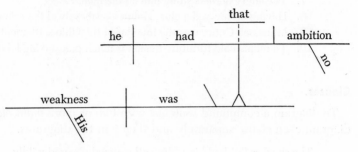

ADJECTIVE CLAUSE

The girl *who won the contest* is a college freshman.

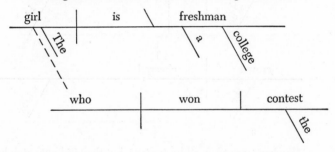

ADVERB CLAUSE

We will meet him *when the train arrives.*

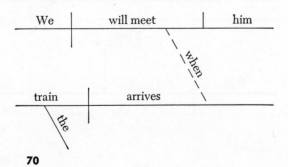

70

EXERCISE 16. Diagram the following sentences.

1. Our main problem was that we had no money.
2. They are refugees who escaped from oppression.
3. When we arrived, the fire was blazing fiercely.
4. This is the new tractor that my neighbor bought.
5. The old gentleman insisted that I take the reward.
6. The land was fertile, but floods ruined the crops.
7. Her promise was that she would read his poems.
8. The man who repaired the shoes could speak many languages.
9. We were eating lunch when the telephone rang.
10. My advice is that you consult a psychiatrist.

9g Independent elements.

In diagraming *absolute phrases, expletives,* interjections, words of direct address, and other independent elements,* set them off above the rest of the sentence.

Generally speaking, he is a good student.

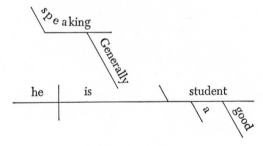

There is a proper time for everything.

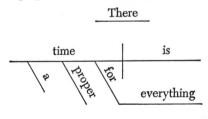

* See Section 50.

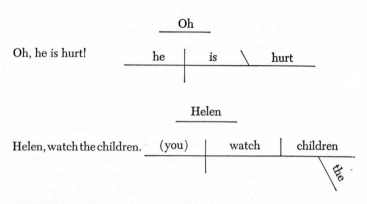

Oh, he is hurt!

Helen, watch the children.

EXERCISE 17. Diagram the following sentences.

1. There was once a very wise old man.
2. Listen, gentlemen, to my story.
3. Help! I am drowning.
4. Considering everything, you have achieved much.
5. Well, the team has finally won a game.
6. There is a small elephant in the garden.
7. I know, fellow Americans, that you will give generously.
8. Hey! Bring back my fountain pen.
9. Your recovery, we hope, will be rapid.
10. Oh, you are surely wrong.

EXERCISE 18. Diagram the following sentences.

1. Having completed our chemical experiment, we studied the results.
2. Following the old Indian trail, we found a good camping site.
3. I know, friends, that you question my intentions.
4. Benson is the president of the insurance company.
5. Dying fish struggled in the polluted water.
6. Help! My hands are slipping off the window ledge.
7. The tattered beggar asked for a dime.
8. The old chief's argument was that Manhattan really belonged to the Indians.
9. After they leave the assembly line the new cars are thoroughly tested.

10. I am tempted to buy a new gazetteer.
11. We visited the house where Lincoln lived.
12. His secret ambition was to find Captain Kidd's buried treasure.
13. The neighbors stubbornly refused to sign his petition.
14. After reading the telegram she collapsed in her chair.
15. To filibuster is an old political stratagem.
16. Who is the spokesman for the rioting prisoners?
17. The marines were ready when the enemy forces attacked.
18. We lit the fuse and waited for the explosion.
19. Wendell Phillips was a famous lecturer during the Civil War years.
20. The carpenter put a new blade on his power saw.

BASIC GRAMMAR REVIEW EXERCISE (Sections 5 through 9). Correct the grammatical errors in the following sentences according to formal usage.

1. The challenger seen at once that the champion was a harder puncher than him.
2. The Turkish battalion were real eager to fight the Chinese invaders of Korea.
3. Now that September is here I wish that summer was only beginning.
4. It was them and not us who forgot the dinner engagement.
5. The second lieutenant ordered Willis and I to report for guard duty.
6. It snowed considerable during the night.
7. He was sure delighted to learn that the damaged car would still run good.
8. The residents forbade foreigners living in the new subdivision.
9. There is seldom a good reason for you being absent from class.
10. The northern states will be grateful to whomever discovers a way to save the deer herds from winter starvation.
11. This information is a secret between you and I.
12. Before the banquet began, the toastmaster asked each of us to introduce ourselves and our wives.
13. He did not say that it was me who he wanted to see.

14. Most of us are annoyed by those kind of people who we know are always trying to get something for nothing.

15. After the play ended, the cast appears for curtain calls.

16. Sheriff Hayes felt badly because he was compelled to arrest a neighbor whom he knew had never stole before.

17. The sailors sprung to the ship's side, drug up the anchor, and fastened it to the cathead.

18. That snake looks as if he was getting ready to strike.

19. In the darkness the police took him to be I.

20. Billy Budd was hung from the main yard, in full view of the ship's company.

21. Do you really think that you are wiser than me?

22. The lifeguard run quick to the pool, dove into the water, and swum toward the screaming girl.

23. I would not have hesitated to have called his bluff.

24. The United Nations protested about China mistreating war prisoners.

25. Whom do you think suffers most in periods of currency inflation?

Basic Sentence Faults =
SEN FLT

Is it correct? Is it effective? These are the two questions we learn to ask of our sentences. And we ask them in just this order, for we like to be sure that the elements of a sentence are in proper grammatical relationship with one another before we concern ourselves with its style. We don't, for instance, worry first about the "effectiveness" of *In Yellowstone Park driving down the road some bears were seen having climbed down from the trees.* We worry first about its "correctness," about eliminating all those basic sentence faults that make the statement such an incoherent mishmash.

10   SENTENCE FRAGMENT = **FRAG**

Do not use fragmentary (incomplete) sentences.

The usual sentence contains both a subject and a verb. But you may sometimes decide, for reasons of emphasis or economy, to omit either the subject or the verb. Conversational language abounds in questions, answers, and exclamations that do not follow the usual sentence pattern. "Really?" "Yes." "How absurd!" Familiar expressions such as "The sooner, the better," or transitional phrases such as "So much for this point. Now for my second argument" are used even in formal English. Although these sentences are fragments, they are understandable in a suitable context.

Writers occasionally omit the verbs in descriptive passages, particularly in recording a series of sense impressions. Here is an example:

> Howland & Gould's Grocery. In the display window, black, over-ripe bananas and lettuce on which a cat was sleeping. Shelves lined with red crepe paper which was now faded and torn and concentrically spotted.
>
> —SINCLAIR LEWIS, *Main Street*

Similarly, writers sometimes omit the verbs in passages that reflect a person's thoughts.

> He looked at the old photograph and was suddenly unhappy. The old gang all split up now. Smitty in L.A., Frank in Berlin, Joe on a two-year stretch in Alaska. Weather observer. Good joke that one. Heard Joe say once he'd never live north of Miami. Serves him right. Never second-guess destiny.

Ordinarily, however, sentences that lack the normal subject-verb sequence are ineffective. A phrase or subordinate clause usually is meaningless unless it is closely related to an independent clause. If you punctuate such phrases and clauses as complete sentences, you sacrifice meaning and effectiveness. Note this example:

> He leaped through the window with a crash. Because there was no other way of escaping the fire.

Here the meaning of the *because*-clause depends directly on the main clause. Punctuating the subordinate clause as though it were a complete sentence results in a "period fault" and sometimes reflects the writer's inability to determine what a complete sentence is. Use of such fragments greatly weakens your writing. Notice the increased clarity of a sentence combining the two clauses from the above example:

> He leaped through the window with a crash, because there was no other way of escaping the fire.

Here is another means of achieving greater clarity:

> He leaped through the window with a crash; there was no other way of escaping the fire.

Or again:

> He leaped through the window with a crash. There was no other way of escaping the fire.

Fortunately, sentence fragments are easy to eliminate from your writing.

EXERCISE 1. In the following sentences eliminate ineffective fragments (1) by combining them with the main clause or (2) by making them into complete sentences.

1. I was frightened. Probably because I had never before seen a gun battle in the street.
2. She used to dislike me. Though I never knew why.
3. The pilot feared that his plane had insufficient fuel. The nearest landing field being nearly a hundred miles away.
4. Prospectors invaded the newly discovered gold field. Some in wagons, some on horseback, and a few in heavily laden canoes.
5. The twins are almost identical. The only difference being a small mole on Judy's cheek.

6. We had a wonderful vacation. Chiefly because the fishing was good.

7. She was constantly making suggestions to her husband. Such as how much soap he should use in the dishwater.

8. No rain for a month. The streams were beginning to dry up

9. She talked almost incessantly. But intelligently nevertheless

10. There shouldn't be any secrets. At least between you and me.

11. Where the corn stands in the sunlight, where the folks eat clabber and blackberries, where the stores charge things to your first name. That's where I want to spend my life.

12. My mother gained twenty pounds and her health improved generally. After she had her tonsils removed.

13. Because I know that my mother will be angry and insist that I never see you again, if we get home after midnight. I think we should go home.

14. In spite of the fact that Hobbes was able to explain rationally almost every phenomenon of the supernatural. He was afraid of the dark.

15. You will serve a specified period in the army. Whether you want to or not.

16. Weaving baskets is an educational and useful hobby. For young or old.

17. Usually trees grow along both banks of a stream, but when they grow only along one bank. The stream very likely flows along a fault line.

18. He struck out three times during the game. Every time he was up.

19. He left without a word of goodbye. And we never heard from him again.

20. A red sunset is not only a beautiful sight. But also is usually a sign of good weather the following day.

11 COMMA SPLICE = **CS** or **CF**
AND RUN-TOGETHER
OR FUSED SENTENCE = **FS**

Avoid comma splices and fused sentences.

11

11a Comma Splice = CS or CF.

Do not use a comma between two main clauses *unless* the clauses are joined by one of the co-ordinating conjunctions: *and, but, for, or, nor, yet.* Use of a comma without the co-ordinating conjunction results in the comma fault or comma splice. Correct the comma splice in one of the following ways:

(1) Connect the main clauses with a co-ordinating conjunction.
(2) Replace the comma with a semicolon.
(3) Make a separate sentence of each main clause.
(4) Change one of the main clauses to a subordinate clause.

COMMA SPLICE	The witness was unwilling to testify, he was afraid of the accused man.
REVISED (1)	The witness was unwilling to testify, for he was afraid of the accused man.
REVISED (2)	The witness was unwilling to testify; he was afraid of the accused man.
REVISED (3)	The witness was unwilling to testify. He was afraid of the accused man.
REVISED (4)	Because he was afraid of the accused man, the witness was unwilling to testify.

Revision (4) is the most effective, for it not only corrects the comma splice but also indicates the relationship between the clauses.

79

A good revision of a comma-splice error often entails reworking the sentence rather than merely inserting a punctuation mark.

11b   Run-together or fused sentence = FS.

Do not omit punctuation between main clauses. Such omission results in run-together or fused sentences—that is, two complete thoughts with no separating punctuation. Correct these errors in the same way as the comma splice.

FUSED	Balboa gazed upon the broad Pacific his heart was filled with awe.
REVISED (1)	Balboa gazed upon the broad Pacific, and his heart was filled with awe.
REVISED (2)	Balboa gazed upon the broad Pacific; his heart was filled with awe.
REVISED (3)	Balboa gazed upon the broad Pacific. His heart was filled with awe.
REVISED (4)	When Balboa gazed upon the broad Pacific, his heart was filled with awe.

EXERCISE 2. Eliminate comma splices and run-together sentences from the following items and be prepared to give the reasons for your corrections.

1. Its tires screaming, the automobile crashed headlong into the bridge culvert then all was quiet.

2. The automobile crashed headlong into the bridge culvert, none of the occupants were injured severely.

3. The automobile was not in good condition it had been wrecked twice and its brakes were completely ineffective.

4. The automobile crashed headlong into the culvert its occupants were all killed.

5. The automobile crashed headlong into the culvert however its occupants were not severely injured.

6. Below us the train rounded a mountain curve, we thought it looked like a mechanical snake.

7. After the blood transfusion the patient was conscious for a short while, the doctor left the hospital for a meal.

8. We used to behave just as wildly I can remember riding my sled in the street without regard for the traffic.

9. Trapped in the center of the court, Charley pivoted and

passed the basketball through his legs from the stands he looked like a football center.

10. This is the reason I stopped reading books, they invariably made me think too much.

11. The hero deserted the army when he realized that the war had no significance for him only one human being meant anything, the nurse he was in love with.

12. I would lie for hours watching the goldfish playing checkers was my only other amusement.

13. My brother must be color-blind, he calls everything from purple to black navy blue.

14. Every day the rooster would fly into the pigpen, he delighted in tormenting the lazy creatures.

15. The Puritans were the source of many of our democratic ideals, however the government of Cromwell was in many ways an absolute dictatorship.

16. Twain knew that Howells was shocked, nevertheless he sent the editor copies of all his coarse productions.

17. In the kitchen are three chairs on the porch are four more.

18. Santa Anna was surprised by the Texan forces at San Jacinto, afterwards he was captured while trying to escape dressed as a common soldier.

19. The rock formations of the Arbuckle Mountains in Oklahoma are gnarled and polished as a geologist told us, these are some of the oldest mountains in the world.

20. No one can say that Walpole had no principles, one of them was that every man had his price.

12 FAULTY AGREEMENT = **AGR**

Agreement is the grammatical relationship between a subject and verb, or a pronoun and its antecedent, or a demonstrative adjective and the word it modifies.

Since modern English nouns and verbs have few inflections, or special endings, agreement usually presents few problems. However, there are some grammatical patterns, such as the agreement in number of a subject and verb, or a pronoun and its antecedent, that you must watch carefully.

12a **Make every verb agree in number with its subject.**

Sometimes a lack of agreement between subject and verb is merely the result of carelessness in composition or revision. But more often, writers use a singular subject with a plural verb or a plural subject with a singular verb, not because they misunderstand the general rule, but because they are uncertain of the number of the subject. This problem in agreement is most likely to arise when other words intervene between the subject and verb.

(1) *Do not be confused by words or phrases that intervene between the subject and verb. Find the subject and make the verb agree with it.*

> The first two *chapters* of the book *were* exciting. (The verb agrees with the subject, *chapters*, not with the nearest noun, *book*.)
>
> The *size* of the bears *startles* the spectators.

Singular subjects followed by such expressions as *with, together with, accompanied by*, and *as well as* take singular verbs. The phrases introduced by such expressions are not part of the subject, even though they do suggest a plural meaning.

> FAULTY   The *coach*, as well as the players, *were* happy over the victory.
>
> REVISED   The *coach*, as well as the players, *was* happy over the victory.
>
> FAULTY   The horse *thief*, with his two accomplices, *have been hanged*.
>
> REVISED   The horse *thief*, with his two accomplices, *has been hanged*.

Again, find the subject and make the verb agree with it. With clearly plural subjects use a plural verb.

> Both the coach and the players were happy over the victory.
> The horse thief and his two accomplices have been hanged.

12

(2) *Remember that singular pronouns take singular verbs.*

> *Everyone is* ready to go.
> *Somebody is* calling from the attic.

Actually, the convention that a singular pronoun must take a singular verb is seldom violated, even by poor writers. No one says, "Everyone are present," or "Nobody win all the time." What does cause some difficulty is remembering to make a pronoun agree with a singular pronoun antecedent such as *anyone, everyone, nobody.* Formal usage prefers "Everyone took off his coat." But violations are common, and "Everyone took off their coats" is acceptable in informal usage. (See Section 12b [1].)

None, either, neither, any may be followed by either a singular or a plural verb, depending on whether you intend a singular or a plural meaning.

> SINGULAR   *None* but a fool *squanders* his time.
> PLURAL   *None* but fools *squander* their time.

(3) *Use a plural verb with two or more subjects joined by* AND.

> A dog and a cat *are* seldom friends.

But use a singular verb when the two parts of a compound subject refer to the same person or thing.

My friend and benefactor *was* there to help me.

(4) *Use a singular verb with two or more singular subjects joined by* OR *or* NOR. *If the subjects differ in number or person, make the verb agree with the subject nearer to it.*

Either the dean or his assistant *was* to have handled the matter.
Neither the farmer nor the chickens *were* aware of the swooping hawk.
Either you or he *has* to be here.

(5) *When the verb precedes the subject of the sentence, be particularly careful to find the subject and make the verb agree with it.*

There *are* only a chair and a table left to auction.
In the balcony there *are* many seats.

In informal English a singular verb is often used when it is followed by a compound subject.

FORMAL   As a result, there *are* confusion, trouble, and uncertainty.
INFORMAL   As a result, there *is* confusion, trouble, and uncertainty.

(6) *Use a singular verb with collective nouns to indicate that the group is considered as one unit. Use a plural verb to indicate that the individual members of the group are acting separately.* (For definition of *collective*, see Section 50.)

The committee *is* meeting today.
The committee *are* unable to agree on a plan of action.

(7) *Make the verb agree with its subject, not with a predicate noun.*

The best part of the program *is* the vocal duets.
Men *are* a necessity in her life.

(8) *With relative pronouns use a singular verb when the antecedent is singular, a plural verb when the antecedent is plural.*

He is the only one of the councilmen who *is opposed* to the plan. (The antecedent of *who* is *one*, not *councilmen*.)

He is one of the best baseball players that *have come* from Texas. (The antecedent of the relative pronoun *that* is *players*, not *one*.)

Expressions like "one of the best baseball players that" commonly take a singular verb in informal usage. Although the antecedent of *that* is the plural noun *players*, the writer or speaker is influenced in his choice of a verb by the fact that *one* is singular.

FORMAL   He is one of those people who *are* afraid to act.
INFORMAL   He is one of those people who *is* afraid to act.

EXERCISE 3. In the following sentences correct any errors in agreement in accordance with formal usage. Place an "I" before the sentences that might be correct in informal English.

1. The poor widow with her five children live in a small flat.
2. Either Johnny or his sister have the measles.
3. His only interest are his studies.
4. There is several ways of skinning a cat.
5. Each of the contestants claim the prize.
6. Fatima is one of the largest elephants that has ever been captured.
7. Does the victor and the vanquished share in the spoils?
8. This is the only one of all his plays that were successful on Broadway.
9. The coach and not the players suffer most in defeat.
10. Ten miles are a long distance to walk.
11. He is one of those fellows who is always whistling at the girls.
12. A fool and his money is soon parted.
13. The first two quarters of the game was evenly fought.
14. Either the candidate or his advisers was wrong about public sentiment before the election.
15. Is there any leaks in the roof?
16. Twelve dollars are too much money for these shoes.
17. Among my favorite plays are *Romeo and Juliet*.
18. There is many good reasons for studying foreign languages.
19. The final two sets of the tennis match was bitterly fought.
20. Tabby, as well as her kittens, are suspicious of strange dogs.

12b **Use a singular pronoun in referring to a singular antecedent. Use a plural pronoun in referring to a plural antecedent.**

SINGULAR   The small *boy* put *his* penny in the collection box.

PLURAL   The *cows* lost *their* way in the storm.

Ambiguity in the use of pronouns is an offense against clarity. The following general rules will help you select proper pronouns:

(1) *In formal writing use a singular pronoun to refer to antecedents such as* PERSON, MAN, WOMAN, ONE, ANY, ANYONE, ANYBODY, SOMEONE, SOMEBODY, EACH, EVERY, EVERYONE, EVERYBODY, EITHER, NEITHER.

In informal English you may use a plural pronoun to refer to antecedents such as *any, every,* and their compounds, and *each, someone, somebody, either, neither,* especially when you want to suggest a plural meaning.

FORMAL   *Everybody* held *his* breath.
INFORMAL   *Everybody* held *their* breath.

FORMAL   He asked *each* of us to bring *his* own lunch.
INFORMAL   He asked *each* of us to bring *our* own lunch.

(2) *With a collective noun as an antecedent, use a singular pronoun if you are considering the group as a unit, a plural pronoun if you are considering the individual members of the group separately.*

The *militia* increased *its* watchfulness.
The *band* raised *their* instruments at the conductor's signal.

(3) *If two or more singular antecedents are joined by* OR *or* NOR, *use a singular pronoun in referring to them; if one of such antecedents is singular and the other plural, make the pronoun agree with the nearer.*

Neither Jack nor Jim has finished *his* work.
Neither the father nor his sons were ready for *their* dinner.

EXERCISE 4. In the following sentences make every pronoun agree with its antecedent in accordance with formal English usage. Then place an "I" before any sentence that would be acceptable in familiar speech or informal writing.

1. Somebody lost their temper in the argument.
2. Nearly everybody has some worthless souvenirs which they would not willingly part with.
3. Each of the Scouts took their turn at keeping up the campfire.
4. Any customer may obtain a refund if they are dissatisfied with the hair restorer.
5. The committee submitted their report.
6. A person usually objects if they think their political beliefs are being attacked.
7. Neither Bill nor Dick have brought their lunch.
8. The longer a man lives, the wiser they become.
9. Each of the witnesses gave their account of the accident.
10. Neither of the recruits failed in their physical examinations.
11. Anyone can attend the meeting if they don't heckle the speaker.
12. Everybody is requested to bring their own food to the picnic.
13. The school board disagreed in its opinions of the superintendent's policies.
14. He can take almost any raw rookie and develop them into an expert player.
15. Neither the farmer nor the hired man has finished their chores.
16. A person should be willing to defend their principles.
17. The student council fined two of their own members for being absent from meetings.
18. If a physician or a lawyer would come to this town, they would make a good living.
19. The Brown family is loyal to every one of their members.
20. Every country is jealous of their rights.

12c **Make sure that a demonstrative adjective** (THIS, THAT, THESE, THOSE) **agrees in number with the noun it modifies.**

These adjective forms seldom cause difficulty. One frequent error, however, occurs when the demonstrative adjective is used with *kind of* or *sort of* followed by plural nouns. Here you must remember that the demonstrative adjective modifies the singular noun *kind* or *sort* and NOT the the following plural noun. Thus a singular demonstrative is used.

SUBSTANDARD	*These kind* of strawberries taste sweet.
STANDARD	*This kind* of strawberry tastes sweet.
SUBSTANDARD	*These sort* of watches are expensive.
STANDARD	*This sort* of watch is expensive.

EXERCISE 5. In the following sentences correct every error of agreement in accordance with formal usage.

1. The influence of journalism is evident in the writing of many American literary artists.

2. The finance committee do not approve the club's policy of low annual dues.

3. Cora is one of those kind of people who sacrifice their happiness for money.

4. Miriam is the only one of the children who are opposed to selling the family home.

5. On my car there is a windshield washer and fog lights.

6. The courage of the rebellious peasants move their enemies to admiration.

7. If one enters politics they must expect partisan criticism.

8. Everybody likes to flatter themselves that their thoughts are original.

9. The solution of the city's traffic problems are certain to require long study.

10. Either the cook or the dinner guest have taken the silver spoons.

11. Radios is a necessity in the modern home.

12. Neither the pianist nor the vocalist were capable of moving the emotions of the audience.

13. Poverty is one of the major forces that encourage crime.

14. In maturity one forgets the romantic world of their childhood imagination.

15. A chorus of jeers and cheers were heard from the theater gallery.

16. The king with his small band of devoted followers have escaped the vengeful mob.

17. The patrol encountered heavy fire and lost two of their men.

18. These sort of planes can exceed the speed of sound.

19. Either lime or commercial fertilizer are useful for fall treatment of lawns.

20. He is one of the finest orators that has come from the South.

13 FAULTY REFERENCE
OF PRONOUNS = REF

Be sure that all pronouns refer clearly and exactly to their antecedents.

A pronoun depends for meaning upon a noun or another pronoun. Insure clarity in your writing by making pronoun antecedents clear and obvious. Place pronouns as close to their antecedents as possible and make pronoun references exact.

13

13a **Avoid sentences in which there are two possible antecedents for a pronoun.**

AMBIGUOUS	Jack told Carl that he was ungrateful. (Does *he* refer to Jack or Carl?)
CLEAR	Jack said to Carl, "You are ungrateful."
CLEAR	Jack said to Carl, "I am ungrateful."
CLEAR	Jack confessed to Carl that he was ungrateful.
CLEAR	Jack accused Carl of being ungrateful.
AMBIGUOUS	After Mrs. Henry scolded little Sylvia, she regretted her rudeness. (To whom do *she* and *her* refer?)
CLEAR	After Mrs. Henry scolded her, little Sylvia regretted her rudeness.
CLEAR	After scolding little Sylvia, Mrs. Henry regretted her own rudeness.

EXERCISE 6. Revise the following sentences by eliminating the ambiguous reference of pronouns.

1. Carol told her mother that she should go to college.
2. I dropped a bottle of vinegar on my toe and broke it.
3. When Aunt Martha visited her sister, she was not feeling well.
4. He put the clock on the mantel which had been repaired.
5. George had a dog with fleas which he was always scratching.

89

6. The instructor gave Warren a copy of *Hamlet,* which was his favorite play.

7. With a worm in its mouth the bird flew to the nest and shoved it down the baby's throat.

8. My children had too many clothes, so I gave them to the Salvation Army.

9. The American people have elected a number of poor presidents, but Congress has generally kept them from ruining the country.

10. Professor Donahue wanted to write a biography of Rutherford B. Hayes with the collaboration of his assistant, Dr. Terence, after he won the Larkins History prize.

13b **Avoid references to remote antecedents.**

REMOTE   The birds sang in the forest where the undergrowth was thick, and a brook wound slowly in the valley. *They* were of many colors. (The pronoun *they* is too far removed from its antecedent, *birds.*)

CLEAR   . . . The *birds* were of many colors. (Confusion in meaning avoided by repetition of the noun.)

CLEAR   The *birds,* which were of many colors, sang in the forest. . . . (Elimination of the remote reference by revision of the sentence. The second sentence of the example has been changed into a subordinate clause.)

EXERCISE 7. Revise all sentences in which pronouns are too remote from their antecedents.

1. Reading is an important means by which a person can acquire an education. Students, business and professional people, and many others find it of great value.

2. The house belongs to my grandfather. The grounds cover several acres and include vineyards and orchards. It is very old.

3. Flowers grew profusely on the hillside. Many people strolled along the path at the foot of the hill on Sunday afternoons. Usually they stopped to admire them.

4. The boy threw the newspaper as he spun headlong down the street on his new bicycle. Making a perfect arc, flying neatly over the fence and between our elm trees, it landed solidly on the stomach of my father, who was asleep on the porch.

5. The curtains by the open window had blown back across the desk and knocked a bottle of red ink into a wastebasket. When we saw them later they appeared to be stained with blood.

13c **Avoid the vague use of** THIS, THAT, **or** WHICH **to refer to the general idea of a preceding clause or sentence.**

In formal usage it is preferable that a pronoun refer to a particular word in the sentence rather than to a whole phrase, clause, or sentence. Informal usage permits such general antecedents.

FORMAL   His *joining* a fraternity, *which* was unexpected, pleased his family. (*Which* refers specifically to *joining.*)

INFORMAL   He joined a fraternity, *which* was unexpected and pleased his family. (The reference is clear, although *which* refers to the entire preceding clause, not to any specific word.)

FORMAL   He pounded my back, an *action that* annoyed me, and I objected strenuously. (*That* refers to *action.*)

INFORMAL   He pounded my back. *That* annoyed me, and I objected strenuously. (*That* clearly refers to the preceding sentence.)

Eliminate a vague pronoun reference by (1) recasting the sentence to eliminate the pronoun, or (2) supplying a specific antecedent for the pronoun.

VAGUE   The profits from the investment would be large, *which* I realized almost immediately.

CLEAR   I realized almost immediately that the profits from the investment would be large. (The pronoun is eliminated.)

CLEAR   The profits from the investment would be large, a *fact that* I realized almost immediately. (A specific antecedent is supplied for the pronoun *that.*)

EXERCISE 8. Revise all sentences in which the reference of pronouns is vague.

1. He makes his own bed daily, which he learned in the army.
2. He was unaware of his own pleasant personality. This made people like him.
3. Some people do not get enough exercise, and they acquire flabby muscles. That will affect their health in later life.
4. The merchant displays the price on every item of his merchandise, which his customers find helpful.
5. There is a large lake near our summer cottage, which is convenient.

6. Jack was very fond of athletics, which influenced him to become a sports writer.

7. People should always vote on election day. This is an indication of their desire to have good government.

8. His slice of pie was smaller than mine, which made him angry.

9. The engine of the car is very noisy, which should be repaired immediately.

10. The granary is bursting with grain. This is due to the fine rains during the growing season.

13d   **Make sure that the antecedent of a pronoun is a noun that can be logically substituted for the pronoun.**

WEAK   Because we put the wire fence around the chicken yard, *they* cannot escape. (*They* cannot logically refer to *chicken,* which here functions as an adjective.)

CLEAR   Because we put the wire fence around the chicken yard, the *chickens* cannot escape.

WEAK   Tom's brother is an engineer, and *this* is the profession Tom wants to study. (*This* cannot logically refer to *engineer.*)

CLEAR   Tom's brother is an engineer, and *engineering* is the profession Tom wants to study.

EXERCISE 9. In the following sentences eliminate all references to unexpressed antecedents.

1. There is a fire station near the school, and we called them when we saw smoke in the basement.

2. Mr. Carson operates a dairy farm, and his son hopes to become one.

3. Because John had never milked a cow, he supposed it was easy.

4. She is a good cook, because she learned it when she was only a child.

5. We removed the fish scales before we fried them.

6. He suffered a slight heart attack, but after a month's rest it was as good as ever.

7. When the political refugee asked for police protection, four of them were assigned to guard him.

8. After reading a book about television engineering, Mr. Foster had great admiration for them.

9. In his youth he was a skillful fisherman, but now he seldom has time to do it.

10. Although Brown likes to talk about politics, he has no personal ambition to be one.

13e Avoid the indefinite use of THEY, YOU, and IT.

The indefinite use of *they, you,* and *it* results in vague, generalized writing, leaving the reader to wonder who or what *they, you,* and *it* are. Always strive for a sharp, clear, definite expression of your meaning. Informal usage permits the indefinite use of these words.

FORMAL   At the state university the rules require all students to take a course in composition.

INFORMAL   At the state university *they* require all students to take a course in composition.

FORMAL   In some states motorists are not permitted to drive faster than fifty miles an hour.

INFORMAL   In some states *you* are not permitted to drive faster than fifty miles an hour.

FORMAL   The newspaper says that Monday will be warmer.

INFORMAL   *It* says in the newspaper that Monday will be warmer.*

EXERCISE 10. Revise the following sentences to avoid the indefinite use of *they, you,* and *it*.

1. In Iowa they grow a great deal of corn.
2. When playing golf, you keep your eye on the ball.
3. In the advertisement it says that the wrist watch is waterproof.
4. They put these stop lights every place but where they are needed.
5. In the Middle West you have cold winters and hot summers.
6. Before you take it, it says to shake the bottle well.
7. In pioneer times you ground your own flour.
8. They deal severely with reckless drivers in this community.
9. In this chapter it states that the Federalists advocated a neutral attitude toward European wars.
10. According to the Puritan law, if a person committed a crime against the theocracy, you had to pay the penalty.

* The indefinite use of *it* is appropriate in such idioms as *it is cloudy, it seems, it is early*.

14 SHIFTS IN POINT OF VIEW = PV
AND MIXED
CONSTRUCTIONS = MIX

*Keep your point of view and grammatical construc-
tion logical and consistent.*

Point of view refers to your use of subject, of person and number,
and of verb tense, voice, and mood. Needless shifts in any of these
elements will impair the effectiveness of your sentences.

14a **Do not shift the subject of a sentence or the voice of the verb.**

FAULTY   Frogs could be heard croaking as we neared the swamp.
(The subject shifts from *frogs* to *we*. The verb shifts
from passive to active voice.)

REVISED   We heard frogs croaking as we neared the swamp.

FAULTY   Ellen stayed at a mountain resort, and much of her
time was spent in painting. (The subject shifts from
Ellen to *much*. The verb shifts from active to passive
voice.)

REVISED   Ellen stayed at a mountain resort and spent much of
her time in painting.

EXERCISE 11. Revise the following sentences by eliminating
all needless shifts in subject or voice.

1. When we approached the burning house, smoke was seen.
2. Mrs. Carey washed the dishes, and then the ironing was done
   by her.
3. Tex is a good swimmer, but his strength was not great enough
   to swim the channel.
4. He held the ruler on the paper, and a long line was drawn.

94

5. After a hot fire was built by the campers, they dried their wet clothing.

6. We entered our first college classroom, and seats were taken by us.

7. Mr. Jones practiced daily, and his golf game was improved.

8. Fish could be seen jumping as we approached the river.

9. The men decided upon a camp site, and the tent was soon pitched.

10. Casey Jones mounted to the engine cab, and the throttle was grabbed.

14b Do not shift person or number.

FAULTY   When *you* have good health, *one* should feel fortunate. (A shift from second to third person.)

REVISED   When *you* have good health, *you* should feel fortunate.

REVISED   When *one* has good health, *he* (or *one*) should feel fortunate.

FAULTY   If a *person* practices diligently, *they* can become an expert archer. (A shift from singular to plural number.)

REVISED   If a *person* practices diligently, *he* can become an expert archer.

EXERCISE 12. Revise the following sentences by eliminating all needless shifts in person or number.

1. I always carry a pocketknife, because they are often useful.

2. I took an aspirin tablet, for I knew they would relieve my headache.

3. If one is willing to help put up the tent, you can get a free ticket to the circus.

4. Everyone should exercise daily, for you derive great benefit from exercise.

5. I like an occasional cup of coffee, for they give me that added boost which I need.

6. After you have finished two sets of tennis, one feels like relaxing in a cool shower.

7. Every young person should learn to drive an automobile, for they will need the ability later in life.

8. I enjoy a novel by Dickens because their plots are so involved.

9. No matter what subject one intends to major in, you should be proficient in writing.

10. I distrust a public opinion poll because they have often been wrong in the past.

14c Do not shift tense or mood.

FAULTY   He *sat* down at his desk and *begins* to write. (The verb shifts from past tense to present tense.)

REVISED He *sat* down at his desk and *began* to write.

FAULTY   *Hold* the rifle firmly against your shoulder, and then you *should take* careful aim. (The verb shifts from imperative mood to indicative mood.)

REVISED *Hold* the rifle firmly against your shoulder and then *take* careful aim.

EXERCISE 13. Revise the following sentences by eliminating all needless shifts in tense or mood.

1. When I met Roger at the street corner, he does not recognize me.

2. First you tie a fisherman's knot, and then you should tighten the loops so that they lie straight in line.

3. Large clouds are drifting in the sky, and suddenly the moon was hidden from view.

4. Spade carefully around the tree, and you should take care not to cut the roots.

5. The book is interesting, although one of the main characters was unrealistic.

6. After I had finished the long explanation, he says he doesn't understand.

7. The cats are playing contentedly, but the family dog was in an angry mood.

8. Heat the grease in the frying pan, and then you should put in the eggs.

9. Without hesitating, he picks up the ball and shot for the wrong basket.

10. I had put a nickel in the juke box, and the fun really starts.

14d Do not use mixed constructions.

A "mixed construction" is a sentence that begins with one construction and changes to another.

We walked slowly up the hill, through the woods to the house stands like a lonely sentinel on the hilltop.

Here the writer forgot that *house* was simply the noun in a prepositional phrase and suddenly boosted it to the rank of subject of the sentence. What he meant was *the house that stands.*

Generally, as in the example above, the shift from one construction to another is absolute; the sentence begins with one construction and ends with another, as in

> The fact that John was a good student he received many offers for well-paying jobs.

This error may occur when you are writing longer or more complex sentences than you commonly write. But once you are aware of the error, you can easily correct it.

MIXED	Take, for example, in the strip-mines of southeastern Ohio, the blaster has one of the best-paying jobs.
REPAIRED	For example, in the strip-mines of southeastern Ohio, the blaster has one of the best-paying jobs.
MIXED	If we here in America cannot live peaceably and happily together, we cannot hope that nations that have different living conditions to live peaceably with us.
REPAIRED	If we here in America cannot live peaceably and happily together, we cannot expect that other nations that have different living conditions will live peaceably with us.
MIXED	Every few hundred feet a test sample of the layer of earth a bit of it is analyzed to determine the distance from oil.
REPAIRED	Every few hundred feet a test sample of the layer of earth is analyzed to determine the distance from oil.

A more specific kind of mixed construction springs from the use of an improper verb tense in indirect questions.

MIXED	The manager told me he would have my car for me as soon as he can get the service garage.
REPAIRED	The manager told me he would have my car for me as soon as he could get the service garage.

EXERCISE 14. Eliminate any mixed constructions in the following sentences.

1. She has a way that makes you feel at home when I am with her.

2. Much help came from the instructor tried a second time to make the students understand.

3. With a slap on the back and a few friendly handshakes the next thing I knew I was on the football field during an actual game.

4. The campus is enormous and one glimpse of it made me feel as a weary traveler must have felt lost in the forbidden mountains.

5. The attitude of forcing the student to make his own decisions is the only way to go to school and learn something.

6. I consider social climbing an evil, for you see many girls look for fellows that can offer security in life.

7. By giving him an education and making him feel wanted will benefit the juvenile delinquent greatly.

8. I am getting acquainted with new friends here, and the friends I had I see them occasionally.

9. Being a girl's boarding school I attended, there were no mixed classes.

10. The law requires you to go to school until of a certain age, besides being an accepted policy that all children go through at least high school.

11. The forestry courses taught here prepare you for a highly technical profession in which it takes four years of very difficult study in order to graduate.

12. The clinic here is very busy, but the way it is handled it doesn't seem to inconvenience the patients.

13. I feel that there is a great need for the integration of education—bring the school, home, and community into a more cooperative program and better understanding of the needs, resources, and meeting the various programs.

14. Compared to the university where your presence in class is not compulsory makes you want to get to class on time.

15. By letting the individual develop as a worthwhile member of society instead of as a member of a reform school is in my way of thinking the way to develop good citizenship.

15 MISPLACED PARTS = **MIS PT**

Place modifiers as close as possible to the words they modify; do not separate related sentence elements needlessly.

Modern English, unlike German or Latin, has few inflections, or special endings, to show relations between words. For example, the Latin sentences *Puella amat agricolam* and *Agricolam amat puella* have the same literal meaning: *the girl loves the farmer.* Even though the positions of the subject and object are reversed, the special endings (*-a* and *-am*) make the meaning of the sentence unmistakable. But if the English equivalents of the Latin words are reversed, so is the English meaning: *the girl loves the farmer; the farmer loves the girl.* In English, therefore, the relation between word order and meaning is fundamental. An awkward or illogical placing of words obscures or alters the meaning.

Logic and clarity require that a modifier be placed as close as possible to the word it modifies. Moreover, its relation to the words that precede or follow it must be clear. Sometimes the unconscious violation of this principle has humorous results:

He bought a horse from a stranger *with a lame hind leg.*

Be sure that adverbs such as ALMOST, EVEN, HARDLY, JUST, MERELY, ONLY, NEARLY, SCARCELY **refer clearly and logically to the words they modify.**

The misplacement of these modifiers—particularly *only*—does not always result in confusion. The misplaced *only*, in fact, is rather common in informal English. However, if you are to avoid ambiguity in meaning you must exercise care in placing modifiers.

99

FORMAL	We caught *only* three fish.
INFORMAL	We *only* caught three fish.
ILLOGICAL	She *nearly* blushed until she was purple.
CLEAR	She blushed until she was *nearly* purple.
MISPLACED	I *almost* read half the book.
CLEAR	I read *almost* half the book.

EXERCISE 15. In the following sentences, place the adverbs nearer the words they modify.

1. I just arrived here last week.
2. She almost seemed tired.
3. We only have club meetings once a month.
4. She merely declined my invitation because she wished to be spiteful.
5. Since I had never attended an opera before, I nearly was sick with excitement when it began.
6. Tickets will only be sold on the day of the game.
7. The pioneers needed men to clear the forests badly.
8. The brass band nearly entertained us for two hours.
9. We scarcely harvested any apples on the farm last year.
10. For a year we almost heard nothing from our former neighbors.

15b   **Be sure that modifying phrases refer clearly to the words they modify.**

ILLOGICAL	Who is the woman who gave you the candy *in the pink dress?*
CLEAR	Who is the woman *in the pink dress* who gave you the candy?
ILLOGICAL	This poison attracts mice *with the smell of cheese.*
CLEAR	This poison *with the smell of cheese* attracts mice.

EXERCISE 16. In the following sentences, place the modifying phrases nearer the words they modify.

1. Jane and I sat and watched the moon rise without saying a word.
2. The roof collapsed soon after we left the building with a great crash.
3. I returned to school after a week's vacation on Monday.

4. Betty looked at the boy eating the sundae with envious eyes.
5. George said that his father was a boy prodigy at my party last week.
6. The yellow cat slowly crept up behind the bird with a bell on his collar.
7. The escaped lion was captured before anybody was clawed or eaten by its keepers.
8. The children looked forward to celebrating Christmas for several weeks.
9. We hope that you will notify us if you can attend the banquet on the enclosed post card.
10. The searchers found the cocker spaniel in a vacant garage with a broken leg.

15c **Be sure that modifying clauses refer clearly to the words they modify.**

ILLOGICAL	She borrowed an egg from a neighbor *that was rotten.*
CLEAR	From a neighbor she borrowed an egg *that was rotten.*
ILLOGICAL	There was a canary in the cage *that never sang.*
CLEAR	In the cage there was a canary *that never sang.*
ILLOGICAL	A dog is good company *that is well trained.*
CLEAR	A dog *that is well trained* is good company.

EXERCISE 17. In the following sentences, place the modifying clauses nearer the words they modify.

1. I heard the train whistle at the crossing that was going to Denver.
2. This book does not describe the Indian wars that I borrowed from the library.
3. The boys bought an old car from a dealer that had no fenders.
4. She put a green bonnet on her head which she had bought at an auction.
5. He secured a job with a department store after he graduated from college which lasted for nearly twenty years.
6. He bought an English setter from a neighbor that was beautifully trained.
7. The fisherman paused to take an artificial fly from his tackle box which had never failed to catch a trout.
8. We listened to the baseball game on the radio which the Yankees won.

9. Dan showed me some beautiful pictures of his trip which he had made with his new enlarger.
10. He told the clerk he wanted to buy a book for his mother that he thought was good.

15d Avoid "squinting" modifiers.

A "squinting" modifier is one that may modify either a preceding word or a following word. It squints at the words on its right and left, and leaves the reader confused.

SQUINTING	His physician told him *frequently* to exercise.
CLEAR	His physician *frequently* told him to exercise.
CLEAR	His physician told him to exercise *frequently*.

EXERCISE 18. Recast the following sentences to eliminate squinting modifiers.

1. I invited her occasionally to visit me.
2. Religious faith without doubt is a great comfort to many people.
3. He asked me the following day to pay my grocery bill.
4. A dog that can do this trick well deserves to be praised.
5. He said today the game would be played.

15e Do not split infinitives awkwardly.

An infinitive is split when an adverbial modifier separates the *to* from the verb. There is nothing ungrammatical about splitting an infinitive, and sometimes a split is necessary to achieve clarity. But most split infinitives are awkward and unnecessary.

AWKWARD	She tried *to* not carelessly *hurt* the kitten.
CLEAR	She tried not *to hurt* the kitten carelessly.
AWKWARD	You should try *to,* if you can, *take* a walk every day.
CLEAR	If you can, you should try *to take* a walk every day.

In the following examples the sentence with the split infinitive is the less awkward.

CLEAR	Needing an advantage in the race, he expected *to* more than *gain* it by diligent practice. (Awkwardness results if *more than* is moved to any other position in the sentence.)
AWKWARD	Needing an advantage in the race, he more than expected *to gain* it by diligent practice.

EXERCISE 19. Revise the following sentences by eliminating awkward split infinitives.

1. He promised to never again go swimming in the old quarry.
2. We agreed to once and for all dissolve our partnership.
3. We expect our guests to not purposely damage our furniture.
4. The general ordered the enemy to completely and unconditionally surrender.
5. The boys intend to, if the weather is fair, play ball tomorrow.
6. After dinner they decided to some day in the near future meet at the same restaurant.
7. Because they quarreled so much they decided to permanently separate.
8. Just as I was about to triumphantly and gleefully slip the net under the biggest trout I have ever seen, he made one last lunge and escaped the hook.
9. There is a legend that Shakespeare had to suddenly and ignominiously leave his boyhood home because of his deer poaching.
10. The marines were able to for three days repel the enemy assaults on Glory Ridge.

15f **In general, avoid separations of subject and verb, verb and object, or parts of verb phrases unless such separations add greatly to the effectiveness of the sentence.**

EFFECTIVE SEPARATION	The *captain,* seeing the ominous storm clouds gathering overhead, *ordered* the crew to take in the sail.
EFFECTIVE SEPARATION	And so Pilate, *willing to content the people,* released Barabbas unto them, and delivered Jesus, *when he had scourged him,* to be crucified. —*St. Mark* 15: 15
EFFECTIVE SEPARATION	Only when a man is safely ensconced under six feet of earth, *with several tons of enlauding granite upon his chest,* is he in a position to give advice with any certainty, and then he is silent. —EDWARD NEWTON
AWKWARD SEPARATION	She *found,* after an hour's search, the *money* hidden under the rug.

103

CLEAR

After an hour's search, she *found* the *money* hidden under the rug.

AWKWARD SEPARATION

At the convention I saw Mr. Ward, whom I *had* many years ago *met* in Chicago.

CLEAR

At the convention I saw Mr. Ward, whom I *had met* many years ago in Chicago.

EXERCISE 20. Revise the following sentences by eliminating the unnecessary separation of related sentence elements.

1. I, realizing that I was in danger, looked for a means of escape.
2. In the spring we saw the songbirds which had some time during the autumn flown south.
3. We shall, if we ever happen to be in St. Louis, call on you.
4. I wrote, after several hours of deliberation, a letter to the president of the corporation.
5. In a pleasant house in Concord, Emerson, who was a neighbor of Thoreau, lived.
6. He discovered, after many years of restless voyaging, an enchanted island in the South Seas.
7. We visited the little park where we had during our childhood lived.
8. The greenhorn was, because he had not been warned against the racketeer's plot, easily fleeced of his money.
9. I sold, although I did not want to do so, my movie camera.
10. At last the scientist perfected the formula which he had been for years and years seeking.

16 DANGLING
CONSTRUCTIONS = DGL

Relate all modifying phrases or clauses logically and grammatically to some word in the sentence.

A dangling construction is a phrase or clause that either modifies nothing in the sentence or that seems to modify a word to which it is not logically related. A dangling construction is most often the result of carelessness in writing or thinking. Eliminate a dangling construction by (1) making the modifier apply clearly to the word it modifies or (2) expanding the dangling phrase into a subordinate clause.

16a   **Avoid dangling participles.**

A participle, though it does not make an assertion, nonetheless does imply an actor. Failure to identify this actor creates misleading—and sometimes humorous—effects.

> Plastic sheeting is used to keep a baby on the rear seat of a car from rolling off and also to protect the seat itself. The sheeting is fashioned to fit the seat and extend upward at the front to fasten to window frames. *Being transparent, the sleeping baby is always visible.*
>
> *Having been shot in the stern,* the captain ordered the ship towed back to the port.
>
> DANGLING   *Driving* through the mountains, several bears were seen. (The participle *driving* modifies nothing, although it seems to modify *bears*, to which it is not logically related.)
>
> REVISED   *Driving* through the mountains, *we* saw several bears. (*Driving* clearly modifies *we*, the subject of the main clause.)

REVISED	When *we drove* through the mountains, *we saw* several bears. (The modifying phrase is expanded into a subordinate clause.)
DANGLING	*Riding* my bicycle, a dog chased me. (*Riding* modifies nothing; it cannot logically modify *dog*.)
REVISED	*Riding* my bicycle, I was chased by a dog. (*Riding* clearly modifies *I*, the subject of the main clause.)
REVISED	While *I was riding* my bicycle, a dog chased me. (The modifying phrase is expanded into a subordinate clause.)

EXERCISE 21. Revise the following sentences to eliminate the dangling participial phrases.

1. My supper was cold, having come home late.
2. Being made of stone, the builder expected the house to stand for a century.
3. Working in the cotton field, the day passed slowly.
4. Sitting in the bus, it was fun watching the passengers.
5. The train ride was tiresome, waiting for morning to come.
6. Expecting dad to send money, the postman brought only disappointment.
7. The house was dark, coming home late last night.
8. Knowing little algebra, the equation was difficult.
9. Watching from the canoe, the moose approached the water's edge.
10. Circling the bend of the river, the bridge loomed before us.

16b Avoid dangling gerunds.

A gerund is an *-ing* verb form used as a noun. Like the participle, the gerund implies an actor, and once again you must identify that actor clearly in order to avoid confused or ludicrous meanings.

DANGLING	After *putting* a worm on my hook, the fish began to bite.
REVISED	After *putting* a worm on my hook, I found that the fish began to bite. (*Putting* clearly refers to *I*, the subject of the main clause.)
DANGLING	Before *exploring* the desert, our water supply was replenished. (*Exploring* cannot logically refer to *supply*, the subject of the main clause.)

REVISED   Before *exploring* the desert, *we* replenished our water supply. (*Exploring* refers to *we*, the subject of the main clause.)

EXERCISE 22. Revise the following sentences to eliminate the dangling gerund phrases.

1. On entering the cave, the bones of a wild animal were seen.
2. By studying hard, his grades improved.
3. On receiving the telegram, our hopes were shattered.
4. By keeping a budget, my bank account increased.
5. In drawing our house plans, a back porch was omitted.
6. After opening the door, the coat rack stood squarely in front of me.
7. In packing the car, a suitcase was forgotten.
8. By working every day, the barn was soon completed.
9. After flying for three hours, the Hudson River appeared in the distance.
10. Before washing the windows, a strong ladder must be obtained.

16c   Avoid dangling infinitives.

DANGLING   *To write* effectively, practice is necessary. (*To write* cannot logically refer to *practice*, the subject of the main clause.)

REVISED   *To write* effectively, *one* must practice. (*To write* logically refers to *one*, the subject of the main clause.)

REVISED   If *one wishes to write* effectively, practice is necessary (*or* he must practice).

DANGLING   *To examine* the brakes, the wheel must be removed. (*To examine* cannot logically refer to *wheel*.)

REVISED   *To examine* the brakes, *one* must remove the wheel. (*To examine* refers to *one*.)

REVISED   If *you wish to examine* the brakes, the wheel must be removed (*or* you must remove the wheel).

EXERCISE 23. Revise the following sentences to eliminate the dangling infinitive phrases.

1. To be a successful salesman, people must like your personality.
2. To become a lawyer, several years of study are required.
3. To grow tomatoes, the plants should be watered regularly.

107

4. To be really scoured, you have to scrub the pans with strong soap.

5. To be well baked, you should leave the potatoes in the oven for forty minutes.

6. To learn how to sing, a good voice teacher should be engaged.

7. To find the trouble, the problem must be carefully studied.

8. To be completely soaked, you have to immerse the sponge in water.

9. To be a financial success, the public must buy a thousand tickets to the class play.

10. To make a good impression, a clean shirt should be worn to the interview.

16d Avoid dangling elliptical clauses.

An elliptical clause is one in which the subject or verb is implied rather than stated. The clause dangles if its implied subject is not the same as the subject of the main clause. Eliminate a dangling elliptical clause by (1) making the dangling clause agree with the subject of the main clause, or (2) supplying the omitted subject or verb.

DANGLING *When a baby,* my grandfather gave me a silver cup.

REVISED *When a baby, I* was given a silver cup by my grandfather. (The subject of the main clause agrees with the implied subject of the elliptical clause.)

REVISED *When I was a baby,* my grandfather gave me a silver cup. (The omitted subject and verb are supplied in the elliptical clause.)

DANGLING *While rowing on the lake,* the boat overturned.

REVISED *While rowing on the lake,* we overturned the boat. (The subject of the main clause agrees with the implied subject of the elliptical clause.)

REVISED *While we were rowing on the lake,* the boat overturned (*or* we overturned the boat). (The elliptical clause is expanded into a subordinate clause.)

EXERCISE 24. Revise the following sentences to eliminate the dangling elliptical clauses.

1. While washing the dishes, somebody knocked on the front door.

2. When well stewed, you remove the bones from the chicken.

3. If found, I shall pay a reward for the dog.
4. While counting the ballots, an argument began at the polling place.
5. If attacked, a planned retreat will be made by the battalion.
6. While shopping, the house burned down.
7. My shoelace broke while hurrying to class.
8. Just after rinsing out the nylon hose, her boy friend rang the doorbell.
9. While flying a kite, the wind stopped.
10. If overstuffed, I will buy the chair.

17 OMISSIONS = OM
AND INCOMPLETE AND
ILLOGICAL COMPARISONS = COMP

Do not omit words and phrases that are necessary to the clarity and logic of the sentence.

Many sentences fail to communicate because necessary words have been omitted.

1. Learning by imitation is one the most common in early life.
2. Television has become a dominating factor in today's children.
3. The opportunities for men the popcorn business are varied.

Sentences 1 and 2 tell us nothing. Sentence 1 needs a phrase like *methods of learning* after *common;* sentence 2 needs a phrase like *the life of* after *in*. This kind of sentence usually results from carelessness. The writer may have *thought out* the complete idea, but he failed to write it all down. In sentence 3 the omission of *in* after *men* is a mechanical error that probably crept into a first draft and was allowed to stand unchecked. The writer's hand is trying too eagerly to catch up with his thought, and words—usually articles, prepositions, and conjunctions—get left out.

17a   **Carefully proofread your manuscripts to catch careless omissions.**

CARELESS	The ball sailed over back fence and out of sight.
CORRECTED	The ball sailed over *the* back fence and out of sight.
CARELESS	The officers of the fraternity were brought before the dean and asked explain the incident.
CORRECTED	The officers of the fraternity were brought before the dean and asked *to* explain the incident.

Some such omissions are acceptable in speech but not in written English.

WRITTEN   We became friends *during* our junior year in high school.

SPOKEN   We became friends our junior year in high school.

WRITTEN   I have *a* great interest in the field of medicine.

SPOKEN   I have great interest in the field of medicine.

EXERCISE 25. Supply the words omitted in the sentences below. Put an "I" before any sentence that you think would be acceptable in informal speech.

1. Orientation week gave the student an idea what was ahead.
2. This type error is difficult to analyze.
3. Since the money was not given me, I had to work my way through college.
4. I was not brought up a rich family.
5. Hard work is the best to earn good marks.
6. Some students make great fuss over having to work hard.
7. World War II was the most costly war in the world.
8. Some people think an athlete does not need sacrifice anything to become a star.
9. Many millions people were unemployed the last depression.
10. Scientific advancement the last twenty years has given us new way of life.

17b **Do not omit or leave incomplete any constructions that are necessary to the clarity of a sentence.**

INCOMPLETE   To go to college for its practical value is a difficult choice in the face of the present economic situation.

COMPLETE   To go to college for its practical value *or to stay at home and take a job in industry is* a difficult choice in the face of the present economic situation.

INCOMPLETE   A period of happiness never lasts long but is interrupted.

COMPLETE   A period of happiness never lasts long but is *inevitably* interrupted *by pain or grief.*

You may discover that the best way to deal with an incomplete construction is not to complete it but to omit it altogether. For instance, the last example above would be fully as meaningful if it were written *A period of happiness never lasts long.*

EXERCISE 26. Improve the following sentences.

1. To make the change from glutton to connoisseur, one must know the difference.
2. The first impression I had when I glanced at the front page of the *Times* was the difference in headlines.
3. The effect of good looks or personality on the total character of an individual is not the only thing.
4. Going into the army is something I never thought would happen.
5. While reading this book I found myself looking at a dictionary to help me understand what I was reading.
6. In college, as compared with high school, teachers are more on an equal basis with students instead of a statue on a high pedestal.
7. Being in class all day is bad, for by the end of the day when a student begins his homework he has forgotten.
8. Having spent most of my first year in college in mathematics and chemistry has made me a bit wary of English courses.
9. At the close of the summer vacation my mind was made for forestry.
10. If you miss chapel, either because of sickness or will power, you have to account for your absence.
11. The competition in business is very keen and requires lots of hard work to keep above the failing point.
12. In running somebody down or building them up when you don't have the facts, you use words with connotations.

17c Provide all necessary transitions.

The adept use of transitional words and phrases is one of the distinguishing marks of a good writer. Use of such transitions as *first, therefore, on the other hand, on the contrary* to introduce sentences or paragraphs helps make your writing move smoothly and logically from one idea to the next. Even within the sentence, transitional words are needed to show the relationships among the sentence elements.

ABRUPT   She wanted to buy a new hat; she could not afford one. (The close relationship between the two ideas is not indicated by a transition.)

REVISED   She wanted to buy a new hat, *but* she could not afford one.

ABRUPT   The captain had had many adventures; he had once been lost in the African jungle.

REVISED   The captain had had many adventures; *for instance*, he had once been lost in the African jungle.

EXERCISE 27. Revise the following sentences by inserting transitions between closely related ideas.

1. The cherries were high in the tree; we borrowed a long ladder.
2. I got up early, went fishing.
3. The snow was deep; the children played indoors.
4. I have lived in several large cities, New York and Chicago.
5. Nancy was ill with pneumonia; she did not attend the party.
6. There were many rabbits in the woods; the hunter saw only one.
7. He lives in Florida; the setting of his poems is in Vermont.
8. When hunting, Jim wears a red jacket; he does not want to be mistaken for a deer.
9. Wilbur likes to ride in the country; his family enjoys going with him.
10. Mel Stevens went off to the University of Idaho to study engineering; his sister stayed home to set her cap for the town's banker.

17d **Avoid the illogical use of** THAN ANY OF **or** ANY OF.

If you say in conversation *I like Wednesday better than any day of the week* when you mean *than any other day of the week,* you are not likely to be called illogical by even your worst enemy; the words disappear quickly into the atmosphere. But if you write *I like "Mending Wall" better than any of Robert Frost's poems* when you mean *better than any other,* you exhibit your careless logic more or less permanently on paper. It is perhaps a slight failing, certainly not crucial to health and happiness, but it does betray a lack of feeling for precision and logic.

ILLOGICAL   He is the best singer of any in the chorus.
REVISED   He is the best singer in the chorus.

17e **Do not compare items that are not logically comparable.**

> ILLOGICAL   The buildings here are as impressive as any other city.
>
> REVISED   The buildings here are as impressive as those in any other city.

17f **Complete all comparisons.**

An incomplete comparison occurs if you make the final part of a comparison depend for its meaning upon a word or words in a preceding parenthetical element. (For example, in the first sentence below, the omission of the parenthetical phrase would result in "He is as strong than I am.") In colloquial English, incomplete comparisons are quite common. But they are seldom appropriate in formal usage.

(1) *Omission of a necessary* AS *or* THAN.

> INCOMPLETE   He is as strong, if not stronger, than I am.
> REVISED   He is as strong as, if not stronger than, I am.
> REVISED   He is as strong as I am, if not stronger.

(2) *Incomplete use of the superlative.*

> INCOMPLETE   She is a very kind, if not the kindest, woman I know.
>
> REVISED   She is one of the kindest women I know, if not the kindest.

17g **Give both terms of the comparison.**

> INCOMPLETE   I admire her more than Jane.
> REVISED   I admire her more than I admire Jane.
> REVISED   I admire her more than Jane does.

17h **State the basis of comparison.***

> INCOMPLETE   Our new automobile uses less gasoline.
> REVISED   Our new automobile uses less gasoline than our old one did.

* Advertisers are especially guilty of violating this rule: "Smoke Dromedaries—they're better!" Here the violation is obviously intentional. In colloquial English, the basis of comparison is often omitted.

EXERCISE 28. In the following sentences make the comparisons logical and complete.

1. She is as tall, if not taller, than her husband.
2. I like "On, Wisconsin" better than any college victory song.
3. I respect him more than John.
4. Her gestures are like an actress.
5. Air travel is much faster.
6. He is the best dancer of any.
7. The students here are as friendly as any other college.
8. Ellen's new boy friend is much more courteous.
9. Mr. Martin's new television set is as good, if not better, than any I ever saw.
10. Henry's "hot rod" will go faster than any of the fellows.

18 AWKWARDNESS = **AWK**
AND OBSCURITY = **OBSC**

Recast awkward or obscure sentences.

Some sentences are so clumsy or meaningless that they cannot be repaired by minor surgery. They contain so many errors in basic structure that statements like "lack of parallelism," "poor subordination," or "vague reference" only begin to diagnose their ills. Such sentences are beyond hope. Discard them, rethink what it is you want to say, and then recast your whole statement. Assume that you have written this:

> The heart, an essential in any organism, to me has the same significance to the organism in comparison with hope and man.

Don't try to touch it up. Strike out the whole sentence and start over again.

Some obscure sentences are not necessarily awkward, but are so absurd as to be meaningless:

> Even though our material possessions are destroyed, we know tomorrow will be different.

This is a perfectly straightforward sentence, grammatically, and no one would accuse it of being awkward. But its meaning is absurd. Again, don't try to touch it up. Discard it, start over, and try to produce a meaningful statement.

18a Recast awkwardly phrased sentences.

AWKWARD   If people know something about color and design they will avoid buying something that they will later say of, "I just don't look as good in it as I thought I would."

RECAST   If people know something about color and design they
            will avoid buying clothes of which they will later say,
            "I don't look as good in this as I thought I would."

AWKWARD   Some farmers plow their land in the fall of the year,
            and this is better they think.

RECAST   Some farmers prefer to plow their land in the fall.

AWKWARD   An education will enable me to read good books which
            in turn will provide happiness on my part.

RECAST   An education will provide me with the opportunity to
            read the good books I feel are necessary to my happi-
            ness.

AWKWARD   Each student has different problems because each has
            a different reason for coming and place to live.

RECAST   The problem of each student is different from that
            of the others because his home life and his reasons for
            coming to college are different.

EXERCISE 29. Recast the following sentences.

1. A fruit substitute for a pastry can make a big difference in
   our general health if we will do this every day.

2. In high school there are few if any fraternities to hinder,
   which they sometimes do, your school work.

3. The thought of becoming a political scientist was brought up
   in the discussion, and the answer given by Professor Beal was
   that one should be able to change his views, if the facts were
   strong enough on another viewpoint, to become a political
   scientist.

4. When I walked through the gates of the university, in the
   best tradition, I was entering something I knew nothing about
   and of which I had no knowledge.

5. A new student entering college will find himself surrounded
   with a completely new way of life and school.

6. Can you overcome some of your weaknesses which you had
   in high school, such as studying, learning to make smart decisions instead of being foolish, and many more weaknesses
   which I can't think of offhand?

7. The students in a technical school are very different because
   most of them are there to learn something instead of because
   they have to be there.

8. To me the course in Latin was a real test, proving a will to
   learn or to be pulled down by weak will power.

9. In college they don't care if you come to class, which makes a person feel it is his duty to do it, but in high school when they said you had to be there that just made you want to try to get away with it.

10. In college I find that there is not the individual help given students as was so in high school.

18b **Rethink and recast sentences whose meaning is obscure or illogical.**

1. It would not do a person any good to boast of a college education if he had accomplished nothing and had nothing at the time.

2. I have always thought that the present time was a rather unhappy time because there are always worries, but as the time went on I looked back at these times as the only happy times.

In sentence 1 the statement "would not do a person any good" is meaningless in its context. *Good* is too ambiguous a word to have real meaning here. The writer of sentence 2 probably meant to say that experience grows more pleasant in retrospect. But his sentence structure does not permit him to move from the present to the future and then to the past, as he wants to. We would have to say of the sentence, as did the confused young boy trying to give directions to some travelers, "You can't get there from here."

There is a kind of illogical sentence which, in a proper context, may make sense—and in fact strike appreciative readers or listeners as sophisticated and witty. For example, the sentence "His bad temper is a lot like his father's, only more so" might impress acquaintances of the father and son as an extremely apt description. Similarly, a sentence like "He is more or less crooked, mostly more" could be either clever or inane, depending on the speaker and the circumstances. But such a sentence as "Our feeling was the closest feeling to love, maybe even closer" is likely to strike readers as absurd. Be sure that your attempted wit reaches its mark.

EXERCISE 30. Recast the following sentences.

1. While I was a salesman traveling hither and yon I ate better yon than hither.

2. Her eyes were not set too far apart or too close together, and the two together, apart from her face, were beautiful.

3. The freshman will always be bewildered at the beginning of school, even if it is high school or college.

4. A large city is not much different, but it sure is bigger.

5. The first impression I had of navy life was very noticeable to me.

6. Most of the unknown facts about psychology are very common; others are complicated.

7. The United States is making some progress in producing synthetic rubber but not enough is produced if the supply were cut off tomorrow.

8. The first difference to enter the mind of a recruit is the lack of freedom he has.

9. When a college teacher has a group of boys and girls of college age, the instructor tends to let them on their own.

10. College life, as compared with high school, is a very great comparison indeed.

BASIC SENTENCE FAULTS REVIEW EXERCISE

(Sections 10 through 18). Indicate what strikes you as the principal error in each of the following sentences (faulty agreement, faulty reference, misplaced parts, etc.) and then revise the sentence.

1. The sportswriters generally pay more attention to Notre Dame than any team in the midwest.

2. Edward R. Murrow said that Senator Jordan showed much ignorance of Asiatic affairs in his broadcast last night.

3. Dushard paused a second and then shot with his famous skill and accuracy the puck straight at the goal.

4. Having been soaked in the experimental pickling solution, the cannery manager decided that the tomatoes had too odd a taste to be used.

5. While counting the day's receipts, two hold-up men entered the cashier's cage.

6. Lake Madison being three miles over to the left of Fort Collier; we had to drive four miles out of our way to pick up Jimmy.

7. An experienced traffic sergeant took over and gave directions and soon the snarl was unravelled by him.

8. Mr. Ash liked Ike Eisenhower better than any of the American generals.

9. The report was filed an hour ago by the new girl with the red dress in the corner cabinet.

10. For tonight's campfire we can use, if they are not too green, the oak branches.

11. Having been fingerprinted and photographed, the guards led Fredericks back into the cell-block.

12. Valdez had some trouble with Wilson in the first three rounds; finally he was too tough for him.

13. Although journalism critics praise it a great deal, the *Morning Post* actually has less circulation.

14. Earl went to work for the Bowman Construction Company after graduating from high school as a bricklayer.

15. Laura sent Bill a letter saying that she had decided not to come; he had planned on this.

16. This new set has a wider screen than the others, being equipped with a new clarity filter, and comes in a nicer cabinet.

17. After the cook has put together the other ingredients, salt and seasonings are added by him to the stew.

18. Captain Hunter watched his inexperienced crew make a confused mess of the mooring gear with many strong and salty observations about today's sailors.

19. Even though everyone in the group had been warned not to go into that part of the building.

20. When a person is nice to a stranger, it always gives them a warm feeling.

21. He felt very strange on the campus coming from a small town he had never seen so many tall buildings.

22. When just nine years old his family moved to Alaska.

23. Running about, gaily splashing in the waves, and building castles in the sand.

24. Even if a student works very hard, they will find that they sometimes still feel discouraged.

25. The roads we have today are very old and just outgrown by the traffic that a city of any size would do.

Punctuation is far from being a mere mechanical device. It is mechanical as a matter of course, like word-spacing or the use of initial capitals; but punctuation is much more than that. It is an integral part of written composition.

—GEORGE SUMMEY, JR.

SECTIONS **19-30**

Punctuation = P

When we speak, we use pauses and gestures to emphasize our meaning, and we vary the tempo and inflection of our voices to mark the beginning and end of units of thought. In other words, we "punctuate" our speech. We punctuate writing for the same purposes. But in writing we can draw on a whole set of conventional devices to give the reader unmistakable clues to what we are trying to communicate.

The first of these devices is *spacing:* that is, closing up or enlarging the space between letters or words. For example, we do not
runwordstogetherthisway
Instead, we identify a word *as a word* by setting it off from its neighbors. Spacing is the most basic of all punctuating devices.

Spacing has other uses as well. Writers of advertising copy use space to focus the reader's eye on the name of a product, a trademark, or a slogan. Novelists and poets manipulate the spacing between words and sentences to produce certain rhetorical effects. John Dos Passos reproduces in words the rush of an assembly line when he writes:

> ... The Taylorized speedup everywhere, reach under, adjust washer, screw down bolt, shove in cotterpin, reachunder adjust washer, screwdownbolt, reachunderadjustscrewdownreachunder-adjust. ...
>
> —"The Big Money," *U.S.A.*

In more ordinary writing, we use spacing for less dramatic effects:

(1) To set off and distinguish words.

(2) To set off paragraphs.

(3) To list items in a series (just as we are doing here).

Though important, spacing is naturally not the only punctuation you need. What, for example, can you understand from this string of words:

> yes madam jones was heard to say to the owl like old dowager without a doubt the taming of the shrew by shakespeare would be a most appropriate new years present for your husband

To make this passage intelligible, we need to add two other kinds of punctuation: (1) *changes in the size and design of letters* (capitals and italics); and (2) *marks or "points"* (periods, commas, quotation marks, apostrophes, and other special signs).

> "Yes, Madam," Jones was heard to say to the owl-like old dowager, "without a doubt, *The Taming of the Shrew* by Shakespeare would be a most appropriate New Year's present for your husband."

Now you know at once that we are reproducing the words of a speaker named Jones; that Jones is probably not a female himself but is addressing someone who is; that Jones is speaking not to an owl but to a lady who looks like one; that *without a doubt* is spoken by Jones and not by the person who is quoting Jones; that Shakespeare did not tame a shrew but wrote a play about one; that *new* is not an ordinary adjective but part of a proper noun; and finally that *years* is not a plural noun but a singular possessive.

This example reveals the four functions of punctuation:

(1) *End punctuation.* Capitals, periods, question marks, and exclamation points indicate sentence beginnings and endings.

(2) *Internal punctuation.* Commas, semicolons, dashes, and parentheses within sentences show the relationship of each word or group of words to the rest of the sentence.

(3) *Direct-quotation punctuation.* Quotation marks and brackets indicate speakers and changes of speaker.

(4) *Word punctuation.* Capitals, italics, quotation marks, apostrophes, and hyphens indicate words that have a special character or use.

The "owl-like old dowager" passage illustrates a conventional, fixed use of each punctuation mark needed to convey accurate meaning. In many instances, however, you may choose with equal correctness among punctuating devices. The statement

> He closed his eyes and jumped. Then he felt the waters close over him.

might just as "correctly" be punctuated

> He closed his eyes and jumped; then he felt the waters close over him.

or even

> He closed his eyes and jumped—then he felt the waters close over him.

Each of these statements makes a slightly different impression on the reader. The first emphasizes the equal importance of the two actions. The second emphasizes their close and immediate relationship. The third emphasizes the element of suspense between the two actions. Yet each interpretation is really the result of our personal tastes and our understanding of the writer's "intention." In questions of punctuation there is often no absolute standard, no authoritative convention, to which you can turn for a "correct" answer. But there are two general rules that serve as reliable guides:

First, remember that punctuation is an *aid to* and *not a substitute for* clear and orderly sentence structure. Before you can punctuate a sentence properly, you must have constructed it properly. No number of commas, semicolons, and dashes will redeem a poorly written sentence.

Second, observe conventional practice in punctuation. Though many of the rules are not hard and fast, still there is a community of agreement about punctuating sentences. Learning and applying the punctuation rules that follow will help you observe these conventions.

19 END PUNCTUATION = END P

Periods, question marks, and exclamation points signal the end of a sentence. Use a period to terminate plain assertions or commands; use a question mark to terminate interrogative statements; use an exclamation point to terminate strongly emotional assertions or ejaculations. Ordinarily, the character of the sentence dictates the proper end punctuation. Occasionally, however, you must determine for yourself just what you *intend* the character of a sentence to be. Notice the different intentions behind these three sentences:

> He struck out with the bases loaded.
> He struck out with the bases loaded?
> He struck out with the bases loaded!

THE PERIOD

19a **Use a period to signal the end of an assertion or a command.**

> ASSERTION He mowed the hay with easy strokes.
>
> COMMAND Mow the hay with easy strokes.

19b **Use a period after an abbreviation.**

> Dr. Mr. Mrs. R.N. C.P.A. Sen. B.A.

You may omit the period after certain abbreviations, particularly those of organizations or government agencies (NEA, AFL, RFC, TVA). If you are in doubt about whether or not to use periods in an abbreviation, consult a good dictionary for the standard practice.

19c **Use a series of three spaced periods [. . .] to indicate an ellipsis within a sentence.**

An ellipsis is an intentional omission of words from quoted material. If you decide that it is unnecessary to reproduce all the words of the author you are quoting, use spaced periods to let your reader know that you have left something out.

For example, the first selection below is taken without any omissions from Donald Keene's *Japanese Literature* (New York, 1955), p. 2. The second selection shows how a writer quoting from the original passage might use the ellipsis. Notice that when the ellipsis comes at the end of sentence, four periods are used. Three indicate the ellipsis, and the fourth is the usual sentence ending.

1. The Korean Confucianists, on the other hand, tended towards extreme orthodoxy, and a chance remark attributed to Confucius, that the superior man did not talk while he ate, resulted in centuries of silent meals in Korea, though not in China, much less in Japan.

2. The Korean Confucianists . . . tended towards extreme orthodoxy, and a chance remark attributed to Confucius, that the superior man did not talk while he ate, resulted in centuries of silent meals in Korea. . . .

THE QUESTION MARK

19d **Use a question mark after a direct question.**

Direct questions often begin with an interrogative pronoun or adverb (*who, when, what,* etc.), and have an inverted word order with the verb before the subject.

1. Did you study *Ivanhoe* in high school?
2. You want to make a good impression, don't you?
3. Do you ever wonder what your future will be?
4. Who do you think will win the game?
5. What are you studying?

19e **Use a question mark inside parentheses (?) to indicate doubt or uncertainty about the correctness of a statement.**

This device shows that even after research, you could not establish the accuracy of the fact. It does not serve as a substitute for checking facts.

John Pomfret, an English poet, was born in 1667 (?) and died in 1702.

Rather than using (?) you may simply say "about":

> John Pomfret, an English poet, was born about 1667 and died in 1702.

Do not use this mark as a form of sarcasm.

> She was a very charming (?) girl.

19f   **Do not use a question mark after an indirect question.**

An indirect question is a statement implying a question but not actually asking one. Though the idea expressed is interrogative, the actual phrasing is not. (See Section 19d for direct questions.)

1. They asked me whether I had studied *Ivanhoe* in high school.
2. He asked me whether I wished to make a good impression.
3. I wonder what my future will be.

Business-letter practice permits the use of a period instead of a question mark after a direct question phrased as a request. The writer's intention determines his choice.

> Will you be sure to let me know if this arrangement does not satisfy you.
>
> BUT   May we hear from you by the end of next week?

THE EXCLAMATION POINT

19g   **Use the exclamation point after a highly emotional or forceful statement.**

1. What! It can't be true! I've never heard of such a thing!
2. Attention!
3. Why, he implies that Shakespeare was a student of Milton's!

19h   **Do not overuse the exclamation point.**

Used sparingly, the exclamation point gives real emphasis to individual statements. Overused, it either deadens the emphasis or introduces an almost hysterical tone in your writing.

> War is hell! Think of what it does to young men to have their futures interrupted and sometimes cut off completely! Think of what it does to their families! Think of what it does to the nation!

EXERCISE 1. Supply the appropriate punctuation marks in each of the following sentences. If you feel that a choice of marks is possible, state why you chose the one you did.

1. He asked whether Jim had come home
2. What do you mean by saying that I lied to Professor Brown
3. Mr T J Roberts, who formerly worked for the G R McBane Co, is now with the U S Army
4. The chairman asked the audience to give careful attention to the speaker
5. The speaker said, "May I have your careful attention please"
6. The sergeant yelled, "Attention"
7. Prof J R Greenbriar, B A, M A, Ph D, lives at 20 N 4th Street, Columbus, O
8. "Has Jim come home yet" he asked
9. "Get out of my way" the driver shouted
10. "Oh, why do you torment me so" she cried
11. He wondered if the severe frost would kill the roses
12. Is Jas the abbreviation for James or Jason
13. The newspaper reported that after the 1st of February Lieut and Mrs J G Todd would live at 467 69th St N W
14. Just as the roller coaster hit the top he frightened us by standing up in his seat and yelling "Here we go"
15. Mr Monroe, who was an analyst for the R F C for many years, is a C P A
16. Assume that in quoting the following passage you wish to omit the following elements: the phrase "At any time"; the sentence beginning "This is the cause"; and the clause "its surface is actually a poor reflector." Show how you would indicate to a reader that you were omitting these elements.

We see the Moon by means of sunlight falling upon it which is reflected back by its surface. At any time one half of the surface is in sunlight and the other half in darkness. Near New Moon the sunlight is mostly falling on the hemisphere that is turned towards us. This is the cause of the varying phases of the Moon. Though the Moon appears very bright, its surface is actually a poor reflector; less than ten per cent of the sunlight that falls on it is reflected back, the remainder being absorbed and going to heat the surface.

—H. SPENCER JONES, *Life on Other Worlds*

20-25 INTERNAL
PUNCTUATION = INT P

Internal punctuation reveals the structure of a sentence. Five punctuation marks are used for this purpose: commas, dashes, parentheses, semicolons, and colons. Here is an example of the skillful use of internal punctuation:

> People who do not understand pigeons—and pigeons can be understood only when you understand that there is nothing to understand about them—should not go around describing pigeons or the effects of pigeons. Pigeons come closer to a zero of impingement than any other birds. Hens embarrass me the way my old Aunt Hattie used to when I was twelve and she still insisted that I wasn't big enough to bathe myself; owls disturb me; if I am with an eagle I always pretend that I am not with an eagle; and so on down to swallows at twilight who scare the hell out of me.
>
> —JAMES THURBER, *There's an Owl in My Room* *

Notice how the use of dashes serves to emphasize the parenthetical thought beginning "and pigeons can be." Commas would have weakened the humorous force of the aside, and parentheses would have made it seem too formal. The second sentence is emphatic because it is brief and simple in contrast to the longer sentences on either side of it. This contrast appears in subject matter, too, with just one bird discussed in the second sentence and four discussed in the third sentence.

* First published in *The New Yorker.*

What is the point of this illustration? Simply that internal punctuation is basically a rhetorical, not a mechanical, matter. In other words, it is impossible to talk about the *punctuation* of a sentence without talking about the *meaning* of that sentence. On any level of writing, punctuation is an integral part of the meaning of a sentence. In studying the punctuation rules that follow, notice not only how each mark is used but also how it contributes to the total meaning of the sentence.

20 MAIN CLAUSES

20a Use a comma to separate main clauses joined with a co-ordinating conjunction (AND, BUT, OR, NOR, FOR, YET, **and** SO).[*]

1. The patrol planes were delayed by a heavy rain, and they barely had enough fuel to get back to the carrier.
2. The patrol planes were delayed by a heavy rain, but they succeeded in making safe landings on the carrier deck.
3. The patrol planes could land near the enemy lines, or they could risk night landings on the carrier deck.
4. The return of the patrol planes must have been delayed, for they made night landings on the carrier deck.

EXCEPTIONS: (1) In short compound sentences you may omit the comma.

I caught the morning train but my neighbor missed it.

(2) You may use a semicolon to separate main clauses joined by a co-ordinating conjunction, especially when you have already used commas within the clauses themselves.

Babe Ruth, the greatest of home run hitters, was the most colorful figure in baseball; but many people think Ty Cobb was a better player.

The life of every man is a diary in which he means to write one story, and writes another; and his humblest hour is when he compares the volume as it is with what he vowed to make it.

—SIR JAMES BARRIE

I first gave it a dose of castor-oil, and then I christened it; so now the poor child is ready for either world.

—SIDNEY SMITH

[*] In formal English *yet* is sometimes used to mean *but*. Informal English often uses *so* as a co-ordinating conjunction.

(3) You may use a semicolon in place of a comma to separate long coordinated clauses or to indicate a stronger pause between clauses.

> We haven't all had the good fortune to be ladies; we haven't all been generals, or poets, or statesmen; but when the toast works down to the babies, we stand on common ground.
> —MARK TWAIN

20b   Use a semicolon to separate main clauses not joined by a co-ordinating conjunction.

> Children begin by loving their parents; as they grow older they judge them; sometimes they forgive them.
> —OSCAR WILDE

> To educate a man is to educate an individual; to educate a woman is to educate a family.

> Okinawa is sixty miles long and from two to ten miles wide; it is the largest of the Ryukyu Islands.

EXCEPTION: You may use a comma to separate very short main clauses not joined by co-ordinating conjunctions.

> I stopped, I aimed, I fired.

20c   Use a semicolon to separate main clauses joined with a conjunctive adverb.

> Americans spend millions of dollars for road-building; however, our roads are rapidly deteriorating.

Conjunctive adverbs are different from *subordinating conjunctions*. A conjunctive adverb is primarily a transitional word carrying the thought from one *main clause* to the next. Subordinating conjunctions introduce *subordinate clauses*. This list, though incomplete, will aid you in distinguishing between the two:

CONJUNCTIVE ADVERBS	SUBORDINATING CONJUNCTIONS
however	when
nevertheless	although
moreover	though
therefore	since
consequently	if
hence	because

indeed	so that
likewise	as
furthermore	after
namely	in order that
still	while
then	unless

20d **Use a colon to separate two main clauses the second of which amplifies or explains the first.***

His reasons are as two grains of wheat hid in a bushel of chaff: you shall search all day ere you find them, and when you do they are not worth the search.

—WILLIAM SHAKESPEARE

A gentleman of our day is one who has money enough to do what every fool would do if he could afford it: that is, consume without producing.

—G B. SHAW

Over the piano was printed a notice: Please do not shoot the pianist. He is doing his best.

—OSCAR WILDE

EXERCISE 2. Separate the main clauses in the following sentences, applying the most appropriate of the above rules in each case.

1. Thompson had made reasonably good grades in introductory French courses however, he almost failed French 34.
2. The *Record* supported Earle but the *Times* was neutral.
3. Conway Motors pays a low dividend rate still it seems entirely safe and has never passed a dividend.
4. During the period around 1950 the T-formation became more and more popular in college circles but some eastern colleges of the conference, notably Winnemac and Southeastern, clung to the old formation.
5. Very few of the office staff had been able to come in on time the morning of the big snow and the manager decided not to go ahead with the interviews planned.
6. The telegram brought him the news he had been hoping for Kenneth had obtained a large contract with the Armstrong Company.

---

* Some writers prefer to use a dash instead of a colon, particularly when they wish to give an emotional emphasis to the amplifying statement. (*See also* 24b.)

7. There were a good many disadvantages in attempting to build on the river lots,moreover the price asked seemed much too great.

8. Then Knox came to realize what his lawyer had meant by his guarded hints his partner had been defrauding the company for years.

9. Sugar stock prices declined alarmingly when the news reached Wall Street,nevertheless the syndicate persisted in its extensive buying operations.

10. The difference between men and women is a simple one,men know that purple and black are not the same as navy blue.

11. When Ziegler died very suddenly the summer before, the company was unable to piece together all the transactions he had conducted,and consequently orders were issued, affecting all executives, that every transaction, in or out of the city, had to be explained in duplicate memoranda.

12. The proposed new bridge would have cost nearly a million dollars,furthermore, extensive changes would have been needed in the streets around Oak Square.

13. The majority of the judges clearly favored the Blue Persian for the grand prize,but a few still held out for the best Siamese.

14. Finally Carter went by train,and Kane drove to the meeting.

15. The invasion of the adjacent small countries, which was carried out with speed and efficiency, stirred some more responsible leaders to action,but unfortunately at that time their efforts, viewed with resentment by some and suspicion by others, came too late to prevent the fall of the country.

16. Mr. Endicott was able to arrange much more favorable rates for the conference at the Nichols Hotel,hence, the committee voted unanimously to meet there.

17. One of Will Rogers' chief assets was a boyish grin,seldom is such a grin seen except on an Oklahoman.

18. The cat attempted to catch a goldfish,but in his eagerness he fell into the bowl and drowned, learning thereby that all that glitters is not gold.

19. The value of the lesson to the cat is, however, doubtful,cats are rarely interested in precious metals.

20. Gray, the author of "Elegy Written in a Country Church-Yard," composed a poem commemorating the cat's death,however,he gave us no indication of the fate of the goldfish.

EXERCISE 3. In each of the following sentences, make the change requested. Then correct the punctuation accordingly.

1. Change *however* to *although*.

   At that time Simmons had seen no cause for alarm; however, he recalled later that the pressure gauge was rising.

2. Change *and* to *also*.

   Mr. Edwards' insurance did not approach covering the loss, and the owners of the adjacent property were filing damage claims.

3. Change *when* to *then*.

   The crowd waited impatiently until 9:30, when they began to become very restless and hiss and boo at the delay.

4. Change *who* to *they*.

   Carlsen was sure that these were the men who had been sitting in the restaurant at the table next to his.

5. Change *otherwise* to *or*.

   Guests' valuables must be kept in the hotel safe; otherwise the managament will assume no responsibility whatever for them.

6. Change *but* to *still*.

   There were a number of trees along the hillside, but the winds last year loosened their roots by blowing the soil away.

7. Omit *because*.

   Because the figures on the left side of the canvas made that side seem bulky, the artist added a cluster of clouds on the right.

8. Change *therefore* to *consequently*.

   The ferry operated with no other power than the current of the river; therefore it had a very low overhead.

9. Change *but* to *still*.

   The psychiatrists announced that television and comics were certainly having an effect upon children, but they were not sure what the effect was or whether it was good or bad.

10. Omit *and*.

    The herd disappeared into the foliage along the creek bank, and the cowboys very soon found themselves scratched and their clothes torn by the low branches of mesquite.

21 SUBORDINATE PHRASES AND CLAUSES

21a **Use a comma to separate long introductory clauses and phrases from a main clause.**

1. When I saw the grizzly bear coming toward me, I raised the gun to my shoulder and took aim.
2. As soon as he finished his dessert, he left.
3. After his long exile to France during the Commonwealth, Charles II returned to England in 1660.
4. In his indifference to criticism from those who could not hurt his political chances, he revealed his callousness and vicious self-interest.
5. If you wish to avoid foreign collision, you had better abandon the ocean.   —HENRY CLAY

Short introductory clauses or prepositional phrases, however, need not be separated from a main clause by a comma.

1. When he arrived she was taking the cat out of the piano.
2. After his defeat he retired from public life.

21b **Use a comma to separate introductory verbal modifiers, regardless of their length, from the rest of the sentence.**

1. Having been a teacher for fifty years, he felt perfectly relaxed among young pople.
2. Exhausted, the swimmer fell back into the pool.
3. To be quite honest about it, that dog has been known to climb trees.

NOTE: Do not confuse verbal modifiers with verbals used as subjects.

Having been a teacher for fifty years made him perfectly relaxed among young people.

21c Use a comma to set off phrases and clauses following the main clause and explaining, amplifying, or offering a contrast to it. Do not set off such clauses if they are closely related to the main clause.

NOT SET OFF

1. She loves me because I tolerate her petty moodiness.
2. The defendant objected to paying income tax while the money was being used for the exploration of outer space.
3. My daughter is seldom in one place long because she married a circus performer who takes her with him from town to town.
4. He has visited all the small towns in Pennsylvania.

SET OFF

1. I know she loves me, because she tolerates my petty moodiness.
2. My neighbor objects to paying income tax, although he seems to approve of the outer space exploration being financed with tax money.
3. Henrietta married a circus performer, which is the reason she travels from town to town.
4. He has visited *all* the small towns in Pennsylvania, in Ohio, in practically every state in the union.
5. It is a common rule with primitive people not to waken a sleeper, because his soul is away and might not have time to get back.   —JAMES FRAZER

EXERCISE 4. Supply commas where necessary.

1. We could see the garden walk from our bedroom window.
2. After he had completed his formal education and had worked in his father's office for two years he went abroad.
3. Having completed his formal education he went abroad for two years.
4. Can you imagine killing a chicken with an automobile?
5. The private began laying out his bedroll over the sergeant's objection.
6. After completing his education he went abroad for two years.

7. He went abroad for two years after completing his formal education.

8. Forced to make an emergency landing the pilot let the plane lose altitude at a rapid rate.

9. When all the returns had come in and had been tallied it was found that Wright was ahead by 154 votes.

10. To view the incident in the most charitable light perhaps we may say that Simmons was unaware of the implications of his comments.

11. That night when he was taking advantage of a period of peace and quiet to reconsider the plan seemed more hopeless than it had before.

12. Since Goldman had won his last three games in September the manager picked him to oppose the Seals in the play-offs.

13. After the flour had been tested and inspected thoroughly by the inspector the workmen on the floor were ready to put it in the sacks.

14. Because he was eager to display his medical knowledge the young doctor interrupted his patient.

15. Rocket ships will avoid landings on the moon's equator which has a noonday temperature of 220 degrees Fahrenheit.

EXERCISE 5. Indicate whether the following sentences are punctuated correctly. If they are not, state why.

1. After plans had been made and supplies accumulated for the proposed invasion, the high command dropped the idea.

2. When investigations were made he remembered that as he was eating the food seemed to have an odd taste.

3. When the car had been raised far enough to remove the tire Harris noticed that the jack was beginning to slip.

4. To explain the matter in more detail, Ingalls was unable at that time to say exactly what the letter did mean.

5. Since the publishers had not expected any great sales for the book, the first printing was exhausted in about ten days.

6. Having turned state's evidence during the trial, Crawford was given a lighter sentence than others in the trial.

7. To finish the report before final grades were given in the course Dorsey would have to work day and night for two days.

8. Fawcett having been found guilty the judge called him a menace to society and gave him the maximum term.

9. Irritated by the sarcastic tone in which he was greeted Harvey was about to answer bitterly, but decided to hold his tongue.

10. As the northern route was uncertain at best in midwinter the Allies had to hold Port Stanley at all costs.

11. He was highly elated, because he had obtained the position he wanted.

12. Frightened the children ran quickly home.

13. Napoleon was joyfully received by the French people, when he returned from Elba.

14. This joy was short-lived as he was soon defeated at the Battle of Waterloo.

15. After being defeated he was permanently exiled to the remote island of St. Helena.

22 NONRESTRICTIVES, OTHER PARENTHETICAL ELEMENTS = NONRESTR

A nonrestrictive element in a sentence is a word or group of words that is an addition to, rather than an integral part of, the basic meaning of the sentence. Such synonyms as *parenthetical, interrupting, nonessential* may be used for *nonrestrictive;* and *central, limiting, restrictive* may be used for *integral.* An illustration will help make our meaning more clear.

RESTRICTIVE   1. A man *who is honest* will succeed.
NONRESTRICTIVE   2. Jacob North, *who is honest,* will succeed.

In sentence 1 the clause *who is honest* is the reader's only means of knowing what kind of man will succeed. In other words, the clause is *restrictive.* It is *not* set off with commas. In sentence 2, however, the clause *who is honest* is only an additional comment on a man already identified as Jacob North. The clause is *nonrestrictive.* It *is* set off with commas.

We have italicized all the nonrestrictives in the following example. We have not italicized the restrictives. Notice that although the nonrestrictives contribute to the humor, they could be eliminated without destroying the basic meaning of the main clauses.

One day not long ago, *idling through the pages of a sophisticated 35-cent monthly while waiting for the barber to give me my sophisticated 65-cent monthly haircut,* I was suddenly oppressed by the characteristic shortness of breath, *mingled with giddiness and general trepidation,* that results whenever one gets too near an advertisement for Tabu. This exotic scent, *in case you have been fortunate enough to forget it,* is widely publicized as "the 'Forbidden' Perfume," which means, *when all the meringue is sluiced away,* that it is forbidden to anyone who doesn't have $18.50 for an ounce of it.

—s. j. perelman, *Keep It Crisp*

22a **Set off nonrestrictive elements with commas, dashes, or parentheses; do not set off restrictive elements.**

Ordinarily you will use commas to set off nonrestrictives, though you may sometimes decide to use dashes or parentheses if you want to indicate a greater break in the sentence.

NONRESTRICTIVE   Zachariah Wheeler, *the town marshal,* was once a professional wrestler.

NONRESTRICTIVE   The town marshal, *Zachariah Wheeler,* was once a professional wrestler.

In each of these sentences the words to which the italicized phrases refer are sufficient by themselves to identify the person being talked about; the italicized phrases simply give additional or extra information about him. These phrases are nonrestrictive.

Now notice the differences among these sentences:

RESTRICTIVE   1. The ex-professional wrestler Zachariah Wheeler is the town marshal.

NONRESTRICTIVE   2. An ex-professional wrestler, Zachariah Wheeler, is the town marshal.

NONRESTRICTIVE   3. This (or that) ex-professional wrestler, Zachariah Wheeler, is the town marshal.

Sentence 1 indicates by the use of the definite article *the* that one particular person is meant. We need to know that person's name to identify him and complete the meaning of the sentence. Thus, *Zachariah Wheeler* here is *restrictive*—it is essential to the meaning of the sentence.

In sentence 2, the indefinite article *an* indicates that the writer's purpose is to make a general statement about an ex-professional wrestler's being town marshal; the marshal's name is merely incidental. Here, then, *Zachariah Wheeler* is *nonrestrictive*—it is not essential to the meaning of the sentence.

In sentence 3, the demonstrative adjective *this* (or *that*) indicates that the person is identified by being pointed out; again his name is incidental. Here again, then, *Zachariah Wheeler* is *nonrestrictive* —it is not essential to the meaning of the sentence.

Here is a rule of thumb to use in identifying restrictives and non-restrictives: If the words in question may be omitted without seriously impairing the sense of the sentence, they are nonrestrictive and must be set off by punctuation marks. If they may not be omitted without impairing the sense of the sentence, they are re-strictive and must not be set off by punctuation marks.

In some cases, depending on the writer's intention, a sentence might be punctuated either way:

NONRESTRICTIVE   Oklahomans, *who have oilwells in their back yards,* can afford the hotel's high prices. (Applies to all Oklahomans.)

RESTRICTIVE   Oklahomans *who have oilwells in their back-yards* can afford the hotel's high prices. (Applies only to those who have oilwells.)

NOTE: Always use *two* commas to set off a nonrestrictive unless it begins or ends the sentence:

NOT   The old mare, half-blind and lame was hardly able to stand in the traces.

BUT   The old mare, half-blind and lame, was hardly able to stand in the traces.

OR   Half-blind and lame, the old mare was hardly able to stand in the traces.

22b   **Set off nonrestrictive appositives with commas or dashes. Do not set off restrictive appositives.**

An appositive is a noun (or group of words used as a noun) that renames another noun in the sentence. Appositives immediately follow the noun they rename. Often they are nonrestrictive because they merely give additional information not essential to the meaning of the sentence. The italicized appositives in the following sentences are nonrestrictive and are therefore set off by commas.

1. The professor, *an elderly and gentle man,* led the student from the class by the ear.
2. Daisy Mae, *our old Irish setter,* has never missed or won a fight.

3. "Hello, Mitty. We're having the devil's own time with Mc-Millan, *the millionaire banker and close personal friend of Roosevelt.*"
   —JAMES THURBER, *The Secret Life of Walter Mitty*

Some appositives are restrictive because they give needed information. They are not set off by commas.

> The poet *Bryant* was a leader in New York literary circles.
> Among the holiday visitors were Doris, Wilma, and my Aunt *Martha.*

BUT NOTICE   Among the holiday visitors were Ted Stevens, Gertrude Williams, and my aunt, Martha Johnson. (The speaker has only one aunt. Had he more than one he might have said "and Martha Johnson, my aunt.")

To prevent confusion, use dashes rather than commas to set off compound appositives. A sentence like the following creates some doubt about what sort of creatures Bill, Dave, and Blacky are:

> Three men, Bill, Dave, and Blacky, were sitting in the office with their feet on the desk.

But when the commas are replaced by dashes, the meaning becomes clear:

> Three men—Bill, Dave, and Blacky—were sitting in the office with their feet on the desk.

22c   **Use commas to set off words or expressions that slightly interrupt the structure of the sentence.**

WORDS IN DIRECT ADDRESS	Yes, Louise, you should file your fingernails.
MILD INTERJECTIONS	Oh, I never get *A*'s—always *C*'s and more *C*'s!
PARENTHETICAL EXPLANATIONS, TRANSITIONS, AND AFTERTHOUGHTS	Horses, *unlike tractors,* must be fed in the winter.
	You may, *if you wish,* leave your teeth in the bathroom.
	Christians, *on the other hand,* are opposed to violence.

143

Come when you can, *the sooner the better*.

"The grave's a fine and private place,
But none, *I think*, do there embrace."
—ANDREW MARVELL, "To His Coy Mistress"

NOTE: There is an increasing tendency to leave very slight pauses unpunctuated.

FORMAL   Thinking is, *nevertheless,* not required for a college degree.

INFORMAL   Thinking is *nevertheless* not required for a college degree.

22d   **Use dashes or parentheses to set off parenthetical expressions that abruptly interrupt the structure of the sentence.**

The choice here is largely one of personal taste. Most writers use dashes to set off statements that they wish to emphasize, and parentheses to set off less emphatic statements.

EMPHATIC
PARENTHETICAL STATEMENT   The power of the *Tribune*—one million people read it daily—is enormous.

UNEMPHATIC
PARENTHETICAL STATEMENT   The power of the *Tribune* (one million people read it daily) is enormous.

NOTE: Always use two commas to set off a parenthetical element unless it begins or ends a sentence.

NOT   She insisted, however that he bring her home before midnight.

BUT   She insisted, however, that he bring her home before midnight.

OR   She insisted that he bring her home before midnight, however.

EXERCISE 6. Punctuate the following sentences. If a choice of marks is possible, explain why you chose the one you did.

1. No one not even his wife knows what Roy paid for his collection of jazz records.

2. Jay Elliott a stocky youth with black hair is an excellent student.

3. The result of his attempt to climb up the roof was as you can guess very unfortunate.

4. Robert Powell an aggressive union leader is a self-educated man.

5. The aggressive union leader Robert Powell is a self-educated man.

6. We submit Mr. Chairman that the effects of the new policy are already detrimental to the institution.

7. These people for reasons unexplained until later were all trying to get possession of the Maltese Falcon the black statuette of a bird.

8. August which is always a hot and humid month in Washington is likely to be even worse than usual this year.

9. Most of the time the man doing the actual steering on commercial ships is not an officer he is only an A. B.

10. The *Solway* an expensive new ship was the first of the Marston Line to be taken over by the government.

11. This peculiar property of small quantities of mercury expanding and contracting with temperature changes is the reason that it is used in thermometers.

12. Captain Ahab who intensely hated the white whale offered a gold doubloon to the first sailor who sighted Moby Dick; however old Ahab himself was the first to spy the whale.

13. Motorists intending to enter the city on 182 were advised to detour on old Route 76 which crossed Heather Creek two miles north.

14. Under the circumstances Professor Sears we may be able to grant you a year's leave of absence.

15. He was playing or rather attempting to play "Home in Tennessee" on his brother's old clarinet.

EXERCISE 7. Indicate which of the following sentences are correctly punctuated. Correct those that are incorrectly punctuated.

1. Children being treated at the clinic were carefully examined for signs of malnutrition.

2. Most of the crew, being dissatisfied with conditions on the ship refused to sign for a second cruise.

3. Girls, working near the drills and presses, received very strict orders against wearing loose-fitting clothing.

4. Carter could not, under the circumstances even hint that he had already read the telegram on her desk.

5. The designs and patterns which had been most popular in the cities, did not sell at all well in the rural districts.

6. Binghampton, the largest city in the area involved, was hard hit by the floods.

7. On Christmas which came on Friday that year, there was a record-breaking snow.

8. Animals, which hibernate during the winter, are usually good fur-bearers.

9. Radium, which is the world's most valuable commodity, has been found in the Urals in fair quantities by Soviet prospectors.

10. Trenton the capital of the state, was the nearest place at which one could obtain comfortable hotel accommodations.

11. No one back in America, on the other hand, had any reliable way of knowing that the news was not correct.

12. Our policy is, as you know to submit bids even though we know that there is little chance of their being accepted.

13. Train Number 22 having been delayed by the wreck at High Falls, arrived in Spokane two hours late.

14. The proprietor of the Green Dragon, having been convicted of negligence, was sentenced to a workhouse term.

15. His right arm which had been crushed in the train wreck was amputated at the city hospital.

23   ITEMS IN A SERIES

23a   **Use commas to separate three or more words, phrases, or clauses that form a co-ordinate series.**

1. He talked fluently, wittily, penetratingly.
2. He is honest, he is courageous, and he is experienced.
3. There is not a more mean, stupid, dastardly, pitiful, selfish, spiteful, envious, ungrateful animal than the Public. It is the greatest of cowards, for it is afraid of itself.
                                                                —WILLIAM HAZLITT

Informal practice permits the omission of the comma before the *and,* unless it is required for clarity.

I'll have roast beef, potatoes and salad.

A comma before the last item in a series, however, is sometimes necessary to prevent an illogical grouping.

Our resort is equipped with comfortable cabins, a large lake with boating facilities and a nine-hole golf course.

I am interested in a modern, furnished apartment with two bedrooms, kitchenette, living room, bathroom with shower and garage.

23b   **Use commas to separate co-ordinate adjectives in a series; do not use commas to separate adjectives that are not co-ordinate.**

Adjectives in a series are co-ordinate if each adjective may be thought of as modifying the noun separately. They are not co-ordinate if each adjective in the series modifies the total concept that follows it.

CO-ORDINATE	1. You are a *greedy, thoughtless, insensitive* prig.
NOT CO-ORDINATE	2. The boys are planning an *exciting holiday canoe* trip.

In sentence 1 each adjective is more or less independent of the other two; the three adjectives might be rearranged without seriously affecting the sense of the sentence: *thoughtless, insensitive, greedy prig; insensitive, greedy, thoughtless prig.* Moreover, the conjunction *and* could be inserted in place of the commas and the basic meaning would remain—*greedy* and *thoughtless* and *insensitive* prig. But in sentence 2 the adjectives are interdependent. Their order may not be changed, nor may *and* be substituted, without making hash of the original meaning—*canoe holiday exciting* trip; *holiday exciting canoe* trip; *exciting* and *holiday* and *canoe* trip. The adjectives in sentence 2 constitute, in effect, a *restrictive* phrase, as distinct from the *nonrestrictive* quality of the adjectives in sentence 1, and therefore are not separated from one another by commas.

It must be said, however, that actual usage in punctuating co-ordinate adjectives varies a great deal. Though few writers would punctuate sentences 1 and 2 above other than we have, many of them would be unable to choose between the punctuation of sentences 3 and 4 below.

3. He presented the ambassador with a *dirty, yellowed, gnarled* hand to shake.
4. He presented the ambassador with a *dirty yellowed gnarled* hand to shake.

Some writers feel that the meaning differs slightly in each case: that sentence 4 suggests a more unified image than sentence 3. That is, they feel that in sentence 4 the three adjectives partake of one another's qualities—*dirty-yellowed-gnarled* rather than *dirty and yellowed and gnarled.*

23c **Use commas to set off items in dates, addresses, and geographical names.**

DATES	I was born on July 17, 1941, the day the municipal hospital burned down.
BUT	I was born in July 1941.

The military services and some other organizations now observe the practice of putting the day of the month before the name of the month, as 17 July 1931, 6 August 1950. If you follow this practice, remember *not* to put a comma after the day of the month.

ADDRESSES

He gave 39 West 46th Street, Olean, New York, as his forwarding address.

GEOGRAPHICAL NAMES

He pretended to make the grand tour in three months, but he spent a whole month at Bremen, Germany, and the rest of the time in Tunbridge Wells, Kent, a small village in England.

23d   **Use semicolons to separate the items of a series if the items themselves contain commas** (*see "Main Clauses," Section 20a (2)*).

The following people were present: John Smith, the doctor; Paul Brown, the dentist; and Elmer Wilson, the psychiatrist.

The bureaucracy consists of functionaries; the aristocracy, of idols; the democracy, of idolaters.

—G. B. SHAW

EXERCISE 8. Supply the appropriate punctuation marks in the sentences below.

1. Among those I visited were the following: James Walley, an author, Harold Wilson, a painter, and Percival Derby, a sculptor.

2. The heading of the letter contained the following information: January 23, 1950, 266 East Longview Road, Susanburg, Alabama.

3. The barn has an aluminum roof, a concrete floor, and steel window sash.

4. He was terribly hungry; all he had eaten that day was a little potato salad, cake with ice cream, and bread and butter.

5. I purchased some nails, a small power saw with an electric motor, and a flashlight.

6. Taking the trip to Denver, paying his income tax, and saving a little left him with almost no ready cash for the rest of the month.

7. The ship touched at Cape Town, South Africa, before going past Madagascar, through the Indian Ocean and the Red Sea, and through the Suez Canal.

8. Her painting was dominated by three blue objects over-hanging what appeared to be a yawning forbidding perhaps bottomless chasm.

9. The house has new copper piping Eckles plumbing fixtures new redwood storm windows with copper screens and electrical outlets in many convenient places.

10. According to this new authoritative American history text by Professor Withers, Benedict Arnold at that time was a brave efficient loyal officer.

11. The men at the convention demonstrated their adherence to the good old American way by snatching a hat from an aged woman by driving an old French boxcar through the streets and by passing a resolution against movies featuring actors whom they termed subversive.

12. The Ellington chief of police reports that the town has no North Ninth Street that there is no similar address on South Ninth and that no one named Edmund Carpenter is known there.

13. This city in southern Yugoslavia has a mixed population of Mohammedan Albanians Roman Catholic Italians and Orthodox Catholic Slavs.

14. The adventurous playful Persian kitten had climbed up on the table and knocked down a very expensive Dellani vase.

15. Frantically twisting the wheel feeding as much gasoline as possible despairingly hoping that the shoulder was firm Craven swung the car sharply to the right.

24 FINAL APPOSITIVES AND SUMMARIES

24a Use a dash to set off a short final appositive or summary.*

1. He had only one pleasure—eating.
2. These are the two culprits—Joe Green and Miller Berg.
3. Each person is born to one possession which overvalues all his others—his last breath.

—MARK TWAIN

4. So I leave it with all of you: Which came out of the opened door—the lady or the tiger?

—FRANK STOCKTON

24b Use a colon to set off a long or formal appositive or summary, or a series or statement introduced by the words "following" or "as follows."

1. Out of these things, and many more, is woven the warp and woof of my childhood memory: the dappled sunlight on the great lawns of Chowderhead, our summer estate at Newport, the bitter-sweet fragrance of stranded eels at low tide, the alcoholic breath of a clubman wafted on the breeze from Bailey's Beach.

—S. J. PERELMAN, *Keep It Crisp*

2. Men hang out signs indicative of their respective trades: shoemakers hang out a gigantic shoe; jewelers, a monster

* A few writers prefer the comma to the dash:

The human species, according to the best theory I can form of it, is composed of two distinct races, the men who borrow, and the men who lend.

—CHARLES LAMB

The use of the dash, however, would appear to make the writer's intention more immediately clear.

151

watch; and the dentist hangs out a gold tooth; but up in the mountains of New Hampshire, God Almighty has hung out a sign to show that there He makes men.

—DANIEL WEBSTER

3. I had three chairs in my house: one for solitude, two for friendship, three for society.

—HENRY DAVID THOREAU

4. Humanity has but three great enemies: fever, famine and war; of these by far the greatest, by far the most terrible, is fever.

—SIR WILLIAM OSLER

5. The great secret, Eliza, is not having bad manners or good manners or any other particular sort of manners, but having the same manner for all human souls: in short, behaving as if you were in Heaven, where there are no third-class carriages, and one soul is as good as another.

—G. B. SHAW

6. If you are interested in reading further on the subject, I would recommend the following books: Mencken, *The American Language;* Baugh, *A History of the English Language;* and Bryant, *Modern English and Its Heritage.*

7. To check out a book from our library, proceed as follows: (1) check the catalogue number carefully, (2) enter the catalogue number in the upper left hand corner of the call slip, (3) fill out the remainder of the call slip information, and (4) hand in the call slip at the main desk.

EXERCISE 9. Supply the appropriate punctuation marks in the sentences below. If a choice of marks is possible, explain why you chose the one you did.

1. He had absolutely no virtues at all:he would lie, cheat, or steal at the slightest opportunity.

2. Of all the things I dislike, this is first—studying.

3. He came out of the war an old man;his health impaired, his nerves shot.

4. He is a fine teacher—good-humored, clever, incisive.

5. There isn't any point in losing your temper:you look foolish and you frighten nobody.

6. Why are you looking so downcast—bad news?

7. These are the marks that give the most difficulty—commas, semicolons, and colons.

8. There is only one teacher who can get any work out of him — Mr. Benson.

9. Do you know how fast he was going when he hit the curve near Atkinson's—eighty miles an hour!

10. He was not without honor in his own country: people there referred to him as an elder statesman.

11. His whole life seems wrapped up in one activity—baseball.

12. Professor Wahlstrom told Harry that only one thing would give him a passing grade in the course—a miracle.

13. You will need the following equipment: skis, ski poles, ski boots, and warm clothing.

14. The instructions read as follows: push Tab A on forward section of launcher down into Groove B on rear section.

15. In the course of our interview he made the following statement: "I believe that college training is essential for success in this field."

25 SUPERFLUOUS INTERNAL PUNCTUATION

Do not use a comma unless you have a definite reason for doing so. Occasionally you will need to use a comma for no other reason than to prevent misreading.

1. Long before, she had left everything to her brother.
2. Pilots who like to see sunbathers, fly low over apartment houses.
3. Inside the house, cats are sometimes a nuisance.

The omission of a comma after *before* in sentence 1 would be momentarily confusing; we get off to a false start by reading *Long-before-she-had-left* without interruption. If there were no comma in sentence 2, we might think we were reading about flying sunbathers. A similar difficulty arises in sentence 3 if *house* is not separated from *cats*. Often it is best to rewrite such sentences to avoid confusion.

Too many punctuation marks, however, clutter sentences and confuse readers. The "comma-rash" is especially prevalent among untrained writers. The reader of the following sentence, for example, is constantly jarred by the unnecessary punctuation:

> The people of this company, have, always, been aware, of the need, for products of better quality, and lower price.

Not one of the commas is necessary.

25a Do not separate a single or final adjective from its noun.

NOT He was a discourteous, greedy, deceitful, boy.
BUT He was a discourteous, greedy, deceitful boy.

154

25b **Do not separate a subject from its verb unless there are intervening words that require punctuation.**

> NOT The worth of real estate, is determined by the demand for it.
>
> BUT The worth of real estate is determined by the demand for it.
>
> OR   The worth of real estate, tangible property, is determined by the demand for it. (The commas set off an appositive.)

25c **Do not separate a verb from its complement unless there are intervening words that require punctuation.**

> NOT After the meeting, Bob was, of the opinion that fraternities should be ruled off the campus.
>
> BUT After the meeting, Bob was of the opinion that fraternities should be ruled off the campus.
>
> NOT The boys always made Peanut, the butt of their pranks.
>
> BUT The boys always made Peanut the butt of their pranks.
>
> OR   The boys always made Peanut, an undersized and immature smart aleck, the butt of their pranks.

25d **Do not separate two words or phrases joined by a co-ordinating conjunction.**

> NOT He is very honest, and patient.
>
> BUT He is very honest and patient.
>
> NOT I decided to work during the summer, and relax in the fall.
>
> BUT I decided to work during the summer and relax in the fall.

25e **Do not separate an introductory word, phrase, or short clause from the main body of the sentence.**

> NOT On Wednesday, the ice in the river began to break up.
>
> BUT On Wednesday the ice in the river began to break up.

Occasionally, however, a comma must be inserted to prevent misreading (see introduction to Section 25).

> NOT Notwithstanding *Drums at Dusk* is a worthy successor to *Black Thunder.*
>
> BUT Notwithstanding, *Drums at Dusk* is a worthy successor to *Black Thunder.*

155

25f **Do not separate a restrictive modifier from the main body of the sentence** (*see "Nonrestrictives," Section 22a*).

NOT   The girl, who slapped my face, also kicked my shins.

BUT   The girl who slapped my face also kicked my shins.

NOT   The band, in the park, played the same tired old marches we had heard, for fifteen years.

BUT   The band in the park played the same tired old marches we had heard for fifteen years.

25g **Do not separate indirect quotations, or single words or short phrases in quotation marks from the rest of the sentence.**

CORRECT   After drinking ten bottles of pop Henry insisted he could drink ten more.

CORRECT   Claude said he was "weary of it all" and that he had "absorbed" his "fill of monotony."

EXERCISE 10. Eliminate any superfluous commas in the sentences below.

1. Violins, viols, and harps, supply the melody during the second part of the sonata, and many critics, who are dubious about this procedure, are likely to object.

2. What Tillotson did in meeting the same attack, was to advance his bishop to the queen's knight's file; he drew his game with Laforgue, the French champion, who was considered a stronger player.

3. The *Dictionary of National Biography,* which is usually correct, agrees with Mendell in stating, that she was born in 1709.

4. The wild, savage, nature of the terrain discouraged early explorers from going far into the LaFayle mountains, and the other ranges to the west.

5. Men from McMaster's, Joyce's, and Kendrick's details were busy on the beach unloading parts of planes, and bringing ashore other supplies.

6. Whatever Ewell bid, his wife was sure to look puzzled, and to re-examine her hand anxiously.

7. Across the river, was a protected cove in which there were anchored, two yawls, two knockabouts, and some dinghys.

8. The troops on Manet and New Hope Islands, were being

156

supplied from Port Osburne, which was about seventy miles away, to the north across the bay.

9. When this edition was printed, Secretary Harris had not yet fired Addison, and announced that Fraley would succeed him.

10. Inspecting the meat and making sure that it comes up to specifications is the next step, according to the procedure of all major packers.

11. Armstrong, holding the king, queen, and jack, unwisely tried to confuse his opponents, and conceal his strength by leading a low card.

12. Two different British armies, the Americans, and several Free French companies, were united in the fighting in Tunisia, and in mop-up operations to the south.

13. The meeting began late, because Blackburn did not know where the Regency Hotel was, or when he was to meet Caldwell there.

14. Allenby's Ford, and his friend's old Chevrolet were parked side by side in the lot in front of the new, cream-colored, Buick, which their supervisor had just bought.

15. The pilot, having received the come-in signal, the plane circled about the field, in preparation for the landing.

16. Cancer and some heart troubles still resist the efforts of research men, but hope runs high, that our century will see great advances in conquering these ailments.

17. At that time, countries allied with Nazi Germany included, Finland, Hungary, and Rumania.

18. A little calico kitten marked with black, yellow, and white, had been mewing on the back porch for over an hour, until she had relented, and had brought it in to feed it.

19. The reports in both the *Sentinel* and the *State,* had distorted, what the secretary of the Chamber of Commerce had said about new industries in the city.

20. The captain of the ship feared an unannounced inspection, and ordered the mates to be careful about the lifeboats, and the davit stanchions on which they hung.

21. The punter, seeing that it was too late to kick, elected to run the ball, and to everyone's surprise, the Wildcats gained fifteen yards, and made their first down after all.

22. In granting the decree, the judge was morally certain, that

there had been collusion between husband and wife, but he did not press the matter.

23. The sturdy, old, oak timbers of the little bridge withstood the force of the flood, until every one had been rescued from the island.

24. The policy offered by the Midwest General Insurance Company, offers the same guarantees, and insures against wind damage also.

25. Melton, Shoemaker, and Parmelee, made up the rest of the regular staff that year, and Terry was justified in being confident, that his pitching would hold up.

26. Robbins decided that he could take the night job, and still take courses in chemistry, math, and English, in the mornings.

27. The ice near the southern bank was too thin, soft, and cracked, to support the child's weight, when he tried skating all the way across the river.

INTERNAL PUNCTUATION REVIEW EXERCISES
(Sections 20 through 25).

EXERCISE A. Correct the internal punctuation of the following sentences where necessary.

1. You may write the examination, in pencil if you wish.

2. Outside the dog scratched on the door.

3. No I have never seen him but I have talked to him, by telephone many times.

4. Jud went hiking Marty saw a movie and Lou stayed home to nurse his cold.

5. The names of the students and their fraternities are as follows John Miller Chi Psi Patrick O'Brien Sigma Nu Peter Cudworth Delta Tau Delta and Ramsden McCosky Phi Gamma Delta.

6. Wendell was last seen walking perilously close to the edge of the dam that was thirty-six hours ago.

7. You can insult him if you wish however I suggest you do so at a distance.

8. His attitude is childish he expects his instructors to give him a magical shortcut to education.

9. Bob Mark our plumber who can bend iron pipe in his bare hands recited Shakespeare as he fixed our leaky faucet.

10. King Charles walked and talked a half hour after his head was cut off.

158

11. No hotel restaurant dining room or kitchen shall be used, as a sleeping or dressing room by an employee.

12. This is merely the cost it does not include any mark up.

13. The comma splice is the least of my worries I think I have it under control now.

14. To a football player I am one myself a student rally is an embarrassing event.

15. The short story was only a pot boiler estimated life one month.

16. The shipping department reported a lag period of ten weeks in its work and more and more orders were coming in.

17. Dormitory regulations stated that each girl had to be in by eleven o'clock otherwise her privileges were restricted for the next week.

18. The regulations say that this grant is available only to persons with a senior standing under the circumstances your request must be refused.

19. There was a good deal of sympathy for the rebels in the eastern sections of the provinces and many volunteers joined their hastily formed armies.

20. Having played in the backfield for two years with the Eagles Garner was surprised to find himself considered as a lineman.

21. Answering the series of questions asked him by the defense attorney Robbins said angrily he was sure of the identification.

22. From underneath the beams seemed to have been weakened a good deal when the charred wood was scraped away.

23. As the miners continued panning and sluicing the claim seemed to become richer and richer.

24. Cigarets which had cork tips became unexpectedly popular at that time among many smokers.

25. The crew of the *Eldorado* to be sure deserves as much praise as any other crew that took part in the battle.

26. The governor refused to everyone's surprise and bewilderment to sign the bill after the senate passed it.

27. The element uranium which is now very important in atomic processes is found in parts of the Belgian Congo.

28. Professor Loganberry has a bachelor's degree from Amherst a master's from Chicago and a Ph.D. from Michigan.

29. The Indians held their lead despite injuries to key pitchers and infielders the suspension of their leading hitter and a long series of tiring doubleheaders.

30. Henry Welch, a brisk, efficient, salesman was put in charge, of the new area, and company officials were quite optimistic.

EXERCISE B. Analyze the internal punctuation in the following passages just as we analyzed the selection from Thurber on pp. 129-130.

1. There is no record in human history of a happy philosopher: they exist only in romantic legend. Many of them have committed suicide; many others have turned their children out of doors and beaten their wives. And no wonder. If you want to find out how a philosopher feels when he is engaged in the practice of his profession, go to the nearest zoo and watch a chimpanzee at the wearying and hopeless job of chasing fleas. Both suffer damnably, and neither can win.

—H. L. MENCKEN

2. The modern miser has changed much from the miser of legend and anecdote; but only because he has grown yet more insane. The old miser had some touch of the human artist about him in so far that he collected gold—a substance that can really be admired for itself, like ivory or old oak. An old man who picked up yellow pieces had something of the simple ardour, something of the mystical materialism, of a child who picks out yellow flowers. Gold is but one kind of coloured clay, but coloured clay can be very beautiful. The modern idolater of riches is content with far less genuine things. The glitter of guineas is like the glitter of buttercups, the chink of pelf is like the chime of bells, compared with the dreary papers and dead calculations which make the hobby of the modern miser.

—GILBERT CHESTERTON

3. The chances and changes, the personal history of any absolute genius, draw us to watch his adventure with curiosity and inquiry, lead us on to win more of his secret and borrow more of his experience (I mean, needless to say, when we are at all critically minded); but there is something in the clear safe arrival of the poetic nature, in a given case, at the point of its free and happy exercise, that provokes, if not the cold impulse to challenge or cross-question it, at least the need of understanding so far as possible how, in a world in which

difficulty and disaster are frequent, the most wavering and flickering of all fine flames has escaped extinction.

—HENRY JAMES

4. Fifty years ago, when I was a boy of fifteen and helping to inhabit a Missourian village on the banks of the Mississippi, I had a friend whose society was very dear to me because I was forbidden by my mother to partake of it. He was a gay and impudent and satirical and delightful young black man— a slave—who daily preached sermons from the top of his master's woodpile, with me for sole audience. He imitated the pulpit style of the several clergymen of the village, and did it well and with fine passion and energy. To me he was a wonder. I believed he was the greatest orator in the United States and would some day be heard from. But it did not happen; in the distribution of rewards he was overlooked. It is the way, in this world.

—MARK TWAIN

5. In those days Sir Austin Feverel was thought a royal man, and was in a fair way to be beloved. He was frank and warm with his friends; generous to the poor, and above all, delicate with them, who have the keenest instinct for a gentleman, and venerated him accordingly. When his disaster befell him, and his home was suddenly desolate, it was as though his tree of life had shrunk under a blight. He shut himself up as he did his Dining-hall; relinquished Parliament, and bade a mute adieu to Ambition. People were astonished at the utter change wrought in so apparently proud and self-reliant a man: but old folks, that knew the family, said they expected it some day or other. It was in the blood, they said: Sir Caradoc, his father, was a strange hand, and so was his father, Sir Algernon, before him: they were all sure to turn out a little wrong some day or other. And the old folks tapped their foreheads meaningly.

—GEORGE MEREDITH

26 PUNCTUATION
OF QUOTED MATERIAL

Quotation marks are the usual sign for indicating quoted material. Brackets also are used in the punctuation of quoted material. One of the purposes of quotation marks and brackets is to signal a change of speaker, usually from the writer himself to someone he is quoting.

> I had gone to the bathroom for a shower, the time he [Elliot Vereker] invited me to his lady's house, when he stalked into the room. "Get out of that tub, you common housebreaker," he said, "or I shall summon the police!" I laughed, of course, and went on bathing. I was rubbing myself with a towel when the police arrived—he had sent for them!
>
> —JAMES THURBER, "Something to Say" *

The quotation marks serve to separate the remarks of Vereker from the descriptive narrative of Thurber, who is telling the story. The brackets permit us, the authors of this handbook, to tell you directly that the antecedent of "he" is Elliot Vereker. In short, punctuation devices in this passage show that there are three different speakers Vereker, Thurber, ourselves.

26a   **Use double quotation marks to enclose a direct quotation whether from a written or spoken source.**

> DIRECT   He said, "Don't dive from that rock."
> DIRECT   Our handbook says, "One of the purposes of quotation marks and brackets is to signal a change of speaker."

Remember *not* to punctuate indirect quotations.

He said not to dive from that rock.

* First published in *The New Yorker.*

Our handbook says that one of the purposes of quotation marks and brackets is to signal a change of speaker.

26b **Use single quotation marks to enclose a quotation within a quotation.**

She turned and said, "Remember Grandfather's advice, 'When other people run, you walk.' "

Notice that the end punctuation of the sentence within single quotation marks serves also as the end punctuation for the entire sentence unit of which it is a part. (The omission of additional end punctuation is sensible; grouping of several punctuation marks ['."] would be awkward.)

26c **If you are quoting several paragraphs, use quotation marks at the beginning of each paragraph and at the end of the final paragraph.**

"The situation in the world today is this: There is a language called 'English.' It is too bad, if you like, that one country should seem to have stolen or to monopolize the claim to the name. But if the English stole the name of a language, the 'American' stole the whole of two continents. Humble people, like the Canadians, and the Eskimos, have to live in 'America' and speak 'English,' without fretting about it.

"English is spoken by the people in England; is also spoken by the Scots, by the unredeemed Irish, the Australians—a lot of other people than Americans. Who speaks it best, no one knows; it's a matter of taste. Personally I think I like best the speech of a cultivated Scot, and perhaps least a certain high-grade English which calls a railroad a 'wailwoad.' I myself talk Ontario English; I don't admire it, but it's all I can do; anything is better than affectation.

"Now by slang is meant the unceasing introduction into language of new phrases, and especially new nouns as names for things. There is no doubt that this peculiar fermentation of language has reached in America higher proportions than ever known anywhere else. For example—and my authority here is Mr. Eric Partridge, who cannot be wrong—a test was taken not long ago in a Wisconsin high school to see how many different words the boys and girls employed to express a low opinion of a person. Their list reads, *mutt, bonehead, guy, carp, highbrow, tightwad,*

26

163

> *grafter, hayseed, hot-air artist, rube, tough-nut, chump,* and *pea-nut.* Perhaps they thought of more after they got home; these no doubt were only some of the things they called their teachers."
>
> —STEPHEN LEACOCK, "Good and Bad Language,"
> in *Essays on Language and Usage*

Ordinarily, however, do not enclose a long quotation in quotation marks. Rather, single-space it and indent it from both the right- and left-hand margins.

> To maintain his standing Carroll was obligated to accept Benton's challenge. Jackson accompanied him to the field. The affair that followed provided Tennessee with a standing jest for many years. Benton fired, and, in a fit of panic, doubled up at the waist so that the most conspicuous part of his person exposed was that covered by the seat of his trousers. Into this target Lieutenant-Colonel Carroll plumped a bullet which did far more injury to the spirit than to the flesh.
>
> —MARQUIS JAMES, *The Life of Andrew Jackson*

26d **Use quotation marks to set off titles of poems, songs, and of articles, short stories, and other parts of a longer work.**

(*For the use of italics to set off titles, see* "Italics," *Section 27a.*)

1. "Preparing the Manuscript" is a chapter in *Report Writing*, a text for engineers.
2. "The Easy Chair" is a section of informal literary review appearing in *Harper's*.
3. "Wintergreen for President" is a song from the play *Of Thee I Sing*.

26e **Use quotation marks to set off words used in a special sense or for a special purpose.**

1. He referred to me as a "briarhopper."
2. Is this what you call "functional" architecture?

This use of quotation marks is often unnecessary. In the examples above, the quotation marks might be omitted without affecting the intention of the sentence. In the sentence

> He told me that my writing was full of "deadwood"—that it read like the work of a "stuffed-shirt."

the quotation marks should be omitted if they are intended as an apology for the use of slang. But if they are meant as the sign of a direct quotation, they should be retained.

26f **Use brackets to set off editorial remarks in quoted material.**

You will sometimes want to insert an explanatory comment in a statement you are quoting. By enclosing such comments in brackets, you let the reader know at once that you are speaking rather than the original author.

> John Dryden, a famous English poet, said, "Those who accuse him [Shakespeare] to have wanted knowledge, give him the greater commendation; he was naturally learned."
> The favorite phrase of their [English] law is "a custom whereof the memory of man runneth not back to the contrary."
> —RALPH WALDO EMERSON

In bibliographical notations, use brackets to enclose the name of a writer reputed to be the author of the work in question. For an illustration of this practice, see line 10 on page 170.

26g **Use the word *sic* ("thus it is") in brackets to indicate that a mistake or peculiarity in the spelling or the grammar of a foregoing word appears in the original work.**

> The high school paper reported, "The students spoke most respectively [*sic*] of Mrs. Higginbottom."

26h **Always place a comma or a period inside the quotation marks.**

Commas are generally used to separate direct quotations from unquoted material.

> 1. "There is no use in working," he complained, "when it only makes me more sleepy than usual."

Note that this rule *always* applies regardless of the reason for using quotation marks.

> 2. According to Shakespeare, the poet writes in a "fine frenzy."
> 3. Now he insists that he is a "beatnik," and I am certainly tired of hearing him say that everything is "cool."

26i Always place a colon or a semicolon outside the quotation marks.

> According to Shakespeare, the poet writes in a "fine frenzy"; by "fine frenzy" he meant a combination of energy, enthusiasm, imagination, and a certain madness.

26j Place a dash, question mark, or exclamation point inside the quotation marks when it applies only to the quotation; place it outside the quotation marks when it applies to the whole statement.

1. He said, "Will I see you tomorrow?"
2. Didn't he say, "I'll see you tomorrow"?
3. "You may have the car tonight"—then he caught himself abruptly and said, "No, you can't have it; I need it myself."

When a mark applies to both the quotation and the sentence, use it only once.

> Has he ever asked, "May I come in?"

26k In punctuating explanatory words preceding a quotation, be guided by the length and formality of the quotation.

NO PUNCTUATION	He yelled "Stop!" and grabbed the wheel.
PUNCTUATION WITH A COMMA	The old man said very quietly, "Under no circumstances will I tell you where my money is hidden."
PUNCTUATION WITH A COLON	The speaker rose to his feet and began: "The party in power has betrayed us. It has not only failed to keep its election promises but has sold out to the moneyed powers."

26l Use a comma to separate an opening quotation from the part of the sentence that follows unless the quotation ends with a question mark or an exclamation point.

1. "The man is dead," he said with finality.
2. "Is the man dead?" he asked.
3. "Oh, no!" he screamed hysterically. "My brother can't be dead!"

26m

When a quotation is interrupted by explanatory words (HE SAID, **or their equivalent), use a comma after the first part of the quotation. In choosing the punctuation mark to place after the explanatory words, apply the rules for punctuating clauses and phrases.**

1. "I am not unaware," he said, "of the dangers of iceboat racing."
2. "I have always worked hard," he declared. "I was peddling newspapers when I was eight years old."
3. "John has great capacities," the foreman said; "he has energy, brains, and personality."

EXERCISE 11. Supply the appropriate punctuation in each of the following sentences.

1. He declared that if I proofread my themes my grades would probably be C's instead of E's.
2. Have you read the chapter on Common Women in Philip Wylie's Generation of Vipers? he asked.
3. He said, I was walking slowly down the street when John stopped me and said, Do you know your house is burning down?
4. Fix the picture in your mind, sir, Charles was always saying. Here's Jackson, a fine figure of a man, the first of the heavies to get up on his toes, faster than Louis and every bit the puncher. And here in front of him is solid Frank, a great rock of a man who's taken everything the black man had to offer and had him on the verge of a kayo in the early rounds. They're locked for a moment in a furious clinch. Jackson, who's made a remarkable recovery, a miraculous recovery, sir, breaks away and nails old Frank with a right that travels just this far—Charles demonstrated, reaching over the bar and rapping me sharply on the side of the jaw—just that far.
   —BUDD SHULBERG, *The Harder They Fall*
5. He said, When you asked me, Where did you get that crewcut? I thought you wore poking fun at me.
6. Andrews never agrees with me, Professor Tapley commented; he subscribes entirely to the McCartney theory of inflation.
7. The notice said curtly, We regret to inform you that your services are no longer needed by the Elliott-Robbins company.

8. Are you entirely sure of the identification of this man as your brother? the chief of police said.

9. McAndrews had also written in his test paper the sentence: It is doubtful whether General Forrest ever said, Git thar fustest with the mostest.

10. The chairman asked, Do we need a formal vote on Martin's suggestion? If so, does any one care to put it in the form of a motion?

11. The Passing of Arthur is one of the last poems in Tennyson's series *The Idylls of the King*.

12. The Cubs are much improved this year, said the new manager, and I am sure we will give the other teams quite a battle.

13. The mayor said, I have every confidence in Commissioner Sellers and have no intention of asking for his resignation.

14. The historian said, President Hoover's exact words about the prohibition amendment were, This is an experiment noble in motive.

15. Lasswell contributed a chapter, Dynamic Socialism, to the collection called *Political Thought of Our Times*.

16. Whatever happens to you and wherever you go, Esmond told his friend, remember that you are always welcome at our house.

17. His secretary asked Howells, Wasn't that number Klondike 3-1981, not Klondike 2-1981?

18. The song Who's Afraid of the Big Bad Wolf was taken from a Disney movie *Three Little Pigs*.

19. We find the defendant guilty as charged, the foreman of the jury said clearly, but we recommend clemency.

20. The F.B.I. asked, Have you any reason to suspect the loyalty of this man?

27-30 WORD PUNCTUATION = **WORD P**

Italics, capitals, apostrophes, and hyphens identify words that have a special use or a particular grammatical function in a sentence.

> Our two-week reading program, assigned in Wednesday's class, is Shakespeare's *King Lear*.

Here the italics set off the two words *King Lear* as a single title. The capitals identify *Wednesday, Shakespeare, King* and *Lear* as proper names. The apostrophes indicate that *Shakespeare* and *Wednesday* are singular possessives and not plurals. The hyphen between *two* and *week* makes the two words function as a single adjective.

27 ITALICS

Strictly speaking, italics are type faces that slope toward the right. In typed or handwritten manuscript, however, we have to indicate italics by underlining.

On the printed page: *italics*
In typewritten copy: <u>italics</u>
In handwritten copy: *<u>italics</u>*

Three centuries ago printers italicized words pretty much as they pleased. They set off important words and phrases in italics and sometimes used italics in place of quotation marks.

> The *Gravity* and *Piety* of their looks, are of great Service to these *American* Christians: It makes strangers that come amongst them, give Credit to their Words. And it is a Proverb with those that know them, *Whosoever believes a* New-England Saint, *shall be sure to be Cheated: And he that knows how to deal with their Traders, may Deal with the Devil and fear no Craft.*
> —[NED WARD], *A Trip to New England* (1699)

Now, however, the use of italics is carefully distinguished from that of capitals and quotation marks.

27a **Italicize the titles of books, newspapers, magazines, and all publications issued separately.**

"Issued separately" means published as a single work and not as an article or story in a magazine, nor as a chapter or section of a book. (For the proper punctuation of such titles, see 26d.)

the New York *World-Telegram*   the *Reader's Digest*
Webster's New Collegiate Dictionary   *Desire under the Elms*
The Winning of Barbara Worth

Be careful not to add the word *The* to titles unless it belongs there, and not to omit it if it does belong.

NOT   *The Saturday Evening Post*
BUT   the *Saturday Evening Post*
NOT   the *Red Badge of Courage*
BUT   *The Red Badge of Courage*

27b **Italicize the names of ships, aircraft, works of art, and movies.**

the *Titanic*   H.M.S. *Queen Mary*   the *Spirit of St. Louis*
the *Sistine Madonna*   *Around the World in 80 Days*

27c **Italicize letters, words, and numbers used as words.**

1. Your *r*'s look very much like your *n*'s.
2. Eliminate the *ain't*'s and *git*'s from your speech.
3. I can't tell your *7*'s from your *1*'s.

27d Italicize foreign words and phrases that have not yet been accepted into the English language.

1. The Communists staged a *coup d'état* in Roumania.
2. He made a great deal of money very quickly and is now a member of the *nouveaux riches.*

You may sometimes feel that a foreign word or phrase expresses your meaning more aptly or concisely than an English one. If you are sure that your readers will understand the expression, use it. But to overuse such words is pedantry. Many foreign words have been accepted into the English language and need no longer be italicized. The following words, for example, are no longer aliens and do not require italics:

| bourgeois | milieu | menu | liqueur |

To determine whether a foreign word should be italicized, consult a good dictionary. Here are a few commonly used words and phrases that require italics:

| *ibid.* | *raison d'être* | *sang-froid* |
| *op. cit.* | *sine qua non* | *i.e.* (*id est*) |

27e Use italics to give a word special stress.

1. "It was a *perfect* day," she said.
2. "You are *so* right," she remarked.
3. I heard him say once that in a democracy (a *democracy,* mind you) a division of opinion cannot be permitted to exist.

27f Avoid the overuse of italics.

Distinguish carefully between a *real* need for italicizing and the use of italics as a mechanical device to achieve emphasis. The best way to achieve emphasis is to write effective, well-constructed sentences. The overuse of italics will only make your writing seem immature and amateurish.

1. Any good education must be *liberal.*
2. America is a *true* democracy, in every sense of the word.
3. This book has what I call *real* depth of meaning.

EXERCISE 12. Italicize words and phrases where necessary in the following sentences.

1. The Cocktail Party, a play by T. S. Eliot, was a tremendous success on Broadway.
2. The letters w and a in the neon sign are broken.
3. During the war he served on the U.S.S. Missouri.
4. The pronunciation of the verb envelop is different from that of the noun envelope.
5. The airplane the Spirit of St. Louis is now in the Smithsonian Institution, Washington, D. C.
6. Your novel The Children of the West has surprised us by its sales.
7. The American Literary Review, the critical periodical published at Denby University, has entirely dropped such scholarly tags as op. cit., loc. cit., passim, etc.
8. There was no justification, according to the statistics in the World Almanac and those in the Department of Agriculture Yearbook, for Senator Cope's comments on wheat imports.
9. The word italics now suggests the country of Italy only to a few students of philology interested in word origins.
10. It is characteristic of midwestern speech not to pronounce the g in the ing ending.

28 CAPITALS

Modern writers capitalize less frequently than did older writers, and informal writing permits less capitalization than formal writing. Two hundred years ago, a famous author wrote:

> Being ruined by the Inconstancy and Unkindness of a Lover, I hope a true and plain Relation of my Misfortune may be of Use and Warning to Credulous Maids, never to put much Trust in deceitful Men.
> —JONATHAN SWIFT, "The Story of the Injured Lady"

A modern writer would eliminate all capitals but the initial *B* and the pronoun *I*.*

28a **Capitalize the first word of a sentence and the first word of a line of poetry.**

1. Education is concerned not with knowledge but the meaning of knowledge.
2. True ease in writing comes from art, not chance,
   As those move easiest who have learned to dance.
   —ALEXANDER POPE, *Essay on Criticism*

---

* The practice of capitalizing nouns persisted long after Swift. The nineteenth-century poet Byron wrote

> Near this spot are deposited the remains of one who possessed Beauty without Vanity, Strength without Insolence, Courage without Ferocity, and all the Virtues of Man without his Vices. This Praise, which would be meaningless Flattery if inscribed over human ashes, is but a just tribute to the Memory of Boatswain, a Dog.

Some modern humorous or satiric writers sometimes capitalize nouns as a way of personifying abstractions and pointing up irony:

> "Well," she said hesitatingly, "the idea is to reduce all employees to a Curve."
> —STEPHEN LEACOCK, *Frenzied Fiction*

Some modern poets ignore the convention of capitalizing each line of poetry, perhaps because they feel that an initial capital letter gives a word unwanted emphasis.

> a man who had fallen among thieves
> lay by the roadside on his back
> dressed in fifteenthrate ideas
> wearing a round jeer for a hat
> —e. e. cummings, "a man who had fallen among thieves"

28b **Capitalize the pronoun *I* and the interjection O.**

Do not capitalize the interjection *oh* unless it is the first word of a sentence.

28c **Capitalize proper nouns, their derivatives and abbreviations, and common nouns used as proper nouns.**

(1) *Specific persons, races, nationalities.*

William	Bob	George A. Smith	Negro
Asiatic	American	Mongolian	Cuban
Canadian	English	Latin	Zulu

(2) *Specific places.*

Dallas	Jamestown	California	Lake Erie
Newfoundland	Iran	Jerusalem	Ohio River

(3) *Specific organizations, historical events and documents.*

Daughters of the American Revolution   the French Revolution
the Locarno Pact   W.C.T.U.
Declaration of Independence

(4) *Days of the week, months, holidays.*

Thursday   April   Christmas   Sunday   Thanksgiving

(5) *Religious terms with sacred significance.*

the Virgin   God   Heavenly Father   the Saviour

(6) *Titles of books, plays, magazines, newspapers, journals, articles, poems.* Capitalize the first word and all others except unimportant prepositions and articles. (*See also Sections* 26d *and* 27a.)

Gone with the Wind	*The Country Wife*	*Pippa Passes*
Paradise Lost	*Atlantic Monthly*	*War and Peace*
Journal of Higher Education	*Much Ado about Nothing*	

(7) *Titles, when they precede a proper noun.* Such titles are an essential part of the name and are regularly capitalized.

Professor Wilson	Secretary Hawkins
Dr. James Spence	Mr. Gottschalk
President Eisenhower	Judge Paul Perry

When titles *follow* a name, do not capitalize them unless they indicate high distinction:

> Robert F. Jones, president of the National Bank
> J. R. Derby, professor of English
>
> BUT Abraham Lincoln, President of the United States
> John Marshall, Chief Justice, United States Supreme Court

"High distinction" is, however, becoming more and more broadly interpreted. Some people write *

> Robert F. Jones, President of the National Bank
> J. R. Derby, Professor of English

(8) *Common nouns used as an essential part of a proper noun.* These are generic names such as street, river, avenue, lake, county, ocean, college.

Vine Street	Fifth Avenue	Pacific Ocean Lake Huron
General Motors Corporation		New York Central Railroad
Hamilton College		Mississippi River

When the generic term is used in the plural, it is not usually capitalized.

> Vine and Mulberry streets   Hamilton and Lake counties
> the Atlantic and Pacific oceans

---

* This practice is at variance with the trend toward less capitalization, but is perhaps explained by (1) a writer's desire to seem polite, and (2) copying the style of capitalization used in formal letters, as

Robert F. Jones
President of the National Bank
West Third Avenue
Kokoma Hills, Georgia

Informal practice sometimes omits the capital in the generic term of proper nouns.

Fifth avenue	Vine street	Mississippi river
Franklin county		New York Central railroad

28d Avoid unnecessary capitalization.

A good general rule is not to capitalize unless a specific convention warrants it.

(1) *Capitalize* north, east, south, west *only when they come at the beginning of a sentence or refer to specific geographical locations.*

> Birds fly south in the winter.
> BUT She lives in the western part of the Old South.,

(2) *Do not capitalize the names of seasons.*

> fall   autumn   winter   midwinter   spring   summer

(3) *Capitalize nouns indicating family relationships only when they are used as names or titles or in combination with proper names. Do not capitalize* mother *and* father *when they are preceded by possessive adjectives.*

> I wrote to my father.
> BUT I wrote Father.

> My uncle has ten children.
> BUT My Uncle Ben has ten children.

(4) *Ordinarily, do not capitalize common nouns and adjectives used in place of proper nouns and adjectives.*

> I went to high school in Cleveland.
> BUT I went to John Adams High School in Cleveland.

> I left for Chicago by railroad.
> BUT I left for Chicago by the New York Central Railroad.

> I am a university graduate.
> BUT I am a Columbia University graduate.

> I took a psychology course in my senior year.
> BUT I took Psychology 653 in my senior year.

EXERCISE 13. Capitalize words as necessary in the following sentences. Remove unnecessary capitals.

1. thousands of university students look forward to the christmas holidays; so do their professors.

2. on a columbia album of records called *i can hear it now* you can hear the actual voices of franklin roosevelt, lou gehrig, arthur godfrey, neville chamberlain, and many other prominent people.

3. william simpson spent the summer writing a book of poetry which he intends to call *a saddle for pegasus.*

4. much of the southern area of texas is devoted to the raising of hereford cattle.

5. the chairmanship of the security council of the u.n. changes each month.

6. After leaving the Suburbs of detroit, we turned North toward Mackinac island for our Summer vacation with my uncle Jim and aunt Sarah.

7. The reverend James Oakley, the Minister of the Third Reformed church, was hurt slightly in the accident at Elm avenue and fourth street.

8. The Doctor told Nurse Praley that she should wait perhaps fifteen minutes before taking Mrs. Connors down to the Delivery room.

9. That Winter the Department offered mathematics 1, a course in Mathematics designed for students with poor High School preparation.

10. Dr. Samuels, the Chemist who has just left whityby college to teach here at this University, has done research work on the inert gaseous elements, such as Neon, Krypton, and Argon.

29 APOSTROPHE = **APOS**

29a **Use an apostrophe to show the possessive case of nouns and indefinite pronouns.**

(1) *If a word (either singular or plural) does not end in* s, *add an apostrophe and* s *to form the possessive.*

the woman's book	the women's books
the child's book	the children's books
the man's book	the men's books
someone's book	people's books

(2) *If the singular of a word ends in* s, *add an apostrophe and* s *unless the second* s *makes pronunciation difficult; in such cases, add only the apostrophe.*

	Lois's book	James's book
BUT	Moses' leadership	Sophocles' dramas

(The addition of a second *s* would change the pronunciation of *Moses* to *Moseses* and *Sophocles* to *Sophocleses.*)

(3) *If the plural of a word ends in* s, *add only the apostrophe.*

the girls' books
the boys' books
the Smiths' books (referring to at least two persons named Smith)

(4) *In compounds, make only the last word possessive.*

father-in-law's book (*singular possessive*)
mothers-in-law's books (*plural possessive*)
someone else's book

(5) *In nouns of joint possession, make only the last noun possessive; in nouns of individual possession, make both nouns possessive.*

178

John and Paul's book (*joint possession*)
John's and Paul's books (*individual possession*)

Here is a list of standard spelling forms:

SINGULAR	PLURAL
child	children
man	men
lady	ladies
father-in-law	fathers-in-law
passer-by	passers-by

POSSESSIVE SINGULAR	POSSESSIVE PLURAL
child's	children's
man's	men's

POSSESSIVE SINGULAR	POSSESSIVE PLURAL
lady's	ladies'
father-in-law's	fathers-in-law's
passer-by's	passers-by's

29b **Use an apostrophe to indicate the omission of a letter or number.**

doesn't   can't   won't   o'clock   the blizzard of '89

In reproducing speech, writers frequently use an apostrophe to show that a word is given a loose or colloquial pronunciation.

"An' one o' the boys is goin' t' be sick," he said.

A too-frequent use of the apostrophe for such purposes, however, clutters up the page and annoys the reader.

29c **Use an apostrophe and s to form the plurals of letters, numbers, and words used as words. (Such forms are also italicized.)**

1. Cross your *t*'s and dot your *i*'s.
2. Count to 10,000 by *2*'s.
3. Tighten your sentence structure by eliminating unnecessary *and*'s.

29d **Do not use the apostrophe with the possessive form of personal pronouns.**

The personal pronouns *his, hers, its, ours, yours, theirs,* and the pronoun *whose* are possessives as they stand and do not require the

29

apostrophe. Be careful not to confuse these forms with *contractions* having other meanings.

THE POSSESSIVES	THE CONTRACTIONS	
its	it's	(it is)
your	you're	(you are)
their	they're	(they are)
whose	who's	(who is)

EXERCISE 14. Insert apostrophes as necessary in the following sentences.

1. Its true that Robert Thomas car was found shortly after it was stolen, but its fenders were smashed and its tires were missing.

2. The presidents secretary has ordered a three-weeks supply of carbon paper.

3. Womens fashions change every year—to everyones satisfaction but their husbands.

4. After working with this company for a years time, you are given a two weeks vacation with pay.

5. This book is Hans, whose collection of dime novels numbers over a thousand items.

6. On the wall is a picture of Jesus Last Supper.

7. Tex McCready, Associated Studios leading western actor, was a childrens and juveniles favorite during the 30s; his income wasnt far from a hundred thousand dollars a year.

8. Dr. Daniels wouldnt have spent his whole years leave trying to establish the Ellins Brothers theory if he hadnt been convinced of its validity.

9. Its too bad that the city of Newbridge cant keep its streets in the condition of those of the wealthier suburbs like Glen Ridge.

10. The Stevenses arent at home this month; theyre visiting their relatives in Florida and wont be back until Christmas.

30 HYPHEN = **HYP**

The hyphen has two distinct uses: (1) to form compound words, and (2) to indicate that a word is continued from one line to the next. The proper use of the hyphen for (2), commonly called "syllabication," is arbitrarily fixed. (See "Syllabication," Section 4.) But the proper use of the hyphen to form compound words is continually changing as the language grows and new word combinations are accepted.

30a **Use a hyphen to form compound words that are not yet accepted as single words.**

The spelling of compound words that express a single idea passes through successive stages. Originally spelled as two separate words, then as a hyphenated word, a compound word finally emerges as a single word.

> base ball *became* base-ball *became* baseball
> post man *became* post-man *became* postman

There is no way of determining the proper spelling of a compound at any given moment. Even the best and most up-to-date dictionaries tend to be too conservative in the matter; they hyphenate many compounds that in actual practice are written as single words. However, the dictionaries are the most authoritative references we have.

30b **Use a hyphen to join two or more words serving as a single adjective before a noun.**

Do not hyphenate such an adjective if it follows the noun.

> a well-known speaker
> BUT   The speaker was well known.

a well-bred child
BUT   The child is well bred.

a grayish-green coat
BUT   The coat was grayish green.

a never-to-be-forgotten moment
BUT   The moment was never to be forgotten.

Omit the hyphen when the first word is an adverb ending in -*ly*.

a slow-curving ball		a quick-moving runner
BUT a slowly curving ball	BUT	a quickly moving runner

30c Use a hyphen to avoid an ambiguous or awkward union of letters.

NOT	reenter	NOT	readdress
BUT	re-enter	BUT	re-address
NOT	preeminence	NOT	preelection
BUT	pre-eminence	BUT	pre-election

In printed copy, the dieresis mark (¨) is often used in place of the hyphen.

reënter   reäddress   preëminence   preëlection

In commonly used words, the hyphen (or dieresis) is sometimes omitted.

coeducational   cooperation   zoology

30d Use a hyphen to form compound numbers from twenty-one through ninety-nine, and to separate the numerator from the denominator in written fractions.

twenty-nine   fifty-five   two-thirds   four-fifths

30e Use a hyphen with the prefixes SELF-, ALL-, EX-, and the suffix -ELECT.

self-important   all-Conference   ex-mayor   governor-elect

Do not capitalize the prefix *ex-* or the suffix -*elect*, even when used in titles that are essential parts of a name.

ex-Mayor Kelley   Governor-elect Jones   ex-President Hoover

EXERCISE 15.   Insert hyphens as needed.

1. Change this ten dollar bill into ten dollar bills.
2. The ¾ inch cable is anchored to a 500 ton concrete pier.

3. The editor in chief owns a well designed house.
4. The tousle headed child poured a whole bottle of ink on our new nine by twelve rug.
5. The secretary elect likes to think of himself as a self made man.
6. Mr. Collins's assistant, a competent although self effacing man named Downes, is in charge of the reinventory of the Woods estate assets.
7. A three way contract permitted the exmayor to operate a fly by night cigar store chain while engaged in his regular employment.
8. There were suggestions that the enlisted men's tight fitting dark blue uniforms be modified.
9. Harold was able to get a part time job with the antihedonism program of the Third Avenue church.
10. My father in law participated in the hundred meter relay, over thirty division; his team went as far as the semifinals.

EXERCISE 16. Supply the necessary italics, capitals, apostrophes, and hyphens in the sentences below.

1. The book review section of the new york times is the bible of liberal american readers.
2. its tail wagging, the little beagle saw its dinner disappear down the throat of the snarling cheshire cat.
3. george lyman kittredge, professor of english at harvard university for many years, was a world renowned scholar.
4. it isnt the cough that carries you off; its the coffin they carry you off in.
5. its a well known fact that baseball players, old timers as well as fresh faced rookies, are the most remarkably successful penny pinchers in professional sport.

EXERCISE 17. Correct the punctuation in the following sentences.

1. Garland's Novel, called Main-travelled Roads, one of the Realistic novels of the latter part of the Nineteenth century, *focussed* attention on the sordidness of the average farmer's existence.
2. The Desk Sergeant, T. A. Wheeler, ordered detective Carpenter and patrolman Winters to make a thorough Investigation into the explosion in the cellar of the *Cranmore Country Club*.

3. The Kintners achieved an *odd* effect by planting American Beauty Roses against a background of Ramblers along the fence.

4. Nickels' next two books, seven hundred page Romantic novels, were'nt reviewed favorably, but they turned out to be popular as clubwomens' choices.

5. Ex Mayor Williams *request* that the Council *improve* conditions in the childrens' playgrounds has'nt received *any* action as yet.

6. Those in the crowd who's ancestors had come from Norway cheered when the Norwegian flag's were unfurled at the King's and Queen's reception in New York.

7. The half dead seaman from the Serapis' first request wasnt about himself; instead he asked what'd happened to his brothers boat.

8. That dog of Mr. Jones' keeps it's tail between it's legs most of the time.

9. The sailor on the bow's appearance was *statuesque.*

10. WSGD's chief television actor that year was Martin Sims, a handsome blond haired singer who hadnt had previous network experience.

11. Mrs. Barry'es many colored calico kitten was awarded it's first blue ribbon as the *Cleveland Cat Club's* best of show.

12. Morris fourteen year old sister, to his familys suppressed delight, was beginning to ridicule his and his friends choice of neckties.

13. The four cylinder sixty horsepower car wasnt able to pull Jones custom built limousine out of the ditch.

14. The Dividends from the supposedly-worthless Flatrock mining company stock were a *real* help to Mrs. Fredericks after the sudden death of her Husband.

15. According to the arrangement made by the committee of the Dean's, the Spring Semester would have started that year on Lincoln's birthday, officially a Holiday in the State.

PUNCTUATION REVIEW EXERCISES (Sections 19 through 30).

EXERCISE A. Supply all necessary punctuation in each of the following sentences.

1. Dobbs hand contained only two sevens and two fives and he wasnt confident when he called Bowers ten chip raise

2. Is not a patron my lord one who looks with unconcern on a man struggling for life in the water and when he has reached ground encumbers him with help

—SAMUEL JOHNSON

3. I like any woman who enjoys a bath insist upon a soap that smells pleasant.

4. His favorite writers are Sinclair Lewis Willa Cather T. S. Eliot and Eugene O'Neill.

5. His favorite writers are modern ones Sinclair Lewis Willa Cather T. S. Eliot and Eugene O'Neill.

6. His favorite writers Sinclair Lewis Willa Cather T. S. Eliot and Eugene O'Neill are modern ones.

7. His favorite writers Sinclair Lewis and Willa Cather novelists T. S. Eliot poet and Eugene O'Neill playwright are modern ones.

8. The first to recover his senses after the explosion he rushed to call an ambulance.

9. The speaker of the evening began his address Ladies and gentlemen we meet here this evening. . . .

10. Harper's Magazine and the Atlantic Monthly which observe high standards of usage are widely read.

11. I am sorry replied Robert I did not mean to be rude.

12. His faults are these an uncontrollable temper inexperience in dealing with people and their problems and indifference to his work.

13. His faults are an uncontrollable temper inexperience and indifference to his work.

14. The tree having been hopelessly damaged we decided to cut it down.

15. He then introduced Thomas Bryce Ph. D. as the speaker of the evening.

16. Although seventy per cent of our english vocabulary comes from the Latin and Greek most of the words in our everyday speech are short vigorous Anglo-Saxon words.

17. John wanted a Ford Jean a Chrysler Bob a Buick Henry a custom made English car.

18. Arizona where the sun shines every day is healthful as a matter of fact any place where the sun shines every day is healthful.

19. If siege is spelled ie why is seize spelled ei asked Tommy.

Because replied his sister seize is one of the exceptions to the rule.

20. The democrats in the senate attacked the secretary of state their object being to embarrass the presidents advisers.

21. The town is not progressive most of the energetic ambitious young people leave it as soon as they finish high school.

22. Designed as a basic text for sophomores in a university Fundamentals of Physics by John Carr of Duke university provides a sound background for advanced study.

23. Mr. Adams who enjoys good conversation dislikes Mrs. Knight whose talk is merely gossip.

24. He is a man who enjoys good conversation and he dislikes women whose talk is merely gossip.

25. All of our clothes which were left outside were stolen.

26. The speaker was faced with a difficult task he had to persuade a skeptical antagonistic audience to a new point of view.

27. Imagine what would happen in this crowded auditorium said the speaker if someone should shout fire.

28. Effective writing has one prerequisite which is inescapable the writer must have something to say.

29. The mutiny having been quelled and the mutineers being all in irons the passengers began to breathe easily.

30. Mother decided that she a friend and I would go to the beach for a short vacation.

31. I believe that Parrington Hall University of Washington Seattle 5 Washington is his correct address.

32. The statement that was issued early in the morning was later confirmed by the same announcer.

33. The members are willing to support any candidate but Mr. Scott who now holds the office.

34. My son John seems too tall for submarine duty however my only nephew Philip Ames has been accepted and he is even taller than John.

35. In his advice to freshmen Dean Carlson made the statement that the trouble with students who stay up half the night studying is that usually theyre either too exhausted the next day to go to class or too sleepy to be much good if they do go

36. The storm having passed our party climbed into two waiting cars and drove on.

37. The audience had been assembled for an hour and was growing more and more restless but still the speaker did not appear.

38. Outside the house looked rather dilapidated within it was very cozy and comfortable.

39. The first thing we notice is that our thought moves with such incredible rapidity that it is almost impossible to arrest any specimen of it long enough to have a look at it.

40. We have found that most students in the dormitory do their work satisfactorily very few fail to pass their tests.

41. If the weight of a medium-sized man were to stand for that of the sun then the weights of most other stars would lie between those of a large man and a ten-year-old boy.

42. This tree is remarkable for its airy widespread tropical appearance which suggests a region of palms rather than of cool resiny pine trees.

43. Larry Brown my former roommate had gone home for the holidays Leo Lamb whose home I had often visited was ill and every other student whom I had known seemed to be busy whenever I called.

44. Dick and Andy changed their clothes put on heavy shoes and brought spades and rakes from the basement then they prepared the soil for planting corn.

45. For want of airplanes MacArthur was forced to a bitter decision make the enemy pay for what it gets.

46. I do not think that Harry will be on time for this concert for he is almost always late when we meet downtown.

47. We started out with every desirable condition for our hunting trip the weather was cool our dogs were well trained and our huntsmen were excellent.

48. Please Alice don't stare at people like that they will think you are very rude her mother said to little Alice who thought watching people was great fun.

49. Many people do not know where their daily milk supply comes from whether cotton grows on a tree a bush or a vine or from what products their cereals plastics and linens are made.

50. It is not a simple task to plan daily meals which are nutritionally valuable attractive as well as palatable reasonable in their demands on time and energy and respectful of the food budget.

51. I found this the hardest question in the whole test What is is the difference between wit and humor?

52. This phrase from The Great Lover one of the poems in our textbook puzzles most students The inenarrable godhead of delight.

53. It isn't the way the words are strung together that makes Lincoln's Gettysburg speech immortal it is the feelings that were in the man who made it.

54. It is more than likely that the student who has imagination and who is able to synthesize facts will some day be the employer of the student who does little except repeat what he reads or what he is told.

55. The boll-weevil the cotton growers' greatest enemy had devastated the cotton crop heavy rains had ruined the wheat which needs dry weather when the grain is forming.

EXERCISE B. Supply all the necessary punctuation in the passages below.

1. the best books are not read even by those who are called good readers what does our concord culture amount to there is in this town with a very few exceptions no taste for the best or for very good books even in english literature whose words all can read and spell even the college bred and so called liberally educated men here and elsewhere have really little or no acquaintance with the english classics and as for the recorded wisdom of mankind the ancient classics and bibles which are accessible to all who will know of them there are the feeblest efforts anywhere made to become acquainted with them i know a woodchopper of middle age who takes a french paper not for the news he says for he is above that but to keep himself in practice he being a canadian by birth and when i ask him what he considers the best thing he can do in this world he says besides this to keep up and add to his english this is about as much as the college bred generally do or aspire to do and they take an english paper for the purpose one who has just come from reading perhaps one of the best english books will find how many with whom he can converse about it or suppose he comes from reading a greek or latin classic in the original whose praises are familiar even to the so called illiterate he will find nobody at all to speak to but must keep silence about it

—HENRY DAVID THOREAU, "Reading"

2. everybody knows that einstein has done something astonishing but very few people know exactly what he has done it is generally recognized that he has revolutionized our conception of the physical world but his new conceptions are wrapped up in mathematical technicalities it is true that there are innumerable popular accounts of the theory of relativity but they generally cease to be intelligible just at the point where they begin to say something important the authors are hardly to be blamed for this many of the new ideas can be expressed in non mathematical language but they are none the less difficult on that account what is demanded is a change in our imaginative picture of the world a picture which has been handed down from the remote perhaps pre human ancestors and has been learned by each one of us in early childhood a change in our imagination is always difficult especially when we are no longer young the same sort of change was demanded by copernicus when he taught that the earth is not stationary and the heavens do not revolve around it once a day to us now there is no difficulty in this idea because we learned it before our mental habits had become fixed einsteins ideas similarly will seem easy to a generation which has grown up with them but for our generation a certain effort of imaginative reconstruction is unavoidable

—BERTRAND RUSSELL, *The A B C of Relativity*

EXERCISE C. In the following sentences determine which marks of punctuation are used correctly, which marks are used incorrectly, and what additional punctuation is needed. Be prepared to give reasons for your decisions.

1. In a city this large, administrative problems range from garbage disposal to school administration, and no one has a ready solution for everything.

2. However, all citizens should be alert to their responsibilities, they can demonstrate their alertness by participating in the forthcoming municipal elections, which will determine who will administer the citys' policies.

3. I first became interested in municipal activities when I took political-science 475; a course called Problems of Municipal Government and Administration.

4. At that time, of course, this area was not so heavily populated as it is now and many of the students in the class said that "they didn't think these problems applied locally."

5. I wonder if they would still say that now that the city's population has increased ten-fold?

6. Probably the worst of the problems to confront us daily is the congested, slow-moving traffic, in which we all must travel to and from work.

7. From 7 a m to 9 a m and again from 4 p. m. to 6 pm., it is virtually impossible to drive faster than 25 mph on many arterials even though the posted speed limit is much higher.

8. Experiencing this congestion morning after morning, exasperated motorists begin to demand action—almost *any* action will do—, and they are likely to be impatient in their demands.

9. Local newspapers also take up the cry for action; the "Star" in a recent editorial entitled *The long walk home* satirized the entire traffic situation quite cleverly, and effectively.

10. The Mayor has now issued this statement: "Prime considerations in current traffic planning are the elimination of bottlenecks from our citys arterial system, and the facilitation of a smoother movement of traffic to and from the downtown and industrial areas".

11. This is a fine sentiment, but I will be interested in seeing if some concrete steps for it's implementation are taken: "The proof of the pudding is in the eating."

12. I suppose i am really unfair to criticize particularly because I have never run for a city' office nor do I intend to do so.

13. I do (indeed) sympathize with these city officials of our's, they have a lot of headaches that I certainly wouldnt want to deal with!

14. Perhaps some of the City Fathers would benefit from taking that Political Science course.

15. We surely have the Problems of Municipal Government and Administration dont we.

If you wish to be a writer, write.

—EPICTETUS

Anyone who wishes to become a good writer should endeavour, before he allows himself to be tempted by the more showy qualities, to be direct, simple, brief, vigorous, and lucid.

—H. W. FOWLER

SECTIONS **31-32**

Larger Elements

31 THE WHOLE COMPOSITION—PLAN

Two difficulties face every writer: Can he say what he really means, and can he make that meaning clear to his readers? There are no pat solutions to this double problem, no easy rules, no short cuts. Every writer has to decide first what he wants to write, and second how he wants to write it. And then, having written it, he has to stand off and look at the results of his labor from the point of view of a reader. Does his writing have readability and clarity? A sense of direction and purpose? If not, he has failed as a writer.

Although there is no safe generalization about "how to write," there are some useful guiding principles:

(1) Decide what you are going to write about. (See Section 31a on selecting a subject, and Section 31b on limiting the subject.)

(2) Make a rough but full list of ideas, assertions, facts, and illustrations that may have some bearing on your subject. (See Section 31c on making a preliminary outline.)

(3) Frame a statement of what you want to say about your subject. (See Section 31d on framing a thesis statement.)

(4) Sort out the items in your rough outline, putting together all the ideas that belong together and eliminating all those that seem irrelevant. (See Section 31e on making a complete outline.)

(5) Try to find a concrete instance, illustration, anecdote, or example for a good opening statement. If you can think of nothing appropriate to your purposes, proceed to the next step immediately. (See Section 31f on beginning the paper.)

(6) Begin to write. Don't let problems of wording and phrasing slow you down, or you will lose momentum and direction. (See Section 31g on writing a first draft.)

(7) Once you have finished the first draft, go back over it and polish your words, sentences, and paragraphs. Check the ending to make sure that it gives the impression of finality and completeness. (See Section 31h on ending the paper and 31i on writing a second draft.)

(8) If possible, put your paper aside for a few days before making final revisions. You will gain perspective in this way and will spot errors in logic and presentation more readily. (See Section 31j on making final revisions.)

In brief, the writing process consists of two basic steps: (1) planning what you are going to say, and (2) writing and rewriting it. Remember that the first step is fully as important as the second. Good writing requires long and careful planning.

31a **Select a subject that interests you.**

Choose a subject that captures your interest and about which you have or want to have ample knowledge. Begin by reviewing your special abilities. Can you clean a gun, take an alarm clock apart, roll a cigarette with one hand, make a coffee table? Such subjects—suggested by the experiences of everyday living—often make interesting papers. Although more abstract subjects are equally interesting, they may lure you into making great billowing generalizations, and they must be managed more carefully. A Francis Bacon may know enough about the abstraction "Prejudice" to write a short paper about it. But most of us know less about "Prejudice" in the abstract than we do about concrete examples of prejudice we have actually observed (for example, "Prejudice Against Traffic Laws in My Home Town").

The list below may be helpful, not only for the specific subjects it gives, but also for those it brings to mind.

SUGGESTED TOPICS FOR COMPOSITIONS

General	*More Specific*
1. How I Learned the Value of Thrift	1. How to Get a Pig Out of a Piggy Bank
2. The Value of Music in the Home	2. We Sing Together Since We Can't Sing Separately
3. How to Be a Baby-Sitter	3. Love Thy Neighbor's Children
4. The Problems of an Oldest Child	4. Why I Nearly Drowned My Baby Sister
5. Does College Teach Self-Reliance?	5. The Housemother Doesn't Wash Our Socks
6. The College Newspaper	6. The Dean of Men Is My Beat
7. Playing the Infield in Softball	7. Leave First Base to Lefties
8. Fishing for Trout	8. Lake Trout and the Dry Fly
9. Fun in Photography	9. Salon Shots for Christmas Cards
10. College Snobs	10. The Trojans Learned to Beware of Greeks
11. The California Gold Rush	11. What Became of Sutter's Mill?
12. Home-Built Furniture	12. A Simple Coffee Table Design
13. Care of the Corn Field	13. Tasseling Hybrid Corn

193

General	More Specific
14. Life of a Ranch Hand	14. "Work? Naw, Them's Just *Chores*"
15. High-School Debating	15. The Art of Making Lies Emphatic
16. Showing Hereford Bulls	16. A Bath for Herodotus III
17. Golfing	17. Approaching the Green
18. Learning to Knit	18. My First Sweater Was a Flop
19. Churches in Local Politics	19. Methodist Ladies and the Boilertown Taverns
20. Are We Progressing Backwards?	20. Bigger and Better Traffic Accidents.
21. Army and the College Student	21. I Study to Avoid the Draft
22. Vocational Guidance in High School	22. They Told Us All to Be Engineers
23. Women Think for Themselves	23. Why Should Girls Have Curfew?
24. Moms and Momma's Boys	24. Crybabies at College
25. Will Small Towns Accept Education?	25. They Call My Uncle "Professor"

EXERCISE 1. Make a list of five titles suggested by your tastes in motion pictures—for example, "Why Are 'Westerns' So Popular?" "Are Double Features Necessary?"

EXERCISE 2. List five titles suggested by the advantages or disadvantages of living in a large city—for example, "Horses: You Can Have Them; I'll Take a Buick," "Keeping a Great Dane in a Small Apartment."

EXERCISE 3. List five titles suggested by your hobbies or your interest in sports—for example, "The World's Most Expensive Stamp," "The Time I Did *Not* Strike Out with the Bases Loaded."

31b **Limit the subject you have chosen so that you can handle it in the time and space at your disposal.**

Don't try to do too much in a paper of three hundred to five hundred words, or you will end up with a series of vague and half-supported generalizations that never come into focus. Experienced writers are constantly aware of the limitations dictated by the time and space at their disposal. For a short paper they reject a subject like "Swimming" in favor of a more restricted topic, such as "How to Swim the Backstroke" or "Developing Speed in Swimming."

Be sure that the title of your paper reflects the limitations you have set on your subject. Don't call a paper on the cleaning of guns simply "Guns," nor a report on the stories of H. P. Lovecraft "Fantasy Fiction."

Another limiting factor is the character of the audience for which you are writing. Always try to fix a specific audience in your mind's eye, even if it is as large a group as "general readers." Then try to decide whether that audience will respond best to a simple or complex, a popular or technical, or a general or specific presentation. If you are honestly trying to communicate, you must adapt the nature of your subject matter, your point of view, the extent of detail and explanation that you introduce, and even your terminology, to the character of the audience you are addressing. All this does not mean that you should try to write "up" or "down," to be pretentious or condescending; you must be yourself, but "being yourself" means first of all that you know what you are trying to say.

You cannot, of course, analyze any audience perfectly (even single members of your family or of your group of friends have their indefinable vagaries as audiences), but you can make a safe guess about its general character. Having an audience in mind will help give direction and clarity to your remarks.

EXERCISE 4. List five topics that would be appropriate for themes of several thousand words. Select a single aspect of each of these topics that would make an appropriate title for a theme of 200-300 words.

EXERCISE 5. Refer to the topics suggested on pages 193-194. Choose five items from the *general* list and devise a *more specific* topic for each.

EXERCISE 6. Write specific titles for five of the general topics listed below.

1. Book Clubs	6. Going on a Hike
2. Going to Church	7. Designing Clothes
3. Teachers	8. Home-made Furniture
4. A Scenic Wonder	9. Detective Stories
5. At the Racetrack	10. Political Conventions

EXERCISE 7. Write a one-paragraph "open letter" on some subject that you think should be of general interest (e.g., taxes, traffic signs, a municipal memorial, fresh air in the classroom). Address it to a very small audience, such as a school board, the city council, your parents, or your fellow students in this course.

31c   Make a preliminary outline.

An outline is a brief working plan of the material you intend to include in a composition. Making an outline is a way of finding out what you have to say on a subject. Suppose you decide to write a short composition on "Trapping the Wily Muskrat." Your preliminary outline might consist of the following ideas:

1. Places to set the traps
2. A dozen #1 traps
3. Trapping the muskrat's feeding grounds
4. Trapping the narrows of streams
5. Need for wearing high boots
6. Demand for pelts
7. Financial profits of trapping
8. Prices of pelts
9. Protective clothing
10. Need for a short, heavy jacket
11. Trapper's equipment
12. Healthful recreation provided by trapping

Clearly this is just a list of notations, without order or logical arrangement. But it is a valuable first step; it gets your ideas down on paper and shows you just what you have to work with.

EXERCISE 8. Make preliminary outlines for two of the theme titles you prepared for Exercises 1-3.

EXERCISE 9. Which of the suggested topics listed on pages 193-194 could you use for a 200-300 word theme without any further study or research? Make preliminary outlines for three of them, to see whether you know as much about them as you think you do.

EXERCISE 10. Make a preliminary outline of one subject you can write about from personal experience (for example, "Problems of an Oldest Child") and one you know about only from hearsay or guess-work (for example, "The Life of a Ranch Hand").

31d **Frame a thesis statement that will help you avoid irrelevancies in planning your composition.***

A "thesis statement" sums up the central idea and purpose of a composition in one or two sentences. It serves as a guide as you begin to re-order and arrange the items in your preliminary outline. The very act of constructing a thesis statement forces you to clarify your thinking, to sift out pointless or irrelevant material, and to keep focused on pertinent detail. The preliminary outline of "Trapping the Wily Muskrat" (31c) suggests some such thesis statement as this: "Profitable trapping of muskrats requires adequate equipment and a knowledge of good trapping places." Notice that the statement catches all the ideas (profit, equipment, places) that are to be dealt with and puts them in meaningful order. You can now begin to re-vise the preliminary outline in the light of a clearly stated purpose.

EXERCISE 11. Make a thesis statement for each of the two themes you outlined in Exercise 8.

EXERCISE 12. Write a thesis statement for an essay or a chapter assigned to you as outside reading.

EXERCISE 13. Write a thesis statement for the paragraph beginning "Another marvelous but sinister invention..." on page 241.

31e **Prepare a complete outline in which you arrange details in logical order and perfect your over-all plan.**

Make it a habit to construct a complete outline for every piece of writing you do. An outline provides you with a working plan for organizing your paper. It insures that your development of the subject will be logical and orderly, and enables you to distinguish clearly between important ideas and less important ones.

---

* Practice in writing précis or brief summaries of other people's works is excellent training for framing clear thesis statements for your own writing. See Section 47.

In constructing your outline, follow some consistent principle of organization—chronological, general to specific (deductive), specific to general (inductive), spatial, and so on. Bring together all related ideas in one place and do not repeat them in other parts of the outline.

In the preliminary outline for "Trapping the Wily Muskrat" (31c), notice that two of the items stand out as general headings: "Places to set the traps" and "Trapper's equipment." Notice too that a third general heading, "Advantages of trapping," must be added; otherwise there would be no place to put such items as "Healthful recreation provided by trapping" and "Financial profits of trapping." If we arrange all the details under these three major headings, we come up with the following outline:

TRAPPING THE WILY MUSKRAT

    I. Advantages of trapping
        A. Financial profit
            1. Demands for pelts
            2. Prices for pelts
        B. Healthful recreation

   II. Trapper's equipment
        A. A dozen # 1 traps
        B. Protective clothing
            1. Boots
            2. Short, heavy jacket

  III. Places to set the traps
        A. Muskrat feeding grounds
        B. Narrows of streams

Such an outline will help you keep your plan in mind as you write your paper (adherence to purpose). It will indicate the order in which you want to discuss each idea (logical development) and the relative importance of each (proportion of material).

If you are to do an efficient job of organizing your material, you must know something of the formal mechanics of outlining, and the various types of outlining that your instructor may require.

(1) Use a consistent method for numbering and indenting major headings and subheadings. For most outlines, it is unnecessary to

divide subheadings more than two degrees. Here is a conventional system of outline notation:

I. . . . .
    A. . . . .
        1. . . . .
           a. . . . .
           b. . . . .
        2. . . . .
    B. . . . .
II. . . . .

(2) Use either the topic, the sentence, or the paragraph form throughout your outline. In a topic outline the separate headings are expressed by a noun, or a word or phrase used as a noun, and its modifiers. In a sentence outline, which has the same structure as the topic outline, the separate headings are expressed in complete sentences. The sentence outline is more informative than the topic outline, because it states ideas more fully; but the topic outline is easier to read. The paragraph outline gives a summary sentence for each paragraph in the theme. It does not divide and subdivide headings into subordinate parts.

Before you start to outline, decide which of the three types of outline you are going to use and then follow it consistently. If, for example, you choose to make a sentence outline, remember that *every* statement in the outline must be expressed as a complete sentence. Remember, too, to make all parts of the outline parallel in structure (see "Parallelism," Section 35), as in the following models.

THE TELEGRAPHER: KEEPER OF THE KEYS
(*Topic Outline*)

  I. Importance of telegraphic communication
    A. International telegraphic networks
    B. Emergency means of communication

 II. Telegrapher's instrument
    A. Manually operated key, or "bug"
        1. Appearance of the key
        2. Operation of the key

    B. Modern teleprinter
        1. Appearance of the teleprinter
        2. Operation of the teleprinter

III. Comparative skills of telegraphers
   A. Complex skills of the "bug" operator
   B. Simple skills of the teleprinter operator

THE TELEGRAPHER: KEEPER OF THE KEYS
(Sentence Outline)

I. Telegraphy is one of our most important means of communication.
   A. The nations of the world are bound together by telegraphic networks.
   B. The telegraph is of great value for sending emergency messages.

II. Telegraphic instruments are of two general types.
   A. The manually operated key, or "bug," is used in small or remote communication centers.
      1. The "bug" resembles a miniature stapler connected to a panel of sockets.
      2. The "bug" produces long and short electrical impulses, or dots and dashes.
   B. The modern teleprinter is used in large communication centers.
      1. The teleprinter is a complicated machine with a manually operated keyboard.
      2. The teleprinter records, or prints, messages.

III. Operators of the "bug" and the teleprinter have different skills.
   A. The "bug" operator sends, receives, and translates the International Morse Code.
   B. The teleprinter operator uses a simple keyboard like that of a typewriter.

THE TELEGRAPHER: KEEPER OF THE KEYS
(Paragraph Outline)

1. Telegraphers are the keepers of a world-wide network of communications.
2. The small key, or "bug," sends electrical impulses through a panel of sockets and out into the atmosphere.
3. The modern teleprinter, operated by a keyboard, records messages in large communication centers.
4. The "bug" operator must employ great skill in sending and receiving messages in the International Morse Code.
5. The teleprinter operator must have only the simple skill of using a typewriter keyboard.

200

(3) Do not use single headings or single subheadings in your outline. Any category of heading or subheading must have at least two parts. If you have a I, you must also have a II. If you introduce an A under a Roman numeral, you must also have a B under that Roman numeral. If you put a 1 under an A, you must also put a 2. And so on for any division. The reason for this procedure is sheer logic. Each breakdown of the outline is a division of a foregoing bigger point, and you cannot logically divide something into just one part. A single subheading reflects poor organization and should be incorporated into the heading of which it is logically a part.

(4) Cast all items in the outline in parallel grammatical constructions. (For a discussion of "Parallelism," see Section 35.) Consistency of grammatical form emphasizes the logic of the outline and gives it clarity and smoothness. Inconsistency of form, on the other hand, makes a perfectly rational ordering of items seem illogical.

NON-PARALLEL	PARALLEL
The Game of Tennis	*The Game of Tennis*

I. The playing court	I. Playing court
A. The surface materials for it	A. Surface materials
1. Made of clay	1. Clay
2. Grass	2. Grass
3. The asphalt type	3. Asphalt
B. Measuring the court	B. Measurements
1. For singles	1. Singles
2. Doubles	2. Doubles
C. Net	C. Net
D. Backstops necessary	D. Backstops
II. Equipment needed	II. Equipment
A. Racket	A. Racket
B. The tennis balls	B. Ball
C. The wearing apparel of players	C. Wearing apparel
III. Rules for playing tennis	III. Playing rules
A. The game of singles	A. Singles
B. Doubles	B. Doubles

NON-PARALLEL	PARALLEL
The Game of Tennis	*The Game of Tennis*

IV. Principal strokes of tennis   IV. Principal strokes
    A. Serving the ball   A. Serving stroke
    B. The forehand   B. Forehand stroke
       1. Drive   1. Drive
       2. Lobbing the ball   2. Lob
    C. The backhand stroke   C. Backhand stroke
       1. The drive   1. Drive
       2. Lob   2. Lob

(5) Avoid vague outline headings such as "introduction," "body," and "conclusion." Not only does the outline serve as a guide in your writing; submitted with your paper, it also serves as a table of contents for your reader. To use such words as "introduction," "body," and "conclusion" as outline headings is meaningless, for they give no clue to what material is to come. If your paper is to have an introduction, indicate in the outline what will be in it. If your paper is to have a formal conclusion, indicate in the outline what conclusion you will draw.

EXERCISE 14. Construct a complete outline for one of the titles suggested in Section 31a. Use each of the three forms just described: (1) topic, (2) sentence, (3) paragraph.

EXERCISE 15. Write a topic outline for one of the theme titles you prepared for Exercises 1-3, Section 31a.

EXERCISE 16. Revise the following topic outline.

THE VALUE OF PUBLIC OPINION POLLS

  I. Introduction
    A. Operation of public opinion polls
      1. Selection of an important issue
      2. Constructing a set of questions
        a. Scientific nature of this construction
      3. A cross section of the population is selected
    B. Replies are tabulated and results summarized

 II. Importance of poll's results
      1. Attitudes of public revealed to lawmakers
      2. Power of present groups revealed
      3. Polls are a democratic process
        a. Polls reveal extent of people's knowledge

31f   **Begin your paper effectively.**

A good beginning serves as a springboard into the subject. If your paper is on how to clean guns, you might say quite simply, "The best method of cleaning guns is. . . ." Or if your paper is entitled "I Hate Cats," you might begin, "Cats are a menace to mankind. They should be exterminated." In each instance you have launched the subject forcefully and can move right along with your development. Here are some other ideas to help you in writing good beginnings.

(1) *Make the beginning self-explanatory.* Give the readers some idea of what you are talking about at the very outset. The following is intelligible only if the title is read as part of the theme.

HOW TO CLEAN A GUN

The first thing to do is to take your gun apart. Then lay all the parts out on the floor in front of you. Next, pick up each piece and clean it in the following manner. . . .

(2) *Avoid a rambling, decorative beginning that simply delays the introduction.*

FATHER KNOWS BEST

You probably wonder from my title what I am going to write about. Well, it's a long story. It started way back in 1942 when I was born. My mother announced to my father that I was a boy! "We're going to send him to State University!" my father exclaimed. So here I am at State, a member of the freshman class.

It was my father's idea from the first that I should come to State. He had been a student here in 1939 when he met my mother. . . .

Here the writer meant well, aiming at what newspapermen call a "human interest" beginning. But he succeeded only in rambling about and wasting the reader's time; he would have done better had he begun his paper with the second paragraph.

(3) *Try one of the following techniques for beginning a paper.*

(a) *Repeat the title.*

FATHER KNOWS BEST

I was not much taken with the idea that I should enter State University this year. After visiting the campus for a few days, however, I became convinced that Father knows best when it comes to matters of his alma mater. . . .

(b) *Repeat a key word in the title.*

THE SACRED HAG

For many years now the American people have felt that Science is the most sacred of man's achievements. We find this feeling expressed almost daily in our newspapers, our magazines. . . .

NOTE: Since a title is not a part of the first paragraph, avoid using a pronoun to refer to the title.

NOT

FATHER KNOWS BEST

I decided this when my father persuaded me that State University was the place to go. . . .

BUT

FATHER KNOWS BEST

I decided that my father knows best after he had persuaded me that State University was the place to go. . . .

(c) *Paraphrase the title.*

COLLEGE FOOTBALL: A GAME OR A BUSINESS?

How much longer must we pay lip service to the notion that big-time college football is a sport played for fun by amateurs? It is time. . . .

(d) *Begin with an anecdote directly related to the subject of the paper.*

FATHER KNOWS BEST

When Mark Twain left home at an early age, he had no great respect for his father's intelligence. When he returned a few years later, however, he was astonished at how much his father had learned in the meantime. Similarly, it was only after I had been away from home for a few years that I became aware that Father knows best. . . .

EXERCISE 17. Choose three titles from the list of suggested topics in Section 31a. Then write a beginning for each, using a different technique each time.

EXERCISE 18. Study the following example of a rough outline. Then make similar outlines for two of the topics suggested in Section 31a.

GAY BLADES: A GUIDE TO HANDSAWS
AND SAWING

   I. Picture of an inexperienced person with a saw: wobbly cut, splintered wood, aching arm. He is using wrong saw and wrong technique.
  II. Quick survey of the kinds of saws and their uses.
 III. Sawing technique: marking wood, beginning cut, leaning into stroke, holding wood to avoid splintering.
 IV. Precautions while sawing.
  V. Another picture of our tenderfoot, impatient with fine points, using machine saw: straight cut, no aching muscles, and losing only unimportant fingers.

31g **Always write a preliminary rough draft of your paper.**

Having completed your outline and having phrased an opening statement, you are ready to proceed with the actual writing of your paper. Be sure to allow time to write your papers at least twice. The first—or rough—draft gives you an opportunity just to *write*. In this draft you need not concern yourself with spelling, punctuation, mechanics, or grammar. Rather, you can devote your attention to getting your ideas, as directed by the outline, down on paper.

31h **End your paper effectively.**

Just as a forceful opening gets your paper off to a good vigorous start, so a strong conclusion lends a finished note to your paper. An effective ending may bring your paper to a logical conclusion or tie it all together. The paper on "How to Clean Guns," for example, might end with this statement:

> If you have followed all the directions given here, you should now have a re-assembled, clean gun ready for another day's shooting.

205

Here are some ideas to help you end your papers effectively:

(1) *Conclude with a restatement of your thesis statement.* In the paper "Father Knows Best" this sort of ending might be effective:

> Now that I have been here and have seen the school for myself, I am convinced that Father *does* know best. I have decided to enroll for the next term at State University.

(2) *Summarize the major ideas you have brought out in the paper.* A summary serves the double purpose of bringing your paper to a good conclusion and of reminding your readers once more of the major points you have made. The paper on "Trapping the Wily Muskrat" could effectively employ this sort of ending:

> Thus, it is clear that muskrat hunting has financial and healthful rewards. With the proper equipment and a knowledge of where to set traps, almost anyone can enjoy this fascinating outdoor sport.

(3) *Draw a logical conclusion, inductively or deductively, from the facts you have presented.* This sort of conclusion is especially effective if you have set out to defend a point of view. If you have, for example, been exploring a controversial topic such as "Should the Franchise Be Extended to Eighteen-Year-Olds?" your conclusion might be a call for action to reinforce whichever side you had defended.

(4) *Avoid weak endings.*

(a) *Don't end your paper with an apology.* Such endings as "This is only my opinion, and I'm probably not really very well qualified to speak" or "I'm sorry that this isn't a better paper, but I didn't have enough time" spoil the effect of whatever you have written. If you feel that you have failed, your reader will probably think so too.

(b) *Don't end your paper by branching off into another aspect of the topic or by introducing new material.* The end of your paper should conclude what you have already said. It is disconcerting to a reader to find new ideas introduced that are not explored further. Avoid such endings as: "There is a lot more I could say about this if I had more time" or "Another aspect of muskrat trapping is the economic, but it would take another paper to tell about it." This type of ending leaves the reader with the feeling that you have led him to no definite conclusion.

31i   Prepare a finished second draft.

After a cooling-off period of several hours, you are ready to check, revise, and rewrite. Test the over-all organization of your first draft by asking yourself the following questions:

(1) Does the title fit the discussion?

(2) Is the material divided into distinct sections?

(3) Are these sections arranged in logical order? (Is there an orderly sequence of thought from one section to the next, and from the beginning to the end?)

(4) Is all the material relevant to the central purpose of the paper?

(5) Is the beginning direct and pertinent?

(6) Does the ending of the paper give an impression of finality and completeness? (Or does it trail off in a cloud of minor details?)

Once you have answered these basic questions to your own satisfaction, check the individual paragraphs—that is, the units of discussion. Be sure that the topic of each paragraph is clear-cut and adequately developed (see Section 32). Test every generalization to insure that it is supported by sufficient evidence—facts, illustrations, examples. When you spot an opinion or assertion that lacks evidence, supply the evidence—or else discard the opinion entirely.

Now you can proceed with your rewriting. Recast clumsy sentences, repair faulty phraseology, make the diction more exact and precise. Supply needed transitions and check existing transitions for accuracy. Scrutinize every mark of punctuation and look up all questionable spellings. Then recopy or retype the whole paper in the required format (see "Manuscript Form," Section 1).

31j   Make final revisions.

Set your manuscript aside for a day or two before making final revisions. Then you can go back to it with some of the objectivity of a reader. Make minor revisions—punctuation, spelling, word substitution—directly (but neatly) on the manuscript. If you find that more fundamental revisions—paragraph and sentence structure—are needed, you may have to recopy one or more pages. Usually the reaction of an unofficial reader—a roommate, a friend, a parent, even a well-disposed stranger—is helpful. Ask whether or not your paper communicates clearly. The revisions your reader suggests may be minor: a word here, a punctuation mark there. If he spots more fundamental flaws, you may have to rewrite the whole paper. One final proofreading—if possible, aloud to yourself—is good insurance against handing in an imperfect paper. Good writers are patient, with an infinite capacity for revision.

> **EXERCISE 19.** On the following pages, you will find three specimen papers, one of which has a critical commentary. After studying the papers carefully, write critical commentaries on the last two.

CRITICAL COMMENTARY

This paper is almost completely unsuccessful. Its real virtues—competent sentence structure, punctuation, spelling—all go begging because of the author's failure to establish the statement he makes in the title. The paper was obviously written without a preconceived plan, an outline; and it teems with unsupported generalizations.

The paper begins effectively; the first sentence repeats the title and states clearly what we assume will be the central purpose of the paper. The second sentence introduces a concrete illustration, to be offered (we suppose) in support of the first sentence. The author then speaks of the speed with which radio gets the news to us. But instead of establishing this generalization with facts and illustrations, he proceeds at once to another idea—that of the accuracy of radio reporting. His comment here is purposeless; the question of the accuracy of radio reporting cannot be dismissed simply by calling it "as accurate as possible." The author then speaks of the "on the spot" quality of radio reporting, a matter which he treats far too summarily. And the last sentence in his first paragraph appears as an afterthought. He should have omitted it, or perhaps worked it into that part of the paragraph concerned with the rapidity of radio as a means of reporting news.

The second paragraph, as the opening sentence informs us, has nothing to do with radio as a source of news. The author has departed completely from his original purpose and is now talking of the value of radio in rescue and patrol work. Moreover, the last sentence of the second

Specimen Paper 1

BEST SOURCE OF NEWS: THE RADIO

The radio is our best means of securing news. Consider the international situation, for example. We would not receive our news as rapidly as we do if it were not for the radio. All the news -- newspaper, radio, television -- is censored before we get it, but the radio provides us with as accurate reporting as is possible. Moreover, radio reports, particularly those coming from "on the spot" observations, are likely to be more exciting than newspaper reports, which are usually written several hours after the event has happened. Yes, speed is the important thing today.

The radio has also saved the lives of many people. Airplanes depend on radio, not only to make their own travel safer, but also to direct the rescue of people marooned by floods, snowstorms, etc. In areas inaccessible by any other means, the airplane is essential for patrolling and observation work.

These facts establish the importance of radio in modern civilization. There is no end to the contribution of radio in making the world safer to live in.

paragraph has very little to do with radio at all; it is simply a comment on the usefulness of the airplane.

The last paragraph is also unrelated to the expressed purpose of the paper. Neither sentence mentions radio as a source of news. Moreover, the first sentence of the last paragraph deserves a special condemnation. The author has not really *established* anything. He has merely written a list of unconnected and unsupported generalizations about radio. To call them "facts" is absurd. Finally, we have only to compare the statement of the last sentence with that of the first sentence of the paper to see how far the author has strayed from his original purpose.

Specimen Paper 2

THE LIGHTEST GAS

Hydrogen is a very important and well-known gas. Its preparation is very simple. There are many ways of preparing it for commercial uses. Cavendish, an Englishman, has been recognized as the discoverer of hydrogen. He was the first to get it into a pure condition and recognize it as an independent substance different from any other known inflammable gases.

Of the many ways hydrogen is prepared, the Bosch process is most common. This process consists of passing steam over hot carbon. The carbon and steam, which is made up of oxygen and hydrogen, unite, and form carbon monoxide and free hydrogen. Another common method is by combining methane, a common natural gas, with steam. The methane gas is composed of carbon and hydrogen. The carbon combines with the oxygen to form carbon monoxide and in turn sets the hydrogen free.

Hydrogen has many uses. One of its uses is inflating balloons and airships. Helium is most frequently used in airships because hydrogen is inflammable and helium is almost as light. Hydrogen is also used in the manufacture of ammonia, which, in turn, has many uses, especially in the production of fertilizers.

Hydrogen has many properties like those of oxygen. It is colorless, odorless, and tasteless. It is slightly soluble in water. And it is the lightest gas or substance known to man. Hydrogen is getting more popular and important every day. An example of this is the H-bomb, the greatest bomb ever created.

Specimen Paper 3

THE IDEAL EDUCATION

More than ever before, a good education is required if one is going to seek the fortunes of opportunity. In the past few years college enrollments have been increasing steadily because people are realizing the importance of higher education. Because the best jobs are held by the persons who have an advanced education, the value of education cannot be stressed too much.

In choosing a college to enter one must consider their differences. For instance, a student considering Normal State must realize that the university has many thousand students. When a student comes to State, he feels as though he is coming into a new town. Right away he finds that he is on his own. He feels that high school was more like kindergarten. The college with a small enrollment is more compact, a circumstance which helps the new student considerably at first. Moreover, the student usually receives more personal attention from the faculty than he would at a college as large as Normal State

Now that we have seen the big differences between the large and small universities, we can probably see that there are advantages to both, or they would not be in existence. At Normal State the student sacrifices personal attention for the better equipment he has to work with. At a small college the situation is reversed. Regardless, the fact remains that the student coming from high school is facing a new situation and may need guidance.

Look to the paragraph and the discourse will look to itself. . . .

—ALEXANDER BAIN

32   EFFECTIVE PARAGRAPHS = ¶ S

The purpose of paragraphing is to reveal the order and unity of the over-all statement. A sentence is a group of words that makes a single statement; a paragraph is a group of sentences which are related to one another, and which, taken together, form a single coherent part of a larger unit.

Let us examine a good paragraph to see how each sentence serves as part of a larger unit. (The sentences are numbered for easy reference.)

> 1. Tourists in Old Ontario often journey out to a cemetery near Chatham on the Thames. 2. They stand by a wooden marker and read with surprise the words: "The grave of Rev. Josiah Henson, the original Uncle Tom of *Uncle Tom's Cabin* by Harriet Beecher Stowe." 3. The famous Negro, after years of labor for his master, escaped from his slavery, endured starvation, fought off wolves in the Indiana and Ohio wilderness, and passed with his wife and child through friendly hands across the border into Canada to become the most notable of the fugitives. 4. He aided 600 Negroes to reach Ontario, he visited Queen Victoria and fanned the flames of war to attain immortality through the pen of Harriet Beecher Stowe. 5. He died at last in peace, and his abused and honored bones lie at the foot of this painted marker.
>
> —HARLAN HATCHER, *Lake Erie*

First, all these sentences serve a single purpose. Sentence 1 provides a physical setting. Sentence 2 identifies Henson as "Uncle Tom." Sentences 3 and 4 describe his adventures. Sentence 5, the last, serves the double purpose of concluding the narrative and referring the reader back to the starting point—the wooden marker in the cemetery. Every sentence after the first one has to do specifically with why the grave of Josiah Henson is of interest and renown. Because all the sentences contribute directly to a single purpose, the paragraph has *unity.*

Second, the individual sentences are not only related to each other in subject matter; they are specifically tied together by logic and grammatical structure. Sentence 2 refers to sentence 1 in two ways: It points out a particular spot in the cemetery named in sentence 1; and the pronoun *They* has its antecedent in the word *Tourists.* Sentences 3, 4, and 5 are bound together by chronology, since they describe Henson's activities in the order of time, from the years of his slavery, through his escape, to his death. The pronoun *He* in sentences 4 and 5 links these sentences with sentence 3, which contains the antecedent *The famous Negro.* The last three sentences are also linked by a uniform verb tense—*escaped, endured, fought off, passed, aided, visited, fanned, died.* In short, the paragraph has *coherence.*

Third, the group of sentences gives ample information about the topic. Our curiosity about the significance of the wooden marker has been satisfied. Less detail would not make Henson's grave a topic worth treating in a separate paragraph; more detail would tend to make the reader forget that his original curiosity concerned a grave marker, not the detailed biography of the man buried under it. The paragraph therefore is *adequately developed.*

The elements of a good paragraph, then, are (1) *unity,* (2) *coherence,* and (3) *adequate development.* For convenience we discuss these elements separately, but all three are interdependent. As the illustration above shows, a coherent paragraph is also unified and adequately developed. In other words, to support a topic sentence clearly and purposively, you must develop a paragraph adequately and connect its sentences logically. Making a good paragraph calls for several closely related skills, none of which is sufficient in itself.

EXERCISE 20. Analyze the following paragraphs just as the paragraph above was analyzed.

1.

1. What people do not seem to realize is that the editors of the various "digests" do not simply delete a word here and there. 2. They do not cut only extraneous material. 3. Instead, they "blue pencil" paragraphs and pages. 4. We depend upon the discretion of these editors, and what seems of importance to them becomes the text we read. 5. We have no idea what has been cut. 6. What we do read may be so removed from its original context that the remainder of the article is completely distorted. 7. The reader, however, has no way of knowing of this distortion and thus reads his digest version in good faith. 8. Consequently, when he tries to discuss his mutilated concept with someone who has taken the time to read the unabridged version, he may find himself unfamiliar with a point which was the basis of the entire thesis.

—Student paragraph

2.

1. It was a very proper wedding. 2. The bride was elegantly dressed; the two bridesmaids were duly inferior; her father gave her away; her mother stood with salts in her hands, expecting to be agitated; her aunt tried to cry; and the service was impressively read by Dr. Grant. 3. Nothing could be objected to when it came under the discussion of the neighbourhood, except that the carriage which conveyed the bride and bridegroom and Julia from the church door to Sotherton was the same chaise which Mr. Rushworth had used for a twelvemonth before. 4. In everything else the etiquette of the day might stand the strictest investigation.

—JANE AUSTEN, *Mansfield Park*

3.

1. It would be difficult to underestimate a foe more dangerously than Britain did the Boers. 2. Because they were generally bucolic, canting, and untutored, they were thought to be a military joke. 3. After all, it was argued, what could these bushmen know of cavalry maneuvers? 4. It was doubted if they could even ride a straight line. 5. What they could do, though, was ride for days on end with little food or rest, cover with dazzling speed a country they knew thoroughly, and think for themselves, according to the rules of common sense rather than those of antiquated army

textbooks. 6. The Boers had been toughened by a code of religious spartanism incomprehensible to the average Britisher. 7. They were a suspicious people, with an implacable God, and were disinclined to frivolity or friendship. 8. If immigrants settled within a day's ride of a man's farm, that neighborhood was viewed as congested, and he picked up and moved. 9. A Boer usually carried a Bible with him and read it as he did his chores, accepting the Old Testament as the Law and discarding the New as untested and disreputable. 10. In the main, a man's chores consisted in caring for huge herds and in hunting, at which he was expert. 11. Most Boers were exceptional shots and could drop an antelope or a wildebeest, in which the country abounded, at distances up to several hundred yards. 12. Agriculture was in bad repute with the Boers; for some reason they thought it sissified. 13. Also, herds were mobile while crops were uncomfortably fixative. 14. Household recreation in the Transvaal depended upon the daily singing of a collection of pretty frightening hymns that left no doubt where a person was likely to lodge if he strayed from the paths of righteousness. 15. Further spicing up life, each family annually made a giddy expedition a hundred or so miles to the nearest church for Holy Communion. 16. And now and then a number of Boers got together to war on nearby natives—the Zulus, the Hottentots, the Tembus, and the Swazis.

—ROBERT LEWIS TAYLOR, *Winston Churchill,
An Informal Study of Greatness*

UNITY IN THE PARAGRAPH = ⊄UN *

32a Write unified paragraphs.

A unified paragraph has a clear intent, and its topic is either summed up in one of its sentences or strongly implied by the subject

---

* An understanding of paragraph "unity" will help make the typical "essay exam" less of a hurdle for you. In your next essay examination rephrase the essay question into a topic sentence and then go about "supporting" it as you would the topic sentence of a regular paragraph. You may have to write two or three actual paragraphs before you feel the topic sentence is completely supported, but the technique (using illustrative detail, sticking to the subject, etc.) is the same as you use in writing a regular paragraph.

matter. Most paragraphs have a *topic sentence*—that is, a sentence that expresses the central idea of the paragraph. The following paragraphs illustrate various ways of placing the topic sentence.

(1) The topic sentence may be the first sentence of the paragraph. Following the deductive method, you may state your topic first and then add supporting details.

> The tea-plant, a native of Southern China, was known from very early times to Chinese botany and medicine. It is alluded to in the classics under the various names of Tou, Tseh, Chung, Kha, and Ming, and was highly prized for possessing the virtues of relieving fatigue, delighting the soul, strengthening the will, and repairing the eyesight. It was not only administered as an internal dose, but often applied externally in the form of paste to alleviate rheumatic pains. The Taoists claimed it as an important ingredient of the elixir of immortality. The Buddhists used it extensively to prevent drowsiness during their long hours of meditation.
>
> —OKAKURA KAKUZO, *The Book of Tea*

(2) The topic sentence may be the last sentence of the paragraph. Following the inductive method, you may give details first and save your main point for the final sentence.

> Along the road walked an old man. He was white-headed as a mountain, bowed in the shoulders, and faded in general aspect. He wore a glazed hat, an ancient boat-cloak, and shoes; his brass buttons bearing an anchor upon their face. In his hand was a silver-headed walking-stick, which he used as a veritable third leg, perseveringly dotting the ground with its point at every few inches' interval. One would have said that he had been, in his day, a naval officer of some sort or other.
>
> —THOMAS HARDY, *The Return of the Native*

(3) The topic sentence may appear first and last.

> The material problems of the war could be solved and the material devastation repaired; the moral devastation was never wholly repaired. The North was demoralized by victory, the South by defeat. During the war violence and destruction and hatred had been called virtues; it was a long time before they were recognized again as vices. The war had been brutalizing in its effects on combatants and non-combatants alike. Ruthlessness

and wastefulness, extravagance and corruption, speculation and exploitation had accompanied the conflict, and they lingered on to trouble the post-war years. Above all, the war left a heritage of misunderstanding and even of bitterness, that colored the thinking and conditioned the actions of men, North and South, for over a generation.

—S. E. MORISON *and* H. S. COMMAGER, *The Growth of the American Republic*

(4) The topic sentence may be implied. Narrative and descriptive paragraphs sometimes do not state a topic sentence directly; instead, the topic may be implicit in the details given. The implied topic of the paragraph below, for example, is "a description of the Grand Ball at Bath, England, in the late eighteenth century."

The hour is just on nine. At six, with the playing of a minuet, the dancing had started; now there is the usual pause for the gentlemen to hand tea to the ladies, and for the musicians to wet their tired throats. Tonight being something of an occasion there will be supper as well, and behind screens footmen are busily laying a long table with cold ham and pheasant, biscuits, sweetmeats, jellies and wine. And now the Master of Ceremonies in plum satin and paste buckles offers his arm to the ranking lady present, Her Grace the Duchess of Marlborough, and together they swing across the room. Behind them rustle the others, Her Grace's inferiors. Countesses and ladyships, wealthy tradesmen's wives and daughters, the mothers and mistresses of bone-setters and shipbuilders and swindling gamesters, all come to Bath to taste the salubrious "Spaw" waters at the Pump Room, to take the cure, to ogle their partners at balls at the Assembly Rooms —and best of all, to be stared at themselves in return.

—ALICE GLASGOW, *Sheridan of Drury Lane*

EXERCISE 21. What is the topic sentence, expressed or implied, in each of the following paragraphs?

1.

1. The columnist is the autocrat of the most prodigious breakfast table ever known. 2. He is the voice beside the cracker barrel amplified to trans-continental dimensions. 3. He is the only non-political figure of record who can clear his throat each day and say "Now, here's what I think . . ." with the assurance that millions will listen. 4. His associates—remembering, it may be, the days before his casual opinions were regarded as canonical—regard him with wonder and a faintly sour envy. 5. The editorial writers of

the papers which buy his work envy his freedom from restraint and the loyalty he engenders. 6. The ranking novelists of the age envy his income. 7. Even his readers, it may be conjectured, envy the facility with which he passes daily judgment upon all the perplexities of life. 8. And in truth, there is something enviable in the daily and profitable projection of an unfettered personality.

—CHARLES FISHER, *The Columnists*

2.

1. The generation that came to maturity between the Peace of Paris and the inauguration of President Washington had to solve more serious and original political problems than any later generation of Americans. 2. It was then that the great beacons of American principles, such as the Declaration of Independence, the Virginia Bill of Rights, and the Federal Constitution, were lighted; it was then that institutions of permanent and profound import in the history of America and of liberty were crystallized. 3. The period was not only revolutionary and destructive, but creative and constructive; moreover the British connection was not the most important thing that was destroyed, nor was national independence the most important thing that was created. 4. A new federal empire was erected on the ruins of the old empire, American ideas proclaimed, and the American character defined.

—S. E. MORISON *and* H. S. COMMAGER, *The Growth of the American Republic*

3.

1. When Captain Rook left the ship he was relieved by Captain John Z. Smith. 2. As a skipper, Captain Smith was just what you'd expect a John Smith to be like: a solid character who knew his business, a plain man, quiet, and very Regulation; the kind of a guy who raises tomatoes in his back yard and takes his family for a drive on Sunday afternoon. 3. Captain Smith was neither an outstandingly good nor bad officer—he stood average. 4. He had no idiosyncrasies and the chances are that most of the men who served with him wouldn't remember his name two years after parting company. 5. But he was a good man, cool in combat, and reasonable.

—W. J. LEDERER, *All the Ship's at Sea*

4.

1. Call me Ishmael. Some years ago—never mind how long precisely—having little or no money in my purse, and nothing particular to interest me on shore, I thought I would sail about a

little and see the watery part of the world. 2. It is a way I have of driving off the spleen, and regulating the circulation. 3. Whenever I find myself growing grim about the mouth; whenever it is a damp, drizzly November in my soul; whenever I find myself involuntarily pausing before coffin warehouses, and bringing up the rear of every funeral I meet; and especially whenever my hypos get such an upper hand of me, that it requires a strong moral principle to prevent me from deliberately stepping into the street, and methodically knocking people's hats off—then, I account it high time to get to sea as soon as I can. 4. This is my substitute for pistol and ball. 5. With a philosophical flourish Cato throws himself upon his sword; I quietly take to the ship. 6. There is nothing surprising in this. 7. If they but knew it, almost all men in their degree, some time or other, cherish very nearly the same feelings towards the ocean with me.

—HERMAN MELVILLE, *Moby Dick*

5.

1. It is the fact that a word not only "means" what its logical definition makes it mean but can call to life all sorts of associative ideas and emotions which makes language such an excellent material for poetry and, at the same time, such an imperfect and even dangerous instrument for any sort of discussion of a scientific or political nature. 2. In poetry, the word *moonlight* is a highly effective word because, apart from meaning "the light of the moon," it also calls up visions of stillness, mystery, beauty, and perhaps love. 3. That these visions are not absolutely the same for each reader of a poem to the moon is no disadvantage to the poet. 4. On the contrary, the more varied the associative values of the word, the greater the number of readers to whom it may appeal in one way or another. 5. In logical discussion, on the other hand, the peripheral elements of meaning represent a constant danger. 6. Even if we tried, we could not keep our language free from words whose emotional value is strong enough to blunt our own mental functions and those of our listeners. 7. As long as words express ideas and conditions about which we are concerned, the word can arouse exactly all the emotion of the thing of which it is the symbol. 8. If, as is often the case, the two parties in a discussion use the same words with different connotations it becomes difficult to reach an agreement. 9. Many scientific discussions have been prolonged and many political conflicts embittered by this insufficiency of language.

—ROBERT M. ESTRICH *and* HANS SPERBER,
Three Keys to Language

EXERCISE 22. Following are three topic sentences, each accompanied by a set of statements. Some of the statements are relevant to the topic, some are not. Eliminate the irrelevant ones, and organize the rest into a paragraph.

1. Given my choice I would sooner be in the Air Force than any other service branch.
    1. I am more interested in flying than in any other military occupation.
    2. Opportunities for advancement are greater in the Air Force.
    3. Wages in certain brackets of the Air Force are higher than in other branches.
    4. There are many opportunities to travel.
    5. The Navy gives one travel opportunities too.
    6. My cousin has been in the Navy for two years, and he has sailed around the whole world.
    7. I think, though, that I still like the Air Force better.

2. The wreck on Route 64 at Mt. Nixon was caused entirely by carelessness and reckless driving by the driver of the Buick.
    1. When the wreck occurred the lights were green for the cars coming off the side road.
    2. A heavy truck loaded with hay was pulling out to cross the highway.
    3. The Buick came speeding down the main road, went through the stoplight, and crashed into the truck.
    4. You could hear the screeching of the tires and then the crashing and grinding of metal a quarter of a mile away.
    5. You could hear it in our house up the road.
    6. Both drivers were killed, and I will never forget how awful the accident was.

3. We owe some of our notions of radar to scientific observation of bats.
    1. Most people hate bats.
    2. Women especially are afraid of them, since they have been told that bats are likely to get into their hair.
    3. Bats are commonly considered unattractive, ugly creatures.
    4. They really look more like mice with wings than anything else.

5. Scientists noticed that bats rarely collided with anything in their erratic flight.
6. Keen eyesight could not be the reason for their flying the way they do, since bats are blind.
7. It was found that bats keep sending out noises inaudible to people and that they hear the echoes of those noises.
8. This principle whereby they fly safely was found to be similar to the main principle of radar.

32b **Be sure that every sentence in a paragraph bears on the central subject.**

Not only must you have a clear intent in writing a paragraph, you must also hold to that intent throughout the paragraph. The writer of the following paragraph, for example, changes his intent three times in the first three sentences; and he tacks on the last sentence as a kind of afterthought:

> Henry James' extensive travel during his early years greatly influenced his later writings. Born in New York in 1843, Henry was destined to become one of the first novelists of the world. He received a remarkable education. His parents took him abroad for a year when he was only an infant. He was educated by tutors until he was twelve, and then taken abroad for three more years by his parents. His father wanted him to absorb French and German culture. His older brother, William, received the same education.

One way of revising this paragraph would be to restrict its subject matter to the one major topic of James's childhood.

> Henry James, the novelist, had an unusual childhood. In 1844, while still an infant, he was taken abroad by his parents for a year. Upon his return, he and his older brother, William, were given private tutoring until Henry was twelve. At that time both boys were taken abroad to spend three years absorbing French and German culture.

Be careful not to violate the principle of unity by introducing new topics or points of view at the end of a paragraph. Notice in the following example how the last sentence, in which the writer deserts his earlier objectivity and takes sides in the argument, breaks the unity.

In the years following World War II there has been much discussion on the question of lowering the minimum voting age to eighteen. Among those people who believe that the age limit should be lowered, the favorite statement is, "If a boy is old enough to die for his country, he's old enough to vote in it." Those people who want the age limit to remain at twenty-one think eighteen-year-olds will be unduly influenced by local ward-heelers who will urge them to vote a "straight ticket." But the young voter who has not had a chance to become a "dyed-in-the-wool" party member will tend to weigh the merits of the individual candidate rather than those of the party itself.

Revised, the paragraph might read:

In the years following World War II there has been much discussion on the question of lowering the minimum voting age to eighteen. Among those people who believe that the age limit should be lowered, the favorite statement is, "If a boy is old enough to die for his country, he's old enough to vote in it." Those people who want the age limit to remain at twenty-one think eighteen-year-olds will be unduly influenced by the promises of dishonest politicians.

EXERCISE 23. Each of the following paragraphs violates the principle of unity. Point out exactly where each paragraph starts to go wrong.

1.

1. Racial discrimination has existed in the United States for many years. 2. It began when the first white settler decided that the Indians were an inferior breed. 3. It was given impetus by the arrival of the first Negro slaves. 4. A civil war was fought largely because the spokesman of the North, Abraham Lincoln, believed that all men are created equal. 5. Slavery was abolished and the Negro set free by act of Congress.

2.

1. The life of Thomas A. Edison illustrates the truth of the old saying "Genius is ten percent inspiration and ninety percent perspiration." 2. Edison was born in Milan, Ohio, and was expelled from school because his teachers thought he was a moron. 3. So Edison was educated at home by his mother, who helped him build a laboratory in the basement. 4. Edison spent long hours here, sometimes working as long as sixteen hours a day.

223

3.

1. Hardy's *The Return of the Native* is one of the finest novels I have ever read. 2. I was amazed to see how Hardy makes his major and minor episodes culminate in a great climax, and how inextricably he weaves the fortunes of his chief characters with those of his lesser characters. 3. Moreover, his handling of the landscape—gloomy Egdon Heath—is masterful. 4. He makes it a genuine, motivating force in the story. 5. My favorite character, however, was Diggory Venn.

4.

1. Many people who use the word *Fascism* in discussing current world problems confuse it with *Communism*. 2. Both Fascism and Communism are totalitarian, but Fascism is the economic antithesis of Communism. 3. Fascism uses military force to sustain capitalism; Communism uses force to suppress capitalism. 4. Obviously, no two systems of government could be more different. 5. But there has never been a clear explanation of the two systems. 6. The popular mediums of information—newspapers, radio, and movies—refer indiscriminately at times to Communism and Fascism in the same terms.

5.

1. The advantages of modern transportation are many. 2. An enormous amount of time is saved by the great speeds at which vehicles of today travel. 3. Cross-country trips are much more comfortable than they were, and they can be made in days rather than months. 4. For land travel today the automobile, motorcycle, and bus have taken the place of the horse and wagon, stage coach, and mule. 5. The railroad has been developed and extended since the use of the diesel. 6. Sailing ships are now chiefly a hobby and few consider them seriously as a means of transportation.

EXERCISE 24. Each of the following paragraphs fails to adhere to a single idea, the idea that the writer evidently had in mind when he started; each of them introduces extraneous material. For each paragraph, write down the numbers of the sentences that threaten the unity of the paragraph.

1.

1. Exhibition cycling is a sport which was popular in America for a time. 2. In the twenties large crowds attended bicycle races in New York and other large cities. 3. As many as thirty thousand

fans might attend motorbike races or six-day bike races. 4. In the first of these, motorcyclists would pace bicyclists who attempted to keep their front wheels touching or very near bars attached to to ends of motorcycles. 5. The bicyclists would thus receive a "tow" which gave them extra speed. 6. This sport was quite dangerous; several bicyclists were killed or injured in motorbike races. 7. Strangely enough, the most dangerous cycling was found in the sprint races. 8. When one cyclist fell in a sprint race, as many as ten others might collide and fall.

2.

1. It is still too early to tell what effect television will have on publishing. 2. Some analysts of publishing have brought out statistics showing some decreases in total receipts, but blaming television alone for these decreases is not plausible. 3. Some consumption analysts conclude that book and magazine buying may fall off in a family for six months after the purchase of a television set, but that it is likely to be resumed after that time. 4. It seems that just as radio did not interfere with the sale of books and magazines, so television may not ultimately. 5. Television is undoubtedly having its effect on American home life. 6. Now the television set is often the center of the family's recreational life. 7. Instead of going out for a good time they are content to stay at home. 8. Whether what they see is always worth while is of course debatable.

3.

1. If you intend to plant a strawberry bed, there are several things that you should consider. 2. Strawberries do best in a sandy loam or sandy clay that has been enriched with humus. 3. Blueberries and blackberries are better in acid soils. 4. Strawberries should be set out in an area which receives adequate drainage. 5. Too much moisture in the soil will kill them or interfere with their growth. 6. Other kinds of plants do better in marshy soils. 7. On account of frost dangers it is better to plant strawberries on a hillside or on a relatively high level area. 8. The effects of frost are rather peculiar; in general, plants in low-lying areas are more likely to be harmed by frost than those on hills. 9. The growth of young strawberries is actually increased if one pinches off the first runners from the plants.

COHERENCE
IN THE PARAGRAPH = ¶COH

32c **To insure coherence in a paragraph, arrange the sentences in a logical order.**

Arrange all sentences within a paragraph according to some pattern that will make for an orderly, natural flow of ideas. One technique is to list events chronologically. Another is to establish a clear cause-and-effect relationship among the ideas. The following examples show how essential some sort of order is to coherence.

INCOHERENT

The Declaration of Independence was the instrument by which the thirteen colonies declared their independence of Great Britain. It was signed originally by only the president and secretary of the Continental Congress. When the declaration was originally voted on, June 28, 1776, the delegates from Pennsylvania and South Carolina refused to approve it until it carried an amendment. The declaration was written by Thomas Jefferson, who was one of a special committee of five assigned by Congress to draw up a form of declaration. The declaration was finally approved on July 4. The signatures of the delegates were added as their states confirmed the action of Congress.

COHERENT (*Chronological order introduced*)

The Declaration of Independence was the instrument by which the thirteen colonies declared their independence of Great Britain. It was written by Thomas Jefferson, one of a special committee of five assigned by the Continental Congress to draw up a form of declaration. When the declaration was originally brought before Congress on June 28, 1776, the delegates from Pennsylvania and South Carolina refused to approve it until it carried an amendment. That amendment was then written into the declaration, which was finally approved on July 4. Originally, only the president and secretary of the Continental Congress affixed their

226

signatures; the delegates added their signatures as their individual states confirmed the action of Congress.

INCOHERENT

Juvenile delinquency is a major problem in this country. The cause of this problem is World War II. Parents of youngsters born during these years either avoided their responsibility or were unable to maintain it. Everywhere we read about the vicious crimes committed by young people. During the war the newspapers and the movies depicted violence, cruelty, and bloodletting as heroic rather than vicious. The war inspired brutality by distorting and twisting humane values. It is no wonder that the younger generation has made a problem of itself. During the war many of them had fathers who were in the service; their mothers were working in war plants. Consquently, they were unhappy and undisciplined. Many of them are organized in gangs and proud of their devotion to a life of crime.

COHERENT (*Clear cause-and-effect relationship introduced*)

Juvenile delinquency is a major problem in this country. Everywhere we read and hear about the vicious crimes committed by younger people. Many of them are organized in gangs and are proud of their devotion to a life of crime. Certainly this unfortunate situation has its roots in the years of World War II. For one thing, the war itself inspired brutality in the young generation by distorting and twisting humane values. The newspapers and the movies depicted violence, cruelty, and bloodletting as heroic rather than vicious. For another, parents of youngsters born during the war either avoided their responsibilities or were unable to exercise them. Many fathers were in the service; mothers were often busy working in war plants. The result was an unhappy, undisciplined group of young people. It was no wonder they soon made a problem of themselves.

EXERCISE 25. Write a coherent paragraph that incorporates, in your own words, all the following information about Eugene Field.

1. He was a reporter on the St. Louis *Evening Journal* at the age of 23.
2. He died in Chicago in 1895.
3. All his life was devoted to journalism.
4. He was born in St. Louis in September, 1850.
5. He collaborated with his brother, Roswell, in *Echoes from a Sabine Farm*, 1893.

6. He wrote literary columns for the Denver *Tribune* and the Chicago *Daily News*.

7. He wrote a great deal of journalistic verse.

EXERCISE 26. Write a coherent paragraph that incorporates all the following information about Robert La Follette. Begin your paragraph with the topic sentence "Robert La Follette truly deserved the epithet 'Fighting Bob.'"

1. When he was twenty-five he ran for district attorney of Madison County, Wisconsin, as a Republican but against the organized Republicans. He was elected.

2. After serving one term as district attorney he ran for Congress and was elected.

3. While a student at the University of Wisconsin he became known as a debater, once winning an interstate contest.

4. In 1924 he ran for president and, though defeated, received 4½ million votes.

5. After serving three terms as Governor of Wisconsin, he was elected to the United States Senate, where he became known as a spokesman for small businessmen and farmers.

6. After graduation from college, he worked in a law office.

7. After serving one term as a Representative, he was elected Governor of Wisconsin, a position he used to help initiate laws of direct primary, referendum, and recall.

8. During the years just preceding the United States entry into World War I, La Follette set himself against the proposed neutrality legislation of Woodrow Wilson, arguing vehemently that such legislation would help get the United States into war.

EXERCISE 27. Because of poor sentence arrangement the following paragraphs lack coherence. Rearrange each group of sentences to form a coherent paragraph.

1.

1. Once upon a time, before 1920, the whole American League hoped that by some freak of fortune the weak New York Yankees might be able to win a pennant. 2. The mighty Red Sox and Athletics, often tail-enders after 1920, were riding high. 3. Things move in cycles in sports, and a weak team five years ago may be a champion now. 4. So let's not lose interest in the home team; they may be up there again soon. 5. Even the Browns, the last

team to play in a World's Series, were very strong in 1922 and finally won the pennant in 1942. 6. The standings are never the same two years straight, and second-division teams of last year often are strong contenders this year. 7. During the last eighteen years Detroit teams have ended up in all eight positions.

2.

1. There were various reasons for the popularity of canasta. 2. It could be played by different numbers of players. 3. Bridge, of course, required no more and no less than four. 4. Many people naturally continued to like bridge. 5. Some players found canasta more dramatic than bridge. 6. They liked the appeal of the different combinations of cards. 7. Canasta became popular about 1950. 8. Many card players liked the freedom of personal choice and independence from a partner's decisions.

3.

1. After World War II our leaders had various problems in framing our foreign policy. 2. Few experts could be sure of the policy of the U.S.S.R. 3. The strength and the determination of our proven allies were questionable. 4. Seemingly no one anticipated developments in Indo-China and Korea. 5. The attitudes of the defeated Germans, Italians, and Japanese were uncertain. 6. Whether the war-time cooperation with the Russians could be continued, no one knew. 7. The attitude of India and Pakistan on future developments was hard to determine.

32d **To insure coherence in a paragraph, make clear the relationships among sentences.**

You can achieve clear relationships among sentences: (1) by *being consistent in point of view;* (2) by *using parallel grammatical structure;* (3) by *repeating words or ideas;* (4) by *using transitional words or phrases.*

(1) *Maintain a consistent point of view.* Avoid unnecessary shifts in person, tense, or number within a paragraph.

UNNECESSARY SHIFT IN PERSON

A pleasant and quiet place to live is essential for a serious-minded college student. If possible, you should rent a room from a landlady with a reputation for keeping order and discipline among her renters. Moreover, a student ought to pick a roommate with the same temperament as his own. Then you can agree to and keep a schedule of study hours.

UNNECESSARY SHIFT IN TENSE

Last summer I finally saw the movie *Around the World in 80 Days,* based on the novel by Jules Verne. I particularly enjoyed the main character, who is played by David Niven. He gives an excellent performance and really seemed intent on winning the wager he has made with his friends. His personal servant was played by the Mexican actor Cantinflas, who is very able in his part, too.

UNNECESSARY SHIFT IN NUMBER

Of great currency at the moment is the notion that education should prepare students for "life." A college graduate no longer goes out into the world as a cultivated gentleman. Instead students feel obliged to prepare themselves for places in the business world. Consequently, we are establishing courses on how to get and keep a mate, how to budget an income, and how to win friends and influence people—that is, how to sell yourself and your product. The study of things not obviously practical to a businessman is coming to be looked upon as unnecessary.

(2) *Use parallel grammatical structure.* Another effective method of connecting sentences is to cast them in parallel grammatical form, as in the following paragraph. Parallelism gives symmetry and balance to your paragraphs.

> Concerning the world and all that is in it man has had many strange opinions, but none more strange than those about himself. From time to time he has been thought the victim of chance or of fate, the sport of gods or of demons, the nursling of divinity or of nature, the "rubbish of an Adam" or evolution's last and fairest animal. He has spun mythical genealogies and embroidered those that were actual. He has mourned lost Edens, golden ages, states of nature; and with equal conviction he has awaited new heavens, new paradises, and new perfections. He has explored the cosmos, and he has mastered the atom. He has seemed to know everything except himself.
>
> —BARROWS DUNHAM, *Man Against Myth*

(3) *Repeat key words and phrases.* This technique emphasizes the major ideas and carries the thought from sentence to sentence. In the following paragraphs the words and phrases repeated for this purpose are italicized.

In discussing the pre-Civil War South, it *should be remembered* that the large plantation owners comprised only a small part of the *total Southern population.* By far the greater part of *that population* was made up of *small farmers,* and of course the Negro slaves themselves. Some *small farmers* had acquired substantial acreage, owned three or four slaves, and were relatively prosperous. But most of the *small farmers* were terribly poor. They rented their land and worked it themselves, sometimes side by side with the slaves of the great *landowners.* In everything but *social position* they were worse off than the Negro slaves. But *it must also be remembered* that they were as jealous of that superior *social position* as the wealthy *landowner* himself.

—Student paragraph

Because they [the colonists] had first of all to survive, they took life with deadly *seriousness.* And in their *seriousness* they were able to record memorably life and living as they knew it. When their writing has distinguished *style,* as it often does, it is *style* which serves a higher purpose than itself; it is *style* which expresses the very *seriousness* of the colonial enterprise. Indeed, when one studies *stylistically* the best of colonial writing, one is studying the *quality* of colonial *seriousness.* The very forms of expression—sermons, histories, diaries, poems, and the like—themselves characterize the men who write, the society to which they write, and the occasion for writing. The difference between the writing of a Mather and of a Byrd, between that of a Sewall and of a Woolman, is in the *style and form* as well as the content. One can see not only what each believes in, but the *quality* of the belief. Theirs is the *style and form* which develop when an idea or an attitude is *seriously put* into action.

—ROY HARVEY PEARCE, *Colonial American Writing*

It is true that *protestantism* spread widely among tradesmen who recognized in it a philosophy which was generally good for business. *Protestantism* was, in part, a *protest* against a large power interfering in *private rights.* Too, it made a virtue of productive labor. The middle classes found in it a warrant for working hard for *private* gains, unhampered by restrictions by outside authority. But even Luther and Calvin recognized the concept of a *fair price.* They believed that it wasn't *fair* to take advantage of a *shortage* of goods, much worse to artificially create such a *shortage.* It wasn't *fair* to exploit ignorance or need. They expected tradesmen to accept only a *fair* return on their risk or on their labor. However these teachings were increasingly disregarded as the element of economic freedom in *protestantism* be-

231

came more pronounced; the notion of a *fair price* limited *private rights,* and if a man said he made a *fair* profit it was likely he was referring not to its justice but to its size.

—Student paragraph

(4) *Use transitional words or phrases.* Here are some suggestions for effective transitions:

TO INDICATE ADDITION
again, also, and, and then, besides, equally important, first, finally, further, furthermore, in addition, last, lastly, likewise, moreover, next, second, secondly, third, thirdly, too

TO INDICATE CONTRAST
and yet, after all, at the same time, although true, but, for all that, however, in contrast, nevertheless, notwithstanding, on the contrary, on the other hand, still, yet, in spite of

TO INDICATE COMPARISON
likewise, in a like manner, similarly

TO INDICATE SUMMARY
in brief, in short, on the whole, to sum up, to summarize, in conclusion, to conclude

TO INDICATE SPECIAL FEATURES OR EXAMPLES
for example, for instance, indeed, incidentally, in fact, in other words, that is, specifically, in particular

TO INDICATE RESULT
accordingly, consequently, hence, therefore, thus, truly, as a result, then, in short

TO INDICATE THE PASSAGE OF TIME
afterwards, at length, immediately, in the meantime, meanwhile, soon, at last, after a short time, while, thereupon, thereafter, temporarily, until, presently, shortly, lately, of late, since

TO INDICATE CONCESSION
at the same time, of course, after all, naturally, I admit, although this may be true

Transitional words and phrases are italicized in the following paragraph.

> *As I have remarked,* the pilots' association was now the compactest monopoly in the world, perhaps, and seemed simply in-

destructible. *And yet* the days of its glory were numbered. *First,* the new railroad, stretching up through Mississippi, Tennessee, and Kentucky, to Northern railway-centers, began to divert the passenger travel from the steamboats; *next* the war came and almost entirely annihilated the steamboating industry during several years, leaving most of the pilots idle and the cost of living advancing all the time; *then* the treasurer of the St. Louis association put his hand into the till and walked off with every dollar of the ample fund; *and finally, the railroads intruding everywhere,* there was little for steamers to do, when the war was over, but carry freights; *so straightway* some genius from the Atlantic coast introduced the plan of towing a dozen steamer cargoes down to New Orleans at the tail of a vulgar little tugboat; *and behold,* in the twinkling of an eye, *as it were,* the association and the noble science of piloting were things of the dead and pathetic past!

—MARK TWAIN, *Life on the Mississippi*

EXERCISE 28. Make a coherent paragraph of the following statements. First, put them in logical order. Second, give them a consistent point of view and link them smoothly with transitional words or phrases. Revise the wording of the statements if necessary, but use all the information given.

1. This attitude shows a naïve faith in the competency of secretaries.
2. Practicing engineers and scientists say they spend half their time writing letters and reports.
3. Many of us foolishly object to taking courses in writing.
4. College students going into business think their secretaries will do their writing for them.
5. A student going into the technical or scientific fields may think that writing is something he seldom has to do.
6. Young businessmen seldom have private secretaries.
7. Our notion that only poets, novelists, and newspaper workers have to know how to write is unrealistic.
8. Other things being equal, a man in any field who can express himself effectively is sure to succeed more rapidly than a man whose command of language is poor.

EXERCISE 29. Using the topic sentence "English is rapidly assuming the character of an 'international language,'" arrange the following statements into a coherent paragraph with a logical order, a consistent point of view, and smooth transitions.

1. It is estimated that well over 500 million people use English as a native or secondary language.

2. The inventions that make communication possible—radio, telephone, telegraph, the motion picture—are largely controlled by English-speaking peoples.

3. English has replaced French as the language of diplomacy.

4. Various corrupt forms of English, like Pidgin English, are widely spoken in the Pacific area.

5. English is made up largely of words from both Teutonic and Romance languages; a good part of its vocabulary is already familiar to those who speak a European language.

6. The 400 million who speak Chinese are separated in innumerable and mutually unintelligible dialectal groups.

EXERCISE 30. Arrange the following statements into a coherent paragraph.

1. Gene Wright, a neighbor of mine, complains to me daily of the corruption and inefficiency of the city officials.

2. The "independent" voter too often shows his independence by not voting at all.

3. One great problem is getting the American people to exercise their voting privilege.

4. It is estimated that less than 70 per cent of the eligible voters go to the polls on election days.

5. Gene Wright did not vote in the last two city elections because he forgot to register.

6. Many people refuse to vote because they say their single votes will make little difference in the outcome of the election.

7. The organized political parties make a point of getting "straight-ticket" voters to the polls.

8. Democracy will work only when all the people accept the responsibilities their liberties give them.

EXERCISE 31. The following paragraphs and paragraph parts are marred and made incoherent by shifts in person, tense, and number. Rewrite the paragraphs to insure consistency and coherence throughout.

1. Every time a nation is involved in a war it must face problems about its ex-soldiers after that war. The veteran is entitled to some special considerations from society, but treating them with complete fairness is a baffling problem. Livy reports that

234

grants to the former soldier caused some troubles in the early history of Rome. There were many disagreements between them and the early Roman senators.

2. Preparing a surface for new paint is as important a step in the whole process as the application of paint itself. First, be sure that the surface is quite clean. You should wash any grease or grime from the woodwork. The painter may use turpentine or a detergent for this. One must be careful to clean off whatever cleanser they have used. Then sand off any rough or chipped paint.

3. One of the books I read in high school English was Dickens' *Tale of Two Cities*. In it the author tells of some of the horrors of the French Revolution. He spent several pages telling about how the French aristocrats suffered. The climax part of the book tells how a ne'er-do-well who had failed in life sacrifices himself for another. He took his place in a prison and went stoically to the guillotine for him.

PARAGRAPH DEVELOPMENT = ¶DEV

32e Construct every paragraph around a topic sentence.

Once you have set forth the point of a paragraph in the topic sentence, you must then give reasons to support it or examples or details to clarify it. Failure to develop every paragraph around a clear-cut topic sentence will give you only a series of short, choppy paragraph fragments.

(1) *Lack of reasons to support topic sentences.*

The president should be elected for an eight-year term. In a four-year term the president cannot establish a smooth-running administration. He has to spend much of his time being a politician rather than being an executive.

Representatives should also be elected for longer terms. Under the present situation, they no more than get elected when they have to begin preparations for the next election.

(2) *Lack of examples and details to clarify topic sentences.*

> English is made up of many words taken from early Church Latin. These words probably came into the language shortly after the Christianization of the British Isles in the seventh century. One such word is *altar;* another is *temple.*
>
> It was the Norman Conquest, beginning in 1066, that had the greatest effect, however, on English. According to one authority about ten thousand French words came into the English language, about three-fourths of which still remain in the language.

32f Avoid excessively long and excessively short paragraphs.

The length of a paragraph is determined by the nature of the subject, the type of topic sentence, the intention of the writer, and the character of the audience. Ultimately, the length of a paragraph is a matter that you must determine for yourself. In general, however, avoid paragraphs that contain less than four or more than eight sentences. Too short a paragraph may mean that you are not developing your topic sentence adequately. Too long a paragraph may mean that you are permitting excessive detail to obscure your central aim.

Excessively long paragraphs may be revised either by a rigorous pruning of details or by division into two or more paragraphs. Insufficiently developed paragraphs usually show lack of attention to detail and an imperfect command of the full idea of the paragraph. The paragraphs below, for example, are all insufficiently developed. The arguments are undirected, and the generalizations are inadequately supported by reasons, examples, and details. Simply stitching these fragments together would not produce a coherent, unified statement; instead, the entire statement would have to be thought through again and then rewritten.

> I am in favor of lowering the minimum voting age to eighteen. I think the average eighteen-year-old has more good judgment to put to use at the polls than the average middle-aged person.
>
> Among the members of the two major parties there is too much straight-ticket voting. I think the candidate himself and not his party should be voted on. The young voter would weigh the virtues of the candidate and not his party.
>
> It is unlikely that the young voter would be influenced by

corrupt politicians. The majority of eighteen-year-olds are high school graduates and would surely have learned enough about current affairs to use good judgment.

If the question of lowering the voting age were put to a nation-wide vote, I am sure it would pass.

In conclusion I say give young Americans a chance. I am sure they will make good.

EXERCISE 32. Group the following sentences into two or three paragraphs. You need not rewrite the sentences, even though they may need revision.

Frederick Winslow Taylor was born in 1856. His mother was a cultured Easterner. She took the family abroad for three years. Fred's father was a lawyer. While at Exeter Fred was a star baseball player and head of his class. Fred began work as a machinist. He liked the men he worked with. He was short, heavily built, and sharp tongued. When he became a foreman he forgot about his working pals. He thought up new ways of doing things. The idea of producing things efficiently went to his head. He divided up jobs. When he was thirty-four, he married. In six years he became chief engineer. Then he went to work for Bethlehem steel. This job did not last long. He began to play golf and entertain. He lectured on production techniques at various colleges. The reason he lost his job was that he was more interested in production than in profit. He died in 1915 of pneumonia. He was one of the first efficiency experts.

EXERCISE 33. Choose two of the following topic sentences and develop each into a meaningful paragraph by supporting it with reasons or examples.

1. There are three great advantages to airplane travel—speed, comfort, thrills.
2. Driving an automobile in big-city traffic requires a nice co-ordination of nerve and skill.
3. The first day of college is a nerve-shattering experience.
4. Making homemade furniture is less difficult than it appears.
5. Our national parks provide excellent and inexpensive camping sites.
6. Keeping a detailed budget is more trouble than it's worth.
7. The greatness of Abraham Lincoln was not in his efficiency as an administrator but in the nobility of his character.

8. Most doctors look upon alcoholism as a disease, not as a mark of immorality.

9. The modern engineer has to be a businessman as well as a technician.

10. A good hitter is far more valuable to a baseball team than a good fielder.

EXERCISE 34. Rewrite the following material as one or two paragraphs, combining relevant ideas and eliminating irrelevant ones.

The word *modern* has many meanings. It may mean something new-fashioned or something characteristic of present or recent times, as modern painting, modern automobiles, or modern poetry.

To be *modern* means something pleasant, hard to understand, or something my grandmother never seemed to be.

A modern painting is a very unrealistic painting of something very realistic. It is unrealistic in the sense that the painter is trying to give you his interpretation of his impression of the object rather than a picture of the object itself. This is sometimes very exciting, but often hard to understand.

To many people, particularly middle-aged and ancient adults, *modern* is a word of condemnation. These people usually speak longingly of "the good old days" and anything modern is a "contraption," a device to make young people either sinful or lazy.

But to young people in general *modern* is a word of high praise. They use it to refer to things and ideas which are up-to-date, clever, speedy.

But I have little doubt that within twenty or thirty years these young people-grown-old will be using the word just as their parents and grandparents use it now—as a word of condemnation.

32g **Choose a method of paragraph development suitable to the subject matter and to your own intent.**

Every paragraph has its own problems of structure, and every writer has his own solutions. But most well-wrought paragraphs depend on one of the following organizational principles or on some slight variation of it: (1) *chronological,* (2) *spatial,* or (3) *logical.*

(1) *Use chronological order to describe events or processes in the sequence of time in which they took place or should take place.*

The opening paragraph of Jonathan Swift's *Gulliver's Travels* is a classic illustration of the chronological method of narrating events, and Benjamin Franklin's famous instructions for making a kite are a classic illustration of the chronological method of describing how something is done.

(a) My father had a small estate in Nottinghamshire; I was the third of five sons. He sent me to Emanuel College in Cambridge at fourteen years old, where I resided three years, and applied myself close to my studies: but the charge of maintaining me (although I had a very scanty allowance) being too great for a narrow fortune, I was bound apprentice to Mr. James Bates, an eminent surgeon in London, with whom I continued four years; and my father now and then sending me small sums of money, I laid them out in learning navigation, and other parts of the mathematics, useful to those who intend to travel, as I always believed it would be some time or other my fortune to do. When I left Mr. Bates, I went down to my father; where, by the assistance of him and my uncle John, and some other relatives, I got forty pounds, and a promise of thirty pounds a year to maintain me at Leyden: there I studied physic two years and seven months, knowing it would be useful in long voyages.

—JONATHAN SWIFT, *Gulliver's Travels* (1726)

(b) Make a small cross of two light strips of cedar, the arms so long as to reach to the four corners of a large thin silk handkerchief when extended; tie the corners of the handkerchief to the extremities of the cross, so you have the body of a kite; which being properly accommodated with a tail, loop, and string, will rise in the air, like those made of paper; but this being of silk, is fitter to bear the wet and wind of a thunder-gust without tearing. To the top of the upright stick of the cross is to be fixed a very sharp-pointed wire, rising a foot or more above the wood. To the end of the twine, next the hand, is to be tied a silk ribbon, and where the silk and twine join, a key may be fastened. This kite is to be raised when a thunder-gust appears to be coming on, and the person who holds the string must stand within a door or window or under some cover, so that the silk ribbon may not be wet; and care must be taken that the twine does not touch the frame of the door or window. As soon as any of the thunder-clouds come over the kite, the pointed wire will draw the electric fire from them, and the kite, with all the twine, will be electrified, and the loose filaments of the twine will stand out every way, and

239

be attracted by an approaching finger. And when the rain has wet the kite and twine, so that it can conduct the electric fire freely, you will find it stream out plentifully from the key on the approach of your knuckle. At this key the phial may be charged; and from electric fire thus obtained, spirits may be kindled, and all the other electric experiments be performed, which are usually done by the help of a rubbed glass globe or tube, and thereby the sameness of the electric matter with that of lightning completely demonstrated.

—BENJAMIN FRANKLIN, Letter to Peter Collinson (1752)

(2) *Use spatial order to describe physical relationships among persons, places, or things.* Spatial order is well suited to stating such relationships as east to west, north to south, small to big, up to down, center to circumference, here to there, and so on. The author of the selection below, which gives an elementary but clear guide to a map of the British Isles, follows an east-to-west organization.

On the east, England is bounded by the North Sea, which is really nothing but an old depression which has gradually run full of water. Again a single glimpse at the map will tell you more than a thousand words. There on the right (the east) is France. Then we get something that looks like a trench across a road, the British Channel and the North Sea. Then the great central plain of England with London in the deepest hollow. Then the high mountains of Wales. Another depression, the Irish Sea, the great central Irish plain, the hills of Ireland, a few lonely rocks further toward the west, rearing their tops above the shallow sea. Finally the rock at St. Kilda (uninhabited since a year ago as it was too hard to reach) and then suddenly down we go, down, down, down, for there the real ocean begins and the last of the vast European and Asiatic continent, both submerged and semi-submerged, here comes to an end.

—HENDRIK WILLEM VAN LOON, *Van Loon's Geography*

(3) *Use logical order to present reasons or arguments in support of the topic sentence.* How the sentences within a paragraph are related to one another depends on the nature of your topic sentence and your intent. Many "logical orders" are possible, but more often than not a logical paragraph develops in one of these ways:

(a) *Definition.* The logic of a paragraph often depends on careful definitions of key objects or terms.

240

1. Another marvelous but sinister invention of science is the lie detector. It does not literally detect lies; it detects emotional changes, such as a catch in the breath, and changes in the blood pressure and heartbeat when making the little effort required to sustain a falsehood. The subject sits, with a cuff round his arm to record blood pressure and pulse rate, a tube round his chest for rate of respiration, and electrodes on his left hand for electrodermal response (or psychogalvanic reflex). He is required to answer a list of questions, beginning with innocuous ones, the nasty one bearing on "who dunnit?" being slipped in later. The same list of questions is given three times over, and a twitch in the various records is not considered significant unless it occurs at the same place all three times. It is not easy to fool the machine, but neither is it entirely foolproof. In any case the results have to be interpreted by a specialist, and a specialist is very uncomfortable to have against you in a law court, because you cannot meet him on his own ground. Lie detectors have been admitted in court many times, when both parties agreed to their use. If either party objects, the evidence obtained from them would probably be ruled inadmissible, but the legal status is not entirely cleared up. Some of the scientists engaged in these matters (but not all) consider the lawyers a bunch of slowpokes for not rushing to accept the wonderful findings of science. Thus, for the immunity from compulsory lie detecting which we enjoy at present, we can thank lawyers rather than scientists.

—ANTHONY STANDEN, *Science Is a Sacred Cow*

2. I ought first of all to explain that when I use the term history I mean knowledge of history. No doubt throughout all past time there actually occurred a series of events which, whether we know what it was or not, constitutes history in some ultimate sense. Nevertheless, much the greater part of these events we can know nothing about, not even that they occurred; many of them we can know only imperfectly; and even the few events that we think we know for sure we can never be absolutely certain of, since we can never revive them, never observe or test them directly. The event itself once occurred, but as an actual event it has disappeared; so that in dealing with it the only objective reality we can observe or test is some material trace which the event has left—usually a written document. With these traces of vanished events, these documents, we must be content since they are all we have; from them we infer what the event was, we affirm that it is a fact that the event was so and so. We do not say "Lincoln is assassinated"; we say "it is a fact that Lincoln

was assassinated." The event *was,* but is no longer; it is only the affirmed fact about the event that *is,* that persists, and will persist until we discover that our affirmation is wrong or inadequate. Let us then admit that there are two histories: the actual series of events that once occurred; and the ideal series that we affirm and hold in memory. The first is absolute and unchanged—it was what it was whatever we do or say about it; the second is relative, always changing in response to the increase or refinement of knowledge. The two series correspond more or less; it is our aim to make the correspondence as exact as possible; but the actual series of events exists for us only in terms of the ideal series which we affirm and hold in memory. This is why I am forced to identify history with knowledge of history. For all practical purposes history is, for us and for the time being, what we know it to be.

—CARL BECKER, "History," from *The American Historical Review* (1932)

(b) *Comparison or contrast, direct or implied.* The logic of a paragraph sometimes resides in a careful statement of the similarities or differences between two or more ideas or things.

1. Speech and language have contrasting advantages and disadvantages. Speech can be changed, even while being uttered, to fit the mood, audience, and occasion; language cannot be so changed, for once printed, it is unchangeable and cannot even be brought up to date without the necessity of a revised edition. Audible speech is augmented by its own possibilities of variation in pitch (intonation), force, volume, and intensity, and by the simultaneous aid of the visible facial, gestural, and postural code; language has none of these aids when read silently, and it is at the mercy of the voice and pantomime of the reader when read aloud. Speech stands or falls on its single momentary utterance—unless, perhaps, the speaker repeats what he has just said, or expounds it—and the hearer cannot stop to think upon a statement, for fear of losing the next statement; language may be read and reread, pondered upon, and discussed at any point, without danger of losing what follows on the next page.

—C. M. WISE *et al., Foundations of Speech*

2. Eventually the whales, as though to divide the sea's food resources among them, became separated into three groups: the plankton-eaters, the fish-eaters, and the squid-eaters. The plankton-eating whales can exist only where there are dense masses of small shrimp or copepods to supply their enormous food require-

ments. This limits them, except for scattered areas, to arctic and antarctic waters and the high temperate latitudes. Fish-eating whales may find food over a somewhat wider range of ocean, but they are restricted to places where there are enormous populations of schooling fish. The blue water of the tropics and of the open ocean basin offers little to either of these groups. But that immense, square-headed, formidable toothed whale known as the cachalot or sperm whale discovered long ago what men have known for only a short time—that hundreds of fathoms below the almost untenanted surface waters of these regions there is an abundant animal life. The sperm whale has taken these deep waters for his hunting grounds; his quarry is the deep-water population of squids, including the giant squid Architeuthis, which lives pelagically at depths of 1500 feet or more. The head of the sperm whale is often marked with long stripes, which consist of a great number of circular scars made by the suckers of the squid. From this evidence we can imagine the battles that go on, in the darkness of deep water, between these two huge creatures—the sperm whale with its 70-ton bulk, the squid with a body as long as 30 feet, and writhing, grasping arms extending the total length of the animal to perhaps 50 feet.

—RACHEL L. CARSON, *The Sea Around Us*

3. In his own person, man represents every aspect of the cosmos. Reduced to his lowest terms, he is a lump of carbon and a puddle of water mixed with a handful of equally common metals, minerals, and gases. But man is likewise a unit of organic life; he is a member of the animal world, and of a special order of the animal world, the vertebrates, with capacity for free movements, for selective intercourse with the environment, for specially canalized responses through a highly developed nervous system. Still further, man belongs to the family of warm-blooded animals, the mammals, whose females give milk to their young and so form a close and tender partnership, often fiercely protective, for the nurture of their offspring; and through his own internal development, his whole life is suffused with emotions and erotic responses which have persisted, like so many other traits of domestication—the cow's milk or the hen's eggs—in exaggerated form. Starting as an animal among the animals, man has stretched and intensified certain special organic capacities in order to develop more fully what is specifically human. In a fashion that has no rivals in other species he thinks: he plays: he loves: he dreams.

—LEWIS MUMFORD, *The Conduct of Life*

(c) *Examples or details.* The logical development of a paragraph sometimes demands carefully marshaled examples or details to support the topic sentence.

1. Lack of variety has often been urged in criticism of American place-names. Certain it is that not only do the European names *Berlin, Cambridge, Belmont, Burlington,* and their kind, appear in endless repetition, but words more distinctively American lose their distinctiveness through constant iteration. Not only do *Washingtons* and *Franklins* and *Jacksons* appear in wearisome numbers, but a name such as *Brooklyn* (a modification of Dutch *Breukelen*) is worn out by adoption in 21 states outside New York. The effectiveness of *Buffalo,* admirably American in quality, is spoiled by its application including compounds, in about 75 different places. Compounds with *Elk-, Bald-, Maple-, Beech-, Oak-, Red-,* and the like are open to similar objection. In many instances inventive power seems to have been entirely lacking. *Disputanta* is said to owe its name to lack of agreement on a name, and in a number of instances settlements have been named like streets by the use of numerals, as in the case of *Seven* (Tennessee), *Fourteen* (West Virginia), *Seventeen* (Ohio), *Seventy-six* (Kentucky and Maryland), *Ninety-six* (South Carolina).

—G. H. MC KNIGHT, *English Words and Their Background*

2. The pyramids were built with sheer muscle-power. Holes were bored in stone in the quarries of the Mokattam Mountains, wooden sticks were driven into them, and these, swelling when soaked with water, cracked apart the rock. On sledges and rollers the resulting blocks were dragged to the site. The pyramids rose layer by layer. Candidates for a doctorate in archaeology write theses on the question of whether one construction plan was used or several. Lepsius and Petrie occupy diametrically opposed positions on this controversy, but modern archaeology inclines to support the Lepsian point of view. Apparently there were several plans of construction, drastic changes being necessitated by suddenly conceived additions. The Egyptians, forty-seven hundred years ago, worked with such precision that mistakes in the lengths and angles of the great pyramids can, as Petrie says, "be covered with one's thumb." They fitted the stone blocks so neatly that "neither needle nor hair" can, to this day, be inserted at the joints. The Arab writer, Abd al Latif, remarked on this in wonder eight hundred years ago. Critics point out that the old Egyptian master builders misjudged their stresses and strains, as for example, when they made five hollow spaces over the burial-

chamber ceiling to reduce the downward pressure, when one would have sufficed. But these fault-finders forget, in our own day of electronically analyzed T-beams, that it was not so long ago that we used to build with a safety factor of five, eight, or even twelve.

—C. W. CERAM, *Gods, Graves, and Scholars*

3. The motor car is, more than any other object, the expression of the nation's character and the nation's dream. In the free billowing fender, in the blinding chromium grilles, in the fluid control, in the ever-widening front seat, we see the flowering of the America that we know. It is of some interest to scholars and historians that the same autumn which saw the abandonment of the window crank and the adoption of the push button (removing the motorist's last necessity for physical exertion) saw also the registration of sixteen million young men of fighting age and symphonic styling. It is of deep interest to me that in the same week Japan joined the Axis, DeSoto moved its clutch pedal two inches to the left—and that the announcements caused equal flurries among the people.

—E. B. WHITE, *One Man's Meat*

(d) *Explanation of causes or effects.* The logical development of a paragraph sometimes calls for a statement of the forces that produce a situation or the results produced by one.

1. Lake Erie, the last of the Great Lakes to be discovered, was the first to take form. In pre-glacial ages a mighty river flowed eastward through what is now the Lake Erie basin. When the ice sheet formed and moved south, it rammed one lobe along the axis of this stream. It gouged heavily into the soft Devonian shales to the east, and it carved deep grooves in the hard, resistant Devonian limestone at Sandusky Bay to the west. These grooves are conspicuous on the islands, especially on Kelleys Island, where one exposed section of this glacial sculpture has been made into a state park. The southwestern lobe of its basin, where the white pioneers found the Black Swamp, was first uncovered when the last of the ice sheets, known as the Wisconsin, began to melt back from the corner of present Ohio, Indiana and Michigan. The sun had beat upon the advancing front of this ice sheet, melting it down and releasing from its frozen grip the billions of tons of rock and gravel which were left piled up in terminal moraines 500 feet deep in places. The water filled in between the moraine and the receding ice sheet and discharged out

of the Maumee lobe down the Wabash River. And when the water was extensive enough to be called a lake, Lake Erie had begun its metamorphosis to its present shore lines.

—HARLAN HATCHER, *Lake Erie*

2. The fading of ideals is sad evidence of the defeat of human endeavour. In the schools of antiquity philosophers aspired to impart wisdom, in modern colleges our humbler aim is to teach subjects. The drop from the divine wisdom, which was the goal of the ancients, to text-book knowledge of subjects, which is achieved by the moderns, marks an educational failure, sustained through the ages. I am not maintaining that in the practice of education the ancients were more successful than ourselves. You have only to read Lucian, and to note his satiric dramatizations of the pretentious claims of philosophers, to see that in this respect the ancients can boast over us no superiority. My point is that, at the dawn of our European civilisation, men started with the full ideas which should inspire education, and that gradually our ideals have sunk to square with our practice.

—A. N. WHITEHEAD, *The Aims of Education*

(e) *Elimination of alternatives.* The logical development of a paragraph sometimes requires that the central proposition be validated by the elimination of alternative propositions.

1. If the Moon had been separated from the Earth at a time when the latter was still completely molten, the liquid would have immediately covered the site of the rupture, and no more trace would have been left on the body of our planet than there is on the surface of a well from which a bucketful of water has been taken. But if at the time of rupture the Earth was already covered with solid crust, the newborn satellite must have carried away a large section of this rocky crust, leaving a clearly visible scar. A glance at the map of the Earth's surface discloses such a scar in the deep basin of the Pacific Ocean, which now covers about one-third of the total surface of the Earth. It would, of course, be rather unwise to draw such a far-reaching conclusion merely from the vast area and roughly circular form of the Pacific, but geologists have discovered an additional fact that lends strong support to the hypothesis that the Pacific basin is really the "hole" left in the Earth's crust by the separation of its satellites. We have already mentioned that the upper crust of the Earth is a layer of granite from 50 to 100 kilometres thick resting on a much thicker layer of heavier basalt. This is true of all the con-

tinents and also of parts of the Earth's crust that are submerged beneath the waters of the Atlantic, Indian, and Arctic oceans where, however, the granite layer is considerably thinner. But the vast expanse of the Pacific is a striking exception—*not a single piece of granite has ever been found on any of the numerous islands scattered through that ocean.* There is hardly any doubt that *the floor of the Pacific is formed exclusively of basaltic rocks, as if some cosmic hand had removed the entire granite layer from all this vast area.* Besides, in contrast to the other oceans, the basin of the Pacific is surrounded by a ring of high mountain chains (Cordilleras, Kamchatka, the islands of Japan, and New Zealand) of pronounced volcanic activity, known as the "ring of fire." This indicates that this roughly circular border line is much more closely connected with the structure of the entire crust than the shore lines of other oceans. It is therefore, quite likely that the area now occupied by the Pacific is the very place where the huge bulk of matter now forming the Moon was torn away from the Earth.

—GEORGE GAMOW, *Biography of the Earth*

2. It is customary to regard the course of history as a great river, with its source in some small rivulet of the distant past, taking its rise on the plains of Asia, and flowing slowly down through the ages, gathering water from new tributaries on the way, until finally in our own days it broadens majestically over the whole world. Men have even personified this flow, made of it a being that develops of its own volition, following its own laws to the achievement of some preconceived goal. They have spoken of the "dialectic of ideas," and regarded men and whole civilizations as the passive instruments employed by this great Being in the working-out of its purposes. The observer not already committed to faith in such an interpretation finds it difficult to discern any such steady sweep in the course of human events, and above all he feels that to look upon humanity as a passive tool to which things are done and with which ends are accomplished, is a falsification of the cardinal fact that it is men who have made history and not history which has made men. Men have built up civilization, men have patiently and laboriously found out every way of doing things and toilingly worked out every idea that is to-day a part of our heritage from the past—men working at every turn, to be sure, under the influences of their environment and with the materials at hand, individual men and races and not even some such being as "humanity." The complex of beliefs and ideals by which the modern world lives and with which it works

247

is not a gift from the gods, as ancient myth had it, but an achievement of a long succession of generations.

—J. H. RANDALL, *The Making of the Modern Mind*

CONSISTENCY
IN THE PARAGRAPH = ¶CON

32h Maintain a consistent tone in developing each paragraph.

When we read effective writers we are often struck by the fact that what seems to hold their sentences together is not merely their adherence to an organizational principle but also an atmosphere of wit or mellowness or serious authority that unites everything they say into a consistent whole. In your own writing, try to maintain a consistent tone throughout each paragraph. A jarring shift of tone may ruin the effect of a paragraph even though your writing meets all the tests of unity, coherence, and adequate development. Notice the consistency of tone in the following examples.

1. What men, in their egoism, constantly mistake for a deficiency of intelligence in woman is merely an incapacity for mastering that mass of small intellectual tricks, that complex of petty knowledges, that collection of cerebral rubber-stamps, which constitute the chief mental equipment of the average male. A man thinks that he is more intelligent than his wife because he can add up a column of figures more accurately, or because he is able to distinguish between the ideas of rival politicians, or because he is privy to the minutiae of some sordid and degrading business or profession. But these empty talents, of course, are not really signs of intelligence; they are, in fact, merely a congeries of petty tricks and antics, and their acquirement puts little more strain on the mental powers than a chimpanzee suffers in learning how to catch a penny or scratch a match.

—H. L. MENCKEN, *In Defense of Women*

2. It is not easy to live in that continuous awareness of things which alone is true living. Even those who make a parade of their conviction that sunset, rain, and the growth of a seed are daily miracles are not usually so much impressed by them as they urge others to be. The faculty of wonder tires easily and a miracle which appears everyday is a miracle no longer, no matter how many times one tells oneself that it ought to be. Life would seem a great deal longer and a great deal fuller than it does if it were not for the fact that the human being is, by nature, a creature to whom *"O altitudo"* is much less natural than "So what!" Really to see something once or twice a week is almost inevitably to have to try—though, alas, not necessarily with success—to make oneself a poet.

—JOSEPH WOOD KRUTCH, *The Desert Year*

3. Outside of the three Rs—the razor, the rope, and the revolver —I know only one sure-fire method of coping with the simmering heat we may cheerfully expect in this meridian from now to Labor Day. Whenever the mercury starts inching up the column, I take to the horizontal plane with a glass graduate trimmed with ferns, place a pinch of digitalis or any good heart stimulant at my elbow, and flip open the advertising section of *Vogue*. Fifteen minutes of that paradisaical prose, those dizzying non sequiturs, and my lips are as blue as Lake Louise. If you want a mackerel iced or a sherbet frozen, just bring it up and let me read the advertising section of *Vogue* over it. I can also take care of small picnic parties up to five. The next time you're hot and breathless, remember the name, folks: Little Labrador Chilling and Dismaying Corporation.

—S. J. PERELMAN, *Keep It Crisp*

4. They talked about religion, and the slack way the world was going nowadays, the decay of behavior, and about the younger children, whom these children always brought at once to mind. On these topics they were firm, critical, and unbewildered. They had received educations which furnished them an assured habit of mind about all the important appearances of life, and especially about the rearing of young. They relied with perfect acquiescence on the dogma that children were conceived in sin and brought forth in iniquity. Childhood was a long state of instruction and probation for adult life, which was in turn a long, severe, undeviating devotion to duty, the largest part of which consisted in bringing up children. The young were difficult, disobedient, and tireless in wrongdoing, apt to turn unkind and undutiful when

249

they grew up, in spite of all one had done for them, or had tried to do: for small painful doubts rose in them now and again when they looked at their completed works. Nannie couldn't abide her new-fangled grandchildren. "Wuthless, shiftless lot, jes plain scum, Miss Sophia Jane; I cain't undahstand it aftah all the raisin' they had."

—K. A. PORTER, "The Old Order"

5. At length as the craft was cast to one side, and ran ranging along with the White Whale's flank, he seemed strangely oblivious of its advance—as the whale sometimes will—and Ahab was fairly within the smoky mountain mist, which, thrown off from the whale's spout, curled round his great Monadnock hump; he was even thus close to him; when, with body arched back, and both arms lengthwise high-lifted to the poise, he darted his fierce iron, and his far fiercer curse into the hated whale. As both steel and curse sank to the socket, as if sucked into a morass, Moby Dick sideways writhed; spasmodically rolled his nigh flank against the bow, and, without staving a hole in it, so suddenly canted the boat over, that had it not been for the elevated part of the gunwale to which he then clung, Ahab would once more have been tossed into the sea. As it was, three of the oarsmen—who foreknew not the precise instant of the dart, and were therefore unprepared for its effects—these were flung out; but so fell, that, in an instant two of them clutched the gunwale again, and rising to its level on a combining wave, hurled themselves bodily inboard again; the third man helplessly dropping astern, but still afloat and swimming.

—HERMAN MELVILLE, *Moby Dick*

6. At first they had come in wagons: the guns, the bedding, the dogs, the food, the whiskey, the keen heart-lifting anticipation of hunting; the young men who could drive all night and all the following day in the cold rain and pitch a camp in the rain and sleep in the wet blankets and rise at daylight the next morning and hunt. There had been bear then. A man shot a doe or a fawn as quickly as he did a buck, and in the afternoons they shot wild turkey with pistols to test their stalking skill and marksmanship, feeding all but the breast to the dogs. But that time was gone now. Now they went in cars, driving faster and faster each year because the roads were better and they had farther and farther to drive, the territory in which game still existed drawing yearly inward as his life was drawing inward, until now he was the last of those who had once made the journey in wagons without feeling it and now those who accompanied him were the sons and

even grandsons of the men who had ridden for twenty-four hours in the rain or sleet behind the steaming mules. They called him "Uncle Ike" now, and he no longer told anyone how near eighty he actually was because he knew as well as they did that he no longer had any business making such expeditions, even by car.

—WILLIAM FAULKNER, "Delta Autumn"

EXERCISE 35. Which of the methods of paragraph development discussed in Section 32g seem to be the most appropriate method of developing each of the following topic sentences into a paragraph? Why? After you have answered this question briefly, choose one of the topics and write a paragraph around it. Is your paragraph developed according to your original notion?

1. The farmer is the backbone of this country's economic prosperity.
2. Attending a big university has disadvantages as well as advantages.
3. A fraternity house is not an ideal place for study.
4. The notion that women are poor automobile drivers is not supported by any real evidence.
5. The most enjoyable book I ever read is . . .
6. Pride in his personal appearance should be one of the chief characteristics of a soldier.
7. To watch a college "prom" is to see every type of human being.
8. Movies are our best entertainment.
9. The construction of a wren house is simple.
10. The farmer uses every possible method to conserve moisture in the soil.
11. The differences in education and social conditioning for boys and girls in our society make for an enormous waste of female talent.
12. Anxiety is an active paralysis.
13. A child who has learned to live and love in the movies will suffer when he enters a world in which there is odor as well as sight and sound.
14. We are too much inclined to measure progress by the number of television sets rather than by the quality of television programs.
15. The people you see at a patriotic rally are not very likely to be the ones that move you to love your country.

16. Good government begins at the local level.

17. Conservation is a farmer's best investment.

18. Fraternities have to watch carefully the line between fellow-ship and snobbishness.

19. A freshman's biggest problem is learning to sever the umbilical cord.

20. Some people come to college wanting to learn, but refusing, at the same time, to change a single idea they came with.

EXERCISE 36. "You cannot do wrong without suffering wrong." Write two separate paragraphs to develop this topic sentence. In the first paragraph, demonstrate by abstract argument or theory that the statement is either true or false. In the second, demonstrate the truth or falsity of the statement by giving examples.

EXERCISE 37. "My reading tastes have changed since I came to college." Write three separate paragraphs to develop this topic sentence. In the first paragraph, show *why* your tastes have changed. In the second, demonstrate *how* they have changed. In the third, contrast specifically your reading tastes in high school with your reading tastes in college.

Paragraphs for Study.

The following paragraphs illustrate the elements of good paragraph structure.

1.

After the coffee is picked it is brought home in sacks, measured, and run through the dispulper, a machine that removes the tough red, outer skin. Every berry (except the pea berry—a freak) is composed of two beans, and these are covered with a sweet, slimy substance known as the "honey," which has to ferment and rot before the beans may be washed. Washing simply removes the honey and those pieces of the outer skin that have escaped the teeth of the machine and flowed from the front end where they weren't wanted. Four or five changes of water are made in the course of the operation, and toward the last, when the rotted honey has been washed away, leaving the beans hard and clean in their coverings of parchment, one of the men takes off his trousers, rolls up his drawers, and knee deep in the heavy mixture of coffee and water drags his feet as rapidly as he can around the cement washing tank until the whole mass is in motion with a swirling eddy in the center. Into the eddy gravitate all the impurities—the foreign substances—the dead leaves and twigs and unwelcome hulls, and when they all seem to be there, the man deftly scoops them up with his hands and tosses them over the side. Then, if it be a fine hot day, the soggy mess is shoveled on the asoleadero (literally, the sunning place), an immense sloping stone platform covered with smooth cement, and there it is spread out to dry while men in their bare feet constantly turn it over with wooden hoes in order that the beans may receive the sun equally on all sides.

—C. M. FLANDRAU, *Viva Mexico!*

2.

It is now over a hundred years since the *Communist Manifesto,* and the course of history has not gone as Marx planned. It is true that the capitalist business cycle of prosperity and depression has gone on, and that possibly depressions have grown worse. There has certainly been a tendency toward the concentration of capital in giant industry, but it has not been uniform even in the German, British and American economies. The formula that the rich are growing richer and the poor are growing poorer has certainly not proved true. Government is intervening to regulate industry even in the United States, and in all industrial countries there has been a tendency to some degree of what is often called "state socialism." And, of course, there was in 1917 in industrially backward Russia—a country Marx himself disliked—the one major revolutionary movement to come to power under Marxist auspices. The Russians have established the dictatorship of the proletariat, but there are as yet not the slightest signs of the withering away of the Russian state. Marx, indeed, supposed that once the revolution was successful in a great nation—he apparently thought it would come first in the most advanced one of his day, Great Britain—it would spread at least to all the rest of Western society, and therefore throughout the world. Faithful Marxists can, of course, point out that until the revolution is world-wide, the state cannot possibly be expected to wither away in beleaguered Russia.

—CRANE BRINTON, *Ideas and Men:*
The Story of Western Thought

3.

Philosophers, scholars, and men of science exhibit a common sensitiveness in all decisions in which their *amour propre* is involved. Thousands of argumentative works have been written to vent a grudge. However stately their reasoning, it may be nothing

253

but rationalizing, stimulated by the most commonplace of all motives. A history of philosophy and theology could be written in terms of grouches, wounded pride, and aversions, and it would be far more instructive than the usual treatments of these themes. Sometimes, under Providence, the lowly impulse of resentment leads to great achievements. Milton wrote his treatise on divorce as a result of his troubles with his seventeen-year-old wife, and when he was accused of being the leading spirit in a new sect, the Divorcers, he wrote his noble *Areopagitica* to prove his right to say what he thought fit, and incidentally to establish the advantage of a free press in the promotion of Truth.

—JAMES HARVEY ROBINSON, *The Mind in the Making*

4.

It is difficult both to define slang and to indicate its relation to other linguistic phenomena. Popular impressions about it are often erroneous: there is no necessary connection, for example, between the slangy and the vulgar, or between the slangy and the ungrammatical; further, there is nothing new about the phenomenon of slang, nor is it anything peculiarly American. Some of these misconceptions we shall return to. In addition, it may be asserted that entirely competent treatments of slang sometimes take in too much territory. One such treatment, Krapp's discussion in *Modern English*, will serve as our point of departure. Incidentally, it is striking testimony to the ephemeral character of a great deal of slang that Krapp's illustrations, brought together only forty-odd years ago, impress the reader as antiquarian specimens, for the most part. Truly, there is nothing so completely dead as last year's slang.

—STUART ROBERTSON *and* FREDERIC G. CASSIDY, *The Development of Modern English* (Second Edition)

5.

Let us spend one day as deliberately as Nature, and not be thrown off the track by every nutshell and mosquito's wing that falls on the rails. Let us rise early and fast, or break fast, gently and without perturbation; let company come and let company go, let the bells ring and the children cry,—determined to make a day of it. Why should we knock under and go with the stream? Let us not be upset and overwhelmed in that terrible rapid and whirlpool called a dinner, situated in the meridian shallows. Weather this danger and you are safe, for the rest of the way is down hill. With unrelaxed nerves, with morning vigor, sail by it, looking another way, tied to the mast like Ulysses. If the engine whistles,

254

let it whistle till it is hoarse for its pains. If the bell rings, why
should we run? We will consider what kind of music they are
like. Let us settle ourselves, and work and wedge our feet downward through the mud and slush of opinion, and prejudice, and
tradition, and delusion, and appearance, that alluvion which covers
the globe, through Paris and London, through New York and
Boston and Concord, through church and state, through poetry
and philosophy and religion, till we come to a hard bottom and
rocks in place, which we can call *reality,* and say, This is, and no
mistake; and then begin, having a point d'appui, below freshet
and frost and fire, a place where you might found a wall or a
state, or set a lamppost safely, or perhaps a gauge, not a
Nilometer, but a Realometer, that future ages might know how
deep a freshet of shams and appearances had gathered from time
to time. If you stand right fronting and face to face to a fact, you
will see the sun glimmer on both its surfaces, as if it were a
cimeter, and feel its sweet edge dividing you through the heart
and marrow, and so you will happily conclude your mortal career.
Be it life or death, we crave only reality. If we are really dying,
let us hear the rattle in our throats and feel cold in the extremities;
if we are alive, let us go about our business.

—HENRY DAVID THOREAU, *Walden*

6.

One evening he and she went up the great sweeping shore of
sands towards Theddlethorpe. The long breakers plunged and ran
in a hiss of foam along the coast. It was a warm evening. There
was not a figure but themselves on the far reaches of sand, no
noise but the sound of the sea. Paul loved to see it clanging at the
land. He loved to feel himself between the noise of it and the
silence of the sandy shore. Miriam was with him. Everything grew
very intense. It was quite dark when they turned again. The way
home was through a gap in the sandhills, and then along a raised
grass road between two dykes. The country was black and still.
From behind the sandhills came the whisper of the sea. Paul and
Miriam walked in silence. Suddenly he started. The whole of his
blood seemed to burst into flame, and he could scarcely breathe.
An enormous orange moon was staring at them from the rim of
the sandhills. He stood still, looking at it.

—D. H. LAWRENCE, *Sons and Lovers*

7.

Nick laid the bottle full of jumping grasshoppers against a pine
trunk. Rapidly he mixed some buckwheat flour with water and

stirred it smooth, one cup of flour, one cup of water. He put a handful of coffee in the pot and dipped a lump of grease out of a can and spread it sputtering across the hot skillet. On the smoking skillet he poured smoothly the buckwheat batter. It spread like lava, the grease spitting sharply. Around the edges the buckwheat cake began to firm, then brown, then crisp. The surface was bubbling slowly to porousness. Nick pushed under the browned under surface with a fresh pine chip. He shook the skillet sideways and the cake was loose on the surface. I won't try to flop it, he thought. He slid the chip of clean wood all the way under the cake, and flopped it over onto its face. It sputtered in the pan.

—ERNEST HEMINGWAY, "Big Two-Hearted River"

8.

He saw, facing him across the spring, a man of undersize, his hands in his coat pockets, a cigarette slanted from his chin. His suit was black, with a tight, high-waisted coat. His trousers were rolled once and caked with mud above mud-caked shoes. His face had a queer, bloodless color, as though seen by electric light; against the sunny silence, in his slanted straw hat and his slightly akimbo arms, he had that vicious depthless quality of stamped tin.

—WILLIAM FAULKNER, *Sanctuary*

9.

It was all over though. The big cat lay tangled in the willows; his head and shoulder raised against the red stems, his legs reaching and his back arched downward, in the caricature of a leap, but loose and motionless. The great, yellow eyes glared balefully up through the willows. The mouth was a little open, the tongue hanging down from it behind the fangs. The blood was still dripping from the tongue into the red stain it had already made in the snow. High behind the shoulder, the black pelt was wet too, and one place farther down, on the ribs. Standing there, looking at it, Harold felt compassion for the long, wicked beauty rendered motionless, and even a little shame that it should have passed so hard.

—WALTER V. T. CLARK, *The Track of the Cat*

10.

At school, he was a desperate and hunted little animal. The herd, infallible in its banded instinct, knew at once that a stranger had been thrust into it, and it was merciless at the hunt. As the lunchtime recess came, Eugene, clutching his big grease-stained bag, would rush for the playground pursued by the yelping pack. The leaders, two or three big louts of advanced age and deficient mentality, pressed closely about him, calling out suppliantly, "You know me, 'Gene. You know me"; and still racing for the far end, he would open his bag and hurl to them one of his big sandwiches, which stayed them for a moment, as they fell upon its possessor and clawed it to fragments, but they were upon him in a moment more with the same yelping insistence, hunting him down into a corner of the fence, and pressing in with outstretched paws and wild entreaty. He would give them what he had, sometimes with a momentary gust of fury, tearing away from a greedy hand half of a sandwich and devouring it. When they saw he had no more to give, they went away.

—THOMAS WOLFE, *Look Homeward, Angel*

PARAGRAPH REVIEW EXERCISE. Discuss the papers on pages 258-260 in terms of their over-all organization and their paragraph organization.

"WHOLE COMPOSITION" REVIEW EXERCISE (Sections 31-32).

1. Study the tentative thesis statement and tentative outline below. Then write a more satisfactory thesis statement and make a complete (and formal) sentence outline.

Tentative thesis statement: A large city is a better place to live than a small town.

Tentative (rough) outline:

Bigger	Cultural services better
Many more activities	Better library
Location	More social activities
Daily newspaper	Medical care better
More stores and shops	Organized athletics
Better schools	More movie theaters
Less prying by neighbors	Cleaner
Better jobs available	Post high school training available
Well known	More interesting people
Transportation to and from is better	

2. Pick out one major section of the sentence outline you have just prepared and build at least one well-constructed paragraph around it.

Specimen Paper 4

THE CRISIS

I have lived through two wars. The First World War came to a close in 1918. This was to be the war that ended all wars. Capable leaders in our government were sincere and honest men. They formed a League of Nations just as the United Nations was formed after World War II. But mankind was not ready for it. The same factions pooled their resources, distrust and dishonesty so it was not possible to cultivate the qualities of trust and love for individuals. Individuals make up a nation.

Humanity's crying needs are for these simple virtues.

The United Nations has done much good. We as individuals can do much to support it. It has certainly held together longer than the League of Nations, and this is very encouraging.

But as a whole the world seems to be hesitating. I believe this is a crisis, a turning point.

This crisis may be a good thing. We are threatened on one hand with atomic bombs and possible destruction. On the other hand, we can discard our worldliness and force ourselves out of our material way of thinking. We are being forced to accept our true selves and live decently with one another, not only in the United States, but throughout the whole world.

In my own experience I have lost a lot of the material and selfish way of looking at things and now try to look at life objectively.

When the whole world does this, we may find our salvation.

Specimen Paper 5

COMIC BOOKS

There are many types of comic books. The four main types are the western, detective, fantastic, and humorous. The stories in each type are very similar. If you have read one, you have read them all. The cowboy hero is practically perfect. He always captures the rustlers single-handed and wins the love of the girl. The detective always gets his man with little or no help. The hero in the fantastic comic can do everything imaginable. He flies and moves buildings, mountains, or countries. The humorous type are very silly and have no point to them, but they are probably the best of the four types.

Most children read comic books because they are inexpensive and they are full of pictures. They don't have to read much to get the story. Also, stories about cowboys, detectives and talking animals appeal to children. Adults probably read comic books because they are very short. They can sit down and read a comic book in a few minutes.

Reading comic books may have a bad effect on some people. It is said that they promote crime because the gangster is built up to be a hero. Some children fail to remember that the gangster is always captured at the end of the story. Some children try to do the things they read about. This practice sometimes leads to trouble. Many times children spend time reading comic books that could be used to read good books. They also stay inside reading when they should be outside getting exercise and fresh air.

There is a good side to reading comic books. They are inexpensive and very short. They try to teach that crime does not pay. The effect they have depends on the person who reads them because some people are more impressed by what they read than others.

Specimen Paper 6

THE PRICE SUPPORT PROGRAM

The farm price support program is essential to the farmer of America. He must compete with other groups that have nearly the same thing as the price support program. For example, the manufacturer has tariffs to help him keep his prices up, and the wage earner has a minimum wage to keep him in some security. If the farmer did not have a price support program he would have to sell his products in a cheap market and buy his products in an expensive one. He would be completely at the mercy of the manufacturer and the businessman.

I fully realize the tremendous cost of the farm price support program, and I am willing to admit that it could be improved, but I am not willing to see it done away with. The farmer has to have some protection against too much food and over-supply, a situation which pushes his prices down and down. And there is no doubt that the price support program has worked, at least in a degree. We have only to compare our recent years with the years just after World War I, when thousands of farmers went bankrupt. When agriculture suffers, the whole national economy suffers, for the production of food is still the greatest industry in this country.

My suggestion is not to argue about the necessity of a farm price support program, but to admit the necessity and then go about finding a way to improve the program we have. We can't let the patient die while we are debating ways of saving him.

S E C T I O N S **33-36**

Effective Sentences = EF

Henry David Thoreau, explaining why he had left "civilized" life for two years, once wrote:

> I went to the woods because I wished to live deliberately, to front only the essential facts of life, and see if I could not learn what it had to teach, and not, when I came to die, discover that I had not lived.

This is a well-written sentence; it is *clear, compact, effective.* Why?

First, the sentence expresses a single thought ("I went to the woods because I wished to live deliberately"), on which all the other statements impinge directly—"front the essential facts," "learn what it had to teach," and "not discover that I had not lived." The main thought is clear and consistently held to; the contributing details never obscure it. In short, the sentence has *unity*.

Second, the sentence is *continuously* clear; we always know where we are. The pronoun "it" refers clearly to "life" and links up the second half of the sentence with the first. The phrases beginning "to live" and "to front" are connected by a parallel grammatical construction. The transition "and" introduces an expansion of the main idea; yet the two parts of the sentence are closely tied by the relationship of the words "live" and "die," "front" and "learn." Because all parts of the sentence are clearly related, the sentence has *coherence*.

Third, the parts of the sentence are arranged effectively. The principal idea, "I wished to live deliberately," gets an emphatic position near the beginning. The least emphatic part of the sentence, the middle, is devoted to supplementary statements. The repetition of the main idea, with its effective balance of "die" and "not lived," gets the most strategic position of all, the end of the sentence. And the words "not lived" provide a stylistic as well as an actual conclusion to the sentence. Because the major ideas of the sentence stand out clearly, the sentence has *emphasis*.

Unity, coherence, and *emphasis* are useful terms when we discuss the effectiveness of a sentence. And the "rules" of effective sentence-writing on the succeeding pages are based on these terms. These "rules" will often tell you where your sentences go wrong. But remember that "effectiveness" is not a mechanical matter. There is no way of divorcing a sentence from the idea it expresses. The idea constructs the sentence, not vice versa. A clumsy sentence is really a badly thought-out idea, and to revise it means, first, to rethink it.

> **EXERCISE 1.** Analyze the following sentences just as the Thoreau sentence was analyzed above.
>
> 1. Here, more than anywhere else in the world, the daily panorama of human existence—the unending procession of governmental extortions and chicaneries, of commercial brigandages and throat-slittings, of theological buffooneries, of aesthetic ribaldries, of legal swindles and harlotries—is so inordinately

262

extravagant, so perfectly brought up to the highest conceivable amperage, that only the man who was born with a petrified diaphragm can fail to go to bed every night grinning from ear to ear, and awake every morning with the eager, unflagging expectations of a Sunday-school superintendent touring the Paris peep-shows.

—H. L. MENCKEN

2. Whenever you hear much of things being unutterable and indefinable and impalpable and unnamable and subtly indescribable, then elevate your aristocratic nose towards heaven and snuff up the smell of decay.

—G. K. CHESTERTON

3. Farmers are interested in science, in modern methods, and in theory, but they are not easily thrown off balance and they maintain a healthy suspicion of book learning and of the shenanigans of biologists, chemists, geneticists, and other late-rising students of farm practice and management.

—E. B. WHITE

33 SUBORDINATION = **SUB**

Put the most important idea of a sentence in the main clause; put less important ideas in subordinate clauses or phrases.

Some sentences have two or more ideas which are co-ordinate, or of equal rank. But more often one idea is dominant, the others of lesser significance. Be sure to arrange your sentences so that the major ideas stand out clearly in the main clauses.

33a **Do not use co-ordinating conjunctions to join subordinate or unrelated ideas to the main clause.**

The co-ordination of unrelated ideas results in a poorly unified sentence. In such sentences it is difficult to tell which idea was intended as dominant (see also Section 33c).

If you use *and* to join a subordinate idea to the main clause, you immediately give the subordinate idea the status of an independent one.

INEXACT	The traffic was heavy *and* we arrived late at the party.
REVISED	*Because* the traffic was heavy, we arrived late at the party. (The lesser idea is subordinated.)
INEXACT	The treaty was signed at Panmunjom in 1953, *and* Korea was still not a united country.
REVISED	*After* the treaty was signed at Panmunjom in 1953, Korea was still not a united country. (The lesser idea is subordinated.)
UNRELATED	My Uncle Bert was a golf instructor and moved here from New Mexico in 1959.

264

| REVISED | My Uncle Bert, a golf instructor, moved here from New Mexico in 1959. |
| REVISED | My Uncle Bert, who moved here from New Mexico in 1959, was a golf instructor. |

33b Do not omit logical steps that seem evident to you but may not to the reader.

| UNRELATED | He was in the army, but he didn't have enough money to finish college. |
| REVISED | Although his service in the army entitled him to some schooling under the GI Bill, he didn't have enough money to finish college. |

33c Do not string out a series of miscellaneous facts as though they were all of equal importance.

"Light-Horse Harry" Lee lived from 1756 to 1818 and was an officer in the Revolutionary War. His army was responsible for quelling the Whiskey Rebellion in Pennsylvania, and he also served his country as governor of Virginia and as a member of Congress. It was "Light-Horse Harry" who described Washington as "first in war, first in peace, and first in the hearts of his countrymen," and was the father of Robert E. Lee.

There is usually little reason for such a collection of ill-assorted facts except in a reference book. However, if you feel that they are necessary, be sure that you subordinate the less important to the more important ones.

The author of the description of Washington as "first in war, first in peace, and first in the hearts of his countrymen," was "Light-Horse Harry" Lee, father of Robert E. Lee. "Light-Horse Harry," having made a reputation as an officer in the Revolutionary War, later became governor of Virginia and led the army which quelled the Whiskey Rebellion.

33d Do not use a co-ordinate conjunction to join items that are not logically of the same kind.

| ILLOGICAL | Entered in the pet show were several dogs, a parrot, a monkey, and a rather mangy cocker spaniel. |
| REVISED | Entered in the pet show were a parrot, a monkey, and several dogs, one of which was a rather mangy cocker spaniel. |

EXERCISE 2. Revise those sentences below that contain faulty co-ordination.

1. We searched for nearly an hour, and we at last found the missing necklace.

2. It began to rain, and we ate our picnic dinner indoors.

3. I did not see the traffic sign and I did not stop.

4. We were tired and the sun was hot, but we did not look for shelter.

5. The dog yelped and then he circled the tree, and the raccoon scrambled to a higher branch.

6. The city was lax in its collection of taxes, and the fire department was unable to cope with several large fires.

7. The Huron Indians were Iroquoian, and they were hated by the main body of the Iroquois.

8. All the miners called the child "The Luck," and were completely transformed by the presence of a baby in a rough mining settlement.

9. "The Star-Spangled Banner" was set to music written by an Englishman, John Stafford Smith, and was used by the army and navy long before it became the national anthem in 1931.

10. Melville served in the navy, and his novel *White-Jacket* exposed many abusive practices in the navy and led to reforms of those abuses.

11. I like any kind of vacation, whether it is to the seashore, to the mountains, or merely over a holiday weekend.

12. In the will he was made heir to a collection of rare stamps, a number of carpentry tools, an old automobile, and his grandfather's favorite handsaw.

13. The last Chief of the Army General Staff under Hitler was General Heinz Guderian, and he was largely responsible for building up the panzer force.

14. He said that he was disgusted with his job of writing propaganda, and that he spent all his time reshuffling ideals to meet the demands of power-politics.

15. The Indian Highway was formerly an Indian trail, but it is now an important thoroughfare, and it is a scenic as well as useful route.

33e **Do not put the principal idea of a sentence in a subordinate construction.**

This practice is called "upside-down" subordination.

INEFFECTIVE   The octopus momentarily relaxed its grip, when the diver escaped.

REVISED   When the octopus momentarily relaxed its grip, the diver escaped.

INEFFECTIVE   He happened to glance at the sidewalk, noticing a large diamond practically at his feet.

REVISED   Happening to glance at the sidewalk, he noticed a large diamond practically at his feet.

E X E R C I S E 3. Revise the following sentences by putting principal ideas in main clauses and by subordinating lesser ideas.

1. He studied hard for his examinations, making high grades.
2. She seized the child as he began to sink, saving him from drowning.
3. My hands trembled and the gun moved, causing me to miss the deer.
4. Mrs. Wood opened the door of the bird cage, when her pet canary escaped.
5. We formed a bucket brigade, putting out the fire.
6. According to the popular ballad, Casey Jones attempted to arrive in "Frisco" on schedule, being prevented by a head-on collision with another train.
7. The original Madison Square Garden, run by P. T. Barnum, was also an auditorium in New York City.
8. William H. Vanderbilt, who once said, "The public be damned," indicated by that statement the attitude which characterized the maneuvers that had made his father, Cornelius Vanderbilt, and himself rich.
9. James Fenimore Cooper was reading a novel to his wife when she challenged his claim that he could write a better one and set him off on his literary career.
10. Our parting at the station consisted of some thirty minutes of kissing, sobbing and exchanging good wishes, and ended with our returning to the house together, since I had missed the train.

Avoid the "primer style" unless you want to achieve a specific effect.

The "primer style" consists of a series of short, simple sentences of similar structure (*e.g.*, subject is followed immediately by predicate, clauses are joined by *and*). (See "Variety," Section 34.) This style tends to give all actions and ideas equal weight and importance, and makes your writing seem monotonous and choppy. Although the skilled narrative writer sometimes uses the "primer style" deliberately and effectively, the beginning writer will do well to avoid it.

CHOPPY   He stood on a street corner. The wind was blowing. He peered into the darkness. He was a stranger. He realized that he had no place to go.

REVISED   Standing on a windy street corner and peering into the darkness, the stranger realized that he had no place to go.

Joining a series of short clauses by *and* to make them into a longer sentence only compounds the error of the "primer style."

And SENTENCE   We approached the river and we looked down from the bluff, and we could see the silvery stream and it wound below in the valley.

REVISED   When we approached the river and looked down from the bluff, we could see the silvery stream winding below in the valley.

EXERCISE 4. Which of the following groups of sentences are effective as they stand? Revise those that could be improved by subordination.

1. I got up later than usual this morning. I had to wait fifteen minutes for a bus. I was late to class.

2. The play was very amusing. I was unable to hear some of the actors' speeches. The people sitting behind me talked incessantly.

3. He entered the hall. He climbed the stairs to the second floor. The door to one of the rooms was partly open. He softly entered.

4. I heard a loud clamor in the street. I ran to the window. I saw a crowd gathered around a shopkeeper. He was gesticulating wildly. He shouted that his store had been robbed.

5. We drove onto a sand road. It led into the woods. It was very narrow. We wondered whether it was safe for travel.

6. I went to a park and sat on a bench, and I fed nuts to the squirrels.

7. The house was very old and it was painted yellow, and the paint was faded and in some places it was cracked.

8. A fly buzzed in the window and a clock ticked on the shelf, and there was no other sound in the room.

9. A car came out of a side road and I pushed hard on the foot brake, and I steered sharply to the left and I narrowly avoided a collision.

10. She crossed the street and she met a policeman and she asked him the way to Monroe Street.

11. Among his other accomplishments Paul Revere designed paper money. It was called Continental Currency. It was issued by the second Continental Congress. In time it became nearly worthless. That's the source of our phrase, "Not worth a Continental."

12. One of the early experimenters with submarines and torpedoes was Robert Fulton, and he built the first successful steamboat as well.

13. John Marshall discovered gold at Sutter's Mill in 1848, and in the gold rush which followed both he and Sutter were financially ruined.

14. Tristram defeated Morault and saved the kingdom of Cornwall and won the gratitude of King Mark.

15. The Barbary Coast was a notorious section of San Francisco. The dancing halls and gambling houses were the scene of vice and crime. The section was almost destroyed in the famous San Francisco earthquake.

33g Do not overload sentences with excessive subordination.

Unessential details in your sentences make your reader lose sight of the points you are trying to make.

EXCESSIVE SUBORDINATION   My fishing equipment includes a casting rod *which Uncle Henry gave me many years ago* and which is nearly worn out, and an assortment of lines, hooks, and bass flies, which make good bait *when I can get time off from work to go bass fishing* at Hardwood Lake.

REVISED   My fishing equipment includes an old casting rod and an assortment of lines, hooks, and bass flies. The flies make good bait when I am bass fishing at Hardwood Lake.

In this particularly ineffective kind of construction, which is called the "House-that-Jack-built" sentence, one dependent clause is tacked on after another, each seeming to be an afterthought:

HOUSE-THAT-JACK-BUILT   The heroine thought the hero was a gambler while he was really a government agent who was investigating the income tax frauds of gamblers who concealed the larger part of their winnings which they took in violation of laws of the state which would arrest them if they made their activity public, which is why she wouldn't marry him, which is why I was disgusted with the movie.

EXERCISE 5. Revise the following sentences by eliminating excessive details and subordination.

1. While I watched a full moon rise above the trees and the fish splash in a nearby stream, a light breeze fanned the embers of the campfire and it was an experience I shall never forget.

2. When I left home early in the morning I did not realize that I had forgotten my railroad ticket until I reached the station and boarded the train and the conductor asked to see my ticket.

3. The policeman stood by the door of the old house, which, I have been told, was once a very handsome dwelling owned by a wealthy importer, and waited for the thief to come home.

4. The conductor raised his baton and Joe picked up his trumpet, which was an expensive instrument given to him by his parents on his eighteenth birthday, and made ready to play his solo.

5. My dog, which I bought from Mr. Hill, a real estate broker who raises dogs as a hobby because he likes dogs, can stand on his hind legs.

6. John Wesley, his brother Charles, and a friend named George Whitefield, were students at Oxford, where they adopted a set of religious exercises which were very precise which is why they were called Methodists, which later became the

accepted term for members of the sect which they founded.

7. As we swung around the curve a truck with glaring headlights which was probably one of the huge cattle trucks carrying livestock into Chicago and traveling late at night to avoid heavy daytime traffic loomed into view.

8. Hearst, who began his career by taking charge of his father's newspaper, the San Francisco *Examiner,* probably had a great deal to do with our entry into the Spanish American War, which was fought during 1897 and 1898 and which is often regarded as having been imperialistic, through his attempts to make sensational news stories which would sell his papers and aggravate international friction.

9. Casting into the lily pads where I often had gigged frogs in the days when I visited Grandfather during my summer vacations from school I snagged one of my best dry flies, a hand tied hackle for which I had paid two dollars, on an overhanging limb.

10. Having escaped from the pendulum, a crescent shaped blade which was razor sharp and which had descended gradually until it cut the ropes in which he had found himself tied upon awakening, he found that the metal walls of his cell were being heated and were closing in, forcing him toward a pit in the center of the room.

33h **Use all connectives** (*e.g.,* BUT, AS, WHILE) **accurately and clearly.**

Careless use of such conjunctions as *and, as, but, so,* and *while* conceals the exact relationship or shade of meaning that you intend to convey.

(1) *Do not use the conjunction* AS *in sentences where it could mean either time or cause.*

AMBIGUOUS　As the river rose to flood stage, many people fled to higher ground. (Time or cause intended?)

REVISED　*When* the river rose to flood stage, many people fled to higher ground. (Time intended.)

REVISED　*Because* the river rose to flood stage, many people fled to higher ground. (Cause intended.)

(2) *Do not use the conjunction* AS *in the sense of* WHETHER *or* THAT.

FAULTY　I do not know *as* I want to go tomorrow.

REVISED　I do not know *whether* (or *that*) I want to go tomorrow.

(3) *Use the conjunction* BUT *to connect contrasted statements.*

> FAULTY He was an All-American in college, *and* today he is in poor physical condition.
>
> REVISED He was an All-American in college, *but* today he is in poor physical condition.

The misuse (intended, of course) of *but, and though,* and *under it all* in the sentence below shows how surprising to a reader an illogical transition can be.

> [Pittsburgh millionaires] are rough but uncivil in their manners, and though their ways are boisterous and unpolished, under it all they have a great deal of impoliteness and discourtesy.
>
> —O. HENRY

(4) *Do not use the preposition* LIKE *as a substitute for the conjunctions* AS IF *or* AS THOUGH *in formal writing.*

> FORMAL He looks *as if* (or *as though*) he were exhausted.
>
> INFORMAL He looks *like* he is exhausted.

(5) *Do not use the conjunction* WHILE *in the sense of* AND *or* BUT.

> INEFFECTIVE John is a doctor, *while* Ray is an engineer.
>
> REVISED John is a doctor *and* Ray is an engineer.
>
> INEFFECTIVE Monday was a cool day, *while* Tuesday was warmer.
>
> REVISED Monday was a cool day, *but* Tuesday was warmer.

(6) *Do not use the conjunction* WHILE *in cases where it is not clear whether time or concession is intended.*

> AMBIGUOUS *While* I was working at night in the library, I saw Jane often. (Time or concession intended?)
>
> REVISED *When* I was working at night in the library, I saw Jane often. (Time intended.)
>
> REVISED *Although* I was working at night in the library, I saw Jane often. (Concession intended.)

EXERCISE 6. In the following sentences replace any connectives that are used weakly or inaccurately.

1. He talks like he is happy.
2. I do not feel as I am qualified for the job.

3. As the ship struck the rocks, several people jumped overboard.

4. She likes sugar in her coffee, while I like cream in mine.

5. Her grape jelly won a prize at the county fair, but it was delicious jelly.

6. While Leander lived across the Hellespont from Hero, he would swim over often to be with her.

7. I don't know as I would have enough energy after such a swim to be good company.

8. The Hellespont is nearly a mile wide at its narrowest point, while a constant current makes swimming very difficult.

9. It seems like Leander would have lost his way swimming at night.

10. Hero carried a torch for him on the opposite shore, but he watched that to be sure of his direction.

34 VARIETY = VAR

Achieve variety in your writing by mixing short simple sentences with longer compound or complex sentences and by varying the beginnings of sentences.

34a   **Avoid the overuse of short simple sentences** (*see* "Subordination," *Section 33f*).

INEFFECTIVE	Jack aproached the mare warily. She saw the bridle in his hand. He stood still. The mare waited. Jack tried to toss the reins over her head. But she galloped away.
REVISED	Jack warily approached the mare, who saw the bridle in his hand. He stood still and the mare waited. But when he tried to toss the reins over her head, she galloped away.

EXERCISE 7. Revise the following sentences to avoid the over-use of short, simple statements.

1. The bookstore was crowded. Martha finally got the attention of a clerk. She asked the price of her history textbook. The price was three dollars. Martha paid the money and left.

2. A company of soldiers marched by. They were led by a burly captain. He gave orders in a thunderous voice. He watched his men with a stern eye.

3. I saw a movement in the deep grass. I stood still. There was a sudden whir of feathers. A pheasant sailed over my head.

4. The pitcher prepared to deliver the ball. The catcher gave him a signal. The pitcher whirled and threw the ball to the first baseman. The baserunner dived safely back to the base.

5. The lecturer looked critically at his audience. He shuffled his notes and cleared his throat. He drank a glass of water. He began speaking in a low voice.

6. Grace is pretty. Her hair is blonde and her eyes blue. She has a fair complexion.

7. I cast my bait into the reed bed. I had seen a large black bass jump there. I felt a powerful jerk on my line. The battle had begun.

8. He picked up the letter. He began to read it. A look of pure bewilderment crossed his face. Then he began to smile. The next moment he was waving the letter in the air and shouting something. He was laughing hard. I couldn't make out what he was saying.

9. The college was small and secluded. It was very old, however. It had an excellent reputation. Its faculty was world famous.

10. Benjamin Franklin achieved his first success as a printer. He was also a practical inventor. The Franklin Stove is named after him. He was also interested in English spelling. He wanted to reform it.

34b **Avoid the overuse of long compound sentences** (*see "Subordination," Section 33g*).

INEFFECTIVE	The stagecoach rounded a bend, but two masked horsemen blocked the road, and they covered the driver with their rifles, and then they ordered him to raise his hands.
REVISED	As the stagecoach rounded a bend, two masked horsemen blocked the road. Covering the driver with their rifles, they ordered him to raise his hands. (In this revision the first co-ordinate clause is reduced to a subordinate clause; the third co-ordinate clause is reduced to a phrase; the second and fourth co-ordinate clauses become the main clauses of separate sentences.)
INEFFECTIVE	He was chief of the volunteer fire company, and he was the town's grocer, but he was never too busy in his store to attend a fire.
REVISED	The chief of the volunteer fire company, who was also the town's grocer, was never too busy in his store to attend a fire. (The first co-ordinate clause becomes a noun phrase, the subject of the main clause in the revised sentence; the second co-ordinate clause becomes a subordinate clause; the third co-ordinate clause becomes the predicate of the main clause.)

275

INEFFECTIVE   She carefully powdered her nose, and then she
               applied her lipstick, and then she smiled at her
               reflection in the mirror.

REVISED   She carefully powdered her nose, applied her lip-
               stick, and then smiled at her reflection in the
               mirror. (The compound sentence is revised to make
               a simple sentence with a compound predicate.)

EXERCISE 8. Revise the following sentences to avoid excessive
or false co-ordination.

1. He had frequent headaches, and he realized that he should
   have his eyes examined, but his meager income did not allow
   him the expense of an examination.

2. The Mortons lived in a residence of impressive size, for they
   believed that large houses were an indication of financial
   success, and they wanted to show some evidence of their
   social position.

3. *Ben Hur* was written by Lew Wallace in 1880, and it is a
   novel of the time of Christ, and it was widely read in America.

4. Arthur was an excellent pianist, and he organized a dance
   orchestra at the university, and he financed his own education, but his long hours of work kept him from making higher
   grades.

5. The social centers of the Puritan community were the church
   and the school, and the Puritans believed that the school
   should exert a religious influence, and they gave a strong
   impetus to moral education in America.

6. I rose early in the morning and I dressed quickly, and then I
   ate breakfast quickly and rushed off to class.

7. The German equivalent of the American high school is the
   Gymnasium, but the word is not connected with athletics, and
   the education is much more formalized than ours.

8. The history of the world is the story of the rise of the common
   man, for the common man has not always enjoyed a voice in
   government, for he was held down by his rulers, and he had
   to fight bitterly for his freedom.

9. The halfback was the star of the game, for after running the
   kickoff back for a touchdown, he recovered a fumble and on
   the next play passed thirty yards for a second touchdown,
   after which he kicked the extra point.

10. Mrs. Tanner talks to my mother over the back fence and they
    go on for hours never really saying anything, but having a

wonderful time, and the dishes sit in the sink and the dust collects and Father wonders where his supper is, and sometimes, I admit, I do too.

34c **Vary the beginnings of your sentences in order to avoid monotony.**

It is easy to fall into monotonous patterns of writing, such as introducing a whole series of sentences with a similar construction. Repetition of a noun subject, for example, is particularly common. This practice is easy to avoid, for there are many ways in which you can begin sentences. Remember, however, that word order is closely associated with meaning and emphasis and that different sentence beginnings will lend slightly different shades of meaning to the whole sentence.

Note how each variant of the following sentence modifies the meaning of the sentence:

> *Deer* grazed peacefully in the valley and were unaware of the advancing hunter.

BEGINNING WITH A PREPOSITIONAL PHRASE
> *In the valley* the deer grazed peacefully and were unaware of the advancing hunter.

BEGINNING WITH A VERBAL PHRASE
> *Grazing peacefully,* the deer in the valley were unaware of the advancing hunter.

BEGINNING WITH AN EXPLETIVE
> *There* were deer grazing peacefully in the valley, unaware of the advancing hunter.

BEGINNING WITH A SUBORDINATE CLAUSE
> *As they grazed peacefully in the valley,* the deer were unaware of the advancing hunter.

BEGINNING WITH A CO-ORDINATING CONJUNCTION
> *And* the deer, grazing peacefully in the valley, were unaware of the advancing hunter.
>
> *But* the deer, grazing peacefully in the valley, were unaware of the advancing hunter.

A sentence beginning with a co-ordinating conjunction usually depends for meaning on the preceding sentence.

EXERCISE 9. Vary the beginning of each of the following sentences in three of the five different ways suggested above.

1. The prisoner looked hopefully at his lawyer and awaited the jury's verdict.
2. Jean hoped her new dress would be pretty and selected the material with great care.
3. The child lost his way in the wilderness but was rescued by a party of searchers.
4. The coach rushed out on the field to protest the umpire's decision.
5. Jumbo was a huge elephant and ate all the peanuts the children gave him.
6. Air pressure is greater on the water in the glass than on the water in the straw, and therefore forces water down in the glass, up the straw and into your mouth.
7. The chair appeared stable until the minister sat down in it, but then one leg crumpled, tipping chair and minister into the swimming pool.
8. We returned home sullen and irritable after a delightful afternoon on the midway.
9. Norm Holden played a good game in left field, but he spent the next three days in bed.
10. The upholsterer, his mouth full of tacks and his magnetic hammer swinging like a piece of machinery, stretched and fastened the chaircover with amazing speed.

EXERCISE 10. Revise the following paragraph by introducing greater variety in sentence structure.

Rod felt better soon as he was out of the house. He sat on the stoop of a nearby apartment house and lighted a cigaret. He knew why his mother screamed at him, and he didn't blame her. She worked a long day, and she spent an hour going and coming on the subway, so naturally she was exhausted when she came home. Rod knew that his mother would be a lot happier if he got a job. He didn't know why he couldn't bring himself to hunt for one, but it seemed as though he couldn't get out of bed before noon. That wasn't the real reason. He was afraid of working because he was afraid he would be fired, like last time. Rod knew that, but he also knew he couldn't tell his mother. They would keep on arguing, and Rod would keep on staying away from home most of the night so that he wouldn't have to face his mother.

EXERCISE 11. Imitate the structures of the following sentences, preserving each grammatical part and keeping the emphasis the same, but substitute different ideas and different words for those given. You may, if you wish, use the prepositions, conjunctions, articles, and demonstratives used in the original sentence.

EXAMPLE: The two sentences immediately below are imitations of the sentences above that give instructions for this exercise. Look at the example sentences carefully and notice how they duplicate the patterns of verb forms, phrasing, punctuation, etc., of the originals. Then try writing similar imitations of the exercise sentences below.

Remember the days of your childhood, nursing each ancient wound and making old victories more glorious, but seek new wounds and new victories without hesitation. Memory can, when it chooses, deaden the spirit, the will, the intent and the effectiveness needed for present action.

Pack the tobacco with your thumb, maintaining even pressure and making the surface flat, but avoid the tight pack or the loose one described in the last paragraph. A pipe will, when packed properly, give the taste, the even draw, the long smoke and the contentment described by seasoned pipe-lovers.

Notice that you may supply or leave out modifying words when you need to. Your sentences need not be related to one another.

1. A sentence is a living thing. (*e.g.* The heat wave was a withering experience.)

2. The good ones have neither too many nor too few parts.

3. And each part, like each organ of a living body, dies when cut off from the source of life.

4. A meaningless fragment shocks the reader as would a dissevered limb.

5. But that same fragment, performing its function in conjunction with the other organs of a good sentence, can be a thing of beauty.

6. Another quality which a sentence shares with an organism is flexibility.

7. With the energetic spurt of a strong verb, with the graceful gesture of an adjective or an adverb, with the persistence of a conjunction or the stubbornness of a noun, a sentence can adapt itself quickly to any demand.

279

8. Like any living thing, every sentence is a proud individual.
9. Although it is necessarily very much like its neighbors in all essentials, it has a life of its own to lead.
10. To conform mechanically to the structures of surrounding sentences would be an indignity to so capable an individual.
11. It might even be said that a sentence is not only a living organism but also a citizen in a community, its paragraph.
12. Two considerations, then, govern the way it is put together.
13. Its first duty is to do its job, as efficiently as possible, in the communicative work of the paragraph.
14. That every writer will make his sentences do this is taken for granted, but the good writer will, in addition, remember the second consideration.
15. He should be able to make each sentence live with harmony and distinction among the other citizens of the paragraph.

35 PARALLELISM = ||

35

Use parallel grammatical structure for sentence elements that are parallel in thought.

Parallel structure puts similar ideas in the sentence in the same grammatical construction. In the sentence below, for example, the phrases *to put ideas* and *to give them* are parallel because they are constructed alike.

> *To put ideas* in the same grammatical construction is *to give them* equal importance.

35a **Use parallel structure for sentence elements joined by co-ordinating conjunctions.**

For balance and smoothness in your writing let the structure of the first of two or more co-ordinate elements set the pattern for the structure of the remaining co-ordinate elements.

> AWKWARD She likes to sew and cooking.
> PARALLEL She likes to sew and cook.
>
> AWKWARD Sam is tall, with blue eyes, and has a congenial manner.
> PARALLEL Sam is tall, blue-eyed, and congenial.

NOTE: *You may point up the parallel structure by repeating a strategic word or words* (see also "Emphasis," Section 36d).

> AMBIGUOUS He wants to write stories that describe the South and study the habits of the Creoles. (Stories which study the habits of the Creoles?)
> REVISED He wants *to* write stories that describe the South and *to* study the habits of the Creoles.

281

AMBIGUOUS	Mr. Gray helps his wife by cooking and ironing his own shirts.
REVISED	Mr. Gray helps his wife *by* cooking and *by* ironing his own shirts.

35b   **Avoid faulty parallelism with** AND WHO, AND WHICH.

Do not use an *and who* or an *and which* clause in a sentence unless you have already used a parallel *who* or *which* clause.

FAULTY	Mary is a graceful dancer, *and who is also an excellent* pianist.
REVISED	Mary is a graceful dancer and also an excellent pianist.
FAULTY	He bought a large farm, *and which* has a productive peach orchard.
REVISED	He bought a large farm which has a productive peach orchard.

EXERCISE 12. In the following sentences, express the co-ordinate ideas in parallel structure.

1. The soldier was told to report to the orderly room and that he was then to do guard duty.
2. He bought a new automobile with an automatic transmission and having a radio and a heater.
3. We stopped at West Branch for food supplies and to inquire about the road to North Point.
4. We did not realize the dangers of the trip, or how long it would take.
5. Playing tennis is more strenuous than to swim or baseball.
6. My work consists of planning the menus, purchasing of the food, supervision of the employees, and keeping a check on the perpetual inventory of the food.
7. Our living room is eighteen feet in length and twelve feet wide.
8. The policeman warned me to drive slowly and that I should be careful.
9. The lecture was long, tedious, and could not easily be understood.
10. The mess sergeant insisted that the pans needed scouring and that the stove be cleaned.

35c Use parallel constructions after correlatives.

The correlatives are *either—or, neither—nor, not only—but also, both—and, whether—or*. When the correlatives *whether—or* are used, *or* is often followed by *not*. (I wondered *whether* he would come or *not*.) In such sentences of course a parallel construction is unnecessary.

FAULTY   You are either *late* or *I am early*. (An adjective made parallel with a clause.)

REVISED   Either *you are late* or *I am early*. (Two parallel clauses.)

FAULTY   Jim not only *has been* outstanding in athletics, but also *in* his studies. (A verb made parallel with a preposition.)

REVISED   Jim has been outstanding not only *in athletics,* but also *in his studies*. (Two parallel phrases.)

EXERCISE 13. Correct the faulty use of correlatives in the following sentences.

1. The book was neither informative nor did I find it entertaining.
2. Pete was undecided whether he should go to the meeting or to stay at home.
3. Mrs. Boggs stayed both longer and gossiped more than I liked.
4. Not only was she unhappy, but also she resented our sympathy.
5. The traffic light was either broken or it had been disconnected.
6. Not only are the lampreys killing the fish in the Great Lakes but also in adjacent lakes and streams.
7. Her birthday is either next week or I am mistaken.
8. The captain was uncertain whether he should ride out the storm or to put in at the nearest port.
9. He was neither properly trained for the work nor did he want to do it.
10. The foreman both watched me and criticized my work more than was necessary.

36 EMPHASIS = EMP

Arrange the parts of a sentence to emphasize important ideas.

36a   **Place important words at the beginning or at the end of the sentence.**

The most emphatic place in a sentence is its ending; the next most emphatic, its beginning; the least emphatic, its middle.

UNEMPHATIC	The nationalist armies won a decisive victory, according to newspaper reports. (An incidental detail is given the most emphatic position in the sentence.)
EMPHATIC	According to newspaper reports, the nationalist armies won a decisive victory.
UNEMPHATIC	If this account is accurate, the results of the chemical experiment were startling, however.
EMPHATIC	If this account is accurate, however, the results of the chemical experiment were startling.

EXERCISE 14. Revise the following sentences by putting important words in an emphatic position.

1. The defendant abused his civil liberties, in my opinion.
2. Moreover, she is a person of wide interests and sympathies, I think.
3. The outcome of the game was decided by lucky breaks, to a large extent.
4. It seems to me that men are more interested in scientific subjects than women are, as a rule.
5. Nevertheless, important scientific discoveries have been made by women, in some cases.

284

6. The terms of the treaty are unacceptable, if I understand the problems correctly.

7. As I see it, the trial was unfair, in the first place.

8. We have an even chance to win the game, if everything goes right.

9. It appears to me that plane accidents are fatal, generally.

10. As a boy, Milton had good eyesight, it is said.

36b Use the periodic sentence for emphasis.

A *periodic sentence* withholds its main idea until the end; a *loose sentence* begins with the main idea and ends with subordinate details. A skillfully written periodic sentence is therefore dramatic; it creates suspense.

> The English poor, broken in every revolt, bullied by every fashion, long despoiled of property, and now being despoiled of liberty, entered history with a noise of trumpets, and turned themselves in two years into one of the iron armies of the world.
> —G. W. CHESTERTON

Similarly in the following sentence: the main idea—*i.e.*, praise of the English jury system—is carefully (perhaps too obviously so) withheld until the end.

> In my mind, he was guilty of no error, he was chargeable with no exaggeration, he was betrayed by his fancy into no metaphor, who once said that all we see about us, kings, lords, and commons, the whole machinery of the State, all the apparatus of the system, and its varied workings, end in simply bringing twelve good men into a box.
> —HENRY PETER

Notice how much more effective the periodic sentence is here:

PERIODIC   After he had stood for five minutes with his arms hanging limply at his sides, a look of beaten humility on his face, the cowboy suddenly reached for his gun and began firing at the two outlaws.

LOOSE   The cowboy suddenly reached for his gun and began firing at the two outlaws after he had stood for five minutes with his arms hanging limply at his sides, a look of beaten humility on his face.

285

Be careful, however, not to use the periodic sentence too often. Too much suspense is wearing. The periodic sentence is effective only when used judiciously—when the subject matter warrants it.

> PERIODIC AND   At the end of a dark alley, three flights down in
> INEFFECTIVE   a dark basement full of grim and evil-looking
>   sailors, I ate my lunch.

In many instances the *periodic* and *loose* constructions are equally effective.

> LOOSE   Balboa reached the Pacific after a long, hazardous
>   journey.
> PERIODIC   After a long, hazardous journey, Balboa reached the
>   Pacific.
>
> LOOSE   He will be a good physician, if enthusiasm is a guar-
>   antee of success.
> PERIODIC   If enthusiasm is a guarantee of success, he will be a
>   good physician.

EXERCISE 15. Change the following loose sentences into periodic sentences.

1. Your money will be returned if, after trying this medicine, you are dissatisfied.
2. The bear turned about suddenly when he heard a noise in the underbrush.
3. Many years ago there was only a wagon trail here, before the highway was built.
4. You must pay the fine unless you can prove that no traffic law was violated.
5. The tomato plants died, although we tried to protect them from the frost.
6. The winning run was scored after two men were out in the last of the ninth inning.
7. You may be killed if you walk into the street without looking.
8. I saw two cars crash head-on several years ago on a three-lane highway just outside a small town in Kentucky.
9. The cavalry force attacked after receiving a message from headquarters telling them to go ahead.
10. The atomic bomb was not perfected until 1945, although atomic fission had been experimented with for many years.

36c　Be sure that all items in a series are in logical order as well as in parallel form.

"Logical order" means using a natural or chronological sequence for the events you want to relate. Thus, you might say, "He ate his dinner, went to a movie, and then retired to his room."

Logical order may sometimes refer to climactic order—that is, building up ideas in rising order of importance. Making the strongest and most striking idea come last is good rhetorical strategy.

> UNEMPHATIC　His life was tragic and brief.
> EMPHATIC　　His life was brief and tragic.

Violation of this principle may result in unintentionally humorous anticlimax.

> Madame, your dinner was superbly cooked, beautifully served, and very good, too.

Intentional anticlimax is a good technique for humor.

> If once a man indulges himself in murder, very soon he comes to think little of robbery; and from robbing he next comes to drinking and Sabbath-breaking, and from that to incivility and procrastination.
>
> —THOMAS DE QUINCEY

Remember that this use is very limited and not generally suitable in your writing.

EXERCISE 16. Revise the following sentences by arranging ideas in logical order.

1. During his vacation Ben acquired a coat of tan, a wife, and a secondhand automobile.
2. Her novel created a furor of controversy and was well written.
3. In the oratorical contest Alan won a college scholarship and a medal.
4. Henry is a capable violinist, a renowned surgeon, and a stamp collector.
5. Mrs. Carey inherited a large farm, some old furniture, and a small insurance policy.

6. After the earthquake one could see tumbled buildings, twisted water pipes, and mangled automobiles.

7. Most students study English in high school, college, and elementary school.

8. Daniel Webster was a great orator and a capable writer.

9. While in college Harry was an "A" student, a waiter in a fraternity house, and a member of the glee club.

10. Metzger finally graduated with honors after almost flunking out in his freshman year and making rather poor grades as a sophomore.

36d Use effective repetition of words and ideas to achieve emphasis.

For a discussion of how words may be repeated to heighten clarity, see Section 41d; for a discussion of ways in which the repetition of words and ideas serves to link sentences together in a paragraph, see Section 32d. Effective repetition is chiefly a matter of repeating key phrases or constructions—in many respects a matter of effective parallelism (see Section 35a). For example, note how Dr. Johnson's "I like their" is effectively repeated in the sentence below.

> I am very fond of the company of ladies. *I like their* beauty, *I like their* delicacy, *I like their* vivacity and *I like their* silence.
> —SAMUEL JOHNSON

The repetition of key constructions in the passage below might strike some modern readers as overly eloquent, but the passage does illustrate how repetition may be used, not only to give continuity to what is being said, but also to bring the reader (or listener) to a rhetorical climax.

> *I would rather have been* a French peasant and worn wooden shoes. *I would rather have* lived in a hut with a vine growing over the door and the grapes growing purple in the kisses of the Autumn sun. *I would rather have been that* poor peasant with my loving wife by my side, knitting as the day died out of the sky, with my children upon my knee and their arms about me. *I would rather have been that* man and gone down to the tongue-less silence of the dreamless dust than to *have been that* imperial impersonation of force and murder known as Napoleon the Great.
> —ROBERT INGERSOLL

EXERCISE 17. Discuss the effectiveness of the repetition of words and phrases in each of the sentences below. (Note how frequently effective repetition and effective parallelism reinforce each other.)

1. No one can be perfectly free till all are free; no one can be perfectly moral till all are moral; no one can be perfectly happy till all are happy.

—HERBERT SPENCER

2. There is no mistake; there has been no mistake; and there shall be no mistake.

—DUKE OF WELLINGTON

3. To know how to say what others only know how to think is what makes men poets or sages; and to dare to say what others only dare to think makes men martyrs or reformers or both.

—ELIZABETH CHARLES

4. It is true that you may fool all the people some of the time; you can even fool some of the people all the time; but you can't fool all of the people all the time.

—ABRAHAM LINCOLN

5. We are always doing something for Posterity, but I would fain see Posterity do something for us.

—JOSEPH ADDISON

36e **In general, for greater emphasis use the active rather than the passive voice.**

Because the active voice of the verb is strong and emphatic, expressing direct action of the subject, it naturally imparts a stronger tone to your writing. The passive voice, stressing the importance of the receiver rather than the doer of the action, is much less emphatic; but it does, of course, have legitimate uses.

In choosing which voice to use, be guided by whether you want to emphasize the doer or the receiver of the action:

PASSIVE 1. He *was struck* on the head by a foul ball.
ACTIVE 2. A foul ball *struck* him on the head.

Sentence 1 emphasizes *who* was struck; sentence 2 *what* struck him. Do not think that the active voice is *always* the more effective.

Even though less emphatic, the passive is more effective in sentences like the following:

> He *was shot* through the heart.
> We *were to be hanged* at midnight.

But in many other instances the passive kills the effect.

> During the morning the equator *was crossed* by the ship.
> A tree *was crashed into* by a car going ninety miles an hour.

If you use very many "weak passive" sentences like those above, you will create a monotonous tone in your writing, and your ideas will appear dull and lifeless.

EXERCISE 18. In the following sentences replace the passive voice with the active voice.

1. Waffles and bacon were ordered by us for supper.
2. Mr. Brown's lawn will be mowed by Johnny on Saturday.
3. A black cotton dress was bought by Susan.
4. No moss is gathered by a rolling stone.
5. My ankles were snapped at by an angry dog.
6. On the opening day of the season a bear was shot by the hunter.
7. Next week my vacation will be begun by me.
8. The radiator of the car became frozen during the cold night.
9. The bone was devoured by the dog.
10. The Battle of Waterloo was lost by Napoleon.

EFFECTIVE SENTENCES REVIEW EXERCISE
(Sections 33 through 36.) Indicate what strikes you as the principal error from the standpoint of effectiveness in each of the following sentences (faulty subordination, lack of emphasis, lack of parallelism, etc.) and then revise the sentence.

1. The vase was a beautiful and priceless illustration of ancient Cretan art, and it was in a glass display case.
2. The dog was casually sauntering down the street when he was hit and instantly killed by a speeding car.
3. While Innis was already deeply in debt, he felt that the bargain was too good to let pass.

4. To make concrete you need cement. This should be of good quality. You also need sand. You should have twice as much sand as concrete. Gravel is the third thing needed. About three times as much gravel as cement goes into concrete. The gravel should be clean. It should not be mixed with soil or dirt.

5. The relief pitcher was a rookie with a good fast ball and who had the coolness and poise of a veteran.

6. The bear was a formidable creature standing over six feet high, with big sharp teeth, and having eyes that glared red in the dark.

7. After looking over the paint charts, Mrs. Cramer decided on light green, and the cottage was finally painted blue.

8. There had been a skunk in the neighborhood and its scent was soon perceived by us as we walked along.

9. Carlsbad Caverns are the largest in the United States, and they were discovered by accident in 1912.

10. After changing her mind several times, Jane finally decided to go to the tea, meeting at it the man she later married.

11. The Buick was speeding down the Mount Quinlan Road when it got out of control, falling sixty feet over a cliff.

12. Frank had always wanted to be able to drive the family car like his brother did.

13. The Sox will be under a new manager next year and they are bringing up two new catchers from their farm system and there will be changes in the infield and the rookie Ziegler is going to play first base.

14. Since Vernon had never been nearly as good in chemistry as his sister Ellen, who had won a scholarship in the subject at West Virginia and who was working in the DuPont laboratories in Wilmington, Delaware, he tried to rearrange his schedule by changing his history section so that he would not be in the chemistry section taught by Professor Welsh, who, everyone agreed, was a very stiff marker.

15. The chief strode ahead of his warlike tribesmen, and he was brandishing a long spear in his hand.

16. The canaries lay inert at the bottom of the cage, showing that the mine gallery was filled with dangerous gases.

17. The *Morning Gazette* was against Saunders. It had many editorials attacking him. The *Star* also opposed him. The afternoon papers were against him too. They supported

Scanlon, his opponent. Scanlon also had the support of the various civic organizations. But Saunders won.

18. As the late afternoon sun lengthened over Tressler Field, which was named for John C. Tressler, who gave it to the school, the Harwood team, which had lost five of its seven games during the year, pushed over the touchdown late in the fourth quarter that beat the Minnequa team and knocked them out of the state championship.

19. First tabulations showed that the majority of the tests contradicted Rinehart's theories, but Randall doubted their accuracy.

20. The bobbin of the sewing machine did not work very well; my aunt always had trouble with them.

21. The melodrama was about a series of murders in an old castle and a Scotland Yard man solved them.

22. Gorgeous Gus put on an act in which he appeared girlish, and he was a bone-crushing wrestler.

23. The industrial growth has been slow and not utilizing the available assets.

24. As the slide blocked the road, the people turned their cars around and returned to town.

25. We have a school system operating on a fulltime basis and which is offering a full curriculum.

In answering he states the question, and expound-
eth the terms thereof. Otherwise the disputants
shall end, where they ought to have begun, in
differences about words, and be barbarians each to
the other, speaking in a language neither understand.
—THOMAS FULLER (1642)

I come from a state that raises corn and cotton and
cockleburs and democrats, and frothy eloquence
neither convinces nor satisfies me. I am from Mis-
souri. You have got to show me.
—WILLARD DUNCAN VANDIVER

SECTION 37

Logic = LOG

**Make sure that the content as well as the structure
of your writing is logical.**

Correct grammatical structure is not an end in itself but a vehicle
for communicating thought clearly. Clear and purposeful writing is
fundamentally a reflection of logical thinking. People who complain
"My ideas are good, but I can't express them clearly in writing" are
usually fooling themselves. Vague and undirected writing reflects
vague and undirected thinking.

The treatment of logic that follows is brief and oversimplified. Space permits a discussion of only those matters that have an obvious relationship to the writing process. You may find more detailed treatments in the following:

Altick, Richard, *A Preface to Critical Reading*. 3rd Edition. New York: Henry Holt and Co., 1956.

Beardsley, Monroe C., *Thinking Straight*. New York: Prentice-Hall, Inc., 1950.

Beardsley, Monroe C., *Practical Logic*. New York: Prentice-Hall, Inc., 1950.

Black, Max, *Critical Thinking*. Second Edition. New York: Prentice-Hall, Inc., 1952.

Boatright, Mody C., *Accuracy in Thinking*. New York: Rinehart & Company, Inc., 1957.

Chase, Stuart, *The Tyranny of Words*. New York: Harcourt, Brace and Company, 1939.

Cohen, Morris, and Ernest Nagel, *An Introduction to Logic and Scientific Method*. New York: Harcourt, Brace and Company, 1934.

Hayakawa, S. I., *Language in Thought and Action*. New York: Harcourt, Brace and Company, 1949.

Johnson, Wendell, *People in Quandaries*. New York: Harper & Brothers, 1946.

Robinson, James H., *The Mind in the Making*. New York: Harper & Brothers, 1921.

Thouless, Robert, *How to Think Straight*. New York: Simon and Schuster, Inc., 1932.

37a **Define terms whose exact meaning is essential to clear and logical communication.**

Clearcut definition is a key feature of logical thinking and writing. Your reader must know how you define your terms before he can comprehend your meaning. Words such as *propaganda, democracy, education, virtue, religion,* for example, may mean vastly different things to different people. Much senseless argument, in fact, arises because people fail to agree on meanings. Your writing will gain in strength and clarity if you are always sure to define important terms.

(1) *In defining a term, first put it into the class of objects* (genus) *to which it belongs.* This process is called *classification.*

TERM		GENUS
A saw	is	a *cutting tool*
A carpet	is	a *floor covering*

In general, the narrower the classification, the clearer the eventual definition.

> NOT A rifle is a *weapon.*
>
> BUT A rifle is a *firearm.*

Though *weapon* is a legitimate classification for *rifle,* for purposes of definition it includes more than is necessary (*knives, spears, bows and arrows, clubs,* etc.).

(2) *Next, distinguish it from other objects in its class.* This process is called *differentiation.*

TERM		GENUS	DIFFERENTIATION
A saw	is	a *cutting tool*	*with a thin, flat blade and a series of teeth on the edge.*
A carpet	is	a *floor covering*	*of woven or felted fabric, usually tacked to the floor.*

(3) *Use parallel form in stating the term to be defined and its definition.* Do not use the phrases "is when" or "is where" to indicate definitions.

> NOT A debate *is when* two people or sides argue a given proposition in a regulated discussion.
>
> BUT *A debate is a regulated discussion* of a given proposition between two matched sides.

(4) *Be sure that the definition itself does not contain the name of the thing defined or any derivative of it.* Nothing is achieved when words are defined in terms of themselves.

> NOT A rifle is a firearm with *riflings* inside its barrel to impart rotary motion to its projectile.
>
> BUT A rifle is a firearm with *spiral grooves* inside its barrel to impart rotary motion to its projectile.

Whenever possible, define a term in words that are more familiar than the term itself. The complexity of Dr. Samuel Johnson's definition of the simple word *network* is notorious:

> *Network:* anything reticulated or decussated, at equal distances, with interstices between the intersections.

Ordinarily, of course, you will define terms without being aware of giving them a genus and a differentiation. But it is always possible to check the logic of a definition against the criteria given above. Consider the following example from a student paper:

> Finally, college is valuable to a person interested in success. By *success* I don't mean what is usually thought of when that word is used. I mean achieving one's goals. Everybody has his own goals to achieve, all of them very different. But whatever they are, college will give one the know-how and the contacts he needs to achieve them successfully.

This definition is obviously unsatisfactory; but the specifications for logical definition will help clarify why and how it breaks down. If the statement which this paragraph makes about *success* is isolated, it comes out like this: "Success is the successful achievement of goals which know-how and contacts gained at college help one achieve." First, this statement violates one of the basic principles of definition because it defines the word in terms of itself—"success is the successful achievement...." Next, the writer does not make it clear what he means by "goals," and the qualifying clause "which know-how and contacts gained at college help one achieve" does nothing to help us grasp his intended meaning because we do not know what his definition would be for "know-how" and "contacts." Hence he has failed in both aspects of good definition. He has neither put the terms into an understandable genus, nor has he made a real differentiation. About all the sense we can make of his paragraph is that success means being successful, a definition of little help indeed. Very likely the writer had no very clear idea of what he was talking about and so could not hope to communicate it to his readers. Had he checked the logic of his definition, he would have discovered this fact for himself.

EXERCISE 1. Discuss the validity of the sentences below *as definitions.* What revisions would you suggest for greater accuracy?

1. Democracy is a government of the people, by the people, and for the people.
2. Humor is to say something funny.
3. Housemaid's knee is a swelling due to the enlargement of the bursa in front of the patella.
4. Walking is when we use our legs as a means of transportation.
5. Swimming is propelling yourself forward in water with a swimming motion.
6. Poetry is when the lines end where they will rhyme with the next one.
7. A touchdown is where the team with the football crosses the goal line of its opponents.
8. Diagnosis means to find out what is wrong with something.
9. A bandsaw is a saw with a cutting blade that revolves in an endless circle.
10. Winter wheat is a species of wheat which is planted in the fall and harvested in the late spring or early summer.

37b **Support or qualify all generalizations.**

A generalization is an assertion that what is true of several particulars (objects, experiences, people) of the same class (genus) is true of most or all of the particulars of that class. For example, the statement "Drinking coffee in the evening always keeps me awake all night" is a generalization based on several particular experiences on separate evenings. Generalization is an essential process in thinking; without it, there could be no evaluation of experience—only the accumulation of isolated facts. Yet generalization has its dangers, as the following examples reveal.

(1) *Base all generalizations on adequate evidence.* We all tend to generalize on the basis of a few striking examples, especially when they accord with what we want to believe.

The hasty generalization—"leaping to conclusions" on the basis of insufficient evidence—is especially dangerous because it can lead you to believe or to make absurd assertions. Test the soundness of this generalization:

PARTICULAR A	My sister Imogene dented the car's fenders yesterday.
PARTICULAR B	Mrs. Elliott has just driven her car through the rear end of the garage.
PARTICULAR C	Did you see that woman drive through that red light!
HASTY GENERALIZATION	Women can't drive.

To protect yourself, as well as to be fair to your readers, never advance a generalization unless you are prepared to support it with ample evidence. How much evidence you need depends on the purpose of your writing. Sometimes you will need to list only three or four examples; sometimes you will need to analyze the evidence itself in detail. Generalizations often take the form of topic sentences in paragraphs (see "Paragraphs," Section 32a).

(2) *Be cautious in using such words as* ALWAYS, NEVER, ALL, NONE, RIGHT, WRONG *in generalizations*. Broad generalizations are as pernicious as hasty generalizations. In fact, the two usually spring from the same desire—to reach a conclusion without going through the effort of collecting evidence. A valid generalization is often rendered invalid by the careless use of *never* instead of *seldom*, of *always* instead of *usually*.

| OVERSTATED | People who are excessively radical in their youth always become conservative when they acquire power and property. |
| QUALIFIED | Even the most radical youths are likely to grow conservative when they acquire power and property. |

EXERCISE 2. Discuss the validity of the following sentences *as generalizations*. Restate those that seem exaggerated.

1. Only intellectuals have nervous breakdowns.
2. That dog understands everything I say.
3. Any man who is honest cannot fail to be successful.
4. A great deal of "realistic" fiction is based on what average people would call "indecent" characters.

5. There isn't a businessman in this country who isn't disgusted with the red tape of government bureaucrats.

6. Professors and preachers are men who cannot succeed in business.

7. Professors and preachers are men who do not care about making money.

8. The number of airplane accidents proves that air travel is not safe.

9. A dog's disposition is simply the reflection of the disposition of the people who own him.

10. American doctors prefer Weedo cigarets.

37c **Base your arguments on honest evidence and present them fairly.**

Consciously or unconsciously in our desire to be right, we tend to falsify, suppress evidence, call names, cheat, and hit below the belt in our arguments.

(1) *Base your judgment on what you know, not on what you want to believe.* Prejudice (prejudgment, or judgment before the facts are examined) is the commonest type of unfairness. Notice in the examples below that a judgment is passed although no *facts* pertinent to that judgment have been stated.

> PREJUDGMENT   I heard that he didn't get in until one A.M. last night, *and you can bet that he was spending his time in some cheap saloon.*

> PREJUDGMENT   Did you hear what Peggy said about her? *It's our duty to ask her to resign from the club immediately.*

(2) *Do not try to dismiss an argument or an opponent by appealing to general prejudice.* Name-calling is an appeal to a reader's emotion, not his reason. It tries to arouse prejudice by attaching unpleasant labels to an idea or person. Labels such as "red," "fascist," "atheist," "low-brow," and "fellow-traveler" carry a heavy emotional charge but little information; to use them loosely and irresponsibly is to be dishonest.

(a) *Do not sidestep an argument by trying to discredit the man who proposed it.* This is known as "argument to the man" (*argu-*

299

mentum ad hominem). It fails to take into account that even though discredited for one thing, the man might be right about others.

> AD HOMINEM   He has no business talking about the responsibilities of a democracy, *because he has just got out of jail.*
>
> AD HOMINEM   Don't pay any attention to what Milton says about divorce. *He just couldn't get along with his wife.*

(b) *Do not associate an idea with a great name or movement in the hope of imbuing your idea with borrowed prestige.* This is the erroneous technique of "transfer" (*argumentum ad verecundiam*). This method usually involves associating an idea with a great name or movement (or, particularly, with an attractive face or figure, as in advertising) in the hope that its prestige or glamour will be transferred to the proposal being argued. The "transfer" device also works in reverse: If a proposal or person can be associated with a movement or name in general disfavor (communism, economic-royalism, and so on), it or he has very little chance of being objectively and logically judged. This technique clouds the issue, for the associations made usually have no real bearing on the conclusions drawn.

> TRANSFER   If Abraham Lincoln were alive today, I am sure he would devote his full energies to seeing our policy made the law of the land.
>
> TRANSFER   She's lovely! She's engaged! She uses X!
>
> TRANSFER   He believes in a high income tax, just as do the Marxists.

(c) *Do not sidestep an argument by appealing to the instincts and ideas of the crowd.* This is known as "argument to the people" (*argumentum ad populum*) or the "bandwagon" approach. It assumes that what the crowd thinks or believes is right. Thus, to be right, one must go along with the crowd. Obviously this is not true, as many incidents of "mob rule" would bear out. Nonetheless it is a favorite approach among advertisers, who are masters of this appeal:

> AD POPULUM   Drink X! For 75 years *it has been the favorite drink of the man in the street. You'll like it too.*

AD POPULUM   Decent, upright citizens will not be interested in anything he says.

EXERCISE 3. Discuss the "fairness" of the statements below.

1. What does Bill know about the responsibilities of business-men? He never met a payroll in his life.

2. George Washington, the Father of our Country, made his position on "foreign entanglements" very clear, and what was good enough in Washington's day is good enough for us.

3. Your neighbor drives a "Wingfoot Special." Why don't you?

4. He's your hit-and-run driver all right; every morning he goes by our house at sixty miles an hour.

5. My parents were like yours: plain, simple hardworking folks, and if you vote for me you can be sure that the rights of the common people will be safeguarded.

6. There is a law against murder in this country, and all mur-derers ought to pay the full penalty of the law.

7. Whenever corruption is found in the federal government the people ought to vote another party into power.

8. I'm sure that Ivan Ivanovitch is a Communist. With a name like that how could he be anything else?

9. Every ambitious citizen should aspire to own a large home because people measure a man's prestige and respectability by the size of his house.

10. The state university has no business using the taxpayers' money to buy books for the library. They haven't read a lot of the books that are already in the library.

37d   **Be sure that statements involving cause-and-effect relationships are logically sound.**

Some of the defects of thinking arise not from prejudice, unfair-ness, or ignorance of the facts, but from lack of training in logical processes. The two major logical processes are *induction* and *deduction*.

In the process of *induction* thinking proceeds from the particular to the general. This means, for example, that when particular facts are shown time after time to be true, or when a particular laboratory experiment time after time yields the same result, or when a wide and varied sampling of people gives the same type of answer to a given question, *then* a general conclusion based on the facts in question may be drawn. Repeated experimentation and testing led to the conclusion that the Salk vaccine would help prevent polio. The scientist uses induction when he tests and retests his hypothesis before stating it as a general truth. The whole "scientific method" proceeds by inductive processes.

In the process of *deduction* thinking proceeds from the general to the particular. This means that from a general conclusion other facts are deduced. Obviously, then, if deduction is to be valid, the conclusion from which you operate must be true. Given sound and valid conclusions from which to draw, deduction is a shrewd and effective logical technique. Knowing that penicillin is an effective weapon against infection, we wisely seek a doctor to administer it to us if we have infections.

Notice that there is an induction-deduction cycle of reasoning. The sound conclusions reached through induction may in turn serve as the bases for deduction. For example, over many years the National Safety Council has kept careful records of holiday highway accidents and has reached the valid conclusion that accidents increase greatly on holiday week ends. From this conclusion, you can deduce that it is safer not to travel on holiday week ends.

The intricacies of induction and deduction as systems of logic would take many pages to explore. The foregoing is designed merely to give a working definition of each, from which we can now proceed to examine a few of the most common errors in logic.

(1) *Do not assume that there is a cause-and-effect relationship between two facts merely because one follows the other in time.* This fallacy is known as *post hoc, ergo propter hoc* ("after this, therefore because of this").

POST HOC   Industrialism was not established until after the Protestant Revolution; therefore Protestantism was the cause of industrialism.

POST HOC   I won't say she's to blame, but I do know that he didn't drink before he married her.

(2) *Do not mistake a mere inference for a logically sound conclusion.* This fallacy is known as *non-sequitur* ("it does not follow").

NON-SEQUITUR   This is the best play I have seen this year and should win the Pulitzer Prize.

(Have you seen *all* the plays produced this year? Are you qualified to judge the qualities that make a Pulitzer Prize play? Does it follow that just because a play is the best you have seen this year, it should therefore win the Pulitzer Prize?)

NON-SEQUITUR   Steven will never get anywhere; he's got his head in the clouds.

(3) *Do not assume the truth of something you are trying to prove.* This fallacy is known as "begging the question."

BEGGING THE QUESTION   His handwriting is hard to read because it is almost illegible.

BEGGING THE QUESTION   I like Buicks because they are my favorite automobiles.

BEGGING THE QUESTION   I don't care what he's done; if he's in jail he's done *something* wrong. Good people don't go to jail.

(4) *Do not assume that because two circumstances or ideas are alike in some respects, they are alike in all other respects.* This is the fallacy of "false analogy"—and perhaps the principal cause of shoddy political thinking.

FALSE ANALOGY   Of course he'll make a good Secretary of Agriculture—hasn't he lived on a farm all his life and hasn't he succeeded in making a profitable business of raising livestock!

(Undoubtedly, the Secretary of Agriculture should have experience with farmers' problems, and undoubtedly he should be a competent man. But a farming background and success in raising livestock are not in themselves proof that a man will be a good administrator or know what is best for all farmers.)

(5) *Avoid contradicting yourself.* This fallacy occurs when you are unwilling or unable to establish a clear conclusion or opinion—when you want to have your cake and eat it too.

SELF-CONTRADICTION   Democracy and communism are widely different political systems, although communism is really an economic system.

303

EXERCISE 4. Discuss the validity of the reasoning in the sentences below. Point out which rules of logic are violated.

1. Good Englishmen should oppose socialized medicine because it violates established British tradition.
2. Democracy has never succeeded in China; therefore immigrant Chinese do not make good American citizens.
3. Don't swap horses in the middle of a stream; don't change presidents during a crisis.
4. Harvey likes reading because books are his favorite pastime.
5. I know a man who had seven years' bad luck because he broke a mirror.
6. Bill's success as a real estate broker is assured; he has a good sense of values.
7. Gentlemen prefer blondes because they are attracted to women with fair hair.
8. The Confederate and Northern states became a united nation after the Civil War. Civil wars are always a unifying force in a country's development.
9. In the state primary election Governor Cameron got the largest number of votes a gubernatorial candidate ever received in this state. This proves that he is the most popular governor in the state's history.
10. Our football team never lost more than three games in a season until last year, when we lost five. It is obvious that the new coach, who came last year, is not as good a coach as his predecessors.

EXERCISE 5. Comment on the logic in the following conversation.

MR. JONES: Newspapers today coddle and spoon-feed the public by such devices as cheesecake, one-syllable words, clichés, jargon, etc. Don't you think it's about time that the public did something about this? It seems to me that our standards of literacy are getting lower and lower. Newspapers used to have a higher standard. They stood for something. Now they depend almost exclusively on cheap devices and sensationalism. All papers must follow this policy if they are to survive.

MR. SMITH: What you're saying is, "Let's go back to the covered wagon era." You don't want to progress. Don't

you think automobiles are a sign of progress? I do.
Similarly, with newspapers. Today they reach many
more people than they used to. Anyone can read
and understand a newspaper today. That's more
than they could do a hundred years ago. If that
isn't progress, then nothing is.

EXERCISE 6. Comment in one or two paragraphs on the logic
(generalization, fairness, reasoning, etc.) of the following selection.

SPORTS VERSUS THE SPORTSWRITER

The trouble with sports is the sportswriters. These tin-horn
sports, these semi-literate dealers in clichés, cram the daily newspapers with misinformation and moronic opinions about athletes,
coaches, and sports themselves. The day after a sports contest
sees the poor sports lover once again a victim in another of the
eternal successions of "mornings-after"—when sportswriters begin
again their assault on the English language, good taste, and
common sense.

One would think that people who pretend to know so much
about the secret workings and inside strategy of sports would be
able to report on a football or baseball game with some objectivity and penetration. But no! The sportswriter goes to great
pains to tell us what we already know: that Old Siwash won.
He tells us further that it is his considered opinion that Old
Siwash played the better game. He then proceeds to indulge in
assorted bits of irrelevancy and viciousness, according to the
state of his ulcers. He gives us the startling news that Old
Siwash's supporters were eager to win the game; that Halfback
Haggerty would not have fumbled the kickoff if he had caught
it instead.

But a sportswriter in front of a typewriter is only an idiot; a
sportswriter in front of a microphone is a jabbering idiot. The
next time you listen to a radio broadcast of a football game, force
yourself to listen to the half-time interviews. Listen to the sportswriters gather to tell one another, in their own substandard idiom,
what marvelous jobs they have done in "bringing you the game."
Listen to them inform you, in voices choked with emotion and
borrowed Scotch, that the game isn't over until the final gun
sounds—"that anything can happen." This is undoubtedly what
sportswriters mean when they speak of "inside dope."

REVIEW EXERCISE. The following problems are designed to direct your attention to some of the violations of logic that we encounter every day.

1. Analyze several automobile advertisements, several cosmetic or drug advertisements, and several cigarette advertisements in current magazines or on television on the basis of the following questions:

    a. What specific appeals are made? (E.g.: automobile advertising makes wide use of the "bandwagon" approach; cosmetic advertising often uses "transfer" methods.) How logical are these appeals?

    b. Are all terms clearly defined?

    c. What kinds of generalizations are used or assumed? Are these generalizations adequately supported?

    d. Is evidence honestly and fairly presented?

    e. Are cause and effect relationships clear and indisputable?

2. Look through copies of your daily newspaper and bring to class letters to the editor or excerpts from political speeches which contain examples of fallacious reasoning. Look for false analogies, unsupported generalizations, name-calling, and prejudices.

3. Read an opinion article in a popular magazine and write a report analyzing the logic underlying the opinions and conclusions stated.

> *Dictionaries are like watches; the worst is better than none, and the best cannot be expected to go quite true.*
>
> —SAMUEL JOHNSON

Words = WDS

38 THE DICTIONARY

The study of words begins with the dictionary, the great storehouse of linguistic information. A good dictionary is a biography of words, recording spelling, pronunciation, part of speech, etymology, meaning, and, when necessary, principal parts, or plurals, or other forms. Very often it includes other information—lists of abbreviations, rules for punctuation and spelling, condensed biographical and geographical information, the pronunciation and source of many given names, and a vocabulary of rhymes. For writers and readers a dictionary is an indispensable tool.

Unabridged Dictionaries.

For English the great standard work is the *New English Dictionary,* sometimes called the NED, a work issued in ten volumes and a supplement between 1888 and 1933 by the Clarendon Press, Oxford, England, and reissued in 1933 as the *Oxford English Dictionary* (OED). A historical work, this dictionary traces the progress of a word through the language, giving dated quotations to illustrate its meaning and spelling at particular times in history. Many pages may be devoted to a single word. *Set,* for example, receives twenty-three pages of closely printed type. Under one of the 150-odd definitions of *set—*"to fix or appoint (a time) for the transaction of an affair"—there are illustrative sentences taken from writings dated 1056, 1250, 1290, 1300, 1387, 1470-85, 1548-77, 1633, 1693, 1753, 1810, 1890, and 1893.

Another unabridged dictionary is *Webster's New International Dictionary of the English Language,* first published in 1909 and reissued in a second edition in 1934 by the G. and C. Merriam Company of Springfield, Massachusetts, a long-established house and the legal inheritor of Noah Webster's copyright. The Merriam-Webster entries are scholarly and exact, though by no means so exhaustive as the OED's. Here is a specimen entry:

jail (jāl), *n.* Also **gaol** (jāl). [ME. *jaile, gail, gayhol,* fr. OF. *jaiole* (F. *geôle*), ONF. *gaiole,* fr. VL. *caveola,* dim. fr. L. *cavea* cage. See CAGE.] **a** Orig., and still often, a prison. **b** A building for the confinement of persons held in lawful custody, esp. for minor offenses or with reference to some future judicial proceeding; a lockup.
☞ COMBINATIONS: **jail′keep′er, jail′mate′, jail′yard′.**
jail, *v. t.;* JAILED (jāld); JAIL′ING.   Also **gaol.**   To confine in or as in a jail; to imprison; to lock up.   "[Bolts] that *jail* you from free life."   *Tennyson.*

Since dictionaries must say much in little space, they use a great number of abbreviations and seemingly cryptic entries. You will find these troublesome unless you take time to read the explanatory pages and acquaint yourself with the symbols used.

In the specimen above, the explanatory symbols tell you that the word *jail* is entered first as a noun (*n.*) and then as a transitive verb (*v. t.*). The pronounciation is indicated by (jāl); if you were to refer to the bottom of the dictionary page on which this entry appears, you would find that *ā* is to be sounded as *a* in *ale*. The variant *gaol*, pronounced exactly as *jail*, is a secondary spelling (as in Oscar Wilde's *Ballad of Reading Gaol*). The material between the brackets shows the origin or etymology of the word: *jail* comes from a word in Middle English (ME.) which was variously spelled *jaile, gail, gayhol*. These forms in turn came from Old French (OF.) *jaiole* and Old Norman French (ONF.) *gaiole*. In modern French the word is *geôle*. The old French words in turn came from the vulgar Latin (VL.) *caveola*, a diminutive (dim.) form of the Latin (L.) *cavea*, which meant *cage*. The editors then suggest that you refer to the word *cage* itself for fuller information. The use of *a* and *b* to number the definitions instead of *1* and *2* indicates that the two meanings are closely related. Because neither of the definitions carries a label (*Brit., U. S., Law*, etc.) you may assume that each is used in general speech or writing. The final item lists combination forms: in each case the main accent (*'*) falls on the first syllable, the secondary accent (*'*) on the second.

The second entry is devoted to the verb *jail*. You may assume at once that it is pronounced in the same way as the noun; otherwise a different pronunciation would be indicated. You learn too that the past tense (and past participle, since no past participle form is given) is *jailed*, the present participle *jailing*. Further, you find that the verb *jail* has the secondary spelling *gaol*, as has the noun. Finally, the meaning of the verb is illustrated by a quotation from the works of the English poet Alfred Tennyson.

Desk Dictionaries.

Unabridged dictionaries are useful as reference works. For everyday purposes a good abridged or desk dictionary is more practical. Here is a list that may help you in selecting a good desk dictionary:

(1) *Webster's New Collegiate Dictionary*, G. and C. Merriam Company, Springfield, Massachusetts, 1949. This is the successor to *Webster's Collegiate Dictionary*, 1941, and like its predecessor is

carefully edited and conservative. Its etymologies are particularly complete. Insofar as possible, the order of definitions under any one word is historical: the original meaning is given first, the second meaning next, and so on.

> **jail** (jāl), *n.* Also **gaol** (jāl). [OF. *jaiole,* ONF. *gaiole,* fr. VL. *cabeola,* dim. fr. L. *cavea* cage.] A building for the confinement of persons held in lawful custody, esp. for minor offenses or pending judicial proceeding; a lockup. — *v. t.* To confine in or as in a jail.
>
> By permission. From Webster's *New Collegiate Dictionary*
> Copyright, 1949,
> by G. & C. Merriam Co.

(2) *The American College Dictionary.* Random House, New York and London, 1947. This dictionary, which is being revised continuously, is edited by a group of outstanding American linguists who recognize that Middle American, Western, and Southern pronunciation and usage contribute as much to the character of the American language as do the pronunciation and usage of New England or the Atlantic seaboard. The word "American" on the title page, therefore, has real significance.

> **jail** (jāl), *n.* **1.** a prison, esp. one for the detention of persons awaiting trial or convicted of minor offenses; gaol. — *v.t.* **2.** to take into or hold in custody. Also, *Brit.,* **gaol.** [ME *jaiole,* t. OF: prison, cage; ult. der. L *cavea* cavity, enclosure, cage. See GAOL] — **jail′less,** *adj.* — **jail′like′,** *adj.*
>
> By permission. From *The American College Dictionary*
> Copyright, 1947, 1949, by Random House.
> Text edition, copyright, 1948, by Harper & Brothers.

(3) *Thorndike-Barnhart Comprehensive Desk Dictionary,* Doubleday and Company, Inc., New York, 1951. This is handy-sized and inexpensive, yet reliable and up-to-date.

> **jail** (jāl), *n.* **1.** Also, *Brit.* **gaol.** prison for people awaiting trial or being punished for minor offenses. **2. break jail,** escape from jail. — *v.* put in jail; keep in jail. [< OF *jaiole,* ult. < L *cavea* coop] — **jail′less,** *adj.* — **jail′like′,** *adj.*
>
> By permission. From *Thorndike-Barnhart Comprehensive Desk Dictionary.* Copyright, 1951, by Doubleday & Company, Inc.

(4) *Webster's New World Dictionary,* The World Publishing Company, Cleveland, 1953. This is the largest and most recently published of the present group of reliable desk dictionaries and is continuously revised.

jail (jāl), *n.* [ME. *jaile, gaile, gayhol;* OFr. *jaiole, jaole, gaole,* a cage, prison; LL. *caveola,* dim. of L. *cavea,* a cage, coop], a building for the confinement of people who have broken the law or are awaiting trial; prison, especially for those convicted of minor offenses. *v.t.* to put or keep in jail; imprison. Also, British, **gaol.**

The Uses of a Dictionary.

(1) *Spelling.* A word is listed in the dictionary under the spelling the editors find most common. You can usually come close enough to the spelling of a doubtful word to find it. Remember, however, the vagaries of English spelling: particularly that *c* and *s* and *sc* are sometimes pronounced alike. When there are alternative spellings, the preferred form is usually given first. The secondary spelling is usually British (as *humour*), or foreign (as *manoeuvre*), or simplified (as *altho, thru*). The general rule is to avoid the secondary spelling except when special circumstances seem to call for it.

The spelling entry also divides the word into syllables, showing how to separate it properly at the ends of lines (see "Syllabication," Section 4). It also gives the proper spelling of compound words— whether the editors found them more often written as two single words (*half brother*), as a hyphenated compound (*quarter-hour*), or as one word (*drugstore*). Dictionaries use special symbols to indicate foreign words that require italics (in manuscript, underlining). The *New Collegiate* marks such words with two vertical bars (‖); *American College* and *Thorndike-Barnhart* as Latin, French, etc.; and *Webster's New World* with a double dagger (‡).

EXERCISE 1. What is the preferred spelling of each of these words?

aeroplane	criticise	humour
aesthetic	daemon	medieval
canceled	enclose	Shakspere
cheque	judgement	theatre

EXERCISE 2. Copy the following compounds, showing which should be written as they are, which hyphenated, and which written as separate words.

ablebodied	selfmade
cleancut	stepson
iceboat	tonguetied
illbred	uptodate
onesided	upperclassmen

EXERCISE 3. Copy the following foreign words and underline those that require italics.

coiffeur	matinee
coup d'état	nouveau riche
debonair	résumé
debut	sine qua non
ibidem	status quo

(2) *Pronunciation.* Dictionaries indicate the pronunciation of words by respelling them with special symbols and letters. Explanation of the symbols is given either at the bottom of the page on which the entry appears or in the prefatory pages or both.

Indicating pronunciations is the most difficult of all the tasks of dictionary editors. *Correct pronunciation* is a very flexible term. Generally speaking, it is the standard of pronunciation prevailing among educated people, but often correctness is a theory rather than a reality. Does a Southerner mispronounce *I* when he says *Ah?* Is a Bostonian incorrect in saying *pa'k* for *park?* Dictionaries do not even attempt to list all the variant pronunciations in use.

The pronunciation of words, moreover, is influenced by the situation. In formal speech, syllables are likely to be more deliberately sounded than in informal speech. Further, the pronunciation of a word is affected by its position in the sentence and by the meaning it carries. Yet dictionary editors have no choice but to deal with each word as an individual entity. They record its formal, or full, pronunciation—what may be referred to as "platform" pronunciation. Certainly, to pronounce every word in our conversation as deliberately as the dictionary recommends would make our speech stilted and pompous.

Dictionaries do, however, make an attempt to show alternatives in pronunciation. Ordinarily, the first pronunciation given is to be preferred, though occasionally the second pronunciation is as acceptable or as "correct" as the first. In the last analysis your preference will be determined by the pronunciation you hear in the cultivated conversation around you.

EXERCISE 4. What is the pronunciation of the following words? Check your dictionary and copy the pronunciations carefully.

alias	exquisite	heinous
bestial	forehead	hyperbole
clique	formidable	mischievous
deference	genuine	municipal
epitome	gondola	superfluous

EXERCISE 5. Is usage divided in the pronunciation of the following words? If so, which pronunciation seems more acceptable to you? Why?

acclimate	decorous	illustrated	process
adult	Don Juan	inquiry	program
amateur	Don Quixote	interesting	research
apparatus	envelope	precedence	vaudeville

(3) *Etymology.* The etymology of a word—that is, its origin and derivation—often helps clarify its present meaning and spelling. Etymological information is sometimes interesting or amusing in its own right. Because the course of history changes or restricts or extends the meanings of words, however, many original meanings have been lost completely. *Presently,* for example, formerly meant *at once, immediately;* because of the human tendency to procrastinate, it now means *shortly, in a little while.*

EXERCISE 6. Trace the etymology of each of the following words.

assassin	egg	nay	shirt
bedlam	edge	neighbor	skirt
chapel	familiar	priest	slogan
draggle	incisive	screech	squelch

EXERCISE 7. From what specific names have the following words been derived?

ampere	macadam
boycott	quisling
chauvinism	shrapnel
dunce	ulster
gardenia	watt

EXERCISE 8. From what language did each of the following words come?

almanac	dory	jute	piano	tulip
canoe	goulash	kerosene	rucksack	turban
cruise	huckster	persimmon	squadron	tycoon

(4) *Meaning.* Strictly speaking, dictionaries do not "define" words; they record the meaning or meanings that actual usage, past and present, has attached to words. When more than one meaning is recorded for a single word, the *Merriam-Webster* dictionaries list them in order of historical use. Most other dictionaries list the more general and present meaning first. Special and technical meanings are clearly labeled. Choosing the appropriate meaning out of the many that are offered is not difficult if you read them *all* and understand their order of arrangement as indicated in the prefatory pages of the dictionary.

EXERCISE 9. How many different meanings can you find for each of the following words?

cut	open
give	out
go	run
hit	sit
light	strike

EXERCISE 10. Trace the changes in meaning that have taken place in each of the following words:

ban	humor
complexion	intern
engine	machine
fond	manufacture
gossip	sincere

EXERCISE 11. Distinguish between the meanings of the words in each of the following groups.

ambitious, aspiring, enterprising	eminent, celebrated
apt, likely, liable	enormous, immense
common, mutual	equanimity, composure
deface, disfigure	restive, restless
diplomatic, politic, tactful	voracious, ravenous

(5) *Grammar.* Grammatically, dictionaries are helpful in several ways. Good dictionaries indicate what part of speech each word is; or, if the word serves as more than one part of speech, the dictionaries will usually list each possibility and give illustrative sentences for each. Dictionaries also list the principal parts of verbs, the plurals of nouns, and the comparative and superlative degrees of adjectives and adverbs, but only when these forms are irregular or present spelling difficulties. The past tense and present participle of a verb are not given when they are regularly formed by adding *-ed* and *-ing* (*walked, walking*). Plurals ending in *-s* or *-es* (*cats, dishes*) are not usually given. And comparatives and superlatives formed by adding *more, most,* or *less, least,* or *-er, -est* are not given, unless the addition of the *-er, -est* endings presents a spelling difficulty (*heavy, heavier, heaviest*).

EXERCISE 12. What are the past tense and the present participle of each of these verbs?

be	prove
broadcast	rely
focus	set
get	teach
lend	wring

EXERCISE 13. What is the plural (or plurals) of each of the following?

alumna	deer
beau	index
bus	madame
crisis	phenomenon
daisy	volley

EXERCISE 14. Write the comparative and superlative forms of each of the following.

bad	often
ill	red
little	refined
lengthy	shyly
much	well

(6) *Labels.* Dictionaries do not label words that belong to the general vocabulary. The absence of a label therefore means that

the word is proper for formal and informal speaking and writing. Other words may have one of three kinds of label:

Subject labels, indicating that the word belongs to a special field: law, medicine, baseball, finance, and so on.

Geographical labels, indicating that the use of the word is generally restricted to a particular region or country: U. S., British, Australian, New England, Southern U. S., and so on.

Usage labels, indicating that the word is classified as archaic, colloquial, dialectal, obsolete, or slang. *Archaic* means that the word is old-fashioned (as *mayhap*); *colloquial* that the word is more suitable for loosely informal than formal use (as *boss*); *dialectal* that the word is restricted to local or provincial use (as *hoecake*); *obsolete* that the word has passed out of use (as *gantelope*); *slang* that the word has not yet been dignified by inclusion in the general vocabulary (as *blockhead*); *illiterate* that the use of the word is limited to vulgar speech (as *ain't*).

EXERCISE 15. Which of the following are standard English, which colloquial, and which slang?

enthuse	milksop
hindsight	natty
jam session	pal
kibitzer	perky
kill-joy	playboy

EXERCISE 16. In what areas of the world are you likely to hear the following?

batsman	mavourneen
billycan	mudcat
coulee	petrol
hoecake	pukka
laager	sourdough

EXERCISE 17. The following questions are designed to test your ability to use the whole dictionary—not only its vocabulary entries but also its various appendices. Any of the desk dictionaries discussed previously will help you find the answers.

1. What is the orthography of the word *embarrass?*
2. What is the preferred orthoëpy of the noun *envelope?*
3. What is the etymology of the word *precise?*

4. What are two homonyms for the word *reign?*
5. What are some antonyms for the word *concise?*
6. What is the syllabication of the word *redundant?*
7. What are some synonyms for the adjective *correct?*
8. Give the meanings of these abbreviations: *syn., v., mus., R.C.Ch.*
9. What do the following phrases mean? *finem respice, ars longa vita brevis, de profundis, honi soit qui mal y pense.*
10. What is the population of Birmingham, Michigan?
11. What is the meaning of the symbol B/E?
12. How long is the Cumberland River?
13. Who was the oldest of the Brontë sisters?
14. From what language does the proper name *Nahum* come?
15. List six words that rhyme with *mince.*

Special Dictionaries.

When you need specialized information about words, check one of the following dictionaries: *

Chambers's Technical Dictionary. Revised Edition with supplement. New York: The Macmillan Company, 1949.

Abbrevs: (A Dictionary of Abbreviations). Compiled by H. J. Stephenson. New York: The Macmillan Company, 1943.

New Rhyming Dictionary and Poet's Handbook. Revised Edition. Burgess Johnson, ed. New York and London: Harper & Brothers, 1957.

A Dictionary of Slang and Unconventional English. Fourth Edition. Eric Partridge, ed. New York: The Macmillan Company, 1952.

The American Thesaurus of Slang. Second Edition. Lester V. Berrey and Melvin Van Den Bark, eds. New York: Thomas Y. Crowell Company, 1953.

Dictionary of Synonyms. Springfield, Massachusetts: G. and C. Merriam Company, 1942.

A Pronouncing Dictionary of American English, J. S. Kenyon and T. A. Knott, eds. Springfield, Massachusetts: G. and C. Merriam Co., 1944.

* See also the list under *Reference Books* ("Dictionaries, Word Books") in "The Library," Section 45.

*The difference between the right word and the
almost-right word is the difference between lightning
and the lightning bug.*

—Attributed to MARK TWAIN

39 VOCABULARY

The English language contains well over a million words. Of
these, about two-fifths belong almost exclusively to special fields:
e.g., zoology, electronics, psychiatry. Of the remaining, the large
dictionaries list about 600,000, the desk dictionaries about 200,000.
Such wealth is both a blessing and a curse. On the one hand, many
English words are loosely synonymous, sometimes interchangeable,
as in *buy* a book or *purchase* a book. On the other hand, the distinctions between synonyms are fully as important as their similarities. For example, a family may be said to be living in *poverty,* or
in *penury,* or in *want,* or in *destitution.* All these words are loosely
synonymous, but only one will describe the family exactly as you
see it and wish your reader to see it. In short, as a writer of English
you must use your resources wisely.

Passive and active vocabulary.

In a sense, you have two vocabularies: a *passive* or *recognition*
vocabulary, which is made up of the words you recognize in the
context of reading matter but do not actually use yourself; and an
active vocabulary, which consists of "working" words—those you use
daily in your own writing and speaking. In the passage below, the
meaning of the italicized words is fairly clear (or at least can be
guessed at) from the context. But how many belong in your *active*
vocabulary?

Has it been been duly marked by historians that the late William Jennings Bryan's last *secular* act on this globe of sin was to catch flies? A curious detail, and not without its *sardonic overtones*. He was the most *sedulous* fly-catcher in American history, and in many ways the most successful. His *quarry*, of course, was not *Musca domestica* but *Homo neandertalensis*. For forty years he tracked it with coo and bellow, up and down the *rustic* backways of the Republic. Wherever the *flambeau* of Chautauqua smoked and guttered, and the bilge of Idealism ran in the veins, the Baptist pastors damned the brooks with the *sanctified*, and men gathered who were weary and heavy laden, and their wives who were full of Peruna and as *fecund* as the shad (*Alosa sapidissima*) —there the *indefatigable* Jennings set up his traps and spread his bait.

—H. L. MENCKEN, *Selected Prejudices*

Measuring your vocabulary.

Measuring the range of your vocabulary with any accuracy is extremely difficult. For one thing, no one knows just how many words make up a normal vocabulary, and estimates vary from eight to twenty thousand words. For another, vocabulary tests themselves are based on "word-frequency counts" that cannot take into account the special vocabulary (business, medicine, engineering, law, and so forth) that almost every individual person has.

The following test * is based on Thorndike's list of the 10,000 words that occur most frequently, grouped in order of their difficulty. It is assumed that a person who knows all the words (111) has a vocabulary of at least 10,000 words; a person who knows only 12 has a vocabulary of about 3,000. This table will help you estimate the size of your own vocabulary:

12	3,000		76	6,500
26	4,000		86	7,000
41	5,000		95	8,000
56	5,500		103	9,000
67	6,000		111	10,000

* From *Concerning Words*, Revised Edition, by J. E. Norwood. Copyright by Prentice-Hall, Inc., and reprinted with permission.

Select in each series the word or word-group that is closest in meaning to the word italicized in the phrase. Then insert its number in the blank.*

1. A *blissful* moment
   ____1. lovely 2. holy
   3. happy 4. uncomfortable 5. sad

2. The crowd was *boisterous*.
   ____1. quiet 2. bold
   3. noisy 4. meddlesome
   5. subdued

3. The men began to *brawl*.
   ____1. quarrel 2. sing
   3. shake hands 4. embrace 5. scrimmage

4. The *brevity* of his reply added to its force.
   ____1. sharpness 2. humor
   3. shortness 4. contrast
   5. prolixity

5. A vote of *censure*
   ____1. blame 2. confidence
   3. census counting
   4. appropriation
   5. commendation

6. *Cherish* the traditions of your school.
   ____1. revive 2. learn
   3. improve 4. question
   5. hold dear

7. A great *clamor* broke out.
   ____1. sweat 2. fight
   3. protest 4. outcry
   5. fire

8. A plea for *clemency*
   ____1. a reprieve 2. justice
   3. mercy 4. extension of
   time 5. partiality

9. The *cloister* of the monastery
   ____1. roof 2. pillar
   3. covered passage
   4. ceiling 5. arches

10. An *implacable* enemy
    ____1. weak 2. unknown
    3. passive 4. disposed to
    forgive 5. not disposed
    to forgive

11. *Adequate* facilities
    ____1. insufficient 2. comfortable 3. convenient
    4. sufficient 5. additional

* Your instructor may wish you to write your answers on a separate paper. Ask for his instructions before you proceed.

12. In a *dilemma*
_____1. frenzy   2. melancholy state   3. stupor   4. fever 5. state of perplexity

13. To *comprehend* the terms of the treaty
_____1. accept   2. understand 3. reject   4. reveal 5. revise

14. His *conjecture* was better than mine.
_____1. gesture   2. plea 3. experience   4. knowledge   5. surmise

15. *Coy* girls
_____1. bold   2. mealy-mouthed   3. immodest 4. coquettish 5. pleasing

16. *Deferred* payment
_____1. prompt   2. postponed 3. easy   4. monthly 5. cash

17. The race had *degenerated.*
_____1. deteriorated   2. gone native   3. improved 4. disappeared 5. changed

18. Labor under a *delusion*
_____1. fancy   2. bondage 3. grievance   4. loss 5. misconception

19. *Extol* his virtues
_____1. minimize   2. praise 3. exaggerate   4. recount 5. call in question

20. *Fallow* ground
_____1. marginal   2. planted 3. sandy   4. fertile 5. uncultivated

21. The accused man was *absolved.*
_____1. unjustly accused 2. insolvent   3. acquitted 4. neglected   5. locked up

22. The question is an *abstract* one.
_____1. moral   2. concrete 3. long drawn out 4. theoretical   5. difficult

23. Food was *abundant* that year.
_____1. scarce   2. expensive 3. cheap   4. inspected 5. plentiful

24. To *acknowledge* a mistake
_____1. admit   2. understand 3. repeat   4. deny 5. repent

25. The jury *acquitted* the accused. ____1. pronounced not guilty 2. found guilty 3. heard evidence against 4. questioned 5. held for trial

26. *Adhere* to the principles of democracy. ____1. desert 2. change 3. hold firmly 4. add 5. re-examine

27. An *eccentric* old man ____1. kindly 2. courteous 3. queer 4. humorous 5. rich

28. The lecturer *reaffirmed* the doctrine. ____1. denied again 2. repeated 3. re-established 4. strengthened 5. reasserted as valid

29. She was *agitated* by the words. ____1. surprised 2. pleased 3. angered 4. perturbed 5. calmed

30. The *alleged* difficulties ____1. legal 2. unacknowledged 3. increased 4. fictitious 5. asserted

31. A state of *anarchy* ____1. lawlessness 2. unhappiness 3. rule of one man 4. rigid enforcement of law 5. peacefulness

32. Mental *anguish* ____1. perplexity 2. satisfaction 3. cruelty 4. distress 5. joy

33. A worthy *antagonist* ____1. sufferer 2. beginner 3. friend 4. opponent 5. revolutionist

34. A strange *apparition* ____1. phantom 2. situation 3. division 4. pair 5. happening

35. To *appease* the crowd ____1. displease 2. arouse 3. feed 4. bless 5. conciliate

36. *Arrogant* in bearing ____1. gracious 2. doubtful 3. humble 4. haughty 5. confident

37. To speak in an *artificial* manner   ____1. natural   2. cultivated
          3. plain   4. affected
          5. unpleasant

38. Vigorously *assailed* the proposal   ____1. questioned   2. carried
          through   3. explained
          4. supported   5. attacked

39. A system of *barter*   ____1. drinking   2. exchanging
          3. gambling   4. exclusion
          5. borrowing

40. *Scrupulous* in all things   ____1. persistent   2. careless
          3. miserly   4. con-
          scientious   5. distrustful

41. The juror showed no *bias*.   ____1. contempt   2. enmity
          3. friendliness   4. preju-
          dice   5. interest

42. He *supplanted* his friend.   ____1. criticized   2. sup-
          ported   3. insulted
          4. took the place of
          5. worked under

43. In a *gruff* voice   ____1. loud   2. soft
          3. harsh   4. unpleasant
          5. pleading

44. Persuaded by *guile*   ____1. profit   2. trickery
          3. eloquence   4. magic
          5. affableness

45. Held as *hostage*   ____1. communist   2. alien
          3. unfriendly person
          4. pledge for payment
          5. indorser

46. Tried to conceal her *humiliation*   ____1. pride   2. discomfort
          3. mortification   4. anger
          5. humble origin

47. The man seemed *incredulous*.   ____1. skeptical   2. believing
          3. gullible   4. believable
          5. in a poor financial
          condition

48. *Impartial* judge   ____1. unfair   2. biased
          3. honest   4. uninformed
          5. fair

49. Of an *impetuous* temperament
    ____1. competitive 2. impulsive 3. lazy 4. stubborn 5. phlegmatic

50. *Implied* criticism
    ____1. deserved 2. undeserved 3. hinted 4. outspoken 5. useful

51. Ashamed of his *indolence*
    ____1. poverty 2. grief 3. ignorance 4. laziness 5. incoherence

52. She has *ruddy* cheeks.
    ____1. wrinkled 2. red 3. pale 4. splotchy 5. fat

53. The *intercession* of a friend
    ____1. reciprocation 2. concession 3. betrayal 4. forgiveness 5. mediation

54. Decide the *issue*
    ____1. next step 2. point in debate 3. result 4. lawsuit 5. problem

55. A *judicious* statement
    ____1. unwise 2. harsh 3. serious 4. legal 5. wise

56. *Latitude* of thought and speech
    ____1. freedom 2. indecency 3. sinfulness 4. slowness 5. boundaries

57. His manner was *solemn*.
    ____1. haughty 2. grave 3. insolent 4. weary 5. nervous

58. The argument lacks *relevancy*.
    ____1. justice 2. vigor 3. applicability 4. consistency 5. importance

59. A *ludicrous* situation
    ____1. embarrassing 2. pleasant 3. tragic 4. laughable 5. exciting

60. *Reconcile* differences
    ____1. change 2. abandon 3. consult about 4. agree to 5. adjust

61. Felt no *remorse*
    ____1. hatred 2. intuition 3. bitter repentance 4. sense of failure 5. revengeful feelings

62. The prince *renounced* his prerogatives.
    ____1. demanded 2. resigned
    3. mistook 4. reclaimed
    5. announced

63. Interrupted her *reverie*
    ____1. musing 2. prayer
    3. revelry 4. spinning
    5. slumber

64. A *rift* in the Democratic Party
    ____1. change 2. reversal
    3. harmony 4. splitting
    5. discussion

65. *Robust* spirit
    ____1. gentle 2. calm
    3. strong 4. brave
    5. bullying

66. *Ruthless* treatment
    ____1. ingenuous 2. dis-
    honest 3. merciful
    4. considerate 5. cruel

67. A *sane* mind
    ____1. just 2. ethical
    3. irrational 4. sound
    5. consistent

68. To *scoff* at the speaker
    ____1. mock 2. shout
    3. be annoyed 4. dis-
    agree with 5. kick

69. Lived a *secluded* life
    ____1. immoral 2. selfish
    3. hard 4. isolated
    5. snobbish

70. A *serene* mood
    ____1. serious 2. gay
    3. artificial 4. tranquil
    5. sad

71. She *shammed* sickness.
    ____1. feared 2. escaped
    3. feigned 4. showed
    signs of 5. was em-
    barrassed by

72. *Specious* reasoning
    ____1. quick 2. plausible
    3. logical 4. specialized
    5. specific

73. *Sprawled* on the desk
    ____1. loafed 2. wrote
    3. lay awkwardly
    4. fought 5. crawled

74. The *stark* narrative
    ____1. vulgar 2. gloomy
    3. tragic 4. thrilling
    5. unadorned

75. An unusual *stratagem*
    ____1. plan to entrap
    2. layer of rock 3. jewel
    4. climax 5. combination

76. *Strenuous* objections
    _____1. thoughtful   2. vigorous
    3. tenuous   4. weak
    5. factitious

77. A *subtle* argument
    _____1. bold   2. unexpected
    3. dull   4. detailed
    5. ingenious

78. A *sullen* mind
    _____1. evil   2. stupid
    3. morose   4. pleasant
    5. menacing

79. The commentary is *superfluous*.
    _____1. essential   2. excessive
    3. fluent   4. detailed
    5. extraordinary

80. Your *surmise* is correct.
    _____1. attitude   2. censure
    3. suggestion   4. conjecture   5. information

81. The king dismissed the *suppliants*.
    _____1. ministers   2. supply men   3. candidates
    4. petitioners
    5. intriguers

82. A *magnanimous* act
    _____1. generous   2. selfish
    3. incredible   4. involving many people
    5. important

83. A *monotonous* tone of voice
    _____1. resonant   2. flexible
    3. low   4. unvarying
    5. high pitched

84. Try to avoid *pedantry*.
    _____1. lowmindedness
    2. sales talk   3. effeminacy   4. scholarliness
    5. display of learning

85. Showed *pique* at his remark
    _____1. lack of interest
    2. resentment   3. fear
    4. interest   5. pleasure

86. A *pompous* manner
    _____1. mild   2. insincere
    3. absurd   4. awkward
    5. pretentious

87. A *portentous* statement
    _____1. invalid   2. important
    3. ominous   4. unimportant   5. exaggerated

88. The judgment of *posterity*
    _____1. old people   2. future
    3. tradition   4. ancestors
    5. successful people

89. A *presumptuous* statement
____1. overbold   2. modest
3. frank   4. false
5. misunderstood

90. *Nettled* by his remark
____1. puzzled   2. irritated
3. exalted   4. illuminated
5. mollified

91. Your fears are *chimerical.*
____1. imaginary   2. real
3. childish   4. hysterical
5. morbid

92. A *thrifty* housewife
____1. frugal   2. careful
3. stingy   4. cheerful
5. tasteful

93. *Tranquil* beauty of Greek sculpture
____1. simple   2. cold
3. quiet   4. fragile
5. restless

94. This *transitory* life
____1. sad   2. fleeting
3. uninteresting
4. transitional   5. long

95. A *trivial* matter
____1. complex   2. petty
3. important   4. boring
5. unpleasant

96. *Ultimate* success
____1. at last   2. complete
3. ulterior   4. present
5. easily achieved

97. *Unscrupulous* competition
____1. zealous   2. untiring
3. fair   4. unprincipled
5. unintelligent

98. *Usurp* authority
____1. seize   2. give up
3. weaken   4. hold
5. defy

99. Spoke kindly to the *vagrant*
____1. tenant   2. vagabond
3. peddler   4. country-
man   5. beggar

100. The *venom* of his glance
____1. secretiveness
2. weariness   3. fierce-
ness   4. malignity
5. displeasure

101. His popularity is *waning.*
____1. increasing
2. decreasing   3. short
lived   4. well-deserved
5. wavering

102. Not *averse* to taking the position

    ____1. disinclined   2. inclined
3. eager   4. fitted
5. unfitted

103. The *excerpt* is typical.

    ____1. condition   2. extract
3. exception   4. choice
5. symptom

104. His desire was *frustrated*.

    ____1. fulfilled   2. dis-
regarded   3. increased
4. thwarted   5. lessened

105. The *tenets* of his faith

    ____1. brethren   2. teachers
3. beliefs   4. sources
5. problems

106. *Immutable* destiny

    ____1. cruel   2. unknown
3. blind   4. unchange-
able   5. fickle

107. Known for his *garrulity*

    ____1. kindness   2. artistic
sense   3. quiet manner
4. sternness
5. talkativeness

108. His reasoning was *fallacious*.

    ____1. logical   2. weighty
3. obvious   4. sensible
5. misleading

109. Displayed *chagrin* at the report

    ____1. pain   2. excitement
3. courage   4. vexation
5. amusement

110. An *affable* person

    ____1. foolish   2. friendly
3. impulsive   4. in-
sincere   5. careless

111. *Circumspect* behavior

    ____1. annoying   2. strange
3. cautious   4. austere
5. courteous

Number of words marked correctly _____.
Corresponding vocabulary range _____.

Increasing your vocabulary.

There are no short cuts to word power. A good vocabulary is the product of years of serious reading, of listening to intelligent talk, and of seeking to speak and write forcefully and clearly. All this does not mean that devices and methods for vocabulary-building are useless. But it does mean that acquiring a good vocabulary is inseparable from acquiring an education.

(1) *Increasing your recognition vocabulary.* English has many words based on a common root form, to which different prefixes or suffixes have been added. The root form *spec-*, for example, from the Latin *specere* (to look) appears in *specter, inspection, perspective, aspect, introspection, circumspect, specimen, spectator.* Knowing the common prefixes and suffixes will help you detect the meaning of many words whose roots are familiar.

(a) *Prefixes.*

PREFIX	MEANING	EXAMPLE
ab-	away from	absent
ad*-	to *or* for	adverb
com*-	with	combine
de-	down, away from, *or* undoing	degrade, depart, dehumanize
dis*-	separation *or* reversal	disparate, disappoint
ex*-	out of *or* former	extend, ex-president
in*-	in *or* on	input
in*-	not	inhuman
mis-	wrong	mistake
non-	not	non-Christian
ob*-	against	obtuse
pre-	before	prevent
pro-	for *or* forward	proceed
re-	back *or* again	repeat
sub*-	under	subcommittee
trans-	across	transcribe
un-	not	unclean

EXERCISE 18. Write words denoting *negation* from the following.

artistic	explicable	revocable
attached	honest	tenable
essential	mutable	workable

* The spelling of these prefixes varies, usually to make pronunciation easier. *Ad* becomes *ac* in *accuse,* *ag* in *aggregate,* *at* in *attack.* Similarly, the final consonant in the other prefixes is assimilated by the initial letter of the root word: *colleague* (*com + league*); *illicit* (*in + licit*); *offend* (*ob + fend*); *succeed* (*sub + ceed*).

EXERCISE 19. Write words denoting *reversal* from the following.

centralize	integrate	please
do	magnetize	qualify
inherit	persuade	ravel

(b) *Suffixes*. These fall into three groups: noun suffixes, verb suffixes, adjectival suffixes.

Noun suffixes denoting "act of," "state of," "quality of."

SUFFIX	EXAMPLE	MEANING
-dom	freedom	*state of* being free
-hood	manhood	*state of* being a man
-ness	dimness	*state of* being dim
-ice	cowardice	*quality of* being a coward
-ation	flirtation	*act of* flirting
-ion	intercession	*act of* interceding
{ -sion	scansion	*act of* scanning
{ -tion	corruption	*state of* being corrupt
-ment	argument	*act of* arguing
-ship	friendship	*state of* being friends
{ -ance	continuance	*act of* continuing
{ -ence	precedence	*act of* preceding
{ -ancy	flippancy	*state of* being flippant
{ -ency	currency	*state of* being current
-ism	baptism	*act of* baptizing
-ery	bravery	*quality of* being brave

Noun suffixes denoting "doer," "one who."

SUFFIX	EXAMPLE	MEANING
{ -eer (male)	auctioneer	*one who* auctions
{ -ess (female)	poetess	*a woman who* writes poetry
-ist	fascist	*one who* believes in fascism
{ -or	debtor	*one who* is in debt
{ -er	worker	*one who* works

Verb suffixes denoting "to make" or "to perform the act of."

SUFFIX	EXAMPLE	MEANING
-ate	perpetuate	*to make* perpetual
-en	soften	*to make* soft
-fy	dignify	*to make* dignified
-ize, -ise	sterilize	*to make* sterile

Adjectival suffixes.

SUFFIX	MEANING	EXAMPLE
-ful	full of	hateful
-ish	resembling	foolish
-ate	having	affectionate
-ic, -ical	resembling	angelic
-ive	having	prospective
-ous	full of	zealous
-ulent	full of	fraudulent
-less	without	fatherless
-able, -ible	capable of	peaceable
-ed	having	spirited
-ly	resembling	womanly
-like	resembling	childlike

EXERCISE 20. Write nouns indicating "act of," "state of," or "quality of" from the following words.

arrange	locate	peace
buoy	occur	promote
judge	pauper	separate

EXERCISE 21. Write nouns indicating "doer" from the following words.

advice	manipulate	profit
conservation	plan	save
help	see (*give masculine and feminine*)	
procrastinate		

EXERCISE 22. Write verb indicating "to make" or "to perform the act of" from the following nouns.

capital	heart	peace
captive	liquid	verse
editorial	moral	victim

EXERCISE 23. Make adjectives of the following words by adding a suffix.

humor	rest	thwart
irony	speed	wasp
mule	talk	whimsey

331

(c) *Combining forms.* Linguists refer to these as "bound forms." They appear generally, but not always, as prefixes.

COMBINING FORM	MEANING	EXAMPLE
anthropo-	man	*anthropo*logy
arch-	rule	*arch*duke, mon*arch*
auto-	self	*auto*mobile
bene-	well	*bene*ficial
eu-	well	*eu*logy
graph-	writing	mono*graph*, bio*graphy*
log-, logue-	word, speech	mono*logue*
magni-	great	*magni*ficent
mal-	bad	*mal*ady
mono-	one	*mono*tone
multi-	many	*multi*plication
neo-	new	*neo*-classic
omni-	all	*omni*bus
pan-, pant-	all	*pan*hellenic
phil-	loving	*phil*osophy
phono-	sound	*phono*graph
poly-	many	*poly*gamy
pseudo-	false	*pseudo*nym
semi-	half	*semi*formal

(2) *Increasing your active vocabulary.* Another way to increase word power is to keep transferring words from your *recognition* vocabulary to your *active* vocabulary. Make a conscious effort to introduce at least one new word a day into your active vocabulary. At the same time be alert to opportunities for increasing your recognition vocabulary. A good system is to enter each new word on a small card: Write the word on one side, the definition and a sentence illustrating its correct use on the other. Then you can quickly test yourself on the meaning of all the new words you collect.

EXERCISE 24. Define each of the following words and use it correctly in a sentence.

extenuate	ostentatious	sensuous
inscrutable	fortuitous	calumny
homogeneous	ritual	finite
disparage	predatory	collate
intrinsic	officious	facetious
prodigious	taciturn	corpulent
palliate	malign	exacerbate

(3) *Strengthening your active vocabulary.* Are you sure that *aggravate, enervate, transpire* mean what you think they mean? You know that *deadly, mortal,* and *fatal* are very much alike in meaning —but do you know the exact distinctions between them? Most good dictionaries group synonyms and point out their differences. Both the Merriam-Webster *New Collegiate* and *The American College Dictionary* are excellent in this respect. The Merriam-Webster *Dictionary of Synonyms* is devoted exclusively to the grouping and differentiating of synonyms. The various editions of Roget's *Thesaurus* must be used cautiously, for they simply group synonymous words without pointing out distinctions in meaning.

The following entry, which appears in the Merriam-Webster *New Collegiate* under *able,* is a good example of the grouping and differentiation of synonyms:

a′ble (ā′b'l), *adj.;* A′BLER (ā′blẽr); A′BLEST (-blĭst). [OF., fr. L. *habilis* that may be easily held or managed, apt, fr. *habere* to have, hold.] **1.** Having sufficient power, skill, or resources of any kind to accomplish an object; capable; competent. **2.** Having intellectual qualifications, or strong mental powers; showing mastery in some department of knowledge or affairs; talented; clever.
Syn. Able, capable, competent, qualified come into comparison when they mean having power or fitness for work. **Able** suggests ability above the average as revealed in promise or performance; **capable** stresses qualities which fit one for work but seldom imply a special ability; **competent** and **qualified** imply the experience or training for a definite employment. — **Ant.** Inept.

EXERCISE 25. Indicate the distinctions in meaning among the words in each of the following groups.

1. anger, ire, rage, fury, indignation, wrath
2. enthusiast, fanatic, zealot, bigot
3. correct, accurate, exact, precise
4. punish, chastise, castigate, chasten, discipline
5. necessary, requisite, essential
6. accidental, casual, fortuitous, contingent, incidental, adventitious
7. ghastly, grisly, gruesome, macabre, grim
8. fool, idiot, imbecile, moron, simpleton
9. abuse, misuse, mistreat, maltreat, ill-treat
10. fragrance, perfume, scent, incense, redolence, bouquet
11. obstruct, hinder, impede, bar, block, dam

12. arise, spring, originate, derive, issue, stem
13. design, plan, scheme, plot
14. benevolent, humane, humanitarian, altruistic, charitable
15. grim, implacable, unrelenting
16. sin, vice, scandal, crime
17. recede, retreat, retract
18. gift, present, gratuity, favor
19. breeding, cultivation, poise, refinement
20. motive, impulse, incentive

Care should be taken, not that the reader may understand, but that he must understand.

—QUINTILIAN

40 EXACTNESS = **EX**

To achieve exactness in writing, choose words that accurately and idiomatically convey the meaning you intend.

To write with precision, you must know both the denotation and the connotation of words. *Denotation* is the core of a word's meaning, sometimes called the "dictionary" or literal meaning; for example, a *tree* is "a woody perennial plant having a single main axis or stem commonly exceeding ten feet in height." *Connotation* refers to the reader's emotional response to a word and to the associations the word carries with it. Thus, *tree* connotes shade or coolness or shelter or stillness. Obviously, the connotation of a word cannot be fixed, for individual responses differ. Some words have fairly standardized connotations (flag > the emotion of patriotism; home > security, the sense of one's own place). But even these words have other and less orthodox connotations. In fact, poets achieve many of their finest effects by avoiding standardized connotations. "Evening," for example, connotes for most of us some quality of beauty, but T. S. Eliot jolts us out of our normal response by seeing

> . . . the evening . . . spread out against the sky
> Like a patient etherised upon a table.

If you ever decide to violate the generally accepted connotations of a word in your own writing, however, be very sure that you know exactly what you are doing. And always take pains to insure that the

335

connotations of your words reinforce and are consistent with their denotative meanings. For example, one of the denotative meanings of *smack* is "to give a hearty kiss," but no one (unless he were trying to be funny) would write

> He looked deep into her eyes, whispered endearing words, and *smacked* her on the ear.

Many words stand for abstractions: *democracy, truth, beauty,* and so on. Because the connotations of such words are both vague and numerous, state specifically what you mean when you use them or make sure that the context makes their meaning clear. Otherwise, the reader will misunderstand your terms, or—what is worse—will *think* he understands them when he does not.

40a Carefully distinguish between words that are nearly synonymous.

The meanings of many words are so similar that occasionally one may be substituted for another. But synonymous words cannot always be used interchangeably, and one of the characteristics of an exact writer is that he uses synonyms carefully, observing their shades of meaning. The careless use of synonyms distorts meaning.

> The man gained great *renown* as a gangster. (*Notoriety* would be more exact.)

Sometimes, unfortunately, a writer chooses the wrong word because he really does not know its meaning and fails to look it up.

> The minister *instigated* love and charity throughout the community. (The writer probably meant *inspired*.)
>
> We admired the speaker for his *sententious* appeal for funds. (*Eloquent* was probably intended.)

EXERCISE 26. Replace the italicized words in the following sentences with more exact ones. Explain why each italicized word is inappropriate.

1. His characters are *garish* and alive; they are people you will remember as old friends.
2. His *obstinancy* in the face of danger saved us all.
3. The ambassador, being treated like a common tourist, sputtered in *intimidation*.

4. We can't blame Margaret for leaving him; certainly she had an ample *pretext*.

5. The school's most honored professor was without fault: a wise mentor to his students, and in addition a scholar recognized as *pedantic* and profound.

EXERCISE 27. Explain the differences in meaning among the italicized words in each of the following groups.

1. an *ignorant*, an *illiterate*, an *unlettered*, an *uneducated* person.

2. a *detached*, a *disinterested*, an *indifferent*, an *unconcerned* attitude.

3. *to condone*, *to excuse*, *to forgive*, *to pardon* a person's actions.

4. an *insurrection*, a *mutiny*, a *rebellion*, a *revolution*.

5. a *barbarous*, a *cruel*, a *fierce*, a *ferocious*, an *inhuman*, a *savage* character.

40b **Do not confuse words with similar sound or spelling but with different meanings.**

Most of these words are approximate *homonyms,* that is, words that have the same pronunciation but different meanings (*idol, idle, idyll; aisle, isle*). You must treat these words as you would any other unfamiliar term: learn the correct spelling and meaning of each as an individual word.

EXERCISE 28. What are the differences in meaning in each of the following groups of words?

1. adapt, adept, adopt	12. canvas, canvass
2. alley, ally	13. carton, cartoon
3. allude, elude	14. chord, cord
4. anecdote, antidote	15. climactic, climatic
5. anesthetic, antiseptic	16. confidently, confidentially
6. angel, angle	17. costume, custom
7. arraign, arrange	18. elicit, illicit
8. bloc, block	19. epic, epoch
9. borne, born	20. flaunt, flout
10. Calvary, cavalry	21. genteel, gentile
11. cannon, canon	22. historic, historical

23. human, humane	27. prescribe, proscribe
24. ingenious, ingenuous	28. receipt, recipe
25. marital, martial	29. statue, statute
26. morality, mortality	30. waive, wave

40c   Generally, avoid "invented" words.

A "coined" word is a new and outright creation (like Gelett Burgess' *blurb*). A "neologism" is either a new word or a new use of an old word or words (like Madison Avenue's "package plans"). A "nonce-word," literally "once-word," is a word made up to suit a special situation and generally not used more than once ("My son," he said, "suffers from an acute case of *baseballitis*"). Because English is an ever-growing language, new words and new functions for words constantly work their way into it. But until you have had a great deal of experience in writing, it is best to leave word-invention to others and to concentrate on learning the meaning of words that have already been established by usage. Be particularly careful to rid your speech and writing of "unconscious" inventions—words that you invent because of spelling errors or an inexact knowledge of word forms (*understandment* for *understanding, multification* for *multiplication*).

> **EXERCISE 29.** In the following sentences correct the italicized words that seem to you to be "needless inventions."
>
> 1. His failure to pay that bill is only one of his many *nonresponsible* acts since he became a campus hero.
> 2. He has spent most of his life studying Indian culture and is now preparing a book on the effects of *savagism* on modern civilization.
> 3. The senator argued that teachers should be *unpolitical* animals; what he really meant was that they should stop campaigning for his opponent.
> 4. Lu described the universe before creation as a tremendous stretch of *unstuff*.
> 5. The weather bureau reported that because of conditions tomorrow's weather was *unforecastable*.
> 6. The newspapers have been full of the *disappearation* of the young man, and no one seems to have any idea where he might be.

7. William Henry has a very *Trumanesque* temper and a very *Swiftian* tongue.

8. Joe considered his older brother a very *affected* young man and would have nothing to do with him.

9. He's never been able to outgrow his *schoolteacherish* attitude toward me, in spite of the fact that I'm now his superintendent.

10. His manner of pronunciation is very *peculiaristic,* to say the least, and sometimes I don't know whether he's speaking English or his native language.

40d **Avoid improprieties.**

An impropriety is a legitimate word wrongly used. In the sentence "He *opinioned* that Edwin was guilty" the word *opinion* is used as a verb, a grammatical function to which it is not accustomed.

IMPROPER   He *carpentered* the doghouse together in less than an hour.

PROPER   He *made* (or *constructed,* or *put together*) the doghouse in less than an hour.

Many words, of course, may function legitimately as more than one part of speech.

PROPER   That garage gives excellent *service.*

PROPER   That garage has agreed to *service* my car.

When in doubt about the grammatical function of a word, always turn to a good dictionary.

EXERCISE 30. In the sentences below correct the italicized words that are improprieties.

1. His fussing at me all the time *aggravates* me.

2. Are you trying to *infer* by that remark that I'm ignorant?

3. In the third grade they *learned* me all the English I need.

4. Mike said his family *raised* him to be a doctor but that the best he could do was pass the third grade.

5. The highway was *stop-lighted* all the way between Seattle and Tacoma and I thought we'd never arrive.

6. The carpenter wanted *to roof* the place before the weather turned cold.

7. The program was *videoed* from coast to coast via the new national cable.

8. We were out *holidaying* when we ran into Ed and Bill and decided to make a foursome of it.

9. The engineer said we could *bulldoze* a clearing on the hillside in a half a day if we could find a way to start the motor.

10. The carpenter *doweled* the joints with half-inch dowels and said they'd never come apart.

40e **Be alert to changes in meaning from one suffixal form of a word to another.**

A roommate whom you *like* is not necessarily a *likable* roommate, nor is a *matter of agreement* an *agreeable matter*. Many words have two, sometimes three, adjectival forms: *e.g.*, a *changeable* personality, a *changing* personality, a *changed* personality. Be careful not to substitute one form for another.

ILLOGICAL   The cook served our *favorable* dessert last night.
LOGICAL   The cook served our *favorite* dessert last night.

ILLOGICAL   He is a good student; he has a very *questionable* mind.
LOGICAL   He is a good student; he has a very *questioning* mind.

EXERCISE 31. Point out the differences in meaning between the italicized words in each of the following groups.

1. an *arguable* point
   an *argued* point

2. a *practical* solution
   a *practicable* solution

3. a *hated* person
   a *hateful* person

4. a *liberal* foreign minister
   a *liberated* foreign minister

5. a *single* effect
   a *singular* effect

6. an *intelligible* writer
   an *intelligent* writer

7. a *godly* man
   a *godlike* man

8. an *informed* teacher
   an *informative* teacher

9. a *peaceful* nation
   a *peaceable* nation

10. a *workable* arrangement
    a *working* arrangement

11. an *amicable* teacher
    an *amiable* teacher

12. a *yellow* piece of paper
    a *yellowed* piece of paper

40f **Avoid "elegant variation."**

Often you will use a variety of synonyms and pronouns in order to avoid the awkward repetition of a word. And that is a perfectly legitimate stylistic device. But when your desire to avoid repetition is so overwhelming that you dig up a synonym or epithet for almost every word you have used previously, you are guilty of "elegant variation."

> Pee Wee Pearce, the Chicago second-baseman, got three hits yesterday. The tiny infielder came up in the first frame and lashed a one-base blow to right field. In the third inning the diminutive keystone sacker knocked a single through the box. In the seventh the little ballhawk reached first safely on a screaming drive to the outer garden.

Here, in the short space of four sentences, we have well over a dozen examples of "elegant variation":

Pee Wee	second-baseman	hits
tiny	infielder	one-base blow
diminutive	keystone sacker	single
little	ballhawk	safety
lashed	right field	first frame
knocked	box	third inning
sent screaming drive	outer garden	seventh

In the first of the examples below, the use of the simple pronoun *he* would have made unnecessary the frantic search for synonyms for *king*. In the second, *visitor* could be omitted and *Two of the other people in attendance* changed to *Two others*.

> The *King* appeared yesterday at the Navy Barracks. *His majesty* was in full dress and escorted by the Home Guards. After inspecting the cadets, the *royal guest* was entertained at the Officers' Club.

> I saw many of my old classmates at your garden party. Two of your *guests* were my fraternity brothers. Another *visitor* played on the same football team with me. *Two of the other people in attendance* were brothers of my old girl friend.

EXERCISE 32. Find a specimen of "elegant variation" in a newspaper or popular magazine and rewrite it to show how the variation might be avoided.

EXERCISE 33. Comment in one or two paragraphs on the "elegant variation" in the following passage.

The outcome of the game was a personal victory for All-American Marty Jerome. The diminutive halfback scored ten times for the Mustangs, five of these coming in the final frame. In the first quarter the pint-sized wingback ran 10 yards for one score, scampered 45 for another, and actually bulled his way over for a third from the two yard stripe. In the second period the little fellow galloped half the length of the field for a marker after intercepting a Longhorn pass on his own fifty. In the third frame the mighty mite was held to one touchdown—that one coming on the last play of the period and featuring a series of fumbles. Lou Zamberg, Longhorn fullback, dropped the ball as he came through the line; Joe Harris, the Mustangs' giant tackle, picked it up, was hit from behind and fumbled. Like a streak of light the tiny Jerome grabbed it just before it hit the ground and dashed 85 long and magnificent yards to paydirt. The last frame was all Jerome's. In a display of ability seldom, if ever, seen the little man ran for five tallies, one of them a 105 yard kickoff return. He scored again on an intercepted pass, then on a 20 yard rabbit-run through center, and twice more on bullet-like plunges from the 5 yard line to home base.

40g Use words and phrases idiomatically.

Idiomatic writing means writing that strikes the reader as natural, smooth, unaffected. It means putting things in an English (or American) way. A Frenchman says *un cheval blanc* and *il fait froid,* but the literal translations, *a horse white* and *it makes cold,* are unidiomatic to us; we say *a white horse* and *it is cold.* In English we use many idiomatic phrase-forms that are justified by custom rather than by logic or grammar, as *look up an old friend, strike a bargain, go down to the sea in ships.* Generally, native users of English unconsciously speak and write idiomatically, though all of us find it hard sometimes to hit upon the right idiomatic prepositions or infinitives or gerunds. Choosing just the right *idiom* is largely a matter of experience—either our own or somebody else's. The following list of a few idiomatic usages is designed to help you find the right phrases in your writing.

ABSOLVE BY, FROM   I was *absolved by* the dean *from* all blame.

ACCEDE TO	He *acceded to* his father's demands.
ACCOMPANY BY, WITH	I was *accompanied by* George. The terms were *accompanied with* a plea for immediate peace.
ACQUITTED OF	He was *acquitted of* the crime.
ADAPTED TO, FROM	This machine can be *adapted to* farm work. The design was *adapted from* a previous invention.
ADMIT TO, OF	He *admitted to* the error. The plan will *admit of* no alternative.
AGREE TO, WITH, IN	They *agreed to* the plan but *disagreed with* us. They *agreed* only *in* principle.
ANGRY WITH, AT	She was *angry with* me and *angry at* the treatment she had received.
CAPABLE OF	He is *capable of* every vice of the ignorant.
COMPARE TO, WITH	He *compared* the roundness of the baseball *to* that of the earth. He *compared* the economy of the Ford *with* that of the Plymouth.
CONCUR WITH, IN	I *concur with* you *in* your desire to use the revised edition.
CONFIDE IN, TO	He *confided in* me. He *confided to* me that he had stolen the car.
CONFORM TO, WITH CONFORMITY WITH	The specifications *conformed to* or *with* his original plans. You must act in *conformity with* our demands.
CONNECT BY, WITH	The rooms are *connected by* a corridor. He is officially *connected with* this university.
DIFFER ABOUT, FROM, WITH	We *differ about* our tastes in clothes. My clothes *differ from* yours. We *differ with* one another.
DIFFERENT FROM *	Our grading system is *different from* yours.

* *Different than* is colloquially idiomatic when the object of the prepositional phrase is a clause.

FORMAL   This town looks *different from* what I had remembered.
COLLOQUIAL   This town looks *different than* I had remembered it.

ENTER INTO, OR, UPON	He *entered into* a new agreement and thereby *entered on* or *upon** a new career.
FREE FROM, OF	He was *freed from* his mother's domination and now he is *free of* her.
IDENTICAL WITH	Your reasons are *identical with* his.
JOIN IN, TO, WITH	He *joined in* the fun *with* the others. He *joined* the wire cables *to* each other.
LIVE AT, IN, ON	He *lives at* 14 Neil Avenue *in* a Dutch Colonial house. He *lives on* Neil Avenue.
NECESSITY FOR, OF NEED FOR, OF	There was no *necessity* (*need*) *for* you to lose your temper. There was no *necessity* (*need*) *of* your losing your temper.
OBJECT TO	I *object to* the statement in the third paragraph.
OBLIVIOUS OF	When he held her hand he was *oblivious of* the passing of time.
OVERCOME BY, WITH	I was *overcome by* the heat. I was *overcome with* grief.
PARALLEL BETWEEN, TO, WITH	There is a *parallel between* your attitude and his. This line is *parallel to* or *with* that one.
PREFERABLE TO	A leisurely walk is *preferable to* violent exercise.
REASON ABOUT, WITH	Why not *reason with* him *about* the matter?
VARIANCE WITH	This conclusion is at *variance with* your facts.
VARY FROM, IN, WITH	The houses *vary from* one another *in* size. People's tastes *vary with* their personalities.
WORTHY OF	That woman is not *worthy of* your trust.

* In many phrases, *on* and *upon* are interchangeable: *depend on* or *depend upon; enter on* or *enter upon.*

EXERCISE 34. Provide the idiomatic prepositions needed in the following sentences.

1. Many students are oblivious _____ the criteria implicit _____ his criticisms.
2. He confided _____ me that he thought me different _____ what he had expected.
3. I agreed _____ his proposal, which had been adapted _____ one I had made previously.
4. The jury absolved Robbins _____ all blame; hence he was acquitted _____ the charge.
5. Lois Bowers said she was angry _____ him because his actions did not conform _____ those of a gentleman.
6. The fence was built parallel _____ the street and connected _____ his neighbor's stone wall.
7. Having been freed _____ his parents' supervision, he saw no necessity _____ (keep or keeping) them informed of his whereabouts.
8. She is not capable _____ (budget or budgeting) her own income, for she is unable _____ (add) 4 and 4 and get 8.
9. My father would admit _____ no disagreement _____ his wishes, and I had to accede _____ his demand that I leave the party at midnight.
10. We entered _____ a contract to buy the house after Mr. Jones agreed _____ our request for a twenty-year mortgage.

EXERCISE 35. Each of the following sentences violates a principle of *exactness*. Find and correct each error, giving reasons for your corrections.

1. I often wondered why I didn't exert more enthusiasm toward my studies.
2. Percival never got accustomed to one respect of college life —the calling of students by "Mr." or "Miss."
3. While in high school I was always challenged to learn by constant threats.
4. I have seen students regardlessly ignore the instructor's lecture and then wonder why they flunked the course.
5. He hadn't been in the army two days when he discovered that his sleeping habits were going to be much shorter.
6. A person has to earn a living in his chosen field if he is going to derive any satisfaction out of it.

7. The first impression I encountered from the neighbor's dog was one of enmity.

8. In spite of his round little face and twinkling eyes the preacher was a very serious and godlike man.

9. "The Charge of the Light Brigade" is a poem about a disasterfull calvary charge in the Crimean War.

10. He went to bed before all the election returns were in, but his confidential manner led us all into believing that he would be the winning candidate.

40h   **Use specific words rather than general words.**

A general word stands for generalized qualities or characteristics, as *color, beast, vehicle*. A specific word singles out more definite and individual qualities, as *red, lion, tricycle*. The context determines whether a particular word is general or specific. For example, *man* is a general word in relation to *Leonard Chapman* and *Barney Rider*, but a specific word in relation to *mammal*. And *beast* is less specific than *lion* but more specific than *creature*.

Try constantly to express your thoughts in concrete and unambiguous terms; search for the most specific words available.

GENERAL	A man walked down the street.
SPECIFIC	An old beggar shuffled along Main Street.
GENERAL	They had a picnic under a tree.
SPECIFIC	They ate pickles and drank lemonade under an old elm.
SPECIFIC	Mateo was a stocky man, with clear eyes and a deeply tanned face. His skill as a marksman was extraordinary, even in Corsica, where everyone is a good shot. He could kill a ram at one hundred and twenty paces, and his aim was as accurate at night as in the daytime.
MORE SPECIFIC	Picture a small, sturdy man, with jet-black, curly hair, a Roman nose, thin lips, large piercing eyes, and a weather-beaten complexion. His skill as a marksman was extraordinary, even in this country, where everyone is a good shot. For instance, Mateo would never fire on a wild ram with small shot, but at a hundred and twenty paces he would bring it down with a bullet in its head or shoulder, just as he fancied. He used his rifle at night as easily as in the daytime, and I was given the following illustration of his skill,

which may seem incredible, perhaps, to those who
have never travelled in Corsica. He placed a lighted
candle behind a piece of transparent paper as big as
a plate, and aimed at it from eighty paces away. He
extinguished the candle, and a moment later, in utter
darkness, fired and pierced the paper three times out
of four.

—PROSPER MÉRIMÉE, *Mateo Falcone*

The need for specific words is not limited to descriptive writing.
Even in general exposition, a good writer leads into a generalization
through images, illustrations, and examples. Note how concretely
Bill Mauldin—no "literary" writer—deals with the abstraction "immigration."

But us champeens of the teeming shores aren't doing a new thing.
The immigration battle has been going on in this country ever
since the flag had thirteen stars. Every generation for 170 years
has produced two schools for thought about immigration: One
has been convinced that the country has reached its saturation
point, that more material for the human melting pot that pro-
duces Americans will result only in lowering the standard of
living, reducing wages, and producing a crop of "furrin ideas."
The other group believes—rightly, I think—that when a country
reaches the stage where it can't expand its population, add new
blood, and realize fresh potentialities, it might as well fold its
flag because it has reached the summit and can only go downhill
until it expires.

—BILL MAULDIN, *Back Home*

40i Avoid "omnibus" words.

One of the chief impediments to exactness in writing is the overuse of words like *aspect, case, cute, factor, field, fine, important,
nice, point, swell, thing, type, wonderful*. These are so general and
inclusive in meaning that they are called "omnibus" words. They
have legitimate uses:

ACCURATE USE   The perfection of the assembly line was an *important factor* in the development of mass-pro-
duction industries.

ACCURATE USE   One interesting *aspect* of Robbins' *case* was the
fervor with which the defense attorney ad-
dressed the jury.

But be careful not to let "omnibus" words lure you from the search for the specific word you need. Overdependence on them will result in triteness, and in time may even rob you of the ability to see things with freshness and to describe them with vigor. (See "Triteness," 42c.)

LOOSE My job has certain *aspects* which I dislike.
REVISED My job has certain *responsibilities* which I dislike.

LOOSE He has a *nice* home overlooking Lake Washington.
REVISED He has a (*large, comfortable, modern, rambling, expensive,* etc.) home overlooking Lake Washington.

EXERCISE 36. Find at least four words that express more specifically the meaning of each of the following italicized words.

SAMPLE: *walked*—trudged, shuffled, sauntered, ambled

1. *spoke* (verb)
2. *wrote*
3. *hit* (verb)
4. *cried*
5. *built*
6. *led*
7. *eat*
8. *correct* (verb)
9. *break*
10. *run*

In composing, as a general rule, run your pen through every other word you have written; you have no idea what vigor it will give your style.

—SIDNEY SMITH

41 DIRECTNESS = DIR

Achieve directness in your writing by choosing words that convey your meaning with economy and precision.

The challenge to *directness* comes from two fronts—wordiness and vagueness. A wordy writer uses more words than are necessary to convey his meaning.

WORDY   He attacks the practice of making a profitable business out of college athletics from the standpoint that it has a detrimental and harmful influence on the college students, and, to a certain degree and extent, on the colleges and universities themselves.

IMPROVED   He attacks commercialization of college athletics as detrimental to the students, and even to the universities themselves.

A vague writer fails to convey his meaning sharply and clearly.

VAGUE   The report asserts the danger from unguarded machines which may lessen the usefulness of workers in later life as well as reducing their life expectancy.

IMPROVED   The report asserts that unguarded machines may severely injure or even kill workers.

Vagueness and wordiness are sometimes indistinguishable, as in the preceding examples. The weight of unnecessary words tends to obscure meaning. But very often wordiness is just awkwardness. The meaning is clear, but the expression is clumsy.

349

AWKWARD	The notion that Communists are people who wear long black beards is a very common notion.
IMPROVED	The notion is common that Communists are people who wear long black beards.

41a   **Eliminate "deadwood" by judiciously reducing clauses to phrases, phrases to single words.**

"Deadwood" consists of words that add nothing to the meaning of a sentence. In the sentence "The football captain, who is an All-American player, played his last game today," *who is* and *player* are deadwood. Sometimes you can prune a sentence simply by changing the position of important words. "*Yesterday's* snow is melting" is more concise than "The snow, *which fell yesterday,* is melting." You can eliminate "deadwood" from your writing by careful proofreading. Remember that simple, direct expression is almost always best, and that all unnecessary words and phrases should be ruthlessly excised.

DEADWOOD	When the time to go had arrived, Jay picked up his suitcase and went to the door.
REVISED	When it was time to go, Jay picked up his suitcase and went to the door.
DEADWOOD	After the close of the war, Phipps Ford entered the university as a special student.
REVISED	After the war, Phipps Ford entered the university as a special student.
DEADWOOD	She is attractive in appearance, but she is a rather selfish person.
REVISED	She is attractive, but rather selfish.
DEADWOOD	There were instances of aggression on the country's frontier in many cases.
REVISED	There were many instances of aggression on the country's frontier.

One kind of deadwood is *circumlocution* (literally, *talking around*) —the use of several words where a single exact one will do. "In this day and age" is a longer "today"; "call up on the telephone" a longer "telephone"; "destroyed by fire" a longer "burned"; "was made the recipient of" a longer "was given."

EXERCISE 37. Eliminate the deadwood from the following sentences.

1. He is an expert in the field of labor relations.
2. He hopes his essay will reinstate in the minds of the people the primary and fundamental purpose of our higher educational schools and colleges.
3. After we had cleaned up the cabin, we explored the surrounding territory for good fishing spots.
4. Blacky Hildreth is a peculiar character; he is interested in several aspects of witchcraft.
5. The fastest type of automobile requires the best quality of gasoline.
6. People have to be educated as to how to plan delicious, inexpensive menus that will meet their nutritional needs.
7. Social life seems to be a very important thing to college students.
8. The rain, which has been coming down steadily for two weeks now, is washing away the young seedlings I planted in the ground last month.
9. After spending four hours of time waiting for his train to come in, I went home and then to bed.
10. Edison spent the majority of the hours of each day tinkering in his laboratory.

41b **Use one exact word for two or more approximate words.**

Deadwood and circumlocutions make sentences clumsy; a more serious violation of directness is the use of two or more loose synonyms for a single precise word.

LOOSE   His *temperament* and *personality* are not very pleasant.
REVISED   His *disposition* is not very pleasant.

LOOSE   He spoke entertainingly of his *deeds* and *doings* as a foreign correspondent.
REVISED   He spoke entertainingly of his *adventures* as a foreign correspondent.

EXERCISE 38. Find a single synonym to express the meaning of the following pairs.

real and *true*	*amazed* and *surprised*
plays and *poems*	*severe* and *strict*
life and *times*	*flat* and *even*
love and *regard*	*proud* and *vain*
costly and *dear*	*conscientious* and *honest*

41c **Do not use words that needlessly repeat the meaning of other words.**

This clumsiness is known as *redundancy* or *tautology*—for example, "seen by the eyes" and "audible to the ears."

NOT He advanced *forward* and told the sergeant that he had captured four enemy spies.

BUT He advanced (or came forward) and told the sergeant that he had captured four enemy spies.

NOT Battalion A retreated *back* to the river bank.

BUT Battalion A retreated to the river bank.

NOT One of the first assignments in English was to write *my own* autobiography.

BUT One of the first assignments in English was to write an autobiography.

Be careful too to avoid unnecessarily long forms of words. *Irregardless* is merely a longer *regardless; preventative* a longer *preventive.* Even when the longer form does exist, as *truthfulness* and *virtuousness,* try substituting the shorter form (*truth, virtue*).

SUPERFLUOUS He is a very *pre-eminent* man, having a reputation as the country's greatest surgeon.

REVISED He is an *eminent* man, reputed to be the country's greatest surgeon.

SUPERFLUOUS In *summarization,* Lewis Doser spoke of the need for a larger library.

REVISED In *summary,* Lewis Doser spoke of the need for a larger library.

EXERCISE 39. Eliminate all redundancies or tautologies from the following sentences.

1. Mrs. Hissong's talk made me realize for the first time in my life the important essential of getting a college education.

2. Barbara Linger's limousine sedan, black in color, has been seen an uncountless number of times parked in front of Blickle's fruit market.

3. The modern business of today is usually a corporation; businesses owned in joint partnership are decreasing in number.

4. It is the consensus of opinion that the total effect of all this government spending, enormous in amount, will not achieve any real prosperity.

5. As a usual rule, the child is in his playpen by nine A.M. in the morning.

6. The life of Thomas Edison provides a good example to illustrate the truth of the old saying, "Genius is ten per cent inspiration and ninety per cent perspiration."

7. I like exciting scenery as well as the next person, but I know that very shortly I would become tired of it, and it would become boring.

8. In good writing there is always a great deal of sincerity in the writer's use of words and phrases.

9. John Dos Passos employs many unconventionalities in his writing, as well as a number of radical and peculiar tricks and devices of style.

10. So far as understanding his meaning is concerned, I would classify James Joyce as a very difficult author to read.

41d Avoid awkward repetition.

Awkward repetition makes a sentence wordy. Effective repetition is a legitimate way of securing emphasis.

EFFECTIVE   All *dullness* is in the mind; it comes out thence and diffuses itself over everything round the *dull* person, and then he terms everything *dull,* and thinks himself the victim of *dull* things.—C. E. MONTAGUE

EFFECTIVE   Don't *join* too many gangs. *Join* few if any. *Join* the United States and *join* the family—but not much in between, unless a college.—ROBERT FROST

EFFECTIVE   A *moderately* honest man with a *moderately* faithful wife, *moderate* drinkers both, in a *moderately* healthy house: that is the true middle class unit.—G. B. SHAW

AWKWARD   Methods of using the harvesting equipment are being *improved* constantly to *improve* efficiency.

AWKWARD   The investigation revealed that the *average teacher teaching* industrial arts in California has an *average* working and *teaching* experience of five years.

AWKWARD   The *important subject* on which I am going to speak is the *subject* of fraternity affairs, a *subject* of great *importance* to college students.

EXERCISE 40. Eliminate awkward repetitions from the following sentences.

1. I was late in leaving the house this morning and so was late for class.
2. He is an industrial engineering student studying the principles of time and motion study.
3. The final chapter of the book is devoted to recounting what happens to the heroine of the book.
4. Undoubtedly the world's tallest building is the Empire State Building.
5. The weatherstripping on the door should provide good protection against the cold weather.
6. People who graduated during the depression found many hardships in the way of finding jobs with adequate pay.
7. The writer's point about the need of making a college education more difficult is one of our points of agreement.
8. I was compelled to read the essay three times before I was prepared to make any kind of decision about the effectiveness of the ideas he presents in his essay.
9. After appearing in the movie *The Four Horsemen,* Rudolph Valentino was hounded the rest of his life by autograph hounds.
10. The formal usage of language is restricted pretty generally to use in academic and technical writing, or what we used to call old-fashioned eloquence.

41e **Use simple, direct expressions in preference to needlessly complex ones.**

This does not mean that *all* writing must be simple. Naturally, highly complex or technical subjects call at times for complex and technical language.

One of the simplest ways of evolving a favorable environment concurrently with the development of the individual organism, is that the influence of each organism on the environment should be favorable to the *endurance* of other organisms of the same type. Further, if the organism also favors *development* of other organisms of the same type, you have then obtained a mechanism of evolution adapted to produce the observed state of large multitudes of analogous entities, with high powers of endurance. For the environment automatically develops with the species, and the species with the environment.

—A. N. WHITEHEAD, *Science and the Modern World* [his italics]

But never be ashamed to express a simple idea in simple language. Remember that the use of complicated language is not in itself a sign of superior intelligence. (See "Appropriateness," Section 42d.)

NEEDLESSLY COMPLEX	Not a year passes without some evidence of the fundamental truth of the statement that the procedures and techniques of education are more complicated and complex than they were two decades ago.
MORE DIRECT	Each year shows that methods of education are more complex than they were twenty years ago.

Mr. Edgar Dale, in his "Art of Confusion," * has satirized the notion that language must be pompous and inflated in order to sound learned.

Young Alvin H. Harrison hesitatingly entered the office of Dr. Maxim S. Kleeshay and timidly inquired about his master's thesis. "What did you think of it?" he asked.

"A worthy endeavor," replied the Doctor, "but it has one major defect. It is written at too elementary a level. I would like to offer somewhat tentatively the pertinent observation that graduate students, research workers, and professors will find it too easy and effortless to read—no disciplinary value. Remember that Chancellor Hutchins once said that good education is painful. Furthermore, you haven't stated any significant challenges in your introductory paragraphs."

"I didn't want to offer any challenges. I just wanted to make my ideas clear."

"That's a worthy primary objective, young man. But no educational writing today should fail to point out that the world is in

---

* Reprinted with permission from *The News Letter* (XIV, No. 3), a publication of the Bureau of Educational Research, The Ohio State University, Columbus, Ohio.

peril, in flux, in conflict, changing, disordered, and disunited. It's either one world or two, you know.

"And another thing—it is interesting to note that you have a mistaken notion about communication on the scholarly level. It is obvious that you are unaware of the appropriate technical terminology in education. Your thesis is too sprightly, too simple."

"You mean that if I am dull enough and labored enough, I'll sound scholarly?"

"A very unfortunate and inaccurate way to put it, young man. I trust that it is not inappropriate to note some examples from your own thesis and to offer some suggestions (tentative, of course) as to how these examples might be shifted into more precise and scholarly language.

"You say on page 59, 'It will be hard to provide enough schools for the three million children entering in 1950.' It would have sounded much better if you had said, 'The phenomenon of fecundity has confronted American education with a challenge of Herculean proportions. An evaluation of the implication to the tax structure of state governments in providing adequate educational facilities is a difficult and complex task.'

"Let me make another point. A critical analysis of your thesis discloses that you are making little use of what is called the adjectival approach in education. You speak of 'thinking.' It would be much better to refer to 'critical thinking.' Change 'an approach to the problem' to 'a constructive approach to the problem.' Instead of 'world citizens' say 'functional world citizens.' At one point here, you say that the teacher is given 'help in working on her problems.' I would say that she had been given 'rather definite assistance in attacking specific difficulties.' You speak of 'reading practices.' Make it 'sound reading practices.' Utilize 'basic fundamentals' and 'desirable goals' a little more. Don't use the word 'function' alone. Say 'basic functions.'"

EXERCISE 41. Find a paragraph or two of "needlessly complex" writing in one of your textbooks. Explain in one or two paragraphs how you think the writing might be made more direct.

EXERCISE 42. Each of the sentences below violates a principle of *directness*. Find and then correct the error.

1. We of the United States cannot expect to spread peace throughout other nations and countries until we can teach and educate our own people to respect each other as equal individuals.

2. Professor Harding respects the ability of students to be able critics.

3. By learning to live with his physical problem, the life of the retarded child is improved, which is in itself a step forward toward recovery.

4. This has been a problem of growing importance which has bothered and troubled the physicists and engineers for a period of over one and one-half decades.

5. During the entirety of the whole fishing trip Morris continually went on thinking about those nice big trout he had caught during the summer before this present one.

6. They were the most beautiful looking fish he had ever seen before in his life.

7. Mr. Walleck used certain words to compliment the Republican Party and other types of words to slander the other party.

8. It has just been in the past couple of years that the Southern colleges have begun to open their doors to the Negro.

9. It was very evident that Pedersen's intention in writing the letter lies in the fact that not enough loyal brothers of the fraternity have been contributing to the upkeep of the fraternity.

10. Individuals who hold low standards of success are generally envious of people who have attained prominence and are constantly dissatisfied with their less fortunate existence which the lack of material success has forced upon them.

> *A speech is composed of three things: the speaker,*
> *the subject on which he speaks, and the audience he*
> *is addressing.*
>
> —ARISTOTLE, *Rhetoric*

42 APPROPRIATENESS = APPR

Be sure that your language is appropriate to the
subject, to the audience, and to yourself.

42a Ordinarily, avoid slang.

Webster's New Collegiate Dictionary defines *slang* as "language comprising certain widely current terms having a forced, fantastic, or grotesque meaning, or exhibiting eccentric humor or fancy." Sometimes slang results from an intentional mispronunciation, as *hoss, dawg;* sometimes from an intentional shortening of a regular word, as *prof, gent;* sometimes from corrupting an ordinary word to cover a different range of meanings, as *lousy, swell, sharp, tough, rugged.* But usually a slang word is an exaggerated metaphor, as *fishface, blockhead, highbrow, cash in your chips, ball and chain.*

To insist that all slang is vulgar * or inappropriate is to be excessively fastidious, if not unrealistic. Slang, after all, is part of the current language pattern, and its creation is inherent in the growth of the language.

Some words move in time from slang to general usage (*rascal, parry*). Clipped forms (*auto, ad, gym, phone*) are entirely appropriate in informal writing. In fact, many skillful writers use slang effectively.

* A slang word is *not* a profanity, an illiteracy, or a provincialism. Not one word in the following sentence is slang: "I reckon them damn apples is rotten."

The admiral jumped from his chair and cleared his throat, his mouth forming a straight, tight line; if anything, the corners turned downward. Clenching his fists, he apparently tried to look as severe and angry as possible. But before he could say anything he lost control and broke into a grin. A second later he started laughing so hard that he couldn't stand up. He chewed on his napkin to try to shut, up but he couldn't stop roaring. The party turned into a wing-ding and we practically blew the roof off the place.

—WILLIAM LEDERER, *All the Ship's at Sea*

But slang has two serious limitations: (1) a little of it goes a long way, and (2) it is not always appropriate. Slang quickly becomes lifeless and dated. Who remembers *Twenty-three skiddoo* and *Oh, you kid?* Then, too, the inherent flippancy of slang makes it inappropriate in formal writing. It is especially poor usage to mix slang and respectable words indiscriminately in the same sentence.

In meeting today in a special session to approve the governor's request for an investigation of the liquor board, the legislators decided to blow the whole shebang sky high.

EXERCISE 43. Almost everyone has his favorite slang terms —*swell, lousy, grand, awful,* and so on. Make a list of your own slang terms and compare the list with those of your classmates to see how "original" your own slang is.

EXERCISE 44. Can you think of a situation or general context in which the following sentences might be appropriate? Explain.

1. The distinguished envoy to the peace conference finished his address by blowing his top.
2. The concert was unfortunately interrupted when a piece of plaster fell near the podium and conked one of the violinists on the noggin.
3. During the congregational meeting the Reverend Mr. Hildreth was called upon to put in his two cents' worth.
4. The beauty of the painting was marred by the artist's tendency to foul up the backgrounds with screwy designs.
5. When heat was applied to the chemical mixture, small particles of zinc were dispersed like crazy.

42b **Avoid substandard English.**

Substandard, or *vulgate*, speech consists of *profanity, provincialisms* (sometimes called *localisms* or *dialecticisms*), and *vulgarisms*. Profanity may be fine for providing an emotional release, but it is inappropriate in formal communication. A *provincialism* is a word whose use is generally restricted to a particular region, as *tote* for *carry; poke* for *bag; spider* for *frying pan; gumshoes* for *overshoes; draw* for *small valley*. A *vulgarism* is an illiteracy: *ain't, could of, he done, we was.* Double negatives (*can't hardly, can't help but, not never*) are considered vulgarisms by many people, though *I cannot help but be confused* is hardly so objectionable an expression as *I can't never seem to git the point.* The vulgarisms that creep most frequently into writing are *improprieties*, good words incorrectly used (see "Exactness," Section 40d).

SUBSTANDARD	He *didn't ought to have* spent the money.
REVISED	He shouldn't have spent the money.
SUBSTANDARD	I wish Irving *had of drove more careful.*
REVISED	I wish Irving had driven more carefully.
SUBSTANDARD	*Let's don't* study tonight.
REVISED	Let's not study tonight.

Of all substandard English forms, the double negative (*can't hardly, scarcely none, don't* want *no,* and so on) is perhaps the most controversial. In the eighteenth century, Englishmen, applying the mathematical principle that two negatives make a positive, ruled out the double negative in grammar. The argument was that a person who says *I don't want nothing to do with you* is really saying *I want something to do with you.* Actually the double (or triple) negative is a means of being emphatic. But since its use is generally frowned upon, you do well to avoid it.

EXERCISE 45. Find at least five examples of *provincialisms* (as "The cat wants in") and describe the circumstances under which they could be used appropriately.

EXERCISE 46. If you are a native of the region in which your college is located, ask a classmate from another region to give you a list of ten words or expressions that strike him as being provincialisms in your speech. If you come from another region yourself, make up your own list of provincialisms of the college area and compare it with your classmate's.

42c Avoid trite expressions.

A trite expression, sometimes called a *cliché,* a *stereotyped,* or a *hackneyed* phrase, is an expression that has been worn out by constant use, as "burning the midnight oil," "Father Time," "raving beauties," "man about town." Words in themselves are never trite—they are only *used* tritely. We cannot avoid trite expressions entirely, for they sometimes describe a situation accurately.* But the writer who burdens his language with clichés runs the risk of being regarded as a trite thinker. What would be your estimate of the person who wrote this?

> A college education develops a *well-rounded personality* and gives the student an appreciation of *the finer things of life.*

Effectively used, triteness can be humorous. Note how the string of trite expressions in the example below explodes into absurdity when the writer transposes the words in the two clichés in the last clause.

> A pair of pigeons were cooing gently directly beneath my window; two squirrels plighted their troth in a branch overhead; at the corner a handsome member of New York's finest twirled his nightstick and cast roguish glances at the saucy-eyed flower vendor. The scene could have been staged only by a Lubitsch; in fact Lubitsch himself was seated on a bench across the street, smoking a cucumber and looking as cool as a cigar.
> —s. j. perelman, *Keep It Crisp*

Watch for trite words and phrases in your own writing. Whenever you discover any, replace them with new, original ways of expressing yourself. As you proofread your manuscripts, be as sensitive to clichés as you are to misspellings.

---

* More fundamentally, of course, triteness is a disease of the personality. If people react to situations in stereotyped ways, their writing will reflect this fact. The next time you prepare a paper on "Why I Came to College" or "What I Expect to Do After Graduation," write what you *really* mean. You will probably avoid triteness.

EXERCISE 47. The selection below contains a number of trite expressions. List as many as you can identify.

The wily Indians, wishing to strike while the iron was hot, converged on the wagon-train at the break of dawn. The hardy pioneers, firing in unison, presented the attacking force with a veritable hail of bullets. Dozens of the pesky red-skins keeled over and bit the dust. The rugged frontiersmen continued to give a good account of themselves until broad daylight. Then the Indians broke through the ramparts. The defenders, their backs against the wall, were slaughtered mercilessly. When the dust had risen from the battlefield and when the smoke had cleared away, the carnage was frightful. Every single white man had gone to meet his maker.

EXERCISE 48. Copy the following passage. Circle all clichés and all expressions that are longer or more involved than they need be. Suggest more appropriate wordings for each.

The American Way is the only feasible route for educational personnel to tread in our educational institutions of learning. Despite its humble origins, this child of adversity, born in a log cabin, has beyond a shadow of a doubt reached the summits in this fair country of ours.

There is too much of a tendency to view this great institution with alarm. But on the other hand people who live in glass houses, which is the type most inclined to cast aspersions and generally be wet blankets, are usually the ones by whom the criticisms are made.

Now I'm just an ordinary schoolteacher, and don't have any complicated ideas on how our schools should be run, but I know that Abe Lincoln, if he were alive, would disapprove of the new-fangled techniques that are making a shambles of our educational system.

Foreigners are at the bottom of the attack on our American heritage and the American Way in education. These notorious radicals have wreaked havoc with our boys and girls.

42d Avoid jargon in writing for a general audience.

The term *jargon* has several meanings. In a famous essay, "On Jargon," Sir Arthur Quiller-Couch defined the term as vague and "woolly" speech or writing that consists of abstract words, elegant variation, and "circumlocution rather than short straight speech."

(Linguists often define jargon as hybrid speech or dialect formed by a mixture of languages. An example would be the English-Chinese jargon known as pidgin-English.)

To most people, however, jargon is the technical or specialized vocabulary of a particular trade or profession—for example, *engineering jargon* or *educational jargon.* Members of the profession, of course, can use their jargon when they are communicating with one another, for it is their language, so to speak. But the use of technical jargon is inappropriate when you are writing for a general audience.

Unfortunately, jargon impresses a great many people simply because it sounds involved and learned. We are all reluctant to admit that we do not understand what we are reading. What, for example, can you make of the following passage?

> ### THE TURBO-ENCABULATOR IN INDUSTRY
>
> ... Work has been proceeding in order to bring to perfection the crudely conceived idea of a machine that would not only supply inverse reactive current for use in unilateral phase detractors, but would also be capable of automatically synchronizing cardinal grammaters. Such a machine is the Turbo-Encabulator. . . . The original machine had a base plate of prefabulated amulite surmounted by a malleable logarithmic casing in such a way that the two spurving bearings were in a direct line with the pentametric fan. . . . The main winding was of the normal lotus-o-delta type placed in a panendermic semiboloid slot in the stator, every seventh conductor being connected by a non-reversible tremie pipe to the differential girdlespring on the "up" end of the grammeters. . . .*

This new mechanical marvel was a joke, the linguistic creation of a research engineer who was tired of reading jargon.

> **EXERCISE 49.** Make a list of twenty words, terms, or phrases that constitute the "jargon" in a field that you know. Define these terms in a way that a general reader could understand; then justify the use of the terms among the people in your field.

* Reprinted by permission of the publishers, Arthur D. Little, Inc., Cambridge, Mass.

42e **Avoid artificial or stilted diction and "fine writing."**

Artificiality is not inherent in words themselves but in the use that is made of them. Simple facts and assertions should be stated simply and directly, or else you will run the risk of making your writing sound pompous and self-conscious, as in the following examples.

ARTIFICIAL   The edifice was consumed by fire.
NATURAL   The house burned down.

ARTIFICIAL   We were unable to commence our journey to your place of residence because of inclement weather conditions.
NATURAL   We could not come because it was snowing.

Many inexperienced writers believe, mistakenly, that an artificial diction makes for "good writing." They shift gears, so to speak, when they go from speaking to writing. They try to make their writing sound like the speech of a Hollywood version of a college professor, and once again the results sound stilted.

ARTIFICIAL   The athletic contest commenced at the stipulated time.
NATURAL   The game began on time.

ARTIFICIAL   I informed him that his advice was unsolicited.
NATURAL   I told him to mind his own business.

Your writing may become artificial simply because you are trying *too* hard to write effectively, because you have grown more concerned with *how* you write than with *what* you write. Writing marked by a continuously artificial diction is called "fine writing."

FINE WRITING   Whenever the press of daily events and duties relaxes its iron grip on me, whenever the turmoil of my private world subsides and leaves me in quiet and solitude, then it is that I feel my crying responsibility as one of God's creatures and recognize the need to speak out loudly and boldly against the greed and intolerance that carry humanity into the terrible destruction of armed conflict.
NATURAL   I am a crusader for international peace.

EXERCISE 50. Find an example of "fine writing" in a newspaper or magazine and explain in a short paper why you think it ineffective.

42f **Avoid mixed and incongruous metaphors and other illogical comparisons.**

One of the most respected and ancient means of reinforcing and enlivening communication is the use of comparisons. An apt figure of speech makes one experience understandable in terms of another.

> The teacher shook her finger in my face as she might shake a clogged fountain pen.

Figurative language, however, has its pitfalls. Unless the figure of speech is clear, logical, and vigorous, it will obscure rather than clarify your meaning. These examples show how meaningless and confusing an inept figure of speech can be.

1. Every field of study is pursued in the hope of finding a universal panacea.
2. Socialists are snakes in the grass, gnawing at the roots of the ship of state.

In the first sentence the "pursuit of a field" sets up an unlikely image; the second is clearly a nonsensical hodgepodge.

Unfortunately, the well-meaning search for fresh comparisons may betray a writer into using figures that are inappropriate to what he is trying to say.

> The minister was not too proud to spend his days visiting the sick and the needy and those rejected by society. He was as little concerned with personal contamination as a pig in a mud puddle when the Lord's work was to be done.

The effective use of figures of speech in your writing is a real challenge. Nothing is more apt, more pointed, more expert than a good figure of speech. Nothing is flatter or more ludicrous than a poor one. Make a habit of reviewing the originality, congruity, logic, and appropriateness of every figure of speech you use.

EXERCISE 51. Replace the mixed or incongruous figures of speech in the following sentences with fresher, more appropriate comparisons.

1. The enemy threw everything at us but the kitchen sink, keeping us on pins and needles.
2. My father was usually on top of the world when he brought home the bacon.
3. Although the first draft of the treaty had received provisional ratification by most of the countries concerned, the diplomats were busy as beavers tidying up the last details.
4. He had to be on the rocks before he would turn over a new leaf.
5. Grandmother's tiny, dried fingers seemed to stitch the material with the rapidity of a pneumatic drill.
6. She may be the last rose of summer, but she's got some vinegar in her yet.
7. It wasn't until Copernicus began re-examining an old cosmology completely in conflict with the Ptolemaic system that he really hit the nail on the head.
8. Table tennis is a good game for you sharp yearlings, but when you're blind as a bat it's a horse of a different color.
9. By a series of such victories, the team was able to roll up a very good foundation for a national reputation.
10. They decided to play the field until the chips were down and then to get behind a single candidate with both barrels.

EXERCISE 52. First assume an "audience" (English teacher, classmates, group of businessmen, parents, etc.); then comment on the "appropriateness" of the language in the following selection in terms of that audience.

Like many other just plain "guys," I just graduated from high school. Being like most of these other guys, I naturally didn't really accomplish much during my previous school years. Yes, I got fair grades, met lots of swell kids, played football. I guess I'm just one of those guys who had the run of the school and never bothered to study.

No, I'm not bragging. I'm just telling you why high school was never like college.

A lot of people graduate from high school every year. A good percentage go to college and the rest go out and get a job. Four years later, the college student graduates. Does that mean he's going to get a better job than the fellow who went from high school directly to a job?

No. It doesn't mean a thing unless the guy in college really studied and hit the books. What I'm trying to bring out is that a person who goes to college and doesn't study is no better off than a guy who goes out and gets a job immediately after high school graduation.

So college for me is the "big jump." I fooled around in high school, and if I don't get right down and study now, I might as well quit school and start that $75.00 a week job.

No, I don't have anything against a $75.00 a week job. It's just that twenty years from now, I'd probably still be there getting the same $75.00. This is it, so I guess it's time for me to bear down and study hard. I think this will be the "big jump."

DICTION REVIEW EXERCISE (Sections 40 through 42). Revise each of the following sentences according to what you have learned in the sections on "Exactness," "Directness," and "Appropriateness."

1. Even though homemaking is an important occupation, only a small number of homemakers have thorough preparation for the task.

2. By reading *Yachting* I am able to keep abreast with the tide of affairs in the sailing world.

3. The sheriff suspicioned that the prisoners had hacksawed their way out of the jail.

4. Coaches are paid for the type of teams they produce or for the number of winning games per season.

5. The principal censored the boy's actions in a meanly manner.

6. I thought I was doing the best thing when I signed up for the army.

7. Her eyes were like limpid pools of clear, crystal water; her skin glowed as though it had been touched by a fairy's wand. She was a knockout.

8. The pup was a nuisance. The little mongrel chased after other curs and followed the dumb brutes to their homes. Then we had to spend our evenings hunting for the hound.

9. Reading every new novel that comes out may give a person a broader aspect of life.

10. The knowledge we receive in our home economics classes is very useful and economical to us.

11. Compared to Johnson, Coleman is a lily-fingered shortstop.

12. He left our domicile a boy; he returned to our outstretched arms a man. His rugged, weather-beaten face had been tanned by the blazing sun of darkest Africa, lined by sorrows and sufferings that would forever remain a secret between him and his God.

13. Child care is taught in the clinic, as well as other matters which the attendants desire.

14. Them people in Washington don't seem to understand that you can't get no blood out of a turnip.

15. My superior, the commanding general of this area, has just instructed me to activate the regiment. I shall implement his directive and communicate with him when his instructions have been carried out.

16. Our language should be adjusted into whatever situation we find ourselves.

17. A college student has to invest most of his time with studying if he is going to be a successful student.

18. Though Jack is able to rationalize very well in the field of philosophy, he has a striking unableness in the field of mathematics.

19. Steinmetz worked with the mysteries of nature, electricity, and science and for years was the most valuable man in the General Electric Company.

20. Professor Catlin's life was poor in terms of remunerative values, but more students in the college remember him than any other teacher.

21. The author was very successful in infiltrating into the minds of his readers the terrible confusion of war.

22. Mr. Morris' frequent forgetfulness of his wife's shopping instructions was the ban of his wife's existent.

23. As we rounded the curve, I could see that a crash was eminent, and I covered my head with my hands.

24. A better job of supervision and management can be done if the administrator knows and can foresee the problems that might arise in the future.

25. The authorship of the novel has not been authenticized, but the existing evidence points to one Joshua Fiddings.

> *"Awfully nice"* is an expression than which few
> could be sillier: but to have succeeded in going
> through life without saying it a certain number of
> times is as bad as to have no redeeming vice.
>
> —H. W. FOWLER

43 GLOSSARY OF USAGE = GLOS

This glossary discusses a number of words that present usage problems. The list is not complete; it includes only the more persistent troublemakers. An unabridged dictionary will give you information on words and expressions that do not appear here.

Many of the judgments and the labels of usage that appear in this glossary are tentative, for usage is sometimes vague and always changing.* Moreover, usage is often a local or sectional matter; errors common in parts of the Middle West may be rare in the East, the South, or the Far West. The following labels of usage occur in the glossary:

Colloquial means often used in informal conversation, but generally avoided in formal writing. Colloquial English has several levels of its own; for example, a low colloquial expression like "being as how" would be considered illiterate by some educated people.

Commercial jargon means the specialized language of business and market place. Such language is unsuitable for most expository writing.

Illiterate means substandard, ignorant.

Informal means the language of familiar, everyday affairs.

* See "The Standards of Modern English" in the Introduction, pp. 6-10.

Jargon means the special language of a particular occupation or group. Jargon is not appropriate for most writing intended for general readers.

Journalese means language suitable only to the commercial press, with its special problems of space and readability.

Legalism means a technical expression used chiefly in legal documents.

Provincial means regularly used in a particular region, but not elsewhere.

Slang means language comprising certain widely current terms having a forced, fantastic, or grotesque meaning. Slang is generally unsuitable for either formal or informal writing.

A, An. *A* is used before words beginning with a consonant sound even though the sound is spelled with a vowel (as in *universe*); *an* is used before words beginning with a vowel sound or with a silent *h*. Some speakers use *an* before words beginning with a pronounced *h*, as *an historian*, but *a* is preferred before such words.

> a dog, a wagon, a habit, a union; an apple, an Indian, an hour, an uproar

Above. *Above* is used chiefly as a preposition ("above the trees") or adverb ("birds flew above"). The use of *above* as an adjective or noun, often found in legal and business writing, is acceptable in standard English, though some writers (and readers) object to it as commercial jargon.

> AS ADJECTIVE   We refer you to the *above* agreement.
> AS NOUN   The *above* is not recorded in our office files.

Accept, Except. These verbs are sometimes confused because of their similarity in sound. *Accept* means "to receive." *Except* (as verb) means "to exclude."

> He *accepted* the gift with pleasure.
> We *excepted* George from the list of candidates.

Ad. A shortened form of *advertisement* inappropriate in formal writing. Other clipped forms include *auto, exam, math, phone, photo.*

Affect, Effect. These words are sometimes confused because of their similarity in sound. As verbs, *affect* means "to influence," and *effect* means "to bring about." As a noun, *effect* means "result."

370

His fame does not *affect* his personality.

We *effected* a truce with our enemies.

Her studying had a good *effect* on her grades.

Aggravate. In formal English *aggravate* means "to intensify" or "to make worse." Colloquially, it is often used as a substitute for *annoy* or *provoke*.

FORMAL   The hot sun *aggravated* his suffering.
COLLOQUIAL   His teasing *aggravated* her.

Aid. *Aid* means "help" and should not be confused with *aide*, "a military assistant."

Ain't. An illiterate form, originally a contraction of "are not," but now used indiscriminately for "am not," "is not," "has not," "have not."

Alibi. In formal English, *alibi* has the technical legal meaning "a plea of having been elsewhere than at the alleged place where an act was committed." Colloquially, *alibi* means "an excuse."

All the farther, All the faster, etc. Unidiomatic when used as a substitute for *as far as, as fast as,* etc. Sometimes used in familiar conversation but not appropriate in writing.

FORMAL   Lane Avenue is *as far as* this bus goes.
COLLOQUIAL   Lane Avenue is *all the farther* this bus goes.

Allusion, Illusion. *Allusion* means "an indirect reference." *Illusion* means "a misleading image" or "a false impression."

The speaker made an *allusion* to the President.

The heat waves from the road produced the *illusion* of a pool of water.

Already, All ready. The adverb *already* means "previously." The adjective phrase *all ready* means "completely prepared."

When he reached the station, his train had *already* gone.

By eight o'clock we were *all ready* to start hiking.

All right. *All right* is the only correct spelling. *Alright,* though occasionally used by writers of advertising and fiction, has not been generally accepted. *All right* in the sense of *satisfactory* or *very well* is a colloquialism that is becoming standard.

Alot. Should be rendered as two words: *a lot.*

Also. Not to be used as a substitute for *and.*

We packed a tent, our guns, *and* (not *also*) our fishing tackle.

Altogether, All together. The adverb *altogether* means "wholly, completely." The adjective phrase *all together* means "in a group."

> I am *altogether* pleased with my new piano.
>
> We were *all together* for the family reunion.

Alumnus, Alumna. An *alumnus* (plural *alumni*) is a male graduate. An *alumna* (plural *alumnae*) is a female graduate.

Among, Between. *Among* implies more than two persons or things; *between* implies only two. To express a reciprocal relationship, or the relationship of one thing to several other things, however, *between* is commonly used for more than two.

> She divided the toys *among* the three children.
>
> Jerry could choose *between* pie and cake for dessert.
>
> An agreement was reached *between* the four companies.
>
> The surveyors drove a stake at a point *between* three trees.

Amount, Number. *Amount* refers to quantity or mass. *Number* refers to countable objects.

> Irrigation requires a large *amount* of water.
>
> The farmer raised a small *number* of beef cattle.

And etc. Etc. (Latin *et cetera*) means "and so forth." The redundant *and etc.* means literally "and and so forth."

And/or. A legalism that should be used with caution.

Angle. Slang for *point of view* or *aspect*. In formal writing *angle* often seems inappropriate: "Newton had a new *angle* on the laws of physics."

Any. *Any* is provincial for *at all* when it modifies a verb.

> PROVINCIAL   It hasn't rained *any* today.

Anyplace. Colloquial for *anywhere*.

Anyways, Anywheres. Colloquial forms of *anyway* and *anywhere*.

Apt, Likely. In formal writing *apt* usually refers to a natural ability or habitual tendency. *Likely* refers to a probability. In informal English, *apt* is often used as a synonym for *likely*.

> FORMAL   Grandma is *apt* at losing her glasses.
>
> FORMAL   The hockey game is *likely* to be exciting.
>
> INFORMAL   The hockey game is *apt* to be exciting.

As. In introducing clauses, *as* is somewhat less precise than *since* or *because.*

> LOOSE *As* we were late, we rode to the theater in a taxi.
> MORE PRECISE *Because* we were late, we rode to the theater in a taxi.

As a method of. Overused and wordy when followed by a gerund.

> WORDY Swimming is useful *as a method of* developing coordination.
> REVISED Swimming is useful *for developing* coordination.

As . . . as, so . . . as. In negative comparisons formal English prefers *so . . . as* to *as . . . as.* This distinction is not usually observed in informal English.

> FORMAL He is *as* tall *as* I am.
>
> FORMAL He is not *so* tall *as* I am.
> INFORMAL He is not *as* tall *as* I am.

As for my part. A confusion of the two idioms *as for me* and *for my part.*

Asset. *Asset* has a specific meaning in law and accounting but may be used informally to mean "value," "merit," or "qualification."

At about, At around. An unnecessary doubling of prepositions. Deadwood may be avoided by using *at, about,* or *around,* whichever is the most exact.

> INEXACT He arrived *at about* one o'clock.
> EXACT He arrived *at* (or *about*) one o'clock.

Auto. *See* Ad.

Badly. Used informally in the sense of *very much* or *greatly* with the verbs *need* and *want.*

> FORMAL I *very much* need a new coat.
> INFORMAL I need a new coat *badly.*

Balance. Colloquial when used to mean "the rest," "remainder" (except when referring to a "bank balance").

> FORMAL I stayed at home for the *rest* of the evening.
> COLLOQUIAL I stayed at home for the *balance* of the evening.

Being that, Being as how. Illogical and illiterate substitutes for the appropriate subordinating conjunctions *as, because, since.*

Beside, Besides. *Beside* is a preposition meaning "by the side of." *Besides,* generally used as an adverb, means "moreover," "in addition to."

He sat down *beside* her.

Besides, we have to wait here for John.

Between, Among. *See* Among.

Blame on, Blame it on. In formal English the verb *blame* is followed by the preposition *for*.

FORMAL   Don't *blame* me *for* it.
INFORMAL   Don't *blame it on* me.

Bursted, Bust, Busted. The principal parts of the verb are *burst, burst, burst*. *Bursted* is an old form of the past and past participle which is no longer considered good usage. *Bust* and *busted* are slang.

But that, But what. In formal usage *that* is preferable to *but what*.

FORMAL   I don't doubt *that* you are right.
INFORMAL   I don't doubt *but what* you are right.

Can, May. In formal English *can* means "to be able"; *may* means "to have permission." Colloquially, *can* is commonly used to imply both ability and permission.

FORMAL   She *can* bake delicious pies.

FORMAL   *May* I go to the church supper with you?
COLLOQUIAL *Can* I go to the church supper with you?

May is also used in the sense of possibility. "This problem *may* be solved as follows."

Can't hardly. A double negative; not considered acceptable usage.

Can't help but. A double negative. Though sometimes found in formal and informal writing, this expression is strongly objected to by many writers.

FORMAL   I *can't help* disliking him.
COLLOQUIAL I *can't help but* dislike him.

Can't seem to. Formal usage prefers *seem unable to*.

FORMAL   He *seems unable* to pass his history courses.
INFORMAL   He *can't seem to* pass his history courses.

Claim. In formal usage *claim* means "to demand as one's right." In informal English *claim* is commonly used as a synonym for *say* or *maintain*.

FORMAL   She *claimed* the fortune found in the old well.
INFORMAL   He *claims* that he is a good horseman.

Complected. Colloquial for *complexioned.*

Considerable. Informal when used as an adjective to indicate *amount;* colloquial when used as a noun.

> INFORMAL   They lost *considerable property* in the flood.
> COLLOQUIAL They lost *considerable* in the flood.

Contact. There is some prejudice, which seems to be disappearing, against the verb *contact* meaning "to meet or talk with." The word is borrowed from commercial jargon. In formal and informal writing a more specific word, such as *meet* or *interview,* is preferable.

Continual, Continuous. *Continual* means "frequently repeated." *Continuous* means "without interruption."

> He was distracted by *continual* telephone calls.
> We heard the *continuous* sound of the waves.

Could of. Illiterate form of *could have.*

Couple. *Couple* in the sense of *two or three* is colloquial, but in any case it should be followed by the preposition *of.*

Credible, Creditable, Credulous. These adjectives are sometimes confused. *Credible* means "believable." *Creditable* means "praiseworthy." *Credulous* means "inclined to believe on slight evidence."

> His story seemed *credible* to the jury.
> She gave a *creditable* piano recital.
> The *credulous* child thought the moon was made of cheese.

Criticizer. Illiterate substitute for *critic.*

Cute. Overused and trite as a vague word of approval.

Data, Phenomena. These nouns are the plural forms of *datum,* "a fact on which an inference is based," and *phenomenon,* "an observable fact or event." In informal usage *data* is frequently treated as a collective noun with a singular verb.

> FORMAL   *This datum is* (or *these data are*) valuable.
> INFORMAL   *This data is* valuable.

Deal. A commercial or colloquial substitute for *bargain* or *transaction.*

Definite, Definitely. Often misspelled *definate, definately,* these words suggest fixed limits and are colloquial as vague intensifiers ("He is definitely handsome").

Different than. *See* "Exactness," Section 40g.

Don't. A contraction for *do not,* not for *does not.*

He *doesn't* (not *don't*) want his dinner.

Doubt but what. *See* But that.

Due to. Since *due* is in origin an adjective, some writers object to the use of *due to* as a preposition introducing an adverbial phrase. It is interesting to note that *owing to,* which developed from a participle to a preposition in the same way, is accepted without question. The prepositional use of *due to* is increasingly widespread, and it is appropriate except in the most formal writing.

due AS AN ADJECTIVE	His failure was *due to* laziness.
FORMAL	The festival was postponed *because of* (or *owing to*) rain.
INFORMAL	The festival was postponed *due to* rain.

Each and every. Wordy jargon.

Each other, One another. Fastidious writers prefer *each other* when referring to two persons or things, and *one another* when referring to more than two, but the distinction is not widely observed. The two expressions are interchangeable.

Educational. Overused and inaccurate as a synonym for *instructive, informative,* etc.

Effect, Affect. *See* Affect, Effect.

Emigrate, Immigrate. *Emigrate* means "to move *from* a country." *Immigrate* means "to move *into* a country."

Erik *emigrated* from Sweden.
Erik *immigrated* to America.

Enthuse. Colloquial for *become enthusiastic.*

FORMAL	We *were enthusiastic* about our vacation.
COLLOQUIAL	We *were enthused* about our vacation.

Environment. *Environment* (often misspelled and mispronounced *enviorment*) is jargon when used to mean "neighborhood," "surroundings," "atmosphere."

Equally as good. The *as* is unnecessary. *Equally good* is more precise.

Etc. Italics are correct but not necessary. This abbreviation for *and so forth* is appropriate in business usage and may be used in formal writing if its meaning is entirely clear. (*See* "Abbreviations," Section 3a (4).)

Everyplace. Colloquial for *everywhere.*

Everyone. Should be written as two words except when used as a synonym for *everybody.*

Every so often. This expression and *every bit as, every once in a while, every which way* are colloquial.

Everywheres. An illiterate form of *everywhere.*

Exam. *See* Ad.

Except, Accept. *See* Accept, Except.

Except for the fact that. Wordy and colloquial substitute for *except that.*

Expect. In colloquial English *expect* is sometimes used to mean "suppose."

FORMAL	I *suppose* I should mow the lawn.
COLLOQUIAL	I *expect* I should mow the lawn.

Extra. There is some prejudice against the use of *extra* as an adverb meaning "unusually."

FORMAL	Monday was an *unusually* warm day.
COLLOQUIAL	Monday was an *extra* warm day.

Farther, Further. In formal English some writers use *farther* when referring to distance and *further* when referring to degree or quantity. In informal English this distinction is not widely observed.

FORMAL	We walked two miles *farther.*
INFORMAL	We walked two miles *further.*

Faze. Colloquial for *disconcert, bother,* or *daunt.*

FORMAL	Ridicule did not *bother* him.
COLLOQUIAL	Ridicule did not *faze* him.

Feel of, Smell of, Taste of. The *of* is unnecessary in these expressions.

The tailor *felt* (not *felt of*) the cloth.

Fellow. Colloquial when used to mean "person."

Fewer, Less. *Fewer* refers to number. In formal English *less* refers only to degree or quantity. In informal English *less* is sometimes used to refer to number.

FORMAL	He is *less* friendly than he used to be.
FORMAL	*Fewer* than half the students could solve the problem.
INFORMAL	*Less* than half the students could solve the problem.

Fiancé, Fiancée. These words, borrowed from the French, are sometimes confused. *Fiancé* (plural *fiancés*) refers to the betrothed man. *Fiancée* (plural *fiancées*) refers to the betrothed woman. In informal writing the accent marks are often dropped.

Fiction book. Illiterate for *novel*.

Fine. As an adjective to express approval ("a *fine* person") *fine* is vague and overused. As an adverb meaning "well" ("works *fine*") *fine* is colloquial.

First-rate. A generally accepted adjective meaning "of the first order." Colloquial as an adverb meaning "very well."

ADJECTIVE USE	He is a *first-rate* swimmer.
FORMAL	He swims *very well*.
COLLOQUIAL	He swims *first-rate*.

Fix. Colloquial when used as a noun meaning "predicament."

FORMAL	John is in a *predicament*.
COLLOQUIAL	John is in a *fix*.

Former, Latter. *Former* refers to the first named of two; *latter* refers to the last named of two. *First* and *last* are used to refer to one of a group of more than two.

Function. Suggests elaborateness or formality when used to describe a social occasion. Pretentious or ironic when used loosely for *activity*.

Funny. Colloquial when used to mean "strange," "queer," or "odd."

Further, Farther. *See* Farther, Further.

Gentleman, Lady. *Man* and *woman* are preferable to the more pretentious *gentleman* and *lady* unless the speaker is intentionally making a distinction between refined and ill-bred persons. "Ladies and Gentlemen" is a conventional expression used in addressing an audience.

Get. The verb *get* is used in many colloquial and slang expressions that are inappropriate in formal writing. Among these are "get going," "get to go," "get at it," "get wise to," "get away with."

Good. An adjective often used colloquially as an adverb in such sentences as "The motor runs *good*." (Formal English would use the adverb *well* to modify the verb *runs*.)

Good and. Colloquial in such expressions as "good and hot," "good and ready."

Guess. Formal usage prefers *suppose* or *think* to the overworked *guess*.

Had of. An illiterate form.

> I wish I *had* (not *had of*) seen the eclipse.

Had ought, Hadn't ought. Illiterate for *ought* and *ought not*.

> He *ought* (not *had ought*) to treat his wife better.

Hanged, Hung. The principal parts of *hang* when referring to death by hanging are *hang, hanged, hanged*. When *hang* is used to mean "suspend," the principal parts are *hang, hung, hung*. In informal English the distinction is not rigidly kept, *hang, hung, hung* being used in all senses.

> FORMAL   The outlaw was *hanged* from a cottonwood tree.
> INFORMAL   The outlaw was *hung* from a cottonwood tree.

Have got. Formal usage prefers *have*.

> FORMAL   I *have* a headache.
> COLLOQUIAL   *I've got* a headache.

Healthful, Healthy. *Healthful* means "giving health." *Healthy* means "having health."

Himself, Myself, Yourself. *See* Myself, Yourself, Himself.

Home. Formal usage prefers *at home*.

> FORMAL   Our neighbors are not *at home*.
> INFORMAL   Our neighbors are not *home*.

Humans. Most careful writers prefer *people* or *human beings*.

Idea. Often vague for *belief, conjecture, intention, plan, theory,* and should be replaced whenever possible by a more specific noun.

If, Whether. Formal English prefers *whether* to *if* after such verbs as *say, ask, know, doubt, wonder, understand*.

> FORMAL   He did not say *whether* he would return.
> INFORMAL   He did not say *if* he would return.

Illusion, Allusion. *See* Allusion, Illusion.

Immigrate, Emigrate. *See* Emigrate, Immigrate.

Imply, Infer. *Imply* means "to hint" or "to suggest." *Infer* means "to draw a conclusion."

> He *implied* that I was ungrateful.
> I *inferred* from his remark that he did not like me.

In, Into. In formal usage *in* denotes location; *into* denotes direction. In colloquial English *in* is often used for *into*.

FORMAL We were studying *in* the library.
FORMAL I fell *into* the pool.
COLLOQUIAL I fell *in* the pool.

In back of. Colloquial for *behind, back of, at the back of.*

Individual, Party, Person. *Individual* refers to one particular person. *Person* refers to a human being in general. *Party* refers to a group of people, except in legal language.

Jefferson defended the rights of the *individual*.
She is a *person* (not *an individual*) of strong character.
You are the *person* (not *party*) I am looking for.

Indulge. *Indulge* means "to be tolerant toward" or "to gratify one's desire"; it is not a synonym for *to take part in.*

ACCURATE The old man *indulged* (*tolerated*) the noisy parrot.
INACCURATE The ladies *indulged in* (*took part in*) a quarrel.

Infer, Imply. *See* Imply, Infer.

Ingenious, Ingenuous. *Ingenious* means "clever." *Ingenuous* means "frank" or "naïve."

Inventors are usually *ingenious* people.
He was too *ingenuous* to suspect that he was being tricked.

In my estimation. Like *in my opinion, in my judgment,* this phrase is often unnecessary, or is pretentious for *I think, I feel, I believe.*

In regards to. A confusion of the British idiom *as regards* with the American idiom *in regard to.*

Inside of. The *of* is unnecessary when *inside* is used as a preposition. *Inside of* is colloquial for *within* when used in reference to time.

FORMAL We stayed *inside* (not *inside of*) the house.
FORMAL He will arrive *within* an hour.
COLLOQUIAL He will arrive *inside of* an hour.

Into, In. *See* In, Into.

Irregardless. A double negative resulting from the confusion of *irrespective* and *regardless.*

Is when, Is where. Noun clauses introduced by *when* or *where* and used to give a definition are avoided by careful writers. (*See* "Logic," Section 37a.)

LOOSE A first down *is when* the football is advanced ten yards in four plays or fewer.

PRECISE A first down *is made when* the football is advanced ten yards in four plays or fewer.

It being. Awkward and colloquial substitute for a clause introduced by *since.*

Its, It's. The possessive pronoun has no apostrophe. *It's* is a contraction of *it is.*

Just. Colloquial for *very, quite.*

FORMAL The customer was *very* indignant.
COLLOQUIAL I was *just* furious.

Kind of, Sort of. Colloquial when used adverbially to mean "somewhat" or "rather."

FORMAL She is *rather* pleased.
COLLOQUIAL She is *kind of* pleased.

Kind of a, Sort of a. The *a* is omitted in formal usage.

FORMAL The child wanted some *kind of* toy.
COLLOQUIAL The child wanted some *kind of a* toy.

Lady, Gentleman. *See* Gentleman, Lady.

Latter, Former. *See* Former, Latter.

Lay, Lie. In colloquial usage, these verbs are often confused. (*See* "Tense and Mood," Section 7d.)

Lead. *Lead* is not the past tense of *to lead; led* is the correct form.

Learn, Teach. *Learn* means "to gain knowledge." *Teach* means "to impart knowledge."

We *learn* from experience.
Experience *teaches* us many things.

Leave, Let. *Leave* means "to depart." *Let* means "to permit."

I must *leave* now.
Will you *let* (not *leave*) me go with you?

Less, Fewer. *See* Fewer, Less.

Lie, Lay. *See* Lay, Lie.

Like, As, As if. *Like* is a preposition; *as* and *as if* are conjunctions. In informal English *like* is often used as a conjunction to introduce clauses. Formal English prefers *as* or *as if* in such constructions.

>   FORMAL   He looks *as if* (or *as though*) he might be tired.
>   INFORMAL   He look *like he* might be tired.

Likely, Apt. *See* Apt, Likely.

Literature. Commercial jargon when used to mean "advertising matter." Used informally in referring to subject matter—"Consult the literature on the subject."

Locate. Colloquial when used to mean "settle."

>   FORMAL   The immigrant *settled* in Iowa.
>   COLLOQUIAL   The immigrant *located* in Iowa.

Loose, Lose. *Loose* means "to free." *Lose* means "to be deprived of."

>   He *loosed* the dog from its leash.
>   Did you *lose* (not *loose*) your money?

Lots, Lots of. Colloquial for *much* or *a great deal.*

>   FORMAL   We had a *great deal* of time for recreation.
>   COLLOQUIAL   We had *a lot of* (or *lots of*) time for recreation.

Mad. Colloquial when used to mean "angry."

Manner. Often unnecessary in phrases like "in a precise manner," where a single adverb ("precisely") or a "with" phrase ("with precision") would do.

Marvelous. Overused as a vague word of approval.

Math. *See* Ad.

May, Can. *See* Can, May.

May of. Illiterate for *may have.*

Might of. Illiterate for *might have.*

Minus. Journalese for *lacking* or *without. See* Plus.

Most. Colloquial when used in sense of *almost.*

>   FORMAL   *Almost* everybody in the hall cheered the speaker.
>   COLLOQUIAL   *Most* everybody in the hall cheered the speaker.

Mr. In American usage *Mr.* is followed by a period and is never written out except humorously or ironically.

Muchly. Illiterate for *much*.

Must of. Illiterate for *must have*.

Myself, Yourself, Himself. In formal English these intensive pronouns are inappropriate as substitutes for the personal pronouns *I, you, him*.

> FORMAL   Jack and *I* trimmed the hedge.
> COLLOQUIAL   Jack and *myself* trimmed the hedge.

They are sometimes appropriate for emphasis.

> The President *himself* will be there.
> She *herself* said so.

Never-the-less. Should be written as a single word: *nevertheless*.

Nice. Overused as a vague word of approval.

No account, No good. Colloquial for *worthless, useless*.

Noplace. Colloquial for *nowhere*.

Nothing else but. Colloquial for *nothing but*.

> FORMAL   There was *nothing but* pity in her voice.
> COLLOQUIAL   There was *nothing else but* pity in her voice.

Nowhere near. Informal and colloquial for *not nearly*.

Nowheres. An illiterate or provincial form of *nowhere*.

O.K. Colloquial for *all right* or *correct*.

Off of. The *of* is unnecessary.

> He jumped *off* (not *off of*) the wagon.

One and the same. Trite and tautological for *the same*.

One another, Each other. *See* Each other, One another.

On the average of. Trite and tautological for *about* or *almost*.

Ought to of. Illiterate for *ought to have*.

Out loud. Informal and colloquial for *aloud*.

Outside of. Colloquial for *except, besides*.

> FORMAL   Nobody was there *except* me.
> COLLOQUIAL   Nobody was there *outside of* me.

Over with. Colloquial for *over, ended.*

> FORMAL   I am glad the cold weather is *over.*
> COLLOQUIAL I am glad the cold weather is *over with.*

Party, Person, Individual. *See* Individual, Party, Person.

Per. Used mainly in commercial expressions, such as "forty hours per week," "thirty cents per yard," or in phrases of Latin origin, such as *per capita, per diem.* In ordinary writing, *per* is less appropriate than *a* or *an:* "twice a day," "forty cents a dozen."

Per cent. This abbreviation, meaning "by the hundred," is not followed by a period and may be written as one word. In formal English, *per cent* usually follows a numeral ("50 per cent") and is not used as a noun synonym for *portion* or *part. Percentage* is the correct noun for formal usage.

> FORMAL   A small *part* of the class was absent.
>
> FORMAL   A small *percentage* of the class was absent.
> INFORMAL   A small *per cent* of the class was absent.

Percentage. Informal for *number, part, portion.*

> FORMAL   The bay is rough a large *part* of the time.
> INFORMAL   The bay is rough a large *percentage* of the time.

Person, Party, Individual. *See* Individual, Party, Person.

Phenomena, Data. *See* Data, Phenomena.

Philosophy. A vague term when used to describe *mental attitude, values, knowledge.*

Phone. *See* Ad.

Photo. *See* Ad.

Plan on. Unidiomatic for *plan to.*

Plenty. Now colloquial when used as an adverb meaning "very" or "amply."

> FORMAL   He is a *very* big man.
> COLLOQUIAL He is a *plenty* big man.

Plus. Journalese for *in addition to. See* Minus.

Poorly. Colloquial or provincial for *unwell, in poor health.*

> FORMAL   Mother is in *poor health* this winter.
> COLLOQUIAL Mother is *poorly* this winter.

Practical, Practicable. *Practical* means "useful, not theoretical." *Practicable* means "capable of being put into practice, feasible."

Franklin's *practical* mind made him a good statesman.

His political schemes were *practicable*.

Practically. Colloquial for *almost*.

FORMAL   The wrestlers were *almost* exhausted.
COLLOQUIAL   The wrestlers were *practically* exhausted.

Principal, Principle. As an adjective *principal* means "chief, main"; as a noun it means "leader, chief officer," or, in finance, "a capital sum, as distinguished from interest or profit." The noun *principle* means "fundamental truth" or "basic law or doctrine."

What is his *principal* reason for being here?

He is the *principal* of the local elementary school.

That bank pays 4% interest on your *principal*.

He explained the underlying *principle*.

Prior to. Usually pretentious for *before*.

Proposition. *Proposition* means "proposal." Colloquial when used to mean "venture, plan, affair."

FORMAL   The community carnival was a successful *venture*.
COLLOQUIAL   The community carnival was a succesful *proposition*.

Proven. A past participle of the verb *prove*, used less often than *proved*.

Put across, Put over, Put in. *Put across* and *put over* are colloquialisms meaning "to accomplish something against opposition." *Put in* is informal for *spend*.

FORMAL   The club was successful in its membership drive.
COLLOQUIAL   The club *put across* its membership drive.

FORMAL   He *spent* a busy day at his office.
INFORMAL   He *put in* a busy day at his office.

Quite a few, Quite a little, Quite a bit. Colloquial for *many, more than a little, a considerable amount*.

Raise, Rise. *Raise, raised, raised* is a transitive verb.

I *raise* flowers. I *raised* flowers. I *have raised* flowers.

Rise, rose, risen is an intransitive verb.

I *rise* at daybreak. I *rose* at daybreak. I *have risen* at daybreak.

Rarely ever. Unidiomatic for *rarely, rarely if ever, rarely or never, hardly ever*.

Real. Colloquial for *really* or *very*.

> FORMAL   The sky was *very* cloudy.
> COLLOQUIAL   The sky was *real* cloudy.

Reason is because. A noun or noun clause should be used instead of "because" in this expression.

> FORMAL   The reason for his absence *is* his illness (that he is ill.)
> ILLOGICAL   The *reason* for his absence *is because* he is ill.

Religion. *Religion* is not a synonym for *sect, cult, denomination,* or *faith*.

> INACCURATE   He belongs to the Presbyterian *religion*.
> ACCURATE   He belongs to the Presbyterian *denomination*.

Remember of. The *of* is unnecessary.

> I *remember* (not *remember of*) seeing you before.

Reverend. The title *Reverend* is properly preceded by *the* and followed by *Mr.*, or followed by the first name or initials of the person referred to.

> The Reverend Mr. Wells (not Reverend Wells)
> Reverend John Wells, The Reverend John Wells
> Reverend J. W. Wells, The Reverend J. W. Wells

Right, Right along, Right away. *Right* is provincial when used to mean "very" or "directly."

> FORMAL   Being *very* tired, we went *directly* home.
> PROVINCIAL   Being *right* tired, we went *right* home.

Right along and *right away* are colloquial for *continuously* and *immediately*.

Rise, Raise. *See* Raise, Rise.

Run. Colloquial for *manage, operate*.

> FORMAL   He *manages* a department store.
> COLLOQUIAL   He *runs* a department store.

Said. The adjective *said* ("the *said* paragraph," "the *said* person") is a legal term and inappropriate in formal writing.

Seeing as how, Seeing that. Low colloquial for *since* or *because*.

Seldom ever, Seldom or ever. Unidiomatic for *seldom, seldom if ever, seldom or never, hardly ever*.

Set, Sit. *See* "Tense and Mood," Section 7d.

Shall, Will, Should, Would. There is a tendency to use *will* and *would* in all persons except when a condition or obligation is expressed. *Should* is used for all persons in conditions and obligations.

> If he *should* come, call me immediately.
> We *should* visit our new neighbors.

Would is used for all persons to express a wish or customary action.

> *Would* that he had listened to my plea!
> I *would* ride on the same bus every morning.

Shape. Colloquial for *condition*.

> FORMAL   Wrestlers must keep themselves in good *condition*.
> COLLOQUIAL   Wrestlers must keep themselves in good *shape*.

Should of. Illiterate for *should have*.

Show up. Colloquial for *appear, expose*.

> FORMAL   He did not *appear* at the office.
> COLLOQUIAL   He did not *show up* at the office.

Sit, Set. *See* Set, Sit.

Size up. Colloquial for estimate, judge.

> FORMAL   We *estimated* our financial needs.
> COLLOQUIAL   We *sized up* our financial needs.

Smell of. *See* Feel of.

So. In clauses of purpose, *so* instead of *so that* is colloquial.

> FORMAL   We camped by a spring *so that* we would have fresh water.
> COLLOQUIAL   We camped by a spring *so* we would have fresh water.

So is colloquial or informal when used to introduce a main clause where formal usage would have a subordinating conjunction introducing a subordinate clause.

> FORMAL   *Because* the rain began to fall, the swimmers left the beach.
> COLLOQUIAL   Rain began to fall, *so* the swimmers left the beach.

The "feminine" *so*, meaning "very," is colloquial and overused.

> FORMAL   She is *very* happy.
> COLLOQUIAL   She is *so* happy.

Some. Colloquial when used as an adverb meaning "somewhat" or "a little."

FORMAL	He seems *somewhat* gayer.
COLLOQUIAL	He seems *some* gayer.

Some is slang when used as an intensive: "He is *some* actor!"

Someplace. Colloquial for *somewhere*.

Something, Somewhat. Colloquial for *slightly*.

COLLOQUIAL	He is somewhat of a liar.
COLLOQUIAL	He is something of a liar.

Somewheres. Illiterate for *somewhere*.

Sort of, Kind of. *See* Kind of, Sort of.

Sort of a, Kind of a. *See* Kind of a, Sort of a.

Stop. Colloquial or informal when used as a substitute for *stay*.

FORMAL	I *stayed* overnight at a hotel.
INFORMAL	I *stopped* overnight at a hotel.

Such. As an intensive, *such* is colloquial.

FORMAL	He told a *very* interesting story.
COLLOQUIAL	He told *such* an interesting story.

No such a is vulgate for *no such*.

FORMAL	There is *no such* place.
VULGATE	There is *no such a* place.

Suspicion. Illiterate when used as a verb.

Take and. Illiterate in such expressions as "I'll *take and* swim across the lake."

Taste of. *See* Feel of.

Teach, Learn. *See* Learn, Teach.

That. Colloquial when used as an adverb. As a relative pronoun *that* may be used only to introduce restrictive clauses. (*Which* may be used for both restrictive and nonrestrictive clauses.)

FORMAL	Nobody can be *so* exhausted after such a short swim.
COLLOQUIAL	Nobody can be *that* exhausted after such a short swim.

There being. *See* It being.

Thing. Whenever possible, *thing* should be replaced with a more specific word.

This here, That there. Illiterate for *this, that.*

Through. Formal usage prefers "finished."

       FORMAL   I have *finished* working.
       INFORMAL   I am *through* working.

Thusly. A pretentious or illiterate form of *thus.*

Transpire. *Transpire* means "to become known." The use of *transpire* in the sense of *to come to pass, happen, occur* is disapproved by some writers, though this meaning is fairly common in informal writing.

Try and. Colloquial for *try to.*

       FORMAL   *Try to* hold your head erect.
       COLLOQUIAL   *Try and* hold your head erect.

Unique. The adjective *unique* cannot logically be compared, since it means "single in kind or excellence." In colloquial English, however, it is sometimes used in the sense of *rare* or *odd* and is compared.

       FORMAL   His deeds are *unique* in history.
       COLLOQUIAL   His deeds are *more unique* in history than people suspect.

Very. In formal English *very* is usually followed by *much, well,* or *greatly* when it modifies a past participle.

       FORMAL   We were *very much* embarrassed.
       INFORMAL   We were *very* embarrassed.

Wait on. Colloquial or provincial in the sense of *wait for. Wait on* means "to serve, attend."

       FORMAL   I *waited for* a bus.
       COLLOQUIAL   I *waited on* a bus.

Want in, Want out, Want off. Colloquial for *want to come in, want to go out, want to get off.*

Want to. Colloquial for *ought, should.*

       FORMAL   You *should* be alert when crossing the street.
       COLLOQUIAL   You *want to* be alert when crossing the street.

Way, Ways. *Way* is colloquial when used to mean "away" ("*way* across the mountains"). *Ways* is used provincially for *way* in such expressions as "a little *ways* up the hill."

Weird. Overused slang for *unusual, queer*.

Where. Colloquial when used for *that*.

> FORMAL I read in the mayor's report *that* many local crimes are unsolved.
>
> COLLOQUIAL I read in the mayor's report *where* many local crimes are unsolved.

Where at. A redundancy.

> ACCURATE *Where* is my pipe?
> REDUNDANT *Where* is my pipe *at?*

Whether, If. *See* If, Whether.

Wonderful. Overused as a vague word of approval.

Would of. Illiterate for *would have*.

Yourself, Myself, Himself. *See* Myself, Yourself, Himself.

Spelling is no longer commonly regarded as a proper field for individuality or experimentation.

—STUART ROBERTSON

44   SPELLING = SP

Language existed first as speech, and the alphabet is basically a device to represent speech on paper. When letters of the alphabet have definite values and are used consistently, as in Polish or Spanish, the spelling of a word is an accurate index to its pronunciation, and vice versa. Not so with English. The alphabet does not represent English sounds consistently. The letter *a* may stand for the sound of the vowel in *may, can, care,* or *car; c* for the initial consonant of *carry* or *city; th* for the diphthong in *both* or in *bother.* Different combinations of letters are often sounded alike, as in *rec(ei)ve, l(ea)ve,* or *p(ee)ve.* In many words, moreover, some letters appear to perform no function at all, as in *i(s)land, de(b)t, of(t)en, recei(p)t.* Finally, the relationship between the spelling and the pronunciation of some words seems downright capricious, as in *through, enough, colonel, right.* **44**

Much of the inconsistency of English spelling may be explained historically. English spelling has been a poor index to pronunciation ever since the Norman Conquest, when French scribes gave written English a French spelling. Subsequent tampering with English spelling has made it even more complex. Early classical scholars with a flair for etymology added the unvoiced *b* to early English *det* and *dout* because they mistakenly traced these words directly from the Latin *debitum* and *dubitum* when actually both the English and the Latin had derived independently from a common Indo-European origin. Dutch printers working in England were responsible for changing early English *gost* to *ghost*. More complications arose when the spelling of many words changed less rapidly than their pronunciation. The *gh* in *right* and *through*, and in similar words, was once pronounced much like the German *ch* in *nicht*. Colonel was once pronounced *col-o-nel*. The final *e* in words like *wife* and *time* was long ago dropped from actual speech, but it still remains as a proper spelling form.

The English tendency to borrow words freely from Latin and French has given us groups like the native English *sight*, the French *site*, and the Latin *cite*. Our word *regal*, with its hard *g*, comes from the Norman French. Our word *regent*, with the *g* sounded as a *j*, comes from Parisian French. Words like *machine, burlesque,* and *suite* come directly from the French, without changes in spelling or in pronunciation. *Envelope*, on the other hand, maintains its French spelling but is given an English pronunciation. From Spanish comes the proper noun *Don Quixote;* its Spanish pronunciation (dǒn kě· hō/tȧ) is still frequently heard, but the English adjective *quixotic* is pronounced kwĭks·ot/ĭk.

The complex history of the English language may help to explain why our spelling is illogical, but it does not justify misspelling. Society tends to equate bad spelling with incompetent writing. In fact, we tend to see only the misspellings and not the quality of the writing, and correct spellings may sometimes blind us to faulty constructions. That particularly American institution—the spelling bee—has for generations put a higher premium on the correct spelling of *phthisis* than on a clearly constructed sentence. To illustrate, we might experiment with our own attitude. Which of the two selections below seems better?

1. Parants should teech childern the importence of puntuallity.
2. The condition of unpunctuality which exists in the character of a great many members of the younger generation should be eliminated by every means that lies at the disposal of parents who are responsible for them.

On first reading, sentence 1 seems inferior to sentence 2. Actually 1 is the better sentence—more direct and succinct. But the misspellings make it difficult for us to take it seriously. Readers have been conditioned to treat misspelling as one of the greatest sins a writer can commit.

44a **Avoid secondary and British spellings.**

Many words have a secondary spelling, generally British. Though the secondary spelling is not incorrect, as an American writer you should avoid it. Here is a brief list of preferred and secondary spelling forms; consult a good dictionary for others.

(1) American *e*	British *ae, oe*
anemia	anaemia
anesthetic	anaesthetic
encyclopedia	encyclopaedia
medieval	mediaeval

(2) American *im-, in-*	British *em-, en-*
incase	encase

But

inquiry	inquiry
insure	insure

(3) American *-ize*	British *-ise*
apologize	apologise

(4) American *-or*	British *-our*
armor	armour
clamor	clamour
flavor	flavour
humor	humour
labor	labour
odor	odour
vigor	vigour

(5) American *-er*	British *-re*
center	centre
fiber	fibre
somber	sombre
theater	theatre

(6) American *-o*	British *-ou*
mold	mould
plow	plough
smolder	smoulder

(7) American *-ction*	British *-xion*
connection	connexion
inflection	inflexion

(8) American *-l*	British *-ll*
leveled	levelled
quarreled	quarrelled
traveled	travelled

(9) American *-e* omitted	British *-e*
acknowledgment	acknowledgement
judgment	judgement

44b **Proofread your manuscripts carefully to eliminate misspelling.**

In writing a first draft, you are forming words into sentences faster than you can write them down. You are concentrating not on the words you are actually writing but on the words to come. A few mistakes in spelling may easily creep into a first draft. Always take five or ten minutes to proofread your final draft to make sure that you do not let them stand uncorrected.

The failure to proofread accounts for the fact that the words most often misspelled are not, for example, *baccalaureate* and *connoisseur*, but *too, its, lose, receive,* and *occurred*. Not trusting ourselves to spell hard words correctly, we consult a dictionary and take pains to get the correct spelling on paper. But most of us *think* we can spell a familiar word. Either we never bother to check the spelling, or we assume that a word pictured correctly in our minds must automatically spell itself correctly on the paper in front of us. This thinking accounts for such errors as omitting the final *o* in *too*, confusing the possessive *its* with the contraction *it's*, and spelling *loose* when *lose* is meant. You will never forget how to spell *receive* and *occurred* if you will devote just a few moments to memorizing their correct spelling.

On pages 402 to 405 is a list of 350 words often misspelled. Almost every one of them is a common word; to misspell any of them in a finished paper denotes carelessness.

44c **Cultivate careful pronunciation as an aid to correct spelling.**

Some words are commonly misspelled because they are mispronounced. The following list of frequently mispronounced words will help you overcome this source of spelling error.

accidentALly		note the AL
accUrate		note the U
canDidate		note the first D
incidentALly		note the AL
mathEmatics		note the E
probABly		note the AB
quanTity		note the first T
represenTAtive		note the TA
sophOmore		note the second O
suRprise		note the first R
aTHLetics	*not*	athEletics
disasTRous	*not*	disastErous
heighT	*not*	heightH
grIE-vous	*not*	grE-vI-ous
ir-reL-e-vant	*not*	ir-reV-e-lant
mis-chIE-vous	*not*	mis-chE-vI-ous

However, pronunciation is not an infallible guide to correct spelling. Although, for example, you pronounce the last syllables of *adviser, beggar,* and *doctor* all as the same unstressed *ur,* you spell each differently. You must, therefore, proceed cautiously in using pronunciation as a spelling aid.

44d **Distinguish carefully between the spellings of words that are similar in sound.**

English abounds in words whose spelling or sound is similar to that of other words: for example, *rain, rein, reign.* The most troublesome of such words are listed below.

ascent: climbing, a way sloping up
assent: agreement, to agree

all ready: everyone is ready
already: by this time

all together: as a group
altogether: entirely, completely

altar: a structure used in worship
alter: to change

breath: air taken into the lungs
breathe: to exhale and inhale

capital: chief; leading or governing city; wealth, resources
capitol: a building that houses the state or national lawmakers

cite: to use as an example, to quote
site: location

clothes: wearing apparel
cloths: two or more pieces of cloth

complement: that which completes; to supply a lack
compliment: praise, flattering remark; to praise

corps: a military group or unit
corpse: a dead body

council: an assembly of lawmakers
counsel: advice; one who advises; to give advice

dairy: a factory or farm engaged in milk production
diary: a daily record of experiences or observations

descent: a way sloping down
dissent: disagreement; to disagree

dining: eating
dinning: making a continuing noise

dying: ceasing to live
dyeing: process of coloring fabrics

formally: in a formal manner
formerly: before

forth: forward in place or space, onward in time
fourth: the ordinal equivalent of the number 4

loose: free from bonds
lose: to suffer a loss

personal: pertaining to a particular person; individual
personnel: body of persons employed in same work or service

principal: chief, most important; a school official; a capital sum
   (as distinguished from interest or profit)
principle: a belief, rule of conduct or thought

respectfully: with respect
respectively: in order, in turn

stationery: writing paper
stationary: not moving

their: possessive form of *they*
they're: contraction of *they are*
there: adverb of place

whose: possessive form of *who*
who's: contraction of *who is*

your: possessive form of *you*
you're: contraction of *you are*

44e **Familiarize yourself with spelling rules as an aid to correct spelling.**

(1) *Carefully distinguish between* ie *and* ei. Remember this useful jingle:

> Write *i* before *e*
> Except after *c*
> Or when sounded like *a*
> As in *eighty* and *sleigh*.

i BEFORE *e*	*ei* AFTER *c*	*ei* WHEN SOUNDED LIKE *a*
thief	receive	weigh
believe	deceive	freight
wield	ceiling	vein

SOME EXCEPTIONS

leisure
financier
weird

(2) *Drop the final* e *before a suffix beginning with a vowel but not before a suffix beginning with a consonant.*

(a) Suffix beginning with a vowel, final *e* dropped:

please + ure	= *pleasure*
ride + ing	= *riding*
locate + ion	= *location*
guide + ance	= *guidance*

EXCEPTIONS

In some words final *e* is retained to prevent confusion with other words.

dyeing (to distinguish it from *dying*)

397

Final *e* is retained to keep *c* or *g* soft before *a* or *o*.

notice + able	= *noticeable*
change + able	= *changeable*
singe + ing	= *singeing*
BUT practice + able	= *practicable* (*c* has sound of *k*)

(b) Suffix beginning with a consonant, final *e* retained:

sure + ly	= *surely*
arrange + ment	= *arrangement*
like + ness	= *likeness*
entire + ty	= *entirety*
hate + ful	= *hateful*

EXCEPTIONS

Some words taking the suffix *-ful* or *-ly* drop final *e:*

awe + ful	= *awful*
due + ly	= *duly*
true + ly	= *truly*

Some words taking the suffix *-ment* drop final *e:*

judge + ment	= *judgment*
acknowledge + ment	= *acknowledgment*

(3) *Final* y *is usually changed to* i *except before a suffix beginning with* i.

defy + ance	= *defiance*
forty + eth	= *fortieth*
ninety + eth	= *ninetieth*
rectify + er	= *rectifier*
BUT cry + ing	= *crying* (suffix begins with *i*)

(4) *A final single consonant is doubled before a suffix beginning with a vowel when* (a) *a single vowel precedes the consonant, and* (b) *the consonant ends an accented syllable or a one-syllable word. Unless both these conditions exist, the final consonant is not doubled.*

stop + ing	= *stopping* (*o* is a single vowel before consonant *p* which ends word of one syllable.)

admit + ed   = *admitted* (*i* is single vowel before consonant *t* which ends an accented syllable.)

stoop + ing   = *stooping* (*p* ends a word of one syllable but is preceded by double vowel *oo*.)

benefit + ed   = *benefited* (*t* is preceded by a single vowel *i* but does not end the accented syllable.)

EXERCISE 1. Spell each of the following words correctly and explain what spelling rule applies. Note any exceptions to the rules.

argue + ment	=	?		change + able	=	?
beg + ar	=	?		change + ing	=	?
bury + ed	=	?		awe + ful	=	?
conceive + able	=	?		precede + ence	=	?
eighty + eth	=	?		shine + ing	=	?
associate + ion	=	?		busy + ness	=	?
hop + ing	=	?		defer + ed	=	?
droop + ing	=	?		peace + able	=	?

(5) *Nouns ending in a sound that can be smoothly united with -s form their plurals by adding -s. (Verbs ending in a sound that can be smoothly united with -s form their third person singular by adding -s.)*

SINGULAR	PLURAL
picture	pictures
radio	radios
flower	flowers
chair	chairs
ache	aches
fan	fans

SOME EXCEPTIONS

buffalo	buffaloes
Negro	Negroes
zero	zeroes

(6) *Nouns ending in a sound that cannot be smoothly united with -s form their plurals by adding -es. (Verbs ending in a sound that cannot be smoothly united with -s form their third person singular by adding -es.)*

SINGULAR	PLURAL
porch	porches
bush	bushes
pass	passes
tax	taxes

(7) *Nouns ending in* y *preceded by a consonant form their plurals by changing* y *to* i *and adding* -es.

SINGULAR	PLURAL
army	armies
nursery	nurseries
sky	skies
mercy	mercies
body	bodies

EXCEPTIONS

The plural of proper nouns ending in *y* is formed by adding *-s*. ("There are three Marys in my history class.")

(8) *Nouns ending in* y *preceded by* a, e, o, *or* u *form their plurals by adding* -s *only.*

SINGULAR	PLURAL
day	days
key	keys
boy	boys
guy	guys

(9) *The spelling of plural nouns borrowed from French, Greek, and Latin frequently retains the plural of the original language.*

SINGULAR	PLURAL
alumna (feminine)	alumnae
alumnus (masculine)	alumni
analysis	analyses
basis	bases
datum	data
crisis	crises
hypothesis	hypotheses
phenomenon	phenomena

The tendency now, however, is to give many such words an anglicized plural. The result is that many words have two plural forms, one foreign, the other anglicized. Either is correct.

SINGULAR	PLURAL (*foreign*)	PLURAL (*anglicized*)
appendix	appendices	appendixes
beau	beaux	beaus
focus	foci	focuses
index	indices	indexes
memorandum	memoranda	memorandums
radius	radii	radiuses
stadium	stadia	stadiums

EXERCISE 2. Spell the plural of each of the following words correctly and explain what spelling rule applies. Note any exceptions to the rules.

1.	frame	6.	branch	11.	echo	16.	Charles
2.	rose	7.	bass	12.	stratum	17.	no
3.	dash	8.	cameo	13.	church	18.	potato
4.	maze	9.	fly	14.	lady	19.	play
5.	table	10.	box	15.	mass	20.	pain

44f **Spell compound words in accordance with current usage.**

Compound words usually progress by stages from being written as two words to being hyphenated to being written as one word. Since these stages often overlap, the correct spelling of a compound word may vary. For the spelling of a compound at any particular moment, take the advice of a good dictionary. (For the general use of the hyphen, see "Hyphen," Section 30. This section gives rules for the spelling of compounds.)

44g **Use drills to help cultivate the habit of correct spelling.**

Spelling is primarily a habit. Once you learn to spell a word correctly, you no longer need to think about it. Its correct spelling becomes an automatic skill. But if you are a chronic misspeller you have the task not only of learning correct spellings but of unlearning the incorrect spellings you now employ. You must train your fingers to write the word correctly until they do so almost without your thinking about it. Here is a suggested drill that will aid you in learning correct spellings:

First, look carefully at a word whose spelling bothers you and say it to yourself. If it has more than one syllable, examine each syllable.

Second, look at the individual letters, dividing the word into syllables as you say the letters.

Third, try to visualize the correct spelling before you write the word. If you have trouble, begin again with the *first* step.

Fourth, write the word without looking at your book or list.

Fifth, look at your book or list and see whether you wrote the word correctly. If you did, cover the word and write it again. If you write the word correctly the third time, you have probably learned it and will not have to think about it again.

Sixth, if you spell the word incorrectly any one of the three times, look very carefully at the letters you missed. Then start over again and keep on until you have spelled it correctly three times.

Spelling Lists.

The following lists contain most of the words whose spelling is troublesome. The words are arranged in alphabetized groups for easy reference and for drill.

Group 1

1 accidentally
2 accommodate
3 achieved
4 accompanied
5 address
6 aggravate
7 anxiety
8 barren
9 believe
10 ceiling
11 confident
12 course
13 disappear
14 disappoint
15 dissipate
16 efficiency
17 emphasize
18 exaggerate
19 exceed
20 fiery
21 finally
22 financial
23 forehead
24 foreign
25 forfeit
26 grief
27 handkerchief
28 hurriedly
29 hypocrisy
30 imminent
31 incidentally
32 innocence
33 intentionally
34 interest
35 legitimate
36 likely
37 manual
38 mattress
39 misspell
40 niece
41 parallel
42 psychiatrist
43 psychology
44 occasion
45 organization
46 piece
47 receive
48 religious
49 severely
50 villain

Group 2

1 arctic
2 auxiliary
3 business
4 candidate
5 characteristic
6 chauffeur
7 colonel
8 column
9 cylinder
10 environment
11 especially
12 exhaust
13 exhilaration
14 February
15 foremost
16 ghost
17 government
18 grievous
19 hygiene
20 intercede
21 leisure
22 library
23 lightning
24 literature
25 mathematics
26 medicine
27 mortgage
28 muscle
29 notoriety
30 optimistic
31 pamphlet
32 parliament
33 physically
34 physician
35 prairie
36 prejudice
37 pronunciation
38 recede
39 recognize
40 reign
41 rhetoric
42 rhythm

43 schedule
44 sentinel
45 soliloquy
46 sophomore
47 studying
48 surprise
49 twelfth
50 Wednesday

Group 3

1 apparent
2 appearance
3 attendance
4 beggar
5 brilliant
6 calendar
7 carriage
8 conqueror
9 contemptible
10 coolly
11 descent
12 desirable
13 dictionary
14 disastrous
15 eligible
16 equivalent
17 existence
18 familiar
19 grammar
20 guidance
21 hindrance
22 hoping
23 imaginary
24 indispensable
25 incredible
26 indigestible
27 inevitable
28 influential
29 irresistible
30 liable
31 marriage
32 momentous
33 naturally
34 nickel

35 noticeable
36 nucleus
37 obedience
38 outrageous
39 pageant
40 permissible
41 perseverance
42 persistent
43 possible
44 pleasant
45 prevalent
46 resistance
47 similar
48 strenuous
49 vengeance
50 vigilance

Group 4

1 allot
2 allotted
3 barbarian
4 barbarous
5 beneficial
6 benefited
7 changeable
8 changing
9 commit
10 committed
11 committee
12 comparative
13 comparatively
14 comparison
15 compel
16 compelled
17 compulsion
18 competent
19 competition
20 conceivable
21 conceive
22 conception
23 conscience
24 conscientious
25 conscious
26 courteous

27 courtesy
28 deceit
29 deceive
30 deception
31 decide
32 decision
33 defer
34 deference
35 deferred
36 describe
37 description
38 device
39 devise
40 discuss
41 discussion
42 dissatisfied
43 dissatisfy
44 equip
45 equipment
46 equipped
47 excel
48 excellent
49 explain
50 explanation

Group 5

1 hesitancy
2 hesitate
3 instance
4 instant
5 intellectual
6 intelligence
7 intelligent
8 intelligible
9 maintain
10 maintenance
11 miniature
12 minute
13 ninetieth
14 ninety
15 ninth
16 obligation
17 oblige
18 obliged

19 occur
20 occurrence
21 occurred
22 omission
23 omit
24 omitted
25 procedure
26 proceed
27 picnic
28 picnicking
29 possess
30 possession
31 precede
32 precedence
33 preceding
34 prefer
35 preference
36 preferred
37 realize
38 really
39 refer
40 reference
41 referred
42 repeat
43 repetition
44 transfer
45 transferred
46 tried
47 tries
48 try
49 writing
50 written

Group 6

1 obstacle
2 operate
3 opinion
4 persuade
5 presence
6 politician
7 practically
8 restaurant
9 region
10 reservoir

11 ridiculous
12 sacrifice
13 sacrilegious
14 safety
15 salary
16 scarcely
17 secretary
18 separate
19 similar
20 supersede
21 tendency
22 temperament
23 temperature
24 tournament
25 truly
26 tragedy
27 unanimous
28 unusual
29 usage
30 valuable
31 yoke
32 yolk
33 quantity
34 tyranny
35 propeller
36 professor
37 recommend
38 representative
39 suppress
40 syllable
41 suffrage
42 symmetry
43 wholly
44 pastime
45 piece
46 relieve
47 science
48 shriek
49 seize
50 siege

Group 7

1 accept
2 across

3 aisle	19 cafeteria	35 exercise
4 all right	20 career	36 extraordinary
5 amateur	21 cemetery	37 fascinate
6 annual	22 completely	38 fraternity
7 appropriate	23 cruelty	39 furniture
8 argument	24 curiosity	40 grandeur
9 arrangement	25 diphtheria	41 height
10 association	26 discipline	42 hypocrisy
11 awkward	27 disease	43 imitation
12 convenient	28 distribute	44 interest
13 definite	29 dormitories	45 livelihood
14 desperate	30 drudgery	46 loneliness
15 eighth	31 ecstasy	47 magazine
16 eliminate	32 eminent	48 material
17 bachelor	33 enemy	49 messenger
18 biscuit	34 except	50 mischievous

EXERCISE 3. Following is a list of words chosen at random to illustrate some of the caprices of English spelling and pronunciation. You might like to try your skill at spelling them. Will any of the spelling rules apply here? How many of these words can you pronounce? How many can you define? Would a knowledge of pronunciations, definitions, or word origins be of help in spelling these words correctly?

1. aardvark	21. connoisseur	41. gneiss
2. abhorrence	22. crescendo	42. heterogeneous
3. alyssum	23. cryptic	43. hieroglyphic
4. apocalypse	24. cyanide	44. homogenous
5. archipelago	25. cyclic	45. hyperbole
6. arpeggio	26. demagogue	46. icicle
7. baccalaureate	27. delicatessen	47. idiosyncrasy
8. bacchanalian	28. diaphragm	48. incarcerate
9. balalaika	29. discomfiture	49. jeopardy
10. baroque	30. disparate	50. jodhpurs
11. bologna	31. doughty	51. khaki
12. bouillon	32. dungeon	52. knell
13. boutonniere	33. ecclesiastical	53. larynx
14. catarrh	34. eerie	54. lymph
15. catechism	35. eucalyptus	55. misogyny
16. charivari	36. flautist	56. moccasin
17. chlorophyll	37. fortuitous	57. myrrh
18. chrysalis	38. fugue	58. niche
19. cinnamon	39. gargoyle	59. nil
20. clique	40. gourmet	60. periphery

61. phthisis
62. pituitary
63. platypus
64. plebiscite
65. porpoise
66. psyche
67. pyrrhic
68. quay
69. queue
70. quinquagenarian
71. quixotic
72. rheumy
73. rhinoceros
74. saccharin

75. salaam
76. salmon
77. sapphire
78. scepter
79. schism
80. sconce
81. scythe
82. suave
83. svelte
84. sylph
85. tableau
86. tarpaulin
87. thyme

88. trauma
89. troglodyte
90. tympany
91. ululate
92. umlaut
93. vaccination
94. vacuum
95. vanilla
96. vitiate
97. whey
98. wreak
99. yacht
100. zephyr

Knowledge is of two kinds: We know a subject our-selves, or we know where we can find information upon it.

A man will turn over half a library to make one book.

—SAMUEL JOHNSON

SECTIONS **45-46**

The Library
and the Research Paper

The processes of "research" range all the way from simple fact-digging to the most abstruse speculations; consequently, there is no one generally accepted definition of the word. *Webster's New Collegiate Dictionary* emphasizes the meaning of the first syllable, "re-": "critical and exhaustive investigation . . . having for its aim the revision of accepted conclusions, in the light of newly discovered facts." The *New World Dictionary* stresses the meaning of the second syllable, "-search": "systematic, patient study and investiga-

407

tion in some field of knowledge, undertaken to establish facts or principles." The second definition more closely describes what is expected of you in your first years in college. True, you will not often revise accepted conclusions or establish new principles. But you can learn to collect, sift, evaluate, and organize information or evidence, and to come to sound conclusions about its meaning. In doing so you will learn some of the basic methods of modern research, and the ethics and etiquette that govern the use the researcher makes of other men's facts and ideas.

When your instructor asks you to prepare a research paper, he is concerned less with the intrinsic value of your findings than with the value you derive from the experience. Writing a research paper demands a sense of responsibility, because you must account for all your facts and assertions. If your results are to be accepted—and that, after all, is a large part of your purpose—you must be prepared to show how you got those results.

It is the citing of sources that distinguishes the research paper from the expository essay in popular magazines. A good journalist undertakes research to assemble his materials, but his readers are primarily concerned with the *results* of his research. He expects to be accepted on faith. The researcher, however, writes for his peers— for readers who are able to *evaluate* his findings; for this reason he uses footnotes to help them check his evidence if they wish to do so.

In preparing a research paper, then, remember that your audience expects and demands that you indicate your sources. It expects you to be *thorough*—to find and sift all the relevant evidence; to be *critical* of your evidence—to test the reliability of your authorities; to be *accurate*—to present your facts and cite your sources with the utmost precision; to be *objective*—to distinguish clearly between your facts and the opinions or generalizations to which your facts lead you.

45 THE LIBRARY

The library is one of the most valuable resources on the college campus, and every successful student draws constantly on its facilities. Learn how to use your college library efficiently—become familiar with the card catalog system, learn where and by what system books are shelved, get acquainted with periodical guides and special indexes. Once you have mastered these skills, you will be able to use your time on concentrated study and research rather than on aimless wandering about the library in search of fugitive items. This section is designed to help you familiarize yourself with your library and its functions.

The library catalogs.

The heart of the library is its card catalog. This is an alphabetical list of all the books and periodicals the library contains. Most libraries have a separate catalog that describes all periodical holdings in complete detail.

The *classification system* on which a card catalog is based serves as a kind of map of library holdings. In libraries where you have direct access to the shelves, familiarity with the classification system enables you to find classes of books in which you are interested without using the catalog. But the chief purpose of a classification system is to supply a *call number* for every item in the library. When you fill out a slip for a book, be sure to copy the call number precisely as it appears on the card.

American libraries generally follow one of two systems in classifying books: (1) the Dewey decimal system, or (2) the Library of Congress system. The system in use determines the call number of any book.

409

The Dewey system, used by most libraries, divides books into ten numbered classes:

000-999	General Works	500-599	Pure Science
100-199	Philosophy	600-699	Useful Arts
200-299	Religion	700-799	Fine Arts
300-399	Social Sciences	800-899	Literature
400-499	Philology	900-999	History

Each of these divisions is further divided into ten parts, as:

800	General Literature	850	Italian Literature
810	American Literature	860	Spanish Literature
820	English Literature	870	Latin Literature
830	German Literature	880	Greek Literature
840	French Literature	890	Minor Literatures

Each of these divisions is further divided, as:

821	English poetry	826	English letters
822	English drama	827	English satire
823	English fiction	828	English miscellany
824	English essays	829	Anglo-Saxon
825	English oratory		

Further subdivisions are indicated by decimals. *The Romantic Rebels,* a book about Keats, Byron, and Shelley, is numbered 821.09 —indicating a subdivision of the 821 English poetry heading.

The Library of Congress classification system—used by large libraries—divides books into lettered classes:

A	General Works
B	Philosophy—Religion
C	History—Auxiliary Sciences
D	Foreign History and Topography
E-F	American History
G	Geography—Anthropology
H	Social Sciences
J	Political Science
K	Law
L	Education
M	Music
N	Fine Arts
P	Language and Literature

Q   Science
R   Medicine
S   Agriculture
T   Technology
U   Military Science
V   Naval Science
Z   Bibliography—Library science

Each of these sections is further divided by letters and numbers which show the specific call number of a book. *English Composition in Theory and Practice* by Henry Seidel Canby and others is classified in this system as PE 1408.E5 (In the Dewey decimal system this same volume is numbered 808.)

The catalog cards.

For most books (not periodicals) you will find at least three cards in the library catalog: an *author* card; a *title* card (no title card is used when the title begins with words as common as "A History of ..."); and at least one *subject* card. Here is a specimen *author* card in the Dewey system; it is filed according to the surname of the author:

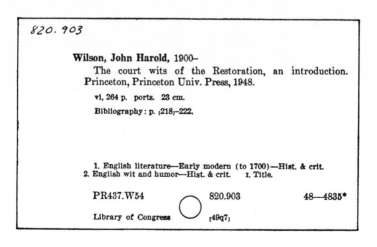

820. 903

>   **Wilson, John Harold,** 1900–
>   The court wits of the Restoration, an introduction.
>   Princeton, Princeton Univ. Press, 1948.
>
>   vi, 264 p.   ports.   23 cm.
>   Bibliography : p. ₍218₎–222.
>
>
>   1. English literature—Early modern (to 1700)—Hist. & crit.
>   2. English wit and humor—Hist. & crit.   ɪ. Title.
>
>   PR437.W54   820.903   48—4835*
>
>   Library of Congress   ₍49q7₎

1. "820.903" gives you the *call number* of the book.

2. "Wilson, John Harold, 1900–" gives you the name of the author and the date of his birth, and tells you that he was still living at the time this card was printed.

3. "The court wits . . . 1948" gives you the full title of the book, the place of publication, the name of the publisher, and the date of publication. (Note that library practice in capitalizing differs from general practice.)

4. "vi, 264 p. ports. 23 cm." tells you that the book contains 6 introductory pages numbered in Roman numerals and 264 pages numbered in Arabic numerals; that portraits appear in the book; and that the book is 23 centimeters high. (An inch is 2.54 centimeters.)

5. "Bibliography: p. [218]-222." tells you that the book contains a bibliography that begins on page 218 and ends on page 222. The brackets around 218 tell you that the page is not actually numbered but appears between numbered pages 217 and 219.

6. "1. English Literature . . . I. Title." tells you that the book is also listed in the card catalog under two subject headings—(1) English Literature, and (2) English Wit and Humor—and under one title heading, "Court wits of the Restoration. . . ." Notice that the subject heading "English Literature" has the subdivision "Early modern (to 1700)" and that this latter heading has the subdivision "Hist. & crit.," the heading under which you will find the first subject card. You will find the second subject card under a division of "English wit and humor" called "Hist. & crit." The Arabic numerals indicate subject headings; the Roman numeral ("I. Title.") indicates a title heading.

7. "PR437.W54" is the Library of Congress call number.

8. "820.903" is the Dewey system call number of the card.

9. "48-4835*" is the order number used by librarians when they wish to order a copy of the card itself.

10. "Library of Congress" tells you that a copy of the book is housed in, and has been catalogued by, the Library of Congress.

11. "[49q⁷]" is a printer's key to the card.

A *title* card is simply a copy of the author card, with the title typed just above the author's name. The title card is filed in the catalog according to the first word of the title that is not an article.

A *subject* card is also a copy of the author card, with the subject typed just above the author's name; it is filed in the catalog alphabetically according to the subject heading. (See item 6 under "The catalog cards," above.) The *subject* cards, which are gathered together in one place in the catalog, help you find all or most books on a particular subject. (To find *articles* on a subject, use the reference tools described on pages 419-420.)

Library holdings.

Libraries have three principal kinds of holdings: (1) a general collection of books; (2) a collection of reference works; (3) a collection of periodicals, bulletins, and pamphlets.

General collection of books.

The general collection includes most of the books in the library—all those that are available for general circulation. Small libraries usually place these books on open shelves and make them available to all who have library privileges. Most large libraries, however, keep these books in stacks, which are closed to everyone except librarians, graduate students, faculty members, and persons holding special permits. If you want to borrow a book from such a library, you must first present a call slip bearing the call number of the book you want, the name of its author, and its title. This information you obtain from the *card catalog*.

Reference books.

Most libraries place these books on open shelves in the main reading room. You are free to consult reference books but you may not remove them from the reading room. If you cannot find the reference book you want, or if you do not know what reference book you need, consult the reference librarian.

Following is a representative list of reference books available in most libraries.

Guides to Reference Books

> Cook, M. G. *The New Library Key.* New York: H. W. Wilson, 1956.

413

Murphey, Robert W. *How and Where to Look It Up; A Guide to Standard Sources of Information.* Consultant: Mabel S. Johnson. Foreword by Louis Shores. New York: McGraw-Hill Book Co., 1958.

Russell, H. G., R. H. Shove, and B. E. Moen. *The Use of Books and Libraries.* Minneapolis: University of Minnesota Press, 1958.

Shores, Louis. *Basic Reference Books.* Chicago: American Library Association, 1954.

Winchell, C. M. *Guide to Reference Books.* Chicago: American Library Association, 1951. Supplements, 1951-52, 1953-55, 1956-58.

General Encyclopedias

Columbia Encyclopedia. 2nd ed. Ed. by William Bridgwater and Elizabeth J. Sherwood. New York: Columbia University Press, 1950.

Encyclopedia Americana. New York: Americana Corporation, 1956. 30 vols.

Encyclopaedia Britannica, 14th ed. New York: Encyclopaedia Britannica, Inc., 1956. 24 vols.

New International Encyclopedia. 2nd ed. New York: Dodd, Mead and Company, 1914-16. 24 vols. Plate revision, 1922. Supplements, 1925, 1930.

Dictionaries, Word Books

Dictionary of American English on Historical Principles. Ed. by Sir W. A. Craigie and J. R. Hulbert. Chicago: The University of Chicago Press, 1936-44. 4 vols.

Fowler, Henry W. *Dictionary of Modern English Usage.* New York: Oxford University Press, 1934.

New Standard Dictionary. New York: Funk and Wagnalls Company, 1952.

Oxford English Dictionary. Ed. by A. H. Murray *et al.* Oxford: The Clarendon Press, 1888-1933. 10 vols. and supplement. Reissue, corrected, 1933. 12 vols. and supplement. The original issue is known as *New English Dictionary.*

Perrin, Porter G. *Writer's Guide and Index to English.* 3rd ed. Chicago: Scott, Foresman and Company, 1959.

Roget's International Thesaurus. New ed. New York: Thomas Y. Crowell, 1946.

Webster's Dictionary of Synonyms. Springfield, Massachusetts: G. & C. Merriam Company, 1942.

Webster's New International Dictionary. Unabridged. Springfield, Massachusetts: G. & C. Merriam Company, 1954.

Year Books

Americana Book of the Year, 1924 to date. New York: Americana Corporation, 1924–.

Britannica Book of the Year, 1938 to date. Chicago: Encyclopaedia Britannica, Inc., 1938–.

Facts on File. A weekly digest of world events. New York: Person's Index, Inc., 1940–.

New International Year Book, 1907 to date. New York: Dodd, Mead and Company, 1908-31; Funk and Wagnalls Company, 1932–.

Stateman's Year Book, 1864 to date. London: The Macmillan Company, 1864–.

World Almanac and Book of Facts, 1886 to date. New York: The New York World-Telegram, 1886–.

Atlases

Columbia-Lippincott Gazetteer of the World. New York: Columbia University Press, 1952.

Commercial Atlas. Chicago: Rand, McNally and Company. Issued annually.

Cosmopolitan World Atlas. 2nd ed. Chicago: Rand, McNally and Company, 1951.

Encyclopaedia Britannica World Atlas. New York: Encyclopaedia Britannica, Inc. Frequently revised.

Webster's Geographical Dictionary. Rev. ed. Springfield, Mass.: G. & C. Merriam Company, 1955.

General Biography

Biography Index. New York: H. W. Wilson Company, 1946–.

Cattell, Jacques. *American Men of Science.* 9th ed. Lancaster, Pennsylvania: The Science Press, 1955. 3 vols.

———. *Directory of American Scholars.* 3rd ed. Lancaster, Pennsylvania: The Science Press, 1957.

Current Biography: Who's News and Why. New York: H. W. Wilson Company, 1940–. Published monthly with half-year and annual cumulations.

Dictionary of American Biography. Ed. by Allen Johnson and Dumas Malone. New York: Charles Scribner's Sons, 1928-37. 20 vols. and index. Supplements, 1944, 1958.

Dictionary of National Biography. Ed. by Leslie Stephen and Sidney Lee. London: Smith, Elder and Company; Oxford University Press, 1885-1937. 63 vols., supplements.

International Who's Who, 1936 to date. London: Europa Publications, 1936–.

Webster's Biographical Dictionary. Springfield, Massachusetts: G. & C. Merriam Company, 1956.

Who's Who, 1848 to date. London: A. & C. Black, 1849–.

Who's Who in America, 1899-1900 to date. Chicago: A. N. Marquis Company, 1899–.

Books of Quotations

Bartlett, John. *Familiar Quotations.* 13th ed. Ed. by Christopher Morley and Louella Everett. Boston: Little, Brown and Company, 1955.

Mencken, H. L. *A New Dictionary of Quotations on Historical Principles from Ancient and Modern Sources.* New York: Alfred A. Knopf, 1942.

Stevenson, Burton. *The Home Book of Quotations.* 5th ed. New York: Dodd, Mead and Company, 1947.

Mythology and Folklore

Cary, M., *et al. The Oxford Classical Dictionary.* Oxford: The Clarendon Press, 1949.

Frazer, Sir James G. *The Golden Bough.* 3rd ed. London: The Macmillan Company, 1911-15. 12 vols. Supplement, 1936.

Funk & Wagnalls Standard Dictionary of Folklore, Mythology, and Legend. New York: Funk & Wagnalls, 1949. 2 vols.

Hamilton, Edith. *Mythology.* Boston: Little, Brown and Company, 1942.

Sandys, John E. *Companion to Latin Studies.* 3rd ed. Cambridge, England: Cambridge University Press, 1938.

Whibley, Leonard. *Companion to Greek Studies.* 4th ed. Cambridge: Cambridge University Press, 1931.

Modern Literature

Cambridge Bibliography of English Literature. Ed. by F. W. Bateson. New York: The Macmillan Company, 1941-1957. 5 vols.

Cambridge History of English Literature. Ed. by A. W. Ward and A. R. Waller. Cambridge, England: Cambridge University Press, 1907-16. 14 vols. Index issued, 1927. Reissued, without bibliographies, 1933. 15 vols. Reissued, 1949.

Hart, J. D. *Oxford Companion to American Literature.* 3rd ed. New York: Oxford University Press, 1956.

Harvey, Sir Paul. *Oxford Companion to English Literature.* 3rd ed. Oxford, England: The Clarendon Press, 1946.

Kunitz, S. J., and Howard Haycraft. *American Authors, 1600-1900.* New York: H. W. Wilson Company, 1938.

————. *British Authors of the Nineteenth Century.* New York: H. W. Wilson Company, 1936.

————. *Twentieth Century Authors.* New York: H. W. Wilson Company, 1942. Supplement, 1955.

Literary History of the United States. Ed. R. E. Spiller, *et al.* New York: The Macmillan Company, 1949. 3 vols. Vol. 3 is bibliography. Reissued, 1953, first two volumes in one.

Millett, Fred B. *Contemporary American Authors.* New York: Harcourt, Brace and Company, 1940.

Millett, Fred B., John M. Manly, and Edith Rickert. *Contemporary British Literature.* 3rd ed. New York: Harcourt, Brace and Company, 1935.

Parrington, V. L. *Main Currents in American Thought.* New York: Harcourt, Brace and Company, 1927-30. Reissued, 1939, 1 vol.

History

Cambridge Ancient History. Ed. by J. B. Bury, *et al.* Cambridge, England: Cambridge University Press, 1923-39. 12 vols.

Cambridge Medieval History. Ed. by H. M. Gwatkin, *et al.* Cambridge, England: Cambridge University Press, 1911-36, 8 vols.

Cambridge Modern History. Ed. by A. W. Ward, *et al.* Cambridge, England: Cambridge University Press, 1902-26. 13 vols. and atlas.

Dictionary of American History. Ed. by J. T. Adams. New York: Charles Scribner's Sons, 1940. 5 vols. Vol. 6 (index), 1941.

Harvard Guide to American History. Cambridge, Massachusetts: Harvard University Press, 1954.

Keller, Helen R. *The Dictionary of Dates.* New York: The Macmillan Company, 1934. 2 vols.

Langer, William L. *An Encyclopedia of World History.* Rev. ed. Boston: Houghton Mifflin Company, 1952.

Schlesinger, Arthur M., and D. R. Fox, ed. *A History of American Life.* New York: The Macmillan Company, 1927-48. 13 vols.

Music, Painting

Bryan, Michael. *Bryan's Dictionary of Painters and Engravers.* Rev. ed. London: George Bell and Sons, 1903-05. 5 vols.

Grove's Dictionary of Music and Musicians. Ed. by H. C. Colles. 5th ed. London and New York: The Macmillan Company, 1954. 5 vols.

Reinach, Solomon. *Apollo: An Illustrated Manual of the History of Art Throughout the Ages.* Tr. by F. Simmonds. Rev. ed. New York: Charles Scribner's Sons, 1935.

Thompson, Oscar. *International Cyclopedia of Music and Musicians.* 5th ed. New York: Dodd, Mead and Company, 1949.

Philosophy, Religion

Catholic Encyclopedia. New York: Catholic Encyclopedia Press, 1907-14. 16 vols. Supplement, 1922. Rev. ed. 1936–.

Encyclopedia of Religion and Ethics. Ed. by James Hastings. New York: Charles Scribner's Sons, 1908-27. 12 vols. and index. Reissued, 1928. 7 vols. Reissued, 1951.

Ferm, Vergilius. *Encyclopedia of Religion.* New York: Philosophical Library, 1945.

Jewish Encyclopedia. New York: Funk & Wagnalls Company, 1901-06. 12 vols. Reissued, 1925.

New Schaff-Herzog Encyclopedia of Religious Knowledge. Ed. by S. M. Jackson. New York: Funk & Wagnalls Company, 1949-50. 12 vols. and index.

Science, Technology

Handbook of Chemistry and Physics. 37th ed. Cleveland: Chemical Rubber Publishing Company, 1955.

Henderson, Isabella F. and W. D. *A Dictionary of Scientific Terms.* 5th ed. New York: D. Van Nostrand Company, 1953.

Hutchinson's Technical and Scientific Encyclopedia. Ed. by C. F. Tweney and I. P. Shirshov. New York: The Macmillan Company, 1936. 4 vols.

Van Nostrand's Scientific Encyclopedia. 3rd ed. New York: D. Van Nostrand Company, 1958.

Social Sciences

Cyclopedia of Education. Ed. by Paul Monroe. New York: The Macmillan Company, 1925. 3 vols.

Encyclopedia of the Social Sciences. Ed. by E. R. A. Seligman and Alvin Johnson. New York: The Macmillan Company, 1930-35. 15 vols. Reissued, 1937.

Fairchild, Henry P. *Dictionary of Sociology.* New York: Philosophical Library, 1944.

Munn, G. G. *Encyclopedia of Banking and Finance.* 5th ed. New York: Bankers Publishing Company, 1949. 2 vols. Supplement, 1956.

Warren, H. C. *Dictionary of Psychology.* Boston: Houghton Mifflin Company, 1934.

Periodicals, bulletins, pamphlets.

A *periodical* is a publication that appears at regular (periodic) intervals. *Bulletins* and *pamphlets* may or may not be periodicals, depending on whether they are issued as parts of a series of publications or as separate, single publications. They are usually kept in the stacks with the main collection of books. Recent issues of magazines and newspapers are usually kept in the open shelves of the reading room. Older issues are bound in volumes and shelved in the stacks.

A library's periodical catalog merely shows what periodicals are available. For guides to the contents of periodicals you must refer to periodical indexes, which are usually shelved in the reference room. A representative list of periodical indexes follows.

General Indexes

Poole's Index to Periodical Literature, 1802-81, supplements through January 1, 1907. This is a subject index only; no author entries are given.

Reader's Guide to Periodical Literature, 1900 to date. This is published monthly; each year the accumulated issues are bound in volumes. The *Reader's Guide* gives entries under author, title, and subject.

International Index to Periodicals, 1907 to date. This index deals with more scholarly publications than the *Reader's Guide*. Although most of the periodicals it indexes are American, it also covers many foreign publications.

Special Indexes. These indexes list articles published in periodicals devoted to special fields. A few also list books.

Agricultural Index, 1916 to date. A subject index, appearing nine times a year and cumulated annually.

Applied Science and Technology Index, 1958 to date. (Formerly *Industrial Arts Index*.)

The Art Index, 1929 to date. An author and subject index.

Articles on American Literature, 1900-1950. (Ed. by Lewis Leary.)

Business Periodicals Index, 1958 to date. Monthly. (Formerly *Industrial Arts Index*.)

Dramatic Index, 1909-1949. Continued in *Bulletin of Bibliography*, 1950 to date. Annual index to drama and theater.

The Education Index, 1929 to date. An author and subject index.

Engineering Index, 1884 to date. An author and subject index.

Essay and General Literature Index, 1900 to date. Semiannual, with annual cumulations.

Industrial Arts Index, 1913-1957. An author and subject index, monthly, with annual cumulations. (In 1958 this index was split into *Applied Science and Technology Index* and *Business Periodicals Index*.)

Index to Legal Periodicals, 1908 to date. A quarterly author and subject index.

The New York Times Index, 1913 to date. A monthly index to news stories in *The New York Times*.

Public Affairs Information Service Bulletin, 1915 to date. Weekly, with bimonthly and annual cumulations. An index to materials on economics, politics, and sociology.

Quarterly Cumulative Index Medicus, 1927 to date. A continuation of the *Index Medicus*, 1899-1926. Indexes books as well as periodicals.

Indexes to Bulletins and Pamphlets

Boyd, Anne M. *United States Government Publications*. 3rd ed. New York: H. W. Wilson Company, 1949.

United States Government Publications: Monthly Catalog, 1895 to date. Washington, D.C.: Government Printing Office, 1895 to date.

Vertical File Service Catalog: An Annotated Subject Catalog of Pamphlets, 1932-34. New York: H. W. Wilson Company, 1935. Supplements, 1935 to date.

EXERCISE 1. Draw a diagram of the reference room of your library, indicating the position of the following reference books and indexes.

1. *Encyclopaedia Britannica*
2. *Encyclopedia Americana*
3. *Encyclopedia of Social Sciences*
4. *Encyclopedia of Religion and Ethics*
5. *Jewish Encyclopedia*
6. *Dictionary of American History* (DAH)
7. *Dictionary of National Biography* (DNB)
8. *Dictionary of American Biography* (DAB)
9. *Current Biography*
10. *Twentieth Century Authors*
11. *British Authors of Nineteenth Century*
12. *American Authors, 1600-1900*
13. *Who's Who*
14. *Facts on File*
15. *World Almanac*
16. *New English Dictionary* (NED) sometimes referred to as *Oxford English Dictionary* (OED)
17. *General Card Catalog*
18. *Reader's Guide to Periodical Literature*
19. *International Index*
20. *The New York Times Index*
21. *Agricultural Index*
22. *Education Index*
23. *Industrial Arts Index*
24. *Art Index*
25. *Drama Index*

EXERCISE 2. Answer each of the following questions by consulting one of the standard reference guides listed in Exercise 1.

1. What occasions did the ancient Hebrews celebrate by dancing?

2. Among which tribe of American Indians is the highest development of shamanism found?

3. What was the minimum equipment of a typical "forty-niner"?

4. When and how did the expression *lime-juicer* originate?

5. How many articles on moving pictures in science education are listed in the *Education Index* for June, 1957–May, 1958?

6. Where can you find listed a scholarly article on the training of nuclear engineers, written in 1958?

7. Where can you find listed a 1945 article on the possibility of blending aralac (a synthetic fabric) with cotton?

8. Where can you find listed articles on French stained glass, printed in 1957 and 1958?

9. What was the first invention of Peter Cooper, American inventor, manufacturer, and philanthropist (*d.* 1883)?

10. What was the occupation of Frances Kyte, an Englishman (*b.* 1710)?

EXERCISE 3. Write a brief paper on one of the following subjects. Be sure to answer all the questions raised. Read the prefaces or introductions to the reference works you are asked to describe, check to see how each work is organized, and make a special point of finding out how to use the works efficiently and effectively. If you have difficulty deciding what particular advantage each work has for research, consult Constance M. Winchell, *A Guide to Reference Books.*

1. Compare the *Dictionary of National Biography* and *Who's Who in America.* On what basis does each work include biographical data about an individual? Nationality? Contemporaneity? Prominence? What kind of prominence? What kinds of information can you get about an individual in each work? Which work is more detailed? What particular research value does each have?

2. Compare the *World Almanac* and *Facts on File.* Both works are known as "year books." How do they differ in methods of compilation of material? How does this difference affect the way in which they are organized? How does it determine the types of information included in each? How do you look up an item in each one? Under what circumstances would you consult the *World Almanac* rather than *Facts on File? Facts on File* rather than the *World Almanac?*

3. Compare the *Oxford English Dictionary* (OED) with the *American College Dictionary* or *Webster's Collegiate Diction-*

ary or *Webster's New World Dictionary*. For illustrative purposes look up the word "kind" in each. What does each work tell you about the derivation of the word? About its history in the English language? How up-to-date is each dictionary? When would you use each one and for what purposes? What does each work tell you about the meaning of "devil" in the phrase "between the devil and the deep blue sea"? What does each work tell you about the sense in which Shakespeare meant the word "prevent"? What does each work tell you about "turbojet"? About "chemist"? About "fancy"?

46 THE RESEARCH PAPER

Choosing and limiting a subject.

Although your own interest or curiosity about a topic is a good motivation in choosing a subject for your research paper, common sense requires also that you choose a subject you can cope with, and that you limit it in accordance with the space and time at your disposal. You might write an informal essay on the following subjects, but *not a research paper:*

1. A History of Medicine
2. Modern Warfare
3. The Great American Sport: Baseball
4. The American Indian

For research purposes, you might limit each subject as follows:

1. A History of the Discovery of Anesthesia
2. The Rival Claims of Types of Army Rifle
3. The Historical Development of Official Rules for Baseball
4. The Relation of the Mohicans to the Five Nations

EXERCISE 4. Write a short research paper in which you answer one of the following questions. Use your ingenuity to determine what the question means and the best way of answering it.

1. Was John Altgeld right in pardoning the Haymarket rioters?
2. Was Margaret O'Neill Eaton unjustly maligned?
3. What part did Theodore Roosevelt really play in the Spanish-American war?
4. Did Alfred really defeat the Danes?
5. How competent a general was Benedict Arnold?

424

6. Was Billy the Kidd really a desperado?
7. Why was Joan of Arc burned at the stake?
8. Why did General Grant write his memoirs?
9. What caused the Reichstag fire?
10. How extensively did the early Algonquians engage in agriculture?
11. Was John Fitch cheated?
12. What differences are there between the poetic and historical accounts of Roland?
13. What was Theodore Roosevelt's attitude toward spelling?
14. Who was Martin Marprelate and what happened to him?
15. Was Samuel Tilden a victim of crooked politics?
16. Where did the American Indians come from?
17. How was Lincoln's "Gettysburg Address" received by his contemporaries?
18. Can a pitcher really curve a baseball?
19. What happened in the Scopes trial?
20. Why did Robert G. Ingersoll turn atheist?
21. What are the present theories on the migratory instincts of birds?
22. Was "Shoeless Joe" Jackson an unfortunate victim of circumstances?
23. Who won the Battle of Hampton Roads?
24. Was Stanton involved in Lincoln's death?
25. What happened to the settlers on Roanoke Island?
26. What was the Teapot Dome scandal?
27. What geographical knowledge did the man of 300 A.D. have?
28. Is the climate really growing warmer?
29. Was Lincoln really a good lawyer?
30. What are the plausible explanations for the statues on Easter Island?
31. Is the human race really growing taller?
32. Does the legend that Pocahontas saved John Smith's life square with the probable facts in the case?
33. Why did Thoreau go to jail?
34. Did Anne Boleyn deserve to have her head chopped off?
35. Did Fulton really invent the steamboat?

36. Did the Norsemen make voyages to America before Columbus?

37. Were Sacco and Vanzetti convicted on the basis of circumstantial evidence?

38. Who won the Battle of the Coral Sea?

39. Did Edgar Allan Poe die intoxicated or insane?

40. What are the reasons for the disappearance of the dinosaur?

Finding and ordering material.

(1) *Bibliographical Aids.* Begin your research by making a preliminary bibliography—that is, a list of source materials compiled from such works as the following:

> Subject cards in the main card catalog.
>
> Bibliographies at the end of pertinent articles in various encyclopedias.
>
> *Reader's Guide to Periodical Literature.*
>
> Appropriate special periodical indexes (*Engineering Index, Education Index,* etc.).
>
> *The New York Times Index.*
>
> Guides to reference books, such as those listed on pages 413-414.

If you need help in selecting the most useful books from a long list, consult such aids as the following:

> *Book Review Digest.* New York: H. W. Wilson Company, 1906 to date.
>
> *Technical Book Review Index.* Pittsburgh: Carnegie Library, 1917-1929. Continued by Special Libraries Association, New York, 1935 to date.

(2) *Bibliography Cards.* The best method of keeping an accurate and useful record of your sources is to make out bibliography cards. The common sizes of cards are 3″ x 5″, 4″ x 6″, and 5″ x 8″. Most students prefer the 3″ x 5″ card for bibliographic entries and one of the larger sizes for note-taking.

Enter each bibliographic item on its own card and gradually build up a bibliographic card file on your subject. Because there are many methods of making out bibliographic entries, your instructor will give you complete directions. The system illustrated here is merely a suggestion:*

(1) *For a book with one author*

> von Neumann, John. The Computer and the Brain. New Haven, Connecticut: Yale University Press, 1958.

(2) *For a book with two or more authors*

> Gaum, Carl G., Harold F. Graves, Lyne S. S. Hoffman. Report Writing. 3rd ed. New York: Prentice-Hall, Inc., 1950.

(3) *For an edited book*

> Beal, Richard S. and Jacob Korg, eds. Thought in Prose. Englewood Cliffs, N. J.: Prentice-Hall, Inc., 1958.

(4) *For a book with an author and editor*

> Swift, Jonathan. Gulliver's Travels. Ed. by Arthur E. Case. New York: The Ronald Press Company, 1938.

(5) *For a book of two or more volumes*

> Morison, S. E., and H. S. Commager. The Growth of the American Republic. 3rd ed. New York: The Oxford University Press, 1942. 2 vols.

(6) *For an article in an encyclopedia*

> "Airship." Encyclopaedia Britannica. (14th ed., 1949), I, 469 ff.

(7) *For a magazine article, author given*

> Nutter, G. W. "Soviet Industrial Growth." Science, CXXX (July 31, 1959), 252-255.

* A common deviation from this system omits the publisher's name from the bibliographical entry. Sample entry (2), for example, would be:

> Gaum, Carl G., Harold F. Graves, Lyne S. S. Hoffman. *Report Writing.* 3rd ed. New York, 1950.

(8) *For a maga-
zine article,
no author given*

> "Society Calls For an End to
> Amateur Rocketry." Science
> News Letter, LXXVI (July 11,
> 1959), 24.

(9) *For a news-
paper article*

> "U. S. Still Leads Russ in
> Nuclear Arms, Says Gates."
> The Seattle Times,
> December 16, 1959, p. 7.

(10) *For a bulletin*

> U. S. Government. Manual of
> Style. Revised ed.
> Washington, D. C.: Govern-
> ment Printing Office, 1945.

(11) *For an un-
published
thesis or
dissertation*

> Rider, Maurice L. Advanced
> Composition for Students in
> Engineering at the Ohio State
> University, Evaluation and
> Proposals. Unpublished
> Doctoral Dissertation.
> Columbus, Ohio: The Ohio
> State University, 1950.

EXERCISE 5. Prepare a short bibliography (on cards) for one of the following topics.

1. Color Television
2. Socialized Medicine
3. The Erie Canal
4. Showboats
5. The Generalship of U. S. Grant
6. Disputed Points about the Life of Poe
7. The Assassination of Lincoln
8. The Early Career of General de Gaulle
9. The Rocket Ship and Interplanetary Travel
10. The Shakespeare-Bacon Controversy

EXERCISE 6. Prepare a short working bibliography for one of the following persons. Hand in a brief biographical sketch with your bibliography.

Charles Steinmetz	Louis Armstrong
Samuel Insull	Andrew Carnegie
Gamal Abdul Nasser	Frank Lloyd Wright
Tennessee Williams	David W. Griffith

James (Jim) Thorpe	George Herman Ruth
Sarah Bernhardt	Henry George
Charles Chaplin	Eugene Debs
George M. Cohan	Douglas Fairbanks, Sr.
Luther Burbank	Eudora Welty
James Thurber	Thorstein Veblen

(3) *Preliminary Organization.* As you are choosing and thinking about your subject, you will probably also work out a rough plan of attack. Then, as you begin to read your source material, your plan will become more and more definite and will eventually crystallize into an outline. Constantly revise this outline as your research progresses; at the outset it may be no more than a set of directions for you to follow as you move ahead. The writer of the specimen research paper at the end of Section 46, for example, began with the following outline.

I. Describe preparations for landing of Hindenburg at Lakehurst.

II. Show what a relatively unimportant affair it was meant to be.

III. Insert remarks of radio announcer.

IV. Describe the crash.
    A. The number killed.
    B. Those who escaped.

V. Describe the effect of the crash on the country at large.
    A. See newspaper accounts.
    B. Look for pictures of the crash in pictorial magazines.

VI. Find the cause of the crash.

VII. See whether the crash had any significance for future airship travel.

With a directive outline such as this, the writer was prepared to go about her research in an organized way.

(4) *Note-taking.* Develop the habit of entering your reading notes on standard-size cards, for they are easier to carry than a notebook and easier to refer to than full sheets of paper. In taking notes, observe the same principles you observed in writing out your bibliography cards; make sure that all your notes are accurate and complete. Nothing is more wearisome and inefficient than second

and third trips to the library to get information that you could have obtained on the first trip.

1. *A sample note card for paraphrasing information.*

Hindenburg measurements and construction details

  803 ft long. 36 longitudinal girders. 15 wire-braced traverse frames. Four 1,100 hp. Mercedes-Benz diesel engines. Max. speed 84 mph. Accommodations for 50 passengers. 8,750-mile range.

"Airship," *Ency. Brit.*, I, 471

2. *A sample note card for recording a direct quotation.* Be sure to indicate on the card what material you are quoting. Otherwise you may forget which are your own words and use a borrowed statement as your own.

Report of Herbert Laughlin, passenger

  "There was very little confusion among the passengers, no screaming.... Nobody knew what was happening.... Everybody just curious."

N.Y. Times, May 7, '37, p. 18

(5) *Footnotes.* One of the purposes of making out accurate bibliography and note cards is to provide you with the information you will need for footnoting your research paper. Footnotes have three main uses:

1. To give information or commentary which, though related to the subject being discussed, would interrupt the flow of the narrative or argument. Some writers use this kind of note skillfully (for example, Van Wyck Brooks in *The Flowering of New England*), but there is a good deal prejudice against it.

2. To give additional evidence or illustration in support of an assertion. For example, if you are arguing that Theodore Roosevelt was essentially a conservative, your footnote might cite one or more other writers who also think so. This device is known as the *See also* footnote, and is the vehicle for much pedantry and pretense. Readers rarely check on the "other writers."

3. To give the source of a fact or quotation.

The third use in particular will give you training in accuracy, authenticity, and honesty. Once you have acquired discipline in these matters, your instructor may encourage you to avoid footnotes as much as possible. The tendency now is away from excessive footnoting, even in formal scholarship. If the specimen library papers printed in this section seem overloaded with notes, it is simply because the editors wish to demonstrate as many footnoting forms as possible.

The rules for footnoting are complex. Most of them were evolved to meet the needs of formal, professional scholarship designed to add to the fund of knowledge. Even though you are chiefly concerned with adding to *your own* knowledge, you are expected to adopt the habits of the professional scholar. Fortunately, many of the conflicts and divergences of the different systems of footnoting have been resolved by the Modern Language Association, whose useful pamphlet, *The MLA Style Sheet,* is available from the Association's offices for a nominal sum.*

* Address: Treasurer, Modern Language Association, 6 Washington Square North, New York 3, New York.

Footnote form. Unless your instructor directs otherwise, place footnotes at the bottom of the page on which the reference occurs and number them consecutively throughout the paper. In type-written manuscript, single-space all footnotes and leave a double space between footnotes (see Specimen Paper A at the end of the section). Indicate the appearance of a footnote by placing a raised figure at the end of the statement to be documented. Then repeat the figure at the beginning of the footnote itself.

TEXT

Since the summer of the previous year, the great dirigible had been observing a regular schedule of flights between Frankfort, Germany, and Lakehurst, N. J.[1]

FOOTNOTE

[1]Commander C. E. Rosendahl, <u>What About the Airship?</u> (New York, 1938), p. 1.

Placing footnotes at the bottom of the page is only one of several ways of handling them. You can place all of them together on a separate page or pages at the end of your paper, or you can insert each in the text directly after the reference to it.

TEXT

All that was of real importance was that this particular flight inaugurated a new series for 1937.[2] It was true of course that

FOOTNOTE

[2]New York <u>Times</u>, May 3, 1937, p. 21.

TEXT

the great German airship expert, Ernst Lehmann, was aboard--

Your instructor will tell you which of these methods he wants you to use.

The following list illustrates the footnote forms recommended by the Modern Language Association. (*Note that the form used for an item in a footnote is different from that used for an item in a bibliography or list of references such as appears at the end of each specimen research paper at the end of this section.*)

1. *For a book with one author, first edition:*

> [1]Norman Lewis, <u>Comprehensive Word Guide</u> (New York, 1959), p. 129.

2. *For a book with one author, later edition:*

> [2]Brian Harold Mason, <u>Principles of Geochemistry</u>, 2nd ed. (New York, 1959), p. 154.

3. *For a book with two or more authors:*

> [3]C. G. Gaum, H. F. Graves, and L. S. S. Hoffman, <u>Report Writing</u>, 3rd ed. (New York, 1950), p. 71.

4. *For an edited book:*

> [4]Charles McCurdy, ed., <u>Modern Art, a Pictorial Anthology</u> (New York, 1959), p. 156.

5. *For a book with an author and an editor:*

> [5]William Shakespeare, "The Tragedy of King Lear," <u>The Complete Works of William Shakespeare</u>, ed. G. L. Kittredge (Boston, 1936), pp. 1203-1205.

6. *For a book consisting of two or more volumes:*

> [6]Bernard Dorival, <u>Twentieth Century Painters</u> (New York, 1959), II, p. 80.

7. *For a signed article in a book by several contributors:*

> [7]Cleanth Brooks, "A Plea to the Protestant Churches," in <u>Who Owns America?</u>, ed. by Herbert Agar (Cambridge, Mass., 1936), p. 105.

8. *For an article in an encyclopedia:*

> [8]"Airship," <u>Encyclopaedia Britannica</u> (14th ed., 1949), I, 470.

9. *For a magazine article, author given:*

> [9]G. W. Nutter, "Soviet Industrial Growth," <u>Science</u> (July 31, 1959), 252-255.

10. *For a magazine article, no author given:*

> [10]"Society Calls for an End to Amateur Rocketry," <u>Science News Letter</u>, LXXVI (July 11, 1959), 24.

11. *For a newspaper article, author given:*

> [11]G. Milton Kelly, "Unfit Canadian Wheat Milled into U. S. Flour," <u>The Seattle Daily Times</u>, LXXVI (January 29, 1953), 1.

12. *For a newspaper article, no author given:*

> [12]"Flying Saucers: Fact or Fancy," <u>Columbus Citizen</u>, LIV (August 10 10, 1952), 11.

13. *For a bulletin:*

> [13]United Nations, <u>Economic Bulletin for Asia and the Far East</u>, X (June, 1959), p. 2.

14. *For an unpublished thesis or dissertation:*

> [14]Maurice L. Rider, <u>Advanced Composition for Students in Engineering at The Ohio State University, Evaluation and Proposals</u> (Unpublished Ohio State University Doctoral Dissertation, 1950), pp. 17-21.

Abbreviations. The abbreviations that you will ordinarily use in footnotes fall into two classes: (1) abbreviations of English words; (2) abbreviations of Latin words. Whenever possible, choose abbreviations of English words.

anon.	anonymous
art., arts.	article(s)
c., ca.	*circa* (about)
cf.	*confer* (compare)
ch., chs.	chapter(s)
col., cols.	column(s)
diss.	dissertation
ed., edn.	edition
ed., eds.	editor(s)
e.g.	*exempli gratia* (for example)
esp.	especially
et al.	*et alii* (and others)

f., ff.	the following page(s)
ibid.	*ibidem* (in the same place)
i.e.	*id est* (that is)
introd.	introduction
loc. cit.	*loco citato* (in the place cited)
MS, MSS, ms., mss.	manuscript(s)
N.B., n.b.	*nota bene* (take notice, mark well)
n.d.	no date given
n.p.	no place given
numb.	numbered
op. cit.	*opere citato* (in the work cited)
p., pp.	page(s)
rev.	revised
tr., trns., trans.	translator, translated, translation
v.	*vide* (see)
vol., vols.	volume(s)

Be particularly careful in your use of *ibid.*, *loc. cit.*, and *op. cit.* Use *ibid.* to refer to the title cited in the note immediately preceding.

```
¹Hugh Allen, The Story of the Airship (Akron, Ohio, 1942), p. 34.
²Ibid., p. 38.
```

If the second note refers to exactly the same page as the first, use only *ibid.*; otherwise give the second page number. The use of the term *ibid.*, however, is rapidly disappearing. Modern practice permits the use of an abbreviated title or the author's name in a second or succeeding note.

```
²Airship, p. 34.
²Allen, p. 34.
```

Similarly with *loc. cit.* and *op. cit.* It is generally easier and clearer to use the abbreviated title or the author's name. Technically *loc. cit.* means "in the same passage referred to in a recent note" and is never followed by a page number.

```
¹Hugh Allen, The Story of the Airship (Akron, Ohio, 1942), p. 34.
²Loc. cit.
```

435

However, the second reference would be clearer this way:

²Allen, p. 34.

The term *op. cit.* is properly used in citing a passage on a different page of a work recently noted.

¹Hugh Allen, The Story of the Airship (Akron, Ohio, 1942), p. 34.

²The New York Times, May 3, 1937, p. 21.

³Allen, op. cit., p. 56.

But, as the *MLA Style Sheet* points out, you may again in such cases use the author's last name alone with the page number or the author's name and a shortened form of the title with the page number:

³Allen, p. 56

or:

³Allen, Airship, p. 56.

(5) *Quoted Material.*

(a) *The Ethics of Quotation.* Footnoting is in part a matter of manners and ethics. At best, a failure to acknowledge one's debt to others for words, facts, and ideas is a breach of manners; at worst, it is a form of theft known as plagiarism, an offense subject to legal action in the courts and to disciplinary action by a university. In the academic world acknowledgement of indebtedness is especially necessary because most researchers are rewarded for what they write not in money but in reputation.

How can you draw the line between material for which you should give credit and material which, through prolonged general use, has become public property? This is a difficult question, and there is no rule to take care of every case. Often you must use your own judgment. Your instructor can help you decide what material should be footnoted.

Here are a few basic rules for the handling of quoted material:

1. When you quote material that is clearly not public property, acknowledge the source whether you quote it *verbatim* or in paraphrase.

2. Always acknowledge a direct quotation unless it can be classified as a "familiar quotation."

3. Transcribe direct quotations precisely and accurately. To omit even a comma may violate the meaning of a statement. *Check and recheck every quotation.*

4. Whenever you want to omit material from a quoted passage, indicate the omission (ellipsis) by using three spaced periods (. . .). If the omission is from the end of a quoted sentence, use four spaced periods (. . . .), the fourth indicating the period at the end of the sentence (see "Punctuation of Quoted Material," Section 26). When you omit material from a quoted passage, be sure that what you retain is grammatically coherent.

5. When you wish to substitute in a quotation words of your own for the original, enclose your own words in square brackets (see Section 26).

Even though you observe these rules, you may still be guilty of misrepresentation and deception in quoting if you are not careful to preserve the key words that indicate the *tone* of the original. Observe the following passage:

> Woodrow Wilson "was more than just an idealist," Herbert Hoover has written. "He was the personification of the heritage of idealism of the American people." He was also the twenty-eighth President of the United States, one of perhaps five or six in the nearly two hundred years of our country's history who can be, by anyone's reckoning, classified as truly great. Perceptive educator, courageous reformer, international leader, Wilson in his time was the spokesman of the future.[1]

The tone of the paragraph is one of praise which comes close to adulation. In quoting from the passage, you can alter the tone as well as the intent of the writer by making small changes in the original. For example, omission of the adjectives "perceptive,"

[1] This and the examples given below are from *The New York Times*, December 13, 1959, Sec. 4, p. 10.

"courageous," and "international" in the last sentence would distort the writer's opinion of Wilson.

(b) *The Technique of Quotation.* (1) Do not quote long, unbroken stretches of material. Such a practice puts the burden of discovering the purpose of your quotation upon the reader, or forces him to re-read the quotation in the light of your subsequent commentary. The *use* you make of a quotation, not the quotation itself, is your research contribution.

Make frequent use of paraphrase, or indirect quotation, whenever you do not need the precise words of the original, or when you can restate its point more briefly in your own words. Interpolate your own commentary and explanations whenever you feel they are needed.

(2) When you work quoted material into a sentence of your own, be sure your words, grammar, and syntax are in logical relation to the quotation. Below are some examples of common errors in quoting material, followed by corrected versions.

INCORRECT	Woodrow Wilson was one of the five or six American Presidents who are "the personification of the history of idealism of the American people." (This confuses the statements of Hoover and the newspaper editor.)
CORRECT	Herbert Hoover describes Woodrow Wilson as "the personification of the heritage of idealism of the American people."
or	The editor describes Woodrow Wilson as one of five or six American Presidents "in the nearly two hundred years of our country's history who can be, by anyone's reckoning, classified as truly great."
INCORRECT	The newspaper declared that Woodrow Wilson was one of the five or six American Presidents that they could classify "as truly great."
CORRECT	The newspaper declared that Woodrow Wilson was one of the five or six American Presidents "who can be, by anyone's reckoning, classified as truly great."
INCORRECT	One of the things Herbert Hoover wrote: Woodrow Wilson "was the personification of the heritage of idealism of the American people."

CORRECT   One of the things Herbert Hoover wrote was that Woodrow Wilson "was the personification of the heritage of idealism of the American people."

SPECIMEN RESEARCH PAPERS

The research papers presented in this section are designed for study. A few minutes spent in checking and evaluating them carefully will help you immeasurably in preparing your own research papers. One paper is given with detailed comment, indicating page by page what is good and what is poor about it. After you have studied this first paper, analyze the other in the same manner. This simple exercise will make you more aware of the mistakes to avoid and the techniques to use in your own papers.

Specimen Research Paper A and critical comment.

Specimen A, though it has real merits, violates several principles in the mechanics and presentation of research. Moreover, the author's handling of source material is far from impeccable. "But why," you might ask, "should I be asked to study a paper that is not absolutely correct in every detail?" Simply because the best way of learning to handle research materials is to observe how another author has failed to handle them successfully. In matters such as this you may profit more by other people's failures than by their successes.

This is an excellent title page; it presents the necessary information in a simple, well-balanced format. Note that the information (sometimes called the "endorsement") answers six basic questions about the research paper:

1. *What* is it about?   (the title)
2. *Who* wrote it?   (the author)
3. *For whom* was it written?   (the instructor assigning it)
4. *For what purpose* was it written?   (the course it was assigned in)
5. *Where* was it written?   (the college or university)
6. *When* was it written?   (the date)

These items are not always arranged precisely as they are here; your instructor may give other directions. This title page simply presents an example of good standard practice.

Specimen Research Paper A

LAST OF THE ZEPPELINS:

THE HINDENBURG

By

Susan Ann Sheldon

For

Professor Mark Roberts

English 401

THE OHIO STATE UNIVERSITY   October 7, 1959

PAGES 1-3

The next three pages give a quick summary of this research paper. Notice that this prefatory material falls into three divisions: (1) *the title*, which is a very general statement; (2) *the statement of purpose*, which explains briefly what the paper attempts to do; and (3) *the outline*, which is a rather full statement of the contents of the paper. You will want to include these three divisions in your own papers.

(1) *The title.* The appearance and position of the title on this page are correct. But, as a moment's glance through the outline will show, the title is not appropriate. Nowhere in her outline or in her paper does Miss Sheldon identify the term *Zeppelin*, and she has no right to assume that her reader knows what it means. More seriously, the title is inaccurate. The *Hindenburg*, as Miss Sheldon must have learned from her research, was not the "last" Zeppelin. Both the American *Los Angeles* and the German *Graf Zeppelin I* were in existence after the *Hindenburg's* crash. Further, the *Graf Zeppelin II*, sister ship of the *Hindenburg*, was completed after 1937 and not dismantled until after 1940. We can appreciate Miss Sheldon's desire for an eye-catching, dramatic title, but not at the sacrifice of accuracy. A better title would be, simply, "The Crash of the *Hindenburg*."

(2) *The statement of purpose.* This statement gives the reader an idea of what to expect in the rest of the outline. Note that Miss Sheldon's statement of purpose is an accurate one; she does as she says.

(3) *The sentence outline.* The sentence outline serves two purposes: (1) it is a kind of table of contents and (2) it is a summary, or abstract, of the paper. In a longer paper, a regular table of contents giving page references, or perhaps a formal summary, would be necessary. In a paper as short as this, the sentence outline alone serves well enough.

Note that this outline is not a *directive* outline; it is meant primarily as a guide to the reader, not to the writer. The major headings (indicated by Roman numerals) are the topic sentences, sometimes rephrased, of the paragraphs appearing in the paper itself. The subdivisions are statements that either support or follow from the topic sentence.

The outline has certain weaknesses. "II. B.," for example, seems less significant than its position in the outline would indicate. And "IV. C." seems inconsistent with its main topic. "V. A." seems similarly inconsistent. Moreover, "VIII. A." and "B." are co-ordinate, not subordinate, to the topic "VIII."; they suggest a poorly developed paragraph. It will be interesting to see their relation to the paragraphs they describe.

442

THE LAST OF THE ZEPPELINS: THE HINDENBURG

Statement of purpose

     The purpose of this paper is to describe the crash of the dirigible Hindenburg at Lakehurst, N. J., and to comment briefly on the implications of that crash to the future of airship travel.

Sentence outline

  I. It was expected that the landing of the Hindenburg at Lakehurst, N. J., on May 6, 1937, would be of minor interest only.

     A. The Hindenburg had been observing a regular schedule of flights between Frankfort and Lakehurst since the previous year.

     B. This particular flight was significant only because it inaugurated a new series of flights for 1937 and because Captain Ernst A. Lehmann, the airship authority, was aboard.

     C. The remarks of radio commentator Herbert Morrison would not go over the air directly but would be played for radio audiences later by electrical transcription.

 II. The Hindenburg appeared over Lakehurst on schedule, shortly after 7:00 p.m.

     A. A fairly large crowd had gathered to see the landing of the world's largest dirigible.

     B. Morrison began to describe the landing in a calm voice.

III. The Hindenburg burst into flames at 7:25 p.m.

     A. The quarter-end of the ship suddenly took fire.

     B. As its front section nosed upward, the dirigible broke in two.

     C. The forward end of the ship then caught fire and the whole ship settled to the ground.

    D. The fire was over in exactly 32 seconds and only a smoking wreckage remained.

IV. In spite of the severity of the fire and the crash, some of the <u>Hindenburg's</u> crew and passengers escaped.

    A. Three members of the crew walked away from the wreckage, completely unharmed.

    B. An elderly woman passenger calmly walked to safety down what remained of the regular hatchway.

    C. One passenger escaped burning only to have another passenger jump on his back, injuring him severely.

    D. The cabin boy escaped burning when one of the dirigible's water tanks let go and drenched him.

V. However, of the 97 persons aboard, 35 perished; of these, 13 were passengers.

    A. Captain Pruss, the commander of the ship, was severely burned.

    B. Captain Lehmann, the airship expert, was brought out alive but died later in a hospital.

    C. John Pannes, a passenger who could have escaped, refused to leave until he had found Mrs. Pannes and thus perished with her.

    D. One man, burned black, walked away from the wreckage and then dropped dead.

VI. The disaster was front-page news for weeks.

    A. <u>Time</u> magazine called it "the worst and most completely witnessed disaster in aviation history."

    B. Dorothy Thompson, the columnist, thought the <u>Hindenburg</u> crash was symbolic of the passing of international peace.

VII. Investigation to determine why the hydrogen in the <u>Hindenburg</u> caught fire did not result in conclusive proof.

- 3 -

A. The official board of investigators decided that leaking gas was ignited by a spark, but they were unable to determine what caused the spark.

B. There was some talk that the spark had been intentionally caused by sabotage.

 1. On his death bed, Captain Lehmann attributed the spark to "an infernal machine."

 2. Commander Rosendahl, U. S. N., thought perhaps an incendiary bullet might have been fired into the Hindenburg as she was preparing to land.

VIII. Airship experts insisted that the crash was due not to a structural failure in the ship but to the use of hydrogen.

A. They suggested that the accident would not have happened had the United States supplied Germany with helium gas.

B. They pointed out that this was the first loss of life in a commercial dirigible and not to be taken as indicative of the danger of airship travel.

IX. The mass of people, however, looked upon the crash as the end of the long and tragic story of dirigible travel.

A. Widely publicized accidents had put dirigible travel in disrepute.

B. Relations between Germany -- the home of the dirigible -- and the United States were becoming more and more strained.

Note the clean, well-balanced format of this page (and the succeeding ones). The title is neatly centered at the top of the page, in capitals; a solid line separates the text proper from the footnotes.

Miss Sheldon begins her paper by pointing out how unimportant this particular landing of the *Hindenburg* was meant to be. In so doing she takes only one liberty with her source material. She does not really know that Morrison thought the job ahead of him would be routine. She knows that he seemed calm when he began to describe the landing and she interprets this calmness to mean that his attitude was casual.

Notice that three statements are documented in the first paragraph. References 1 and 2 are not really necessary. The information in the statements appears in several different publications, not merely in the ones Miss Sheldon gives in her footnotes. Actually, the information is the result of her general reading in preparation for the paper and would have been adequately acknowledged by her listing of "References Consulted" at the end of her paper. Reference 3, on the other hand, is a necessary one; it documents information found in only one source, *Time* magazine.

The footnotes themselves follow standard practice. They are separated from the text of the paper with a heavy black line, and the information they give is complete and precise. In the absence of a final bibliography or list of "References Consulted," the form of the entry would be different. Footnote 1 would then appear as

[1]Commander C. E. Rosendahl, What about the Airship? New York: Charles Scribner's Sons, 1938, p. 1.

And the titles and dates in footnotes 2 and 3 would be separated by periods, not commas.

LAST OF THE ZEPPELINS: THE HINDENBURG

It was shortly after seven o'clock on the evening
of May 6, 1937. For radio commentator Herbert Morrison,
assigned to Lakehurst, New Jersey, to cover the landing
of the dirigible Hindenburg, the job ahead appeared to be
routine. Since the summer of the previous year, the
great dirigible had been observing a regular schedule of
flights between Frankfort, Germany, and Lakehurst, N. J.[1]
All that was of real importance was that this particular
flight inaugurated a new series for 1937.[2] It was true
of course that the great German airship expert, Ernst
Lehmann, was aboard -- a celebrity to be welcomed -- but
this was hardly of sensational interest. In fact, Morrison
was not even going to broadcast directly; his voice would
be transcribed and played back for radio audiences at some
more convenient time.[3]

A fairly large crowd was at hand, made up mostly
of vacationers come to gape at the world's largest

---

[1] Commander C. E. Rosendahl, What about the Airship?
(New York, 1938), p. 1.

[2] "Hindenburg Is Off for U.S. Tomorrow," New York
Times, LXXXVI (May 3, 1937), 21 (col. 7).

[3] "Oh, the Humanity!" Time, XXIX (May 17, 1937), 37.

- 4 -

Reference 4 illustrates one of the special uses of footnotes—adding information which, had it been inserted in the text of the paper, would have interrupted the flow of the narrative. Note that the information presented in the footnote itself is also documented.

Reference 5 raises a question. If Miss Sheldon had spoken of the time as exactly 7:20, she would have needed documentation. But she generalizes about the time by writing "A few minutes before 7:20" and thereby eliminates any real need for specific documentation. Her general list of "References Consulted" would have been sufficient acknowledgment.

On the other hand, Miss Sheldon has used Commander Rosendahl's *What About the Airship?* as her chief source of information. She refers to it nine times. She might have indicated her reliance on Rosendahl more precisely and yet more simply by the use of an "omnibus" footnote, as

---

[1]Unless otherwise indicated, information on the details of the landing and burning of the Hindenburg are drawn from Commander C. E. Rosendahl, What about the Airship? (New York, 1938), pp. 1-30.

Miss Sheldon's handling of Morrison's remarks is excellent. She indents and single-spaces them, identifying them immediately as direct quotations. Her bracketing of the word *comes* shows that the word is her own insertion; she could not make out exactly what word Morrison did use, so she guessed at it and told the reader she was guessing. The use of the three periods [. . .] indicates that she is omitting some words, either because she did not think them necessary to her purpose or because she could not understand them. Her capitalizing all the letters in "IT BURST INTO FLAMES!" is an attempt to show the force with which Morrison made the statement.

We have discovered by this time that part "II. B." of Miss Sheldon's outline, "Morrison began to describe the landing in a calm voice," is really far more significant than we first assumed. Actually, Miss Sheldon built her first three pages around Morrison's remarks, and the weakness of her outline is that it does not indicate this fact clearly enough.

- 5 -

airship.[4] Navy ground crewmen, a few photographers and
reporters were scurrying about, getting their equipment
in proper places. Customs officials were getting ready
to pass the Hindenburg's 36 passengers through the
necessary red tape. A few minutes before 7:20 a shout
went up from the crowd: the great silver ship broke through
the clouds and began to reduce speed in preparation for
landing.[5] Morrison turned to his microphone and in calm,
professional tones began to describe the landing.

> ...it comes majestically
> toward us like some great feather.
> . . .It's practically standing still
> now. They have dropped ropes out
> of the nose of the ship. The rain
> has slacked up a little bit. The
> back motors of the ship are just
> holding it just enough to keep it
> from -- IT BURST INTO FLAMES!
> Get this Charley. Get this
> Charley. It's crashing and it's

---

[4] The Hindenburg, 803 feet long, was the largest
airship ever built, with a capacity of 7,070,000 cubic
feet of gas. The largest American dirigibles, the Akron
and the Macon, each had a capacity of 6,500,000 cubic
feet. See Hugh Allen, The Story of the Airship (Goodyear
Tire and Rubber Company, Akron, Ohio, 1938), p. 25. Also
the article "Airship," Encyclopaedia Britannica (1949
ed.) I, 471.

[5] What about the Airship?, p. 2.

Miss Sheldon's use of the bracketed *sic,* meaning "thus it is," after *plane* shows that she wants her readers to understand that the error is Morrison's, not hers. Reference 6 is necessary; it gives the source of Morrison's remarks. The footnote itself is interesting: in referring to a recording, Miss Sheldon had no model to guide her. She had to use her own judgment. Note that she describes the recording quite precisely.

Reference 7 is unnecessary. In the formal report the exact time the fire started would be important. In a journalistic account such as this, it is hardly of great moment. Reference 8, on the other hand, is quite essential and quite correct. It documents a direct quotation.

Note the form in which Rosendahl's book is cited in footnotes 7 and 8. The author has referred to this book previously (footnote 1, p. 4). She need not repeat all this information in subsequent references to the book; the abridgement she uses here is correct. She might have used the form "Rosendahl, p. 2." had she not planned to make a subsequent reference to another book in which Rosendahl had a hand (see next page).

- 6 -

smashing. It's crashing. Terrible.
Oh my. Get out of the way please. It's
burning, bursting into flames and it's
falling on the mooring mast and all
the folks. . . .This is terrible.
This is one of the worst catastrophes
in the world. Oh it's. . . Four or
five hundred feet into the sky. It
is a terrific crash ladies and
gentlemen. It's smoke and it's flames
now and the plane [sic] is crashing
to the ground not quite to the mooring
mast. Oh the humanity.[6]

At 7:25[7], just four minutes after the first landing

rope had touched the ground, the middle section of the

dirigible burst into flames, resembling, according to one

spectator,"a mushroom-shaped flower bursting into bloom."[8]

In a matter of seconds the whole quarter-end of the ship

was in flames. The forward part, still buoyant, nosed

upward 45 degrees; the dirigible broke in two. Fire then

shot forward, igniting one gas partition after another.

The whole ship settled on the ground. The Hindenburg was

_____

[6] Morrison's description of the crash is now part
of the Columbia Recording Corporation's Album I Can Hear
it Now...., ed. by Edward R. Murrow and Fred W. Friendly,
set #MM800. Except for the indicated omissions, Morrison's
remarks are exactly transcribed here.

[7] This is the time Rosendahl gives (What about the
Airship?, p. 6). The New York Times (May 7, 1937, p. 1.)
gives the time as exactly 7:23.

[8] What about the Airship?, p. 6.

PAGE 7

Reference 9 illustrates one way of documenting information summarized from several paragraphs of original source material; rather than document each sentence, Miss Sheldon completes the description and then gives a single reference. Footnote 9 seems rather lengthy, but the book's varied authorship needed comment. Footnote 10 is necessary to document the precise statement, "... exactly 32 seconds," and the explanatory sentence in the footnote gives necessary information. Reference 11 and its footnote are also in good order.

The statement documented by footnote 11 illustrates the danger of unconscious plagiarism. In her note-taking Miss Sheldon prepared this card:

> *Effect of the Hindenburg's burning*
>
> "The heat was so great that thermometers rose at the Naval Aerological School 500 yards away."
>
> *Time,* 17 May '37, p. 36

Her paraphrase of this quotation is too close; she simply adds the word *momentarily* and substitutes *intense* for *great*. She has borrowed *Time's* sentence structure and vocabulary without acknowledging the loan properly. She would have been wiser to say:

```
Momentarily, "the heat was so great that thermometers rose
in the Navy Aerological School 500 yards away." 11
```

The organization of the paragraph that begins on this page is not completely satisfactory. Miss Sheldon does not tell us how many people escaped; she merely lists some of the more sensational escapes. Moreover, the statement of the man who escaped only to be severely injured by another passenger hardly follows from her topic "there were many survivors, some of them completely uninjured."

- 7 -

a twisted skeleton of girders and smoking wreckage.[9] The
fire had lasted exactly 32 seconds.[10]

For a moment spectators and ground crewmen either
stood in dumb wonder or fled for cover. The heat was
momentarily so intense that thermometers rose in the Navy
Aerological School 500 yards away.[11] Then ground crewmen
rushed to the wreckage to save what lives they could,
despairing of finding anyone alive. But strangely enough,
there were many survivors, some of them completely
uninjured. Three members of the Hindenburg's crew walked
out of the smoking wreckage, unharmed. An elderly woman
passenger calmly walked down what remained of the regular
hatchway to safety. A male passenger, who had jumped to
safety a moment before the ship crashed, was getting to his
feet when another passenger jumped squarely on his back,
injuring him severely. The fourteen-year-old cabin boy

---

[9]   C. E. Rosendahl, "The Last Flight," the final
chapter in Zeppelin: the Story of Lighter-than-Air Craft
(London and New York, 1937), p. 357. Earlier chapters
were written by Ernst Lehmann, who perished in the
Hindenburg crash, in collaboration with Leonard Adelt,
a surviving passenger. Zeppelin was translated into
English by Jay Dratler.

[10]   Time (May 17, 1937), 37. One of the reporters
carried a stop watch and timed the fire exactly.

[11]   Ibid., 36.

Reference 12 is not necessary. The story of the cabin boy's miraculous escape appeared in almost all the news accounts of the disaster. At first glance, reference 13 also appears unnecessary. It takes but a moment to see, however, that Miss Sheldon's real purpose here is to bring in Rosendahl's comment. Strictly speaking, she should have placed her 13 after "... death in the cabin," for that is the statement it explains. O'Laughlin's statement in footnote 13 is hardly justified. Rosendahl simply said it was unfortunate that passengers had gathered on the starboard side; he did not imply that they knew what was happening to them.

Reference 14 is puzzling. It implies that Adelt's article was the only one of Miss Sheldon's sources that gave the information. But this implication is simply not true. The incident was mentioned in most of the news accounts of the disaster. Reference 15 is also unnecessary. The heroic death of John Pannes was described in many news accounts.

The paragraph beginning on this page contains one sentence that belongs more properly in the preceding paragraph. The topic sentence of the former suggests that the paragraph will recite a list of fatalities. But the first instance given is that of Captain Pruss, who was rescued alive.

- 8 -

jumped through a hatch in the bottom of the ship; just
as the flames of the wreckage began to choke him, one of
the dirigible's water tanks directly above him let go and
drenched him. He emerged wringing wet but totally
unharmed.[12]

Many of the others were not so lucky. Some passengers
were burned to death in the cabin; others were killed when
they jumped.[13] The commander of the ship, Captain Max Pruss,
though severely burned, was rescued. Ernst Lehmann, the
airship expert, broke his back in jumping,[14] and though
brought out alive, died later in a hospital. John Pannes,
who could have jumped to safety, turned his back to the
escape window to search for his wife. He found her and
perished with her.[15] One man, burned black, walked away
from the wreckage, said "I'm all right," and then fell to

---

[12] What about the Airship?, pp. 8-9.

[13] Rosendahl, Zeppelin, p. 358, thinks more passengers would have been saved had not they been gathered on the
starboard side of the main cabin. The wind was blowing in
that direction and driving the flames directly onto the
passengers. But the passengers, according to Herbert
O'Laughlin, who was one of those who escaped, "never knew
what happened" until it was all over (New York Times,
May 7, 1938, p. 18).

[14] Leonhard Adelt, "Last Trip of the Hindenburg,"
Reader's Digest, XXXI (November, 1937), 72.

[15] What about the Airship?, p. 11.

Reference 16 is necessary, since *Time* was the only publication Miss Sheldon saw that carried this particular piece of information. Reference 17 is also necessary; the statement gives precise figures. Reference 18 documents, correctly, a direct quotation. Reference 19, on the other hand, is superfluous. Note that the reference is not used to document the statement—for which Miss Sheldon herself is the best authority—but to permit Miss Sheldon to make an additional, and unnecessary, comment. As a pictorial magazine, *Life* would be expected to devote many pages of pictures to such a sensational crash.

Reference 20 illustrates poor research technique. If Miss Sheldon wanted to include a statement by Dorothy Thompson, she should have gone directly to Miss Thompson's article. She has used a secondary source (*Time*) when a primary source (Miss Thompson's own article) was available in several newspapers. Reference 21 is technically correct, but the statement it documents does not follow logically from the topic sentence of the paragraph. Miss Sheldon has again sacrificed the unity of her paper in order to bring in a rather sensational bit of information.

- 9 -

the ground dead.[16] Of the 97 persons aboard, 35 perished

immediately or died of their wounds; of these, 13 were

passengers.[17]

So ended what _Time_ magazine called "the worst and

the most completely witnessed disaster in the history of

commercial aviation."[18] For weeks the public press

carried eye-witness stories and pictures of the crash.[19]

Columnists commented on the significance of the accident.

Dorothy Thompson spoke of the _Hindenburg_ as one of the symbols

of international peace: of its passing as the passing of an

era.[20] For the German Chancellor Adolf Hitler, the news

was a tremendous shock. When informed of the disaster, he

paced his room all night, unable to sleep.[21]

Investigation to determine the cause of the burning

centered chiefly on the combustible characteristics of

---

[16] _Time_ (May 17, 1937), 37.

[17] _What about the Airship?_, p. 10. Ordinarily the
crew totalled a few over 40, but unfortunately this trip
was a training cruise and the _Hindenburg_ carried about 20
extra men.

[18] _Time_ (May 17, 1937), 37.

[19] _Life_ (May 17, 1937), for example, devoted 5 pages
to pictures of the crash.

[20] _Time_ (May 17, 1937), 42.

[21] _Ibid._, p. 40.

Reference 22 illustrates competent research technique. Almost all of the publications Miss Sheldon consulted contain some information on the investigation of the *Hindenburg* disaster. But Rosendahl's account was the fullest and the most expert. He had ideal qualifications to speak as an authority: he was a recognized expert in airship construction; he saw the crash of the *Hindenburg;* and he was technical adviser to the board that investigated the crash.

The statement documented by reference 23, on the other hand, does not show clearly what Miss Sheldon thinks it does. The words of Lehmann, "I don't understand it, etc.," are not evidence in support of sabotage. They are simply the pathetic remarks of a man who was dying of injuries suffered in a crash whose cause he did not understand. The statement supported by reference 24, though vague and inconclusive, is more satisfactory. Rosendahl's statement, reference 25, is correctly documented, but inaccurate. Miss Sheldon has oversimplified Rosendahl's comments on the causes of the disaster; he spoke of an incendiary bullet as only one of many possible causes.

- 10 -

hydrogen, the gas with which the Hindenburg had been
inflated. A board of investigators finally decided, incon-
clusively, that one of the gas partitions sprang a leak,
that a spark ignited the gas, and that the extremely
combustible nature of hydrogen did the rest.[22] The investigators could only guess at what caused the spark. There was
talk for a while of sabotage. Captain Lehmann, as he was
carried off the field, repeated again and again "I don't
understand it, I don't understand it."[23] Just before he
died, he told Commander Rosendahl of the U. S. Navy that "it
must have been an infernal machine."[24] Rosendahl himself
thought that perhaps an incendiary bullet might have been
fired into the dirigible just before it landed.[25]

But the cause of the spark was never really determined. Airship experts attributed the disaster to the use
of hydrogen and not to a structural failure in the ship
itself. Some of them suggested that the real guilt rested
with the United States, which was too suspicious of

[22] What about the Airship?, p. 23.

[23] Time (May 17, 1937), 40.

[24] What about the Airship?, p. 28.

[25] Ibid., p. 24.

The paragraph that ends on this page does not focus clearly on any single point. It is a series of topic sentences no one of which is properly developed. Each of the final two sentences, for example, is tantalizingly brief. The reader would like supporting information for each statement.

Reference 26 is in good order. A number of airship experts made statements similar to Campbell's, and Miss Sheldon might have used any one of them. But Campbell's article, published a full year after the crash, represents a generalization of the attitudes of airship experts toward the *Hindenburg* crash. Miss Sheldon was wise to use such an article.

Reference 27 represents a very unscholarly use of source material. Miss Sheldon takes Teale's words and gives them an interpretation directly the reverse of what he intended. Teale's whole article is a refutation of the notion that the story of the dirigible is closed. Miss Sheldon, inadvertently or not, has misused her source.

Reference 28 illustrates how a footnote may be used for material that would be intrusive if placed in the text.

- 11 -

Germany's motives to relax its monopolistic control of
helium and had thereby forced Germany to use a dangerous
gas in the <u>Hindenburg</u>. They were also quick to point out
that this accident represented the first loss of life in
a commercial dirigible and should not therefore be taken
as proof of the danger of airship travel.[26]

But most people the world over accepted the crash
of the <u>Hindenburg</u> as bringing to a close the long and
tragic story of the dirigible.[27] In spite of the fact that
tens of thousands of people had traveled safely in airships,[28]
the commercial dirigible was in disrepute. Previous
airship disasters had been too widely publicized -- that of
the <u>Shenandoah</u> in 1925, the <u>Akron</u> in 1933, the <u>Macon</u> in 1935,

---

[26]   G. N. Campbell, "They Won't Stay Down,
<u>Collier's</u>, CI (May 28, 1938), 13.

[27]   Edwin Teale, "Can the Zepplin Come Back?"
<u>Popular Science</u>, CXXXII, No. 4 (April, 1938), 29.

[28]   Campbell, p. 13. See Allen, p. 38, who
commented ". . .the <u>Graf Zeppelin</u> and the <u>Hindenburg</u>,
in the years 1930-36, made a record of regularity
which no other vehicle of transportation has approached."
See also "Airship," <u>Ency. Brit.</u>, I, 471.
The <u>Graf Zeppelin</u>, at the time of its decommission in 1937,
had made 590 trips, had crossed the ocean 144 times, and
had carried 13,110 passengers over a total of 1,000,000
miles, all without a serious mishap.

Miss Sheldon was obviously in a hurry to conclude her paper. True, her major concern was to describe the crash, not to discuss its significance. But her final two paragraphs cover too much ground too rapidly.

- 12 -

to mention only the American ones.[29] That fact, coupled
with the ever-widening break between Germany -- the home
of the dirigible -- and the United States, was more than
the proponents of airship travel could overcome. The
Zeppelin was doomed, its place shortly to be taken over
completely by giant, ocean-spanning airplanes.

[29] "Airship," Ency. Brit., I, p. 73

Note first the heading, *References Consulted*. This is a more accurate heading than *Bibliography* or *Selective Bibliography*. The first would imply that Miss Sheldon's list of books and articles was exhaustive; the second that she was listing only those sources she thought most important. The heading *References Consulted*, on the other hand, indicates that the listing is neither full nor critical. It shows that Miss Sheldon has purposely limited herself to listing the source material she actually used in writing her paper.

Note that the items are arranged in alphabetical order and that each item is described more completely in the final bibliography than in the footnotes.

- 13 -

REFERENCES CONSULTED

Adelt, Leonhard. "Last Trip of the Hindenburg," Reader's
        Digest, XXXI (November, 1937), 69-72.

"Airship," Encyclopaedia Britannica, I (14th edition,
        1949), I 469-476.

Allen, Hugh. The Story of the Airship. Akron, Ohio:
        Goodyear Tire and Rubber Company, 1942.

Campbell, G. N. "They Won't Stay Down," Collier's, CI
        (May 28, 1938), 12-13.

Lehmann, Captain Ernst A. Zeppelin: The Story of Lighter-
        than-Air Craft. With collaboration of Leonhard
        Adelt, translated by Jay Dratler, preface and
        final chapter by Comdr. C. E. Rosendahl, U. S. N.
        London and New York: Longmans, Green and Co., 1937.

Life, II, No. 20 (May 17, 1937), 25-30.

New York Times, LXXXVI (issues May 3-10, 1937 inclusive).

"Oh, the Humanity!" Time, XXIX (May 17, 1937), 35-42.

Rosendahl, Comdr. C. E. What about the Airship? London
        and New York: Charles Scribner's Sons, 1938.

Teale, Edwin. "Can the Zeppelin Come Back?" Popular
        Science, CXXXII, No. 4 (April, 1938), 29-31.

Time, May 17, 1937.

Specimen Research Paper B.

Specimen Research Paper B concentrates on a single, closely defined problem. The writer describes an archeological "mystery," and reports on three theories concerning it. Although the paper is a good one in several respects, the following questions will guide you in reading it critically and determining how the material could have been presented better.

(1) Is the title precisely appropriate for this paper?

(2) The central statement in paragraph 1 is that the past culture of Easter Island was "far superior" to that of the present. This is the only mention of the present: is some information about it needed?

(3) In paragraph 2 the claim that the early islanders had unusual engineering skill is based in part on the statement that the statues, weighing ten to fifty tons, were transported a considerable distance. The *Columbia Encyclopedia* (2nd edition) gives the weight as five to eight tons, and the height as thirty to forty feet. Make a search for *all* the evidence about weight and height, and decide how this information should have been used in the paper.

(4) In paragraph 2 the material of the statues is described as "lava or tufa." Tufa has been defined as very light, porous, easily worked material. Find out if Easter Island stone is of this type. If it is, is the fact relevant to paragraph 2?

(5) The images are described by the writer as "heads." Is this description in accord with the quotation from Wolff?

(6) The crucial statement in paragraph 3 (second sentence) is that Easter Island was (is? does the tense make a difference?) "barren" and "isolated." The assumption of the theorists (which seems to be shared by the writer) is that because the island is barren and isolated the culture that produced the statues must have come from somewhere else. Examine the logic of this assumption. The *Columbia Encyclopedia* states that Easter Island has heavy rainfall, and that the natives raise potatoes, bananas, and sugar cane. Find and evaluate the evidence on this matter of fertility, and determine its relevance.

(7) In paragraphs 4, 5, and 6 the writer seems to give as much weight to native "traditions" (myths, legends, place names) as to geographical and geodetic evidence. He has obviously absorbed his respect for such tradition from the anthropological sources he has used, but has

failed to give his readers the ground for using tradition as evidence. Look up some such source as "Polynesian Mythology" in the Funk & Wagnalls *Standard Dictionary of Folklore, Mythology, and Legend* and write a footnote that might have been used in this paper to show how anthropologists make use of "tradition."

(8) Paragraph 7 refers to "symbolism as used in the art, statues, and script of the island." This is the writer's only allusion to art other than statues; and "script" presumably refers to the famous petroglyphs with which the monuments are decorated and which archeologists have never been able to decipher. Is some description of this art and script needed to support the claim of an advanced culture?

(9) "References Consulted." In a subject of this sort the expertness of the testimony cited is important. Using the bibliographical tools listed in section 45, especially those that will help you find authoritative reviews of books on anthropology, discover what you can about the competence of the writers cited.

(10) The latest reference given was published in 1948. Using the appropriate bibliographical tools, make a list of the more important subsequent studies of Easter Island.

Specimen Research Paper B

EASTER ISLAND, MYSTERY OF THE PACIFIC

(1) A present-day adventurer in the South Seas would have to
travel far off the main trade routes to reach Easter Island, the
mystery of the Pacific. This small, triangular Polynesian island,
located 1,400 miles east of Pitcairn and 2,000 miles west of
Chile, presents one of the most interesting problems in cultural
anthropology. Evidences remain today of a past culture far
superior to that of the natives now living on Easter Island. The
present inhabitants are the descendants of a race who carved at
least 550 huge lava statues, erecting some of them on masonry
platforms 200 to 300 feet long and thirty feet high. Modern
Easter Islanders know little about their ancestors, or how the
images were carved.

(2) The carving and transporting of the images show a degree
of artistic and engineering skill not often found among primitive
peoples. The great stone heads crowned with flat red hats standing
on Easter Island all seem to portray the same person or god, and
all exhibit similar workmanship. They range in size from ten to
over fifty tons, with characteristically jutting eyebrows, hollows
for eyes, pouting lips, and long ears. The heads were carved from
lava or tufa from a quarry in the crater of an extinct volcano,
Rano Raraku. Routledge in The Mystery of Easter Island describes
the carving of the images as follows:

> The face and anterior aspect of the statue
> were first carved, and the block became gradu-
> ally isolated as the material was removed in
> forming the head, base, and sides.... When
> the front and sides were completed down to
> every detail of the hands, the under-cutting
> commenced. The rock beneath was chipped away

- 2 -

by degrees till the statue rested only on
a narrow strip of stone running along the
spine.[1]

Some of the images are still in an unfinished state in the crater;

others are standing along the side of the volcano facing the sea;

and the third group has been moved in a way not yet determined

down the mountain to the shore, where they were placed on huge

masonry burial vaults called ahus. All of the statues which orig-

inally stood on the ahus have now fallen, perhaps from volcanic

eruptions, earthquakes, lack of care, or through willful destruction.

(3) Although it has been proved beyond a doubt where the

statues were made, and how they were carved, the mystery of who

made them remains. Many hypotheses have been offered which attempt

to explain how a few thousand people at most, living on a barren

island isolated from the rest of the world, could have developed

a culture capable of making the statues. One of the more romantic,

but unfounded, theories of the origin of the Easter Island culture

is the belief that the island is the last remains of a continent

which sank in the Pacific. This idea would explain very neatly

how the Polynesian culture could have spread over the Pacific area,

but unfortunately for those who believe in the legend of Mu, no

evidence of a sunken plateau can be found in that part of the

ocean. If Easter Island were raised until the ocean floor reached

sea level, the quarry would be 13,000 feet above sea level, and

the whole island would be snow covered.[2] The sea walls on the

------

[1] Quoted in Werner Wolff, Island of Death (New York, 1948), p. 155.
[2] Robert Casey, Easter Island (New York, 1931), p. 238.

- 3 -

shores of the island also indicate that the coastline is the same
as it was when the walls were erected.

(4) Another theory concerning the early inhabitants of
Easter Island states that the island is the last of a sunken archipelago from which the people originally came. Tales of islands
near Easter which have appeared and then disappeared, according to
early navigators in the area, seem to encourage this conjecture.
The native name for the island, Te Pito Te Henua, 'the navel of
the world,' indicates that those who named it believed the island
was surrounded by other lands. "Thus, tradition, legend, and the
observation of modern European sailors combine to indicate Easter
Island as the center of an archipelagic world that surrounded it
at various distances."[3]

(5) Not all of those who have studied Easter Island hold
this theory, however. The lack of native tradition concerning
the sinking of the archipelago, and the chart of the depth of the
Pacific Ocean again seem to make it questionable.[4]

(6) The theory which most conforms with the geography and
traditions of Easter Island, and is most widely accepted among
anthropologists, explains the migration of the Polynesians across
the Pacific by boat. Evidences of similarities in the cultures
of the Maoris of New Zealand, the Tahitians, the Easter Islanders,

- - - - -

[3]J. M. Brown, The Riddle of the Pacific (Boston, 1924), p. 45.

[4]Casey, p. 239.

- 4 -

and the Peruvians suggest a relationship exists among the groups.
Traditions of the long voyages taken by the Polynesians in the
Pacific with only the stars to guide them also support this
hypothesis. According to Easter Island legends, the first king
and founder of the culture, Hotu Matua, came from the Southwest
with his followers in long canoes. One investigator places this
migration at about 850 A.D.[5] Since the statues which have been
found all seem to be the work of experienced carvers, many
anthropologists believe that the images were carved during the
time of Hotu Matua by sculptors who had come with him. Recently
the age of the statues has been placed at not more than 800 years,
because of their well-preserved condition.[6] This estimate would
suggest a later migration than 850. While the date of the migration is not definitely established, most anthropologists believe
that one did take place.

The question of who built the statues on Easter Island is
still not satisfactorily answered. Until much more is learned
about migrations in the Pacific, symbolism as used in the art,
statues, and script of the island, and the early history of the
culture, Easter Island will remain the unsolved mystery of the
Pacific.

- - - - -

[5]Wolff, p. 15.

[6]"New Light on Easter Island Mystery," Science Digest, XIX
(April, 1946), 32.

REFERENCES CONSULTED

Braunholtz, H. J. "Easter Island," Encyclopedia Britannica, 14th ed., VII, 860-1.

Brown, J. M. The Riddle of the Pacific. Boston: Small, Maynard & Co., 1924.

Casey, R. J. Easter Island, Home of the Scornful Gods. New York: Blue Ribbon Books, Inc., 1931.

"Easter Island Relics Only a Few Centures Old," Science News Letter, XLIX (Feb. 9, 1946), 83.

Metraux, Alfred. "Easter Island," Encyclopedia Britannica, 14th ed. IX, 508-9.

Ethnology of Easter Island. Honolulu, Hawaii: The Museum, 1940.

"New Light on Easter Island Mystery," Science Digest, XIX (April, 1946), 32.

Wolff, Werner. Island of Death. New York: J. J. Augustin, 1948.

Writing Summaries

The formal summary or précis (pronounced pray-sée) has had a long history as a useful technique for condensing material. During the reign of Queen Anne (1702-1714) English diplomats began the practice of having their undersecretaries condense long documents in order to simplify the conduct of daily business. As a result précis-writing was established as a formal tradition in English diplomacy.

Naturally, we are not concerned here with training English diplomats, but over the years the effective summary has proved itself an extremely useful tool to many people—and particularly to college students. Often during your years in college you will need to reduce

47

chapters of books to short, manageable statements for purposes of review and study.

Literally, the word précis means "cut down" or "trimmed"; making a précis is very much like trimming a bush down to its trunk and main branches: beauty of style, illustration, and detailed explanation are all eliminated, leaving the gist of the material unadorned. Unlike a restatement or a paraphrase, a précis retains the original author's thought and approach, sometimes in his own words. The writer of a précis speaks in the author's voice—it is never necessary to say, "in this paragraph the author says. . . ." Rather you simply proceed with your condensation of his actual words.

Practice in preparing summaries will also help you to read with greater accuracy and to write with greater conciseness and directness. You cannot summarize effectively if you have not read carefully, discriminating between principal and subordinate ideas. Such discrimination, in turn, will help you to sharpen your own style and to avoid the prolixity that creeps into careless writing.

Procedure.

Before you try to summarize a passage, read it carefully to discover the author's purpose and his point of view. As you read, pick out his central ideas and notice how he arranges them. Be on the lookout for the author's own compact summaries, either at the beginning or end of a passage or at points of transition.

After studying the passage, you are ready to organize your summary. Ordinarily you will be able to reduce a paragraph—or sometimes a whole group of paragraphs—to a single sentence. Very complex paragraphs, however, may require more than one sentence.

Use a simple or complex sentence (Section 50) rather than a compound sentence to summarize a paragraph—unless the original paragraph itself is poorly organized. A compound sentence implies that there are two or more equally dominant ideas in the paragraph. If you find that you have written a compound summarizing sentence, re-check the paragraph to make sure that the author did not imply some subordinating relationship that you have missed. In determining the author's intent, be alert to such writing techniques as parallel clauses and phrases, which indicate ideas of equal weight, and transitional words and phrases, which show relationships among ideas.

Summarize the author's ideas in the order in which he has presented them, but avoid following his wording too closely. If you are overly scrupulous in trying to preserve the "flavor" of the original, you will find that your summary will be far too long. Do not hesitate, however, to pick up the author's key terms and phrases, for they are useful in binding the précis together. Discard any figures of speech, digressions, or discussions that are not essential to the "trunk and main branches." When you are all through, you should find that you have reduced the material to not over one-third of its original length.

Example.

> We very rarely consider, however, the process by which we gained our convictions. If we did so, we could hardly fail to see that there was usually little ground for our confidence in them. Here and there, in this department of knowledge or that, some one of us might make a fair claim to have taken some trouble to get correct ideas of, let us say, the situation in Russia, the sources of our food supply, the origin of the Constitution, the revision of the tariff, the policy of the Holy Roman Apostolic Church, modern business organization, trade unions, birth control, socialism, the League of Nations, the excess-profits tax, preparedness, advertising in its social bearings; but only a very exceptional person would be entitled to opinions on all of even these few matters. And yet most of us have opinions on all these, and on many other questions of equal importance, of which we may know even less. We feel compelled, as self-respecting persons, to take sides when they come up for discussion. We even surprise ourselves by our omniscience. Without taking thought we see in a flash that it is most righteous and expedient to discourage birth control by legislative enactment, or that one who decries intervention in Mexico is clearly wrong, or that big advertising is essential to big business and that big business is the pride of the land. As godlike beings why should we not rejoice in our omniscience?
>
> —JAMES HARVEY ROBINSON, *The Mind in the Making*

Notice that this paragraph hinges on the sentence beginning "And yet most of us have opinions on all these. . . ." This sentence suggests the pattern that your summarizing sentence should probably take. The central idea of the paragraph is that we do not ordinarily take pains in forming our convictions on important matters, *but* we nevertheless express our opinions as a matter of right and even take delight in our apparent omniscience. The main clause of your summarizing sentence will express the second part of the central idea, retaining the author's ironic approach.

> We are godlike beings who delight in our ability to form and express convictions on birth control, on intervention in Mexico, or on the role of big business, without a moment's thought.

To preserve the author's qualification in the first part of the paragraph, however, you must precede the main clause with a subordinate clause.

> Although the few pains we take to understand such things as the situation in Russia, the sources of our food supply, the origin of the Constitution, the revision of the tariff, the policy of the Holy Roman Apostolic Church, modern business organization, trade unions, birth control, socialism, the League of Nations, the excess profits tax, preparedness, and advertising in its social bearings give us little reason to have confidence in our opinions on these matters, we are godlike beings who delight in our ability to form and express convictions on birth control, on intervention in Mexico or on the role of big business, without a moment's thought.

But this "summary" is almost half as long as the original. To reduce it further, replace the specific examples with general terms.

> Although the few pains we take to understand such things as social, political, economic, religious and medical issues give us little reason to have confidence in our convictions on these matters, we are godlike beings who delight in our ability to form and express such convictions without a moment's thought.

This summary, less than one-third the length of the original, would be acceptable for most purposes. But occasionally even a shorter summary is desirable.

> Although we have little reason to trust our convictions on the important issues of life, we delight in forming and expressing such opinions without a moment's thought.

Clearly this last sentence does not express everything in Robinson's paragraph, where the concreteness and the vigor of the short sentences are perhaps even more striking than its central thought. But a summary is concerned only with the central thought, not necessarily with retaining the author's style, and the central thought is preserved even in the shortest statement above.

EXERCISE 1. Write a two-sentence précis of the paragraph beginning "Speech and language have contrasting advantages ..." on page 242.

EXERCISE 2. Write a one-sentence précis of the same paragraph.

EXERCISE 3. Try to write a one-sentence précis of the following paragraph. Does the effort tell you anything about the weakness of the paragraph itself?

Among the many interesting aspects of dietary training is the living together of the students. This allows each to get acquainted with people from all over the States and to exchange ideas and viewpoints from different sections of the country. By living in such a home, many girls grow into more mature individuals. It proves a good chance for girls who have always lived at home to become more independent. It also helps to establish feelings of self-sufficiency in those who have never before been on their own.

EXERCISE 4. Write the briefest précis you can of the following paragraph.

Great care and attention is given in the organisation of pageants and other popular feasts, and of these a Russian crowd is particularly appreciative, throwing itself wholeheartedly into the enjoyment of every detail. The "crowd sense," which is just another expression of the corporate instinct, is peculiarly strong in Russia, and it is often curiously reminiscent of an English crowd, particularly in its broad and jolly sense of humor. But Russians of any class have a much stronger artistic sense than we have. This was so before the revolution, and it comes out in the organisation of these festivals. They are all out to enjoy themselves, and anything particularly clever or pretty gets them at once. In Kiev, still as always a beautiful city on its lovely site, in the late summer of 1936, I saw a march past of all the wards in turn. They swung past with splendid vigour, squads of men or of women—one squad of women had in the middle of it a fine old man with a long beard who looked very pleased with his company. There were flowers and dancing everywhere; each ward was preceded by a dancing band of girl skirmishers in the picturesque Ukrainian costume, sometimes singing the charming Ukrainian folk songs. At one point various forms of recreation and amusement were represented: the fishermen carrying long fishing rods with coloured paper fish hooped to them, the chess players carrying enormous cardboard knights, bishops and castles. Interspersed between the detachments came curious and fanciful constructions, sometimes very ingenious; an effigy of Trotsky with long nose and black eyes and curls made an excellent Mephistopheles. It was a family feast of old and young, and we all exchanged our comments as each new surprise went past. With the usual courtesy to guests there was a chair set for me, and when I wanted to let a lady have it, I was genially told "that I had to submit to the will of the majority." At one time a torrent of rain came down, but the marchers swung past with all the more vigour and enjoyment. And so it was with the onlookers. After several hours of it, I asked a neighbouring policeman whether I couldn't go away: "No," he said very nicely, "you must stay and enjoy it." And enjoy it they certainly did, for in spite of more downpours of rain, from my room in my hotel I could hear them singing and dancing on the square outside till two in the morning. The one thing that fell below the level of all the rest was the exhausting reiteration of the portraits of Stalin and the other "big noises" of Communism. There must have been about forty of Stalin alone: one ten foot high, of the face alone. I noticed a sympathetic cheer when there came past a single portrait of Lenin.

—BERNARD PARES, *Russia: Its Past and Present*

Mend your speech a little,
Lest you may mar your fortunes.
—WILLIAM SHAKESPEARE

SECTION **48**

Business and Social Correspondence

BUSINESS LETTERS

Business letters are cast in forms that emphasize clarity, neatness, and symmetry. They are usually typewritten on letter paper 8½ by 11 inches in size; the letter is folded twice across to fit a long envelope; or folded once across and twice in the other direction to fit a small envelope.

Although the style used in business letters varies greatly in its degree of formality, the tendency in most modern business firms is

479

to avoid the clichés that once made business English seem quite different from ordinary English (*Yrs. of 4th inst., Your esteemed favor, I beg to inform,* etc.). Now, the successful writer of business letters, like any other successful writer, uses a language that is appropriate to his reader. He is direct and exact. Realizing that he will be judged by his letter, he is particularly careful about his punctuation, grammar, and spelling.

Parts of the business letter.

The six parts of a business letter are as follows:

1. The Heading
2. The Inside Address
3. The Salutation
4. The Body of the Letter
5. The Complimentary Close
6. The Signature

(1) *The Heading.* Included in the heading are the writer's full address and the date of the letter. The heading is (1) blocked with open punctuation, or (2) indented with open punctuation, or (3) indented with closed punctuation. Though all three methods are correct, (1) is most commonly used.,

Blocked, with open punctuation:	617 Lake Street Tucson, Arizona April 7, 1960
Indented, with open punctuation:	617 Lake Street Tucson, Arizona April 7, 1960
Indented, with closed punctuation:	617 Lake Street, Tucson, Arizona, April 7, 1960.

If the paper has a letterhead carrying your address, type the date directly under the letterhead or flush with the right-hand margin.

(2) *The Inside Address.* The inside address gives the name and full address of the person written to. Personal titles, as Mr., Mrs., Messrs., Dr., may be used before the name of the person addressed. Use the form Mr. James C. Smith or Mr. James Smith, or Mr. J. C. Smith; never use the form Mr. Smith or Mr. Jas. Smith. Use either

the blocked or the indented form, depending on which form you used in the heading. But whatever your choice, be consistent throughout the letter. Type the first line of the inside address flush with the left-hand margin.

Blocked, with open punctuation:

```
Mr. J. C. Smith
School of Veterinary Medicine
Michigan State University
East Lansing, Michigan
```

Indented, with open punctuation:

```
Mr. J. C. Smith
   School of Veterinary Medicine
      Michigan State University
         East Lansing, Michigan
```

Indented, with closed punctuation:

```
Mr. J. C. Smith,
   School of Veterinary Medicine,
      Michigan State University,
         East Lansing, Michigan.
```

(3) *The Salutation. Dear Sir:, Dear Mr. Howe:,* or *Gentlemen:* is the usual business salutation. If you are addressing a woman, use the forms *Dear Madame:, Dear Miss (or Mrs.) Walker:,* or *Mesdames:. My dear Sir: (or Madame:), My dear Mr. (or Mrs.) Kane:, Sir:,* or *Madam:* are more formal salutations. When you are in doubt about the sex or rank of your addressee, you may safely use *Dear Sir:.*

Type the salutation flush with the left-hand margin and use a colon after it. The comma after the salutation appears only in business letters of the most informal kind.

(4) *The Body of the Letter.* Most business letters are single-spaced with double spaces between paragraphs; only very short letters are double-spaced throughout. Keep all paragraph indentations equal. General practice indents the first sentence of each paragraph five spaces from the left-hand margin. However, if you use the block form, you may make the first sentence of each para-

graph flush with the left-hand margin. Indentation is not logically necessary, for the spacing between paragraphs sets them off sufficiently.

In writing business letters, observe the principles of good writing: unity and clarity. Avoid cumbersome clichés and unconventional abbreviations, and express facts and opinions in simple, direct English. Above all, remember the importance of *proofreading* and (if necessary) of revising: Have you made any careless mistakes in grammar or spelling? Any omissions of essential information? Have you said exactly what you meant to say? Will the form and neatness of the letter make a good impression?

(5) *The Complimentary Close.* It is customary to close a business letter with one of several courteous phrases. The most common are *Yours truly, Very truly yours,* and *Yours very truly.* More formal, and used only in appropriate circumstances, are *Respectfully yours* and *Yours respectfully.* Informal business letters, such as those addressed to friends or acquaintances, often close with *Sincerely yours, Yours sincerely, Cordially yours, Faithfully yours,* or simply *Yours.*

Capitalize the first word of the complimentary close, and put a comma after the entire phrase. Type the complimentary close two spaces below the body of the letter, beginning near the center of the page or flush with the left margin.

(6) *The Signature.* Write your signature with pen and ink and type your name below it. Do not use professional titles or academic degrees with a signature. A married woman signs her own given names rather than her husband's: *Mary Jane Hale,* not *Mrs. John D. Hale.* The following signature is also appropriate:

Mary Jane Hale
(Mrs. John D.)

Specimen Letter.

The following letter of application shows the form of a typical business letter. The address on the envelope should follow the pattern of the inside address. The return address should appear in block form in the upper left-hand corner.

100 Corbin Street
Mackton, Indiana
May 27, 1960

Mr. J. R. Darwin
The Calvinsville Courier
212 Holmes Street
Calvinsville, Indiana

Dear Mr. Darwin:

Please consider me an applicant for the position which
you have recently advertised, that of news reporter for
the Courier.

In June I will graduate from the Journalism School of
Holton College. You will find enclosed a transcript of
my academic record.

I am twenty-two years old and unmarried. Last summer I
worked for the Hillton Times, which is owned and published
by Mr. R. I. Dana. While employed by the Times, I worked
at a variety of jobs, including reporting, copy reading,
and feature writing. I feel that this experience has
helped to qualify me for a position with your newspaper.

Further information about my academic record can be obtained from Professor D. O. Homer, Head of the Journalism
School, Holton College. Mr. Dana will gladly write you
about my practical work with his newspaper.

If I qualify for the position with the Courier, and if you
will let me know when it will be convenient for you to see
me, I will be glad to come to Calvinsville for an interview.

Very truly yours,

Roger Preston

Roger Preston

PERSONAL LETTERS

The form of a personal letter is similar to that of a business letter. It is simply more relaxed. Personal letters often omit the inside address, and follow the salutation with a comma instead of a colon. A great variety of phrases may be used for the complimentary close, depending on the intimacy of the correspondents. The effect of a personal letter depends largely on the personality of the writer and his ability to write interestingly. A simple, cordial, informal style is a part of that ability.

Following is a specimen personal letter, a "bread-and-butter" note.

207 Lilac Road
Martin, Wisconsin
August 24, 1960

Dear Mr. and Mrs. Bell,

Since my arrival home on Tuesday I have thought many times of my pleasant stay with you last weekend. It was certainly considerate of you to take me in, because I know my sudden appearance with your son Dick must have caused you some inconveniences.

Here at home I found everyone well and very busy. In one way, I arrived at a bad time. Mother was canning tomatoes — bushels of them — and immediately put me to work in the assembly line. However, that job is nearly finished, and in another day or two I'll have plenty of time to do some of the things I want to do before school starts.

Cordially, yours,
Jim Rust

SOCIAL NOTES

Formal social notes follow established patterns of form and style. They are usually engraved or handwritten rather than typed. They are written from the point of view of the impersonal third person. Abbreviations are not used, except for *Mr., Mrs., Dr.* and *R.S.V.P.* (*please reply*). Numbers, except street numbers, are written out. Here is a specimen invitation:

> Mr. and Mrs. John Peele request the pleasure of Mr. and Mrs. Henry Tyler's company at dinner on Thursday, May the eleventh, at eight o'clock.
>
> 931 King Road
> May the fourth

Acceptances and regrets repeat the details of the invitation, including the date and hour.

> Mr. and Mrs. Henry Tyler accept with pleasure the kind invitation of Mr. and Mrs. John Peele to dinner on Thursday, May the eleventh, at eight o'clock.
>
> 323 Oakhurst Drive
> May the fifth

> Mr. and Mrs. Henry Tyler regret that another engagement prevents their acceptance of Mr. and Mrs. John Peele's kind invitation to dinner on Thursday, May the eleventh, at eight o'clock.
>
> 323 Oakhurst Drive
> May the fifth

Informal invitations are written in a simple, friendly style. There are, of course, various degrees of informality, as the following examples illustrate.

Dear Mrs Trent,

My husband and I are giving an informal dinner at home on Thursday, May the eleventh, at seven o'clock. We shall be pleased if you can come.

Sincerely yours,
Helen Carson
(Mrs J. S.)

101 Kay Street
May fourth

---

101 Kay Street
May 4, 1950

Dear Jane,

George and I are having a few friends in for dinner on Thursday evening, May 11, at seven. We hope you can come.

Sincerely,
Helen

Supplementary Exercises

The eight one-page papers that follow are specimens of writing done in freshman English classes. Analyze them on the basis of the following questions.

General organization (Section 31)

1. Does the title fit the discussion?
2. Is the material organized into distinct sections?
3. Are these sections arranged in logical order? (Is there an orderly sequence of thought from one section to the next and from the beginning to the end of the paper?)
4. Is all the material relevant to the central purpose of the paper?
5. Is the beginning direct and pertinent?
6. Does the ending of the paper give an impression of finality and completeness?

Paragraphing (Section 32)

1. Does each paragraph have a clearly stated or implied purpose? (Sections 32a, 32b, "Paragraph Unity")

2. Is each paragraph coherent? (Does each sentence proceed logically and clearly from the preceding one to the one that follows? (Sections 32c, 32d, "Paragraph Coherence")

3. Is the idea of each paragraph developed sufficiently? (Section 32e, "Paragraph Development")

Sentence structure (Sections 10-18; 33-36); **Logic** (Section 37)

1. Are less important ideas in the sentences clearly subordinated to the principal one? (Section 33a, 33b, "Subordination")

2. Does unnecessary detail obscure the main thought of any sentence? (Section 33d, "Subordination")

3. Are the parts of each sentence arranged in a natural, clear order? (Section 15, "Misplaced Parts"; Section 16, "Dangling Constructions")

4. Do pronouns refer clearly to their antecedents? (Section 13, "Reference of Pronouns")

5. Is the grammatical point of view established in the opening sentences of the paper maintained consistently? Are the lapses justifiable? (Section 14, "Shifts and Mixed Constructions")

6. Is the sentence pattern monotonous? Does the writer know how to vary short emphatic sentences with longer, more complex ones? (Section 36, "Emphasis"; Section 34, "Variety")

Word choice (Sections 39-43)

1. Does the word choice seem precise? Does the writer seem able to find the word that expresses his meaning exactly? (Section 40, "Exactness")

2. Is the writer's use of words economical? Does he express his meaning quickly and cleanly? (Section 41, "Directness")

3. Does the writer use standard English terms? Is his choice of words appropriate for the tone and subject matter of his paper? (Section 42, "Appropriateness")

Grammar (Sections 5-18)

1. Are there any clumsy, incomplete sentences? (Section 10a, "Sentence Fragment")

2. Is there any confusion in the use of adjectives and adverbs? (Section 8, "Adjectives and Adverbs")

3. Is there any violation of agreement of subject and verb, of pronoun and antecedent? (Section 12, "Agreement")

Specimen Paper 7

THE CONSTRUCTION OF A MODEL AIRPLANE

The first thing to do is to obtain the proper model kit. If you have not had previous experience with these kits, the best model for you is the R.O.G. If you have built models before and know what you can do, you can choose from a large assortment ranging from radio-controlled models to microfilm floaters.

When you are ready to assemble the kit, you should clear a table of all but the necessary equipment. Take all parts from the box. You should read the instructions at least twice before starting to work on the model. Follow the instructions step by step. Always allow sufficient time for the glue to dry before adding another part. If the model is supposed to be light, go easy on the glue. If you are trying to make a strong and sturdy model, be quite free in the use of type B glue.

After you have completed the basic inner frame, you may find it difficult to apply the covering tissue properly. For curved surfaces, use small pieces of tissue so that you can avoid wrinkles in the surface. When you have finished covering the model, water should be sprinkled on the tissue quite liberally. This will give a tight fit.

The last and most interesting phase is the painting and decorating phase. This applies only to the heavier models. Ordinarily two clear base coats should be applied before the two coats of color paint. It is best to use sandpaper after each coat except on the outside one. In order to keep your paint brushes pliable, clean them thoroughly after each job. Use scotch tape as masking tape. Various decorations can be applied by using decals made and sold especially for the purpose.

Specimen Paper 8

MY FIRST JOB

One summer day, when I was eleven years old, I was sitting on the
front porch in deep thought, dreaming about the paper route I hoped to
acquire. Suddenly I was brought to my senses by a truck stopping in the
driveway. He had arrived, the route man whom I had been waiting for
anxiously. He had offered me the job a couple days before, and when I
told him I needed my father's approval, he said he would speak to him
in a couple days. He walked up on the porch, asked for my father, and I
knew that in a few minutes I would know the result.

Inviting the route man in, and introducing him to my father,
I waited anxiously while they talked. My father wanted to know how
heavy the papers were, what sort of district I would have, whether I
would have to cross a lot of busy intersections. Finally my father
gave his approval, and I was thrilled that the route was mine.

Before departing, the route man gave me a few final instructions
and wished me luck. It was Saturday and I wouldn't start my deliveries
until Monday. It seemed as though that day was very far off. But before
I knew it, Monday had arrived.

The first thought that entered my mind upon rising Monday was my
newspapers. I dashed downstairs and there were the newspapers on the
front porch. I carried them inside, counted them, and then went in
to eat with great speed, for which my mother scolded me, although
in an understanding way.

After eating breakfast, I bid farewell to my parents, loaded the
newspapers on my wagon and very proudly started out on my first job,
an experience that I will always remember.

Specimen Paper 9

THE BIG SNOW

Let it snow, let it snow, let it snow. This was the theme song of Brookville residents last weekend. For the first time since 1935, Brookville had sixteen inches of snow. The big snow hit Friday afternoon and continued to fall for three days. Stores closed, transportation came to a standstill, garage owners had nervous breakdowns, citizens pleaded with hardware dealers to sell them snow shovels and tire chains.

No one, looking at stalled cars practically covered with snow, could help remarking that grandfather's mode of transportation was the best and safest after all. Grandfather could really depend on old Dobbin to get him from one place to the next. A slippery road only makes a sleigh more efficient than ever.

But today a heavy snow is a paralyzing thing. People can't get to work without walking, and walking means a trip of two to five miles, for people now live far from their place of employment. And stores can't open because clerks can't get to work. Food and milk supplies run short. The farmer can get the milk out of the cow but he can't get it to the dairy.

In Brookville most people stayed in their homes and listened all day to radio accounts of the storm. They shoveled their driveways and waited for one of the town's half-dozen snowplows to begin plowing their own particular street. When the driveways and streets were cleared, people got out their cars and got stuck in slippery spots. The man who depended on an automobile was one mass of solid frustration for three days.

Specimen Paper 10

PROBLEMS OF A COMMERCIAL FISHERMAN

The first thing that anyone who starts in commercial fishing needs is a boat. Just any boat will not do, it must be seaworthy and have a powerful motor. A new boat that fits this description costs in the neighborhood of seven thousand dollars. There are many boat builders around Lake Erie who build nothing but this kind of boat.

Next in importance to the commercial fisherman is his nets. The average trap net costs about one thousand dollars; a fisherman needs about sixteen. It would not be profitable to start commercial fishing with less than this amount. The fisherman works on the law of average. He places his nets here and there, hoping that he will get a good catch in a few of them at least.

After you have the boat and the nets, you have to know where the fish are feeding. This knowledge is really gained only through years of working around the lake on fish boats. The hardest part is learning where the fish are during the different seasons of the year.

The worst thing about commercial fishing is the weather in which you must work. In the spring the cold rains numb your hands, and in the winter the cold winds chill you to the bone. But you are forced to go out on the lake even in the roughest weather, for you must check your nets constantly. Your investment is too great to be neglected.

So you can see that commercial fishing is not a business for fly-by-night promoters and tenderfeet. Commercial fishing requires a large capital investment and a rugged constitution. Above all, it requires "know-how" -- an attitude compounded largely of a willingness to work, courage, and patience.

Specimen Paper 11

MY IDEA OF INTELLIGENT READING

Intelligent reading is a very important medium by which a person may educate himself and be well informed. Students, professional people, laborers, and people in all walks of life find intelligent reading to be a great asset. Intelligent reading is a way of getting an education, and if a person cannot afford a conventional kind of education he can always educate himself by intelligent reading.

But what is intelligent reading? It means the kind of reading that forces a person to think. Intelligent reading is not just reading for fun. People who want to educate themselves by reading should select their materials carefully. They should select something that interests them, about which they wish to know more.

When a person has selected the right material, he should make himself comfortable. This means a comfortable chair and a good reading light. If the book is his own, he should read with a pencil in his hand, marking in the margin of the page or underscoring the important parts. He should make sure that he understands where the writer is taking him. When he begins to tire, he should stop reading, for that is a sign that his mind is tired and unable to absorb any more information.

The habit of reading a little each day is a good one. It provides a pattern and a direction, and a person who gets himself into such a habit will be surprised at the end of a year how much he has learned, how different he is intellectually from what he was before. He will know a great many more words and he will also know much more language in general. For he has exposed himself to a liberal education, and the effects of that exposure are more telling on him than he thought possible.

Specimen Paper 12

WOMEN DRIVERS

The other day as I was driving along Green Street I happened to get behind a woman driver. I followed her for a few blocks and since the traffic was heavy that day I could not pass her. There I was stuck behind her with the worst yet to come. Then I noticed that her turn signal was on for a right turn and her arm was out for a left turn. I didn't know what she was going to do. As I approached the corner, I waited to see what her next move would be; she went straight ahead. I guess she was drying her nail polish and conducting calisthenics for her turn signal at the same time.

Another incident, rather accident, that I happened to observe was when an aunt of a friend of mine was trying to back out of a parking space. She was parked with the front bumper against the curb rather than in the legal way for this town with the side of the car to the curb. The car had a hydromatic transmission, and when the lady pulled down the gearshift lever for reverse she was looking backwards and didn't notice that the lever stopped at low instead of at reverse. She then tramped on the accelerator, and the car went bounding up over the curb, knocking over a parking meter and smashing into the side of the adjoining bank building. What a way to rob a bank!

Now I realize that these are only two incidents to illustrate my thesis, but they are so typical and there are so many others that I could give, that I think they will suffice. A woman behind the wheel of an automobile is not to be trusted, not merely because she doesn't have the proper awareness of the mechanical monster she is sitting in, but also because she won't pay attention to what she's doing.

Specimen Paper 13

TELEVISION

Television is a great threat to the future intelligence of the
American public. In the last few years television has become one of the
most time-consuming pastimes of many people. Those who have sets use
most of the time they previously spent on hobbies, reading, and in
friendly conversation watching television. The programs they watch are:
wrestling show, cheap vaudeville acts, and many programs that represent
the lowest form of entertainment.

Television has put an end to many of the friendly visits that people
once made to see one another. Even if one does go to visit a friend now,
he must sit silent watching a twenty-year-old movie or some other program
just as unenlightening. No more do people talk about politics, the
state of the world, or the latest happenings around town. Instead they
laugh together at some foolish comedian or wear themselves out watching
one man twist another man's arms, or something just as meaningless.

One can read or at least look at the pictures in a magazine while he
is listening to radio, but he cannot do so while watching television. Also
to watch television is hard on the eyes. TV manufacturers may not admit
this, but they are constantly experimenting to develop a tube which is
not so hard on the eyes. This may have little effect on the present
generation, but it may harm the eyes of our children and ultimately affect
their ability to read. People who do not read can never make an intelligent, informed public.

The increasing popularity of television is discouraging reading and
intellectual conversation, and it is affecting the coming generation
greatly. If this trend continues and the quality of the programs does
not improve, television -- a great step forward in science -- can do
the American people more harm than good.

Specimen Paper 14

SUCCESS IN THE MODERN WORLD

Have you ever stopped to think about yourself? To think about what you, as an individual, are fitted for and will be able to do as your occupation in later life? Surely at one time or another everyone has and at that time charts his course in life. Every course of life has a destination, some higher than others, but still a definite goal to work and strive to reach. As you and I charted this course and the many steps along the way, doubtless one major step was education. Why is this? Why is education such a major step?

The major portion of our education is acquired in the period from childhood to manhood. Its' purpose is to help make a place for every individual in life. By this, I mean to reach the goal of the individual.

Let us take my own case, as a young child I wanted to be a policeman, then a fireman, then a truck driver. When I matured I set my goal, I decided I would like to work in the field of radio, however if I did not attain that goal I will not consider myself a failure. If I am success-ful in another field, I will be happy. Here I believe we come to the key word of human life, Success.

There are many kinds of success; business, financial, social and many others. A well rounded education paves the way for success, no matter what the type.

Many people ridicule modern education, however I believed that as the modern world is modernized, so much education be modernized. Quoting a contemporary businessman we find "Many of my former college mates are in fields of activity which did not exist twenty years ago." So as the world improves and progresses, education must do likewise.

In conclusions, I think it is safe to say that education is the key to success; and to be a success in the modern world the individual must possess a modern education.

An Index
to Grammatical Terms

This index gives brief definitions of common grammatical terms. Refer to specific sections of the handbook for fuller discussions.

Absolute. An expression that is grammatically independent of the rest of the sentence. An absolute phrase, usually consisting of a noun followed by a participle, is often called the *nominative absolute.*

> *The hour being late,* we hurried home.
> *The job finished,* we put away our tools.

Adjective. A word used to describe or limit the meaning of a noun or pronoun. *Descriptive adjectives* name some quality of an object: *white* house, *small* child, *leaking* faucet. *Limiting adjectives* restrict the meaning of a noun to a particular object or indicate quantity or number. There are five kinds of limiting adjective:

POSSESSIVE	*my* suit, *their* yard
DEMONSTRATIVE	*this* carriage, *those* people
INTERROGATIVE	*whose* cat? *which* boy?
ARTICLES	*a* picture, *an* egg, *the* book
NUMERICAL	*one* day, *second* inning

(*See also* Section 8, "Adjectives and Adverbs.")

Adjective Clause. A subordinate, or dependent, clause used as an adjective.

> The man *who lives here* is an Irishman. (The adjective clause modifies the noun *man.*)
>
> Dogs *that chase cars* seldom grow old. (The adjective clause modifies the noun *dogs.*)

Adverb. A word used to describe or limit the meaning of a verb, an adjective, or another adverb. Classified by meaning, adverbs may indicate:

PLACE	Put the cat *outside.* (Outside *modifies* the verb *put.*)
TIME	He was *never* healthy. (*Never* modifies the adjective *healthy.*)
MANNER	She was *secretly* envious. (*Secretly* modifies the adjective *envious.*)
DEGREE	I was *quite* easily angered. (*Quite* modifies the adverb *easily.*)

(*See also* Section 8, "Adjectives and Adverbs.")

Adverb Clause. A subordinate, or dependent, clause used as an adverb.

> *When you leave,* please close the door. (The adverb clause, indicating time, modifies the verb *close.*)
>
> The sheep grazed *where the grass was greenest.* (The adverb clause, indicating place, modifies the verb *grazed.* Adverb clauses also indicate manner, purpose, cause, result, condition, concession, and comparison.)

Adverbial Objective. A noun used adverbially.

> We walked *home.* I ran a *mile.*

Agreement. Correspondence in person and number between a subject and verb; in person, number, and gender between a pronoun and its antecedent; and in number between a demonstrative adjective and its noun. (*See also* Section 12, "Agreement.")

Antecedent. A word or group of words for which a pronoun stands.

> She is a *woman who* seldom complains. (*Woman* is the antecedent of the pronoun *who*.)
>
> *Uncle Henry* came for a brief visit, but *he* stayed all winter. (*Uncle Henry* is the antecedent of the pronoun *he*.)

Appositive. A substantive (a word or group of words used as a noun) placed beside another substantive and denoting the same person or thing.

> *John*, my younger *brother*, is visiting in *Albany*, the state *capital*. (*Brother* is in apposition with *John*, and *capital* is in apposition with *Albany*.)

Most appositives are *nonrestrictives* (*i.e.*, not essential to the basic meaning of the sentence) and so are set off with commas. *Restrictive* appositives limit the meaning of the sentence and are not set off with commas.

> NONRESTRICTIVE   Tom Edison, *the inventor*, often worked sixteen hours a day.
>
> RESTRICTIVE   The *inventor* Edison often worked sixteen hours a day.

Article. The articles *a, an,* and *the* are used as adjectives. The definite article is *the*. The indefinite articles are *a* and *an*.

Auxiliary. A "helping verb," used to make the form of another verb. The common auxiliaries are *be* (and its various forms), *have, shall, will, should, would, may, can, might, could, must, ought,* and *do*.

> I *am* studying.   He *may* return.   You *must* leave.

Case. The inflectional form of nouns and pronouns showing their relation to other words in the sentence. In English the three cases are nominative (*boy, I*), possessive (*boy's, my*), and objective (*boy, me*). (*See also* Section 6, "Case.")

Clause. A grammatical unit containing a subject and verb. Clauses are of two kinds: *main* or *independent,* and *subordinate* or *dependent*. A *main clause* makes an independent assertion.

> When the moon shone, *the dog barked*.

A *subordinate clause* is used as a noun, adjective, or adverb and is dependent on some other element in the sentence.

> *That he would survive* was doubtful. (The subordinate clause is the subject of the verb *was.*)

(*See also* Section 5, "Sentence Sense.")

Collective Noun. The Merriam-Webster *New Collegiate* defines this term as "a noun naming a collection or aggregate of individuals by a singular form (as *assembly, army, jury*). It takes a singular verb when the group is thought of as a unit, and a plural when the component individuals are in mind; as, the majority *decides;* the majority *were* slaves."

Common and Proper Nouns. A *common noun* names the general class to which a person, place, or thing belongs, as *man, country, state, river, ocean, dog, pencil, beauty.* A *proper noun,* on the other hand, distinguishes an individual person, place, or thing, as *Wallace, Europe, Massachusetts, Amazon, Atlantic, Rover, Parker, Beethoven's Fifth.*

Comparison. A term used to describe the changes in the forms of adjectives or adverbs to show degrees of quality or quantity. The three degrees are positive, comparative, and superlative.

POSITIVE	COMPARATIVE	SUPERLATIVE
loud	louder	loudest
bad	worse	worst
slowly	more slowly	most slowly

(*See also* Section 8, "Adjectives and Adverbs.")

Complement. A term used to describe the word or words that complete the meaning of a verb. A complement may be a *direct object,* as

> The sexton rang the *bell.*

An *indirect object,* as

> Give *me* the dollar.

A *predicate noun* (as *subjective complement*), as

> Harry is a *baker.*

A *predicate noun* (as *objective complement*), as

> We made him our *secretary.*

A *predicate adjective* (as *subjective complement*), as

> The man was *silent.*

A *predicate adjective* (as *objective complement*), as

> Tom painted the fence *white.* (The adjective *white,* modifying the direct object *fence,* is also called the *objective complement.*)

An *infinitive,* as

> We had George *cook* pancakes.

Conjugation. A term used to describe the changes in the inflectional forms of a verb to show tense, voice, mood, person, and number. (For the conjugation of the verb *choose,* see Section 7, "Tense and Mood.")

Conjunction. A word used to connect words, phrases, and clauses. Conjunctions are of two kinds: *co-ordinating* and *subordinating. Co-ordinating conjunctions* (*and, but, or, nor, for,* etc.) join words, phrases, or clauses of equal grammatical rank. *Subordinating conjunctions* (*after, as, because, if, when,* etc.) join subordinate clauses with main clauses. (*See also* Correlative Conjunctions *and* Section 35, "Parallelism.")

Conjunctive Adverb. An adverb used to join main clauses in a sentence. Common conjunctive adverbs are *also, besides, consequently, furthermore, however, likewise, moreover, nevertheless, then, thus.*

Co-ordinate. Having equal rank, as two main clauses in a compound sentence.

Correlative Conjunctions. Conjunctions used in pairs to join sentence elements of equal rank. Common correlatives are *either . . . or, neither . . . nor, not only . . . but also.*

Declension. *See* Inflection *and* Case.

Direct Address. A noun or pronoun used parenthetically to point out the person addressed, sometimes called *nominative of address* or *vocative.*

> *George,* where are you going?
>
> I suppose, *gentlemen,* that you enjoyed the lecture.

Direct and Indirect Quotations. A direct quotation is an exact quotation of a speaker's or writer's words (sometimes called direct discourse). In indirect discourse the speaker's or writer's thought is summarized without direct quotation.

> DIRECT   He said, "I must leave on the morning train."
> INDIRECT   He said that he had to leave on the morning train.

Elliptical Expression. An ellipsis is an omission of words necessary to the grammatical completeness of an expression but assumed in the context. The omitted words in elliptical expressions may be supplied by the reader or hearer.

> He is older than I (am).
>
> Our house is small, his (house is) large.

Expletive. The word *it* or *there* used to introduce a sentence in which the subject follows the verb.

> *It* is doubtful that he will arrive today. (The clause *that he will arrive today* is the subject of the verb *is.*)
>
> *There* are two ways of solving the problem. (The noun *ways* is the subject of *are.*)

Finite Verb. A verb form that makes an assertion about its subject. Verbals (infinitives, participles, gerunds) are not finite forms.

Gender. The classification of nouns and pronouns as masculine (*man, he*), feminine (*woman, she*), and neuter (*desk, it*). Some English nouns have special forms to indicate gender: *salesman, saleswoman; hero, heroine.*

Genitive Case. The possessive case. (*See* Section 6, "Cases.")

Gerund. A verbal used as a noun. Gerunds, which end in *-ing*, have the functions of nouns, such as subject or object of a verb.

> *Fishing* is an interesting sport.
> He enjoyed *hiking*.

Idiom. An expression established by usage and peculiar to a particular language. Many idioms have unusual grammatical construction and make little sense if taken literally. Examples of English idioms are "by and large," "catch a cold," "have a try at," "look up an old friend."

Independent Element. An expression that has no grammatical relation to other parts of the sentence. (*See* Absolute.)

Indirect Discourse. *See* Direct and Indirect Quotations.

Infinitive. A verbal usually preceded by *to* and used as a noun, adjective, or adverb.

NOUN	*To swim* is relaxing. (Subject.)
	We didn't dare (to) *leave*. (Object.)
	(*To* is usually omitted in infinitives after *dare, hear, make, see,* and some other verbs.)
ADJECTIVE	I have nothing *to say*. (*To say* modifies the noun *nothing*.)
	There is no time *to waste*.
ADVERB	We were ready *to begin*. (*To begin* modifies the adjective *ready*.)
	He came *to inspect* the house. (*To inspect* modifies the verb *came*.)

Inflection. Variation in the form of words to show changes in meaning or to indicate case (*he, him*), gender (*aviator, aviatrix*), number (*man, men*), tense (*walk, walked*), etc. *Declension* is the inflection of nouns and pronouns; *conjugation* the inflection of verbs; and *comparison* the inflection of adjectives and adverbs.

Interjection. A word used to express emotion. An interjection is grammatically independent of other words in the sentence.

> *Oh,* you startled me.
>
> *Ouch!* You are stepping on my foot.

Irregular Verb. *See* Strong Verb.

Linking Verb. A verb that shows the relation between the subject of a sentence and an adjective or a noun in the nominative case. The chief linking verbs are *be, become, appear, seem,* and the verbs pertaining to the senses (*look, smell, taste, sound, feel*).

> He *seems* timid.   The cake *tastes* sweet.   He *is* a thief.

Modification. Describing or limiting the meaning of a word or group of words. Adjectives and adjective phrases or clauses modify nouns; adverbs and adverb phrases or clauses modify verbs, adjectives, or adverbs. (*See also* Section 8, "Adjectives and Adverbs.")

Mood. The form of the verb used to show how the action is viewed by the writer or speaker. English has three moods: *indicative, imperative,* and *subjunctive.*

The *indicative mood* states a fact or asks a question.

> The wheat *is* ripe. *Is* breakfast ready?

The *imperative mood* expresses a command or request.

> *Report* to the office at once. Please *give* me your attention.

The *subjunctive mood* expresses doubt, supposition, concession, probability, a condition contrary to fact, a regret, or wish.

> The grass looks as if it *were* dying.
>
> I wish that he *were* more congenial.

(*See also* Section 7, "Tense and Mood.")

Nonrestrictive Modifier. A modifying phrase or clause that is not essential to pointing out or identifying the person or thing modified. Nonrestrictive modifiers are set off with commas.

> Mr. Smith, *who was watching from the window,* saw the boys stealing the apples.

505

Television, *which is growing in popularity,* has great educational value.

Noun. A word used to name a person, place, or thing. A *common noun* names any one of a class of persons, places, or things.

> *man, table, valley, carrot*

A *proper noun* names a specific person, place, or thing.
> *Stephen, Kansas, Canada, Labor Day, Last Supper*

A *collective noun* names a group by using a singular form.
> *committee, herd, jury*

A *concrete noun* names something that can be perceived by the senses.
> *house, lake, flower*

An *abstract noun* names an idea or quality.
> *hope, tragedy, kindness*

Noun Clause. A subordinate clause used as a noun.
> *What I saw* was humiliating. (Subject.)
> I shall accept *whatever he offers.* (Object of the verb.)
> We will be ready for *whatever happens.* (Object of the preposition *for.*)

Number. The form of a noun, pronoun, verb, or demonstrative adjective to indicate one (*singular*) or more than one (*plural*).

Object. A word, phrase, or clause that is affected by the action of a transitive verb. A *direct object* receives directly the action of a transitive verb.
> I followed *him.*
> You may keep *whatever you find.*

An *indirect object* receives indirectly the action of a transitive verb.
> Give *me* the money. (*Money* is the direct object of *give; me* is the indirect object.)

The *object of a preposition* is a substantive that follows the preposition.
> We sat on the *porch.* (*Porch* is the object of *on.*)
> The horse galloped across the *meadow.* (*Meadow* is the object of *across.*)

Parenthetical Expression. An inserted expression that interrupts the thought of a sentence. Parenthetical items are set off by commas, dashes, or parentheses.

506

His failure, *I suppose*, was his own fault.

I shall arrive—*this will surprise you*—on Monday.

The old seaman (*actually he was only forty*) loved children.

Parse. To analyze the function of a word or group of words in a sentence.

Participle. A verbal used as an adjective. Though a participle cannot make an assertion, it is derived from a verb and can take an object and be modified by an adverb. As an adjective, a participle can modify a noun or pronoun. The present participle ends in *-ing: running, seeing, trying.* The past participle ends in *-d, -ed, -t, -n, -en,* or changes the form of the vowel: *walked, lost, seen, rung.*

Parts of Speech. The classification of words on the basis of their function in the sentence. The eight parts of speech are: *noun, pronoun, adjective, verb, adverb, preposition, conjunction,* and *interjection.* Each of these is discussed in this Index to Grammatical Terms.

Person. The form of a pronoun and verb used to indicate the speaker (first person—*I am*); the person spoken to (second person—*you are*); or the person spoken about (third person—*he is*).

Phrase. A group of related words lacking both subject and predicate and used as a noun, adjective, adverb, or verb. On the basis of their form, phrases are classified as *prepositional, participial, gerund, infinitive,* and *verb* phrases.

PREPOSITIONAL	We walked *across the street.* (Adverb)
PARTICIPIAL	The man *entering the room* is my father. (Adjective)
GERUND	*Washing windows* is tiresome work. (Noun)
INFINITIVE	*To see the sunset* was a pleasure. (Noun)
VERB	He *has been educated* in Europe. (Verb)

Predicate. The part of a sentence or clause that makes a statement about the subject. The predicate consists of the verb and its complements and modifiers.

Preposition. A word used to relate a noun or pronoun to some other word in the sentence. A preposition and its object form a prepositional phrase.

The sheep are *in* the meadow.

He dodged *through* the traffic.

Principal Clause. A main or independent clause. *See* Clause.

Principal Parts. The three forms of a verb from which the various tenses are derived.

PRESENT INFINITIVE	PAST TENSE	PAST PARTICIPLE
join	joined	joined
go	went	gone

(*See also* Section 7, "Tense and Mood.")

Progressive. The form of the verb used to describe an action occurring, but not completed, at the time referred to.

I *am studying.* (Present progressive.)

I *was studying.* (Past progressive.)

Pronoun. A word used in place of a noun. The noun for which a pronoun stands is called its *antecedent.* (For a discussion of the relation of pronouns and antecedents, *see* Section 12, "Agreement.") Pronouns are classified as follows:

PERSONAL	*I, you, he, she, it,* etc. (*See the declension in* Section 6, "Case.")
RELATIVE	*who, which, that* I am the man *who* lives here. We saw a barn *that* was burning.
INTERROGATIVE	*who, which, what* *Who* are you? *Which* is your book?
DEMONSTRATIVE	*this, that, these, those*
INDEFINITE	*one, any, each, anyone, somebody, all,* etc.
RECIPROCAL	*each other, one another*
INTENSIVE	*myself, yourself, himself,* etc. I *myself* was afraid. You *yourself* must decide.
REFLEXIVE	*myself, yourself, himself,* etc. I burned *myself.* You are deceiving *yourself.*

Regular Verb. *See* Weak Verb.

Relative Clause. A clause introduced by a relative pronoun.

Restrictive Modifier. A modifying phrase or clause that is essential to pointing out or identifying the person or thing modified. Restrictive modifiers are not set off with punctuation marks.

People *who live in glass houses* shouldn't throw stones.

The horse *that won the race* is a bay mare.

(*See also* Nonrestrictive Modifier.)

Sentence. A group of words expressing a unit of thought and normally containing a subject and predicate. Sentences are classified on the basis of their form as *simple, compound, complex,* or *compound-complex.* A *simple sentence* has one main clause. Either the subject or the verb may be compound.

> The sun rises.
>
> The boys and girls are playing tag.

A *compound sentence* has two or more main clauses.

> He went to the store, but I stayed at home.

A *complex sentence* has one main clause and one or more subordinate clauses.

> The twins ran when they heard their father coming.

A *compound-complex* sentence has two or more main clauses and one or more subordinate clauses.

> He seized the reins, and the horses reared because they were frightened.

Sentences are classified as *declarative, interrogative, imperative,* and *exclamatory.* A *declarative sentence* states or asserts something.

> John smiled. The crowd cheered.

An *interrogative sentence* asks a question.

> Where are you going? What is his name?

An *imperative sentence* expresses a request or command.

> Please pass the bread. Watch your step.

An *exclamatory sentence* expresses strong emotion and is followed by an exclamation point.

> What a temper he has! I will not go!

Strong Verb. A verb that forms its past and past participle by a vowel change or by other individual spelling changes. (*See* Sections 7 *and* 7d.)

> begin, *began, begun;* spring, *sprang, sprung.*

Subject. The person or thing about which the predicate of a sentence or clause makes an assertion.

Substantive. A word or group of words used as a noun. Substantives include nouns, pronouns, infinitives, gerunds, and noun clauses.

Substantive Clause. A subordinate clause used as a noun. *See* Noun Clause.

Syntax. The relationship between words in a sentence.

Tense. The time or the state of the action expressed by a verb. (For a discussion of verb tenses, *see* Section 7, "Tense and Mood.")

Verb. A word or phrase used to assert an action or state of being. A *transitive verb* is one that takes an object.

Jack *mowed* the grass.

An *intransitive verb* is one that does not require an object.

The children *are laughing*.

Some verbs may be either transitive or intransitive.

The whistle *blew*. (Intransitive.)
Tom *blew* the whistle. (Transitive.)

(*See* Finite Verb.)

Verbal. A word derived from a verb, but unable to make an assertion. *See* Infinitive, Gerund, *and* Participle.

Vocative. *See* Direct Address.

Voice. The property of a verb that shows whether the subject acts (*active voice*) or is acted upon (*passive voice*).

ACTIVE   Ed *is taking* a walk.
PASSIVE   A walk *is being taken* by Ed.

ACTIVE   Grace *bought* some flowers.
PASSIVE   Some flowers *were bought* by Grace.

Weak Verb. Also called a regular verb. A verb that forms its past and past participle by adding *-d, -ed,* or *-t* to the infinitive: *move, moved, moved; kneel, knelt, knelt.*

Index